Lecture Notes in Computer Science 12321

More information about this series at http://www.springer.com/series/7407

Heike Jagode · Hartwig Anzt ·
Guido Juckeland · Hatem Ltaief (Eds.)

High Performance Computing

ISC High Performance 2020 International Workshops
Frankfurt, Germany, June 21–25, 2020
Revised Selected Papers

Springer

Editors
Heike Jagode 🆔
University of Tennessee at Knoxville
Knowville, TN, USA

Guido Juckeland 🆔
Computational Science
Helmholtz-Zentrum Dresden Rossendorf
Dresden, Sachsen, Germany

Hartwig Anzt 🆔
Department of Mathematics
KIT für Technologie Karlsruhe
Karlsruhe, Baden-Württemberg, Germany

Hatem Ltaief
Extreme Computing Research Center
King Abdullah University of Science
and Technology
Thuwal, Saudi Arabia

ISSN 0302-9743   ISSN 1611-3349 (electronic)
Lecture Notes in Computer Science
ISBN 978-3-030-59850-1   ISBN 978-3-030-59851-8 (eBook)
https://doi.org/10.1007/978-3-030-59851-8

LNCS Sublibrary: SL1 – Theoretical Computer Science and General Issues

This Springer imprint is published by the registered company Springer Nature Switzerland AG
The registered company address is: Gewerbestrasse 11, 6330 Cham, Switzerland

Preface

Without a doubt, 2020 has been a different kind of year for all of us, and so it was for the 35th ISC High Performance conference, which became known as ISC 2020 Digital. As the name suggests, the organizing team around David Keyes (KAUST, Saudi Arabia) successfully adapted the conference to an all-digital format by providing a significant portion of the program via web conferencing. While we should not forget the importance of in-person interaction and socializing, the video streaming of the accepted papers, focus sessions, and invited talks enabled unprecedented access and dissemination of new research findings for the high-performance computing community.

The ISC High Performance workshop series has been a complementary component of the main conference since 2015, and – sustained by its continued success – a renewed workshop program was presented at the ISC 2020 Digital event under the leadership of workshops chair Heike Jagode (The University of Tennessee at Knoxville, USA) and deputy chair Hartwig Anzt (Karlsruhe Institute of Technology, Germany). Guido Juckeland (Helmholtz-Zentrum Dresden-Rossendorf, Germany) and Hatem Ltaief (KAUST, Saudi Arabia) joined the team as proceedings chair and deputy chair, respectively, and managed the organization of the workshops' proceedings.

All workshops were selected with a peer-review process by an international committee of 21 experts in the field from all over Europe, the USA, and Asia. For the digital version of the conference, we offered all of the accepted workshops the flexibility to postpone their workshop to ISC 2021 and run a virtual workshop in the ISC 2020 edition. In the end, 10 of the 23 accepted workshops decided to organize a virtual version of their event, which we greatly appreciate given the extra effort put forth by everyone involved.

Like in the 2019 edition, the ISC workshops were composed of two types of workshops: workshops with proceedings (early deadline) and workshops without proceedings (later deadline). While we had 16 workshops with proceedings accepted, only 7 out of those decided to offer a digital version this year. Given all of these challenges, the quality of this year's ISC workshops proceedings is impressive. In total, we have 25 high-quality papers that all underwent thorough reviews. Each chapter of the book contains the accepted and revised papers for one of the workshops. For some workshops, an additional preface describes the review process and provides a summary of the outcome.

With the hope that, perhaps next year, we will be able to once again host ISC High Performance in person, we want to thank our Workshops Committee members, organizers of workshops, and all contributors. We are proud to present the latest findings on topics related to research, development, and the application of large-scale, high-performance systems.

August 2020

Heike Jagode
Hartwig Anzt
Guido Juckeland
Hatem Ltaief

Organization

Workshops Committee

Emmanuel Agullo	Inria, France
Hartwig Anzt	Karlsruhe Institute of Technology, Germany, and The University of Tennessee, Knoxville, USA
Richard Barrett	Sandia National Laboratories, USA
Roy Campbell	Department of Defense, USA
Florina Ciorba	University of Basel, Switzerland
Anthony Danalis	The University of Tennessee, Knoxville, USA
Manuel F. Dolz	Universitat Jaume I, Spain
Nick Forrington	Arm, USA
Karl Fuerlinger	Ludwig Maximilian University of Munich (LMU), Germany
Judit Gimenez Lucas	Barcelona Supercomputing Center, Spain
Thomas Gruber	University of Erlangen-Nuremberg, Erlangen Regional Computing Center, Germany
Joachim Hein	Lund University, Sweden
David Henty	The University of Edinburgh, UK
Marc-Andre Hermanns	RWTH Aachen University, Germany
Kevin Huck	University of Oregon, USA
Sascha Hunold	TU Wien, Austria
Heike Jagode	The University of Tennessee, Knoxville, USA
Eileen Kühn	Karlsruhe Institute of Technology, Germany
Diana Moise	Cray, HPE, Switzerland
Tapasya Patki	Lawrence Livermore National Laboratory, USA
Jelena Pjesivac-Grbovic	Verily Life Sciences LLC, Google LLC, USA
Philip Roth	Oak Ridge National Laboratory, USA
Ana Lucia Varbanescu	University of Amsterdam, The Netherlands

Proceedings Chairs

Guido Juckeland	Helmholtz-Zentrum Dresden-Rossendorf (HZDR), Germany
Hatem Ltaief	KAUST, Saudi Arabia

Contents

15th Workshop on Virtualization in High-Performance Cloud Computing (VHPC'20)

First Workshop on Compiler-Assisted Correctness Checking and Performance Optimization for HPC (C3PO'20)

Preface to the First Workshop on Compiler-assisted Correctness Checking and Performance Optimization for HPC (C3PO'20)

Peter Pirkelbauer[1] and Emmanuelle Saillard[2]

[1] Lawrence Livermore National Laboratory, Livermore, CA 94550
pirkelbauer2@llnl.gov

[2] Inria Bordeaux Sud-Ouest, Talence, France
emmanuelle.saillard@inria.fr

Introduction

Changing HPC architecture and software stack create enormous challenges for HPC application developers that need to write performance portable code and keep existing applications up to speed. Purely manual solutions are cost prohibitive. Source-to-source translators are poised to address these challenges automatically or with user input semi-automatically. Practical compiler-enabled programming environments, applied analysis methodologies, and end-to-end toolchains are crucial to performance portability in the exascale era.

C3PO is a new workshop at the intersection of compilers/translators, HPC middleware, and HPC applications. The workshop brings together researchers with a shared interest in applying compilation and source-to-source translation methodologies to enhance parallel programming, including explicit programming models such as MPI, OpenMP, and hybrid models.

Organization

Five papers were submitted, and after a double-blind review process, four papers were accepted. The workshop was held virtually with live presentations on June 24, 2020.

Organizing Committee

Peter Pirkelbauer	Lawrence Livermore National Laboratory and University of Central Florida
Emmanuelle Saillard	Inria Bordeaux Sud-Ouest
Anthony Skjellum	University of Tennessee at Chattanooga
Martin Ruefenacht	University of Edinburgh

Purushotham Bangalore   University of Alabama at Birmingham
Julien Jaeger   French Alternative Energies and Atomic Energy
                                  Commission
Peter Thoman   University of Innsbruck

Program Committee

Hadia Ahmed   Lawrence Berkeley National Laboratory
Ritu Arora   Texas Advanced Computing Center
Protonu Basu   Facebook
Ira Baxter   Semantic Design
Benson Muite   Kichakato Kizito
Elisabeth Brunet   Telecom Sud Paris
Patrick Carribault   French Alternative Energies and Atomic Energy
                                  Commission
Thomas Fahringer   University of Innsbruck
Chunhua Liao   Lawrence Livermore National Laboratory
Reed Milewicz   Sandia National Laboratories
Christina Peterson   University of Central Florida
Joachim Protze   RWTH Aachen University
Sara Royuela   Barcelona Supercomputing Center
Markus Schordan   Lawrence Livermore National Laboratory
Prema Soundararajan   University of Alabama at Birmingham
Aravind Sukumaran Rajam   Washington State University
Amalee Wilson   Stanford University

Program

The workshop content was built on two tracks: invited talk and research paper presentations. All presentations were performed live using zoom and the audience could (and did) ask questions at any time via the zoom chat.

Invited Talk

Computational scientists face numerous challenges when trying to exploit powerful and complex high-performance computing (HPC) platforms. These challenges arise in multiple aspects including productivity, performance, correctness etc.

Chunhua Liao presented a source-to-source transformation-based approach to address such challenges. His work is based on a unique compiler framework named

ROSE. Developed at the Lawrence Livermore National Laboratory, ROSE encapsulates advanced compiler analysis and optimization technologies into easy-to-use library APIs so developers can quickly build customized program analysis and transformation tools for C/C++/Fortran and OpenMP programs. Chunhua Liao showed several tools, including an AST inliner, an AST outliner, and a variable move tool. He briefly mentioned ongoing work related to benchmarks, composable tools, and online training for compiler/tool developers.

Research Papers

The research papers presentations were organized in two sessions with two talks each: correctness and optimization.

The first speaker was Jan Patrick Lehr from TU Darmstadt. He presented TyCart, a tool for type-safe checkpoint/restart that extends the memory allocation sanitizer tool TypeART with type asserts. In TyCart, type asserts are used to implement a typesafe interface for the existing checkpoint libraries FTI and VeloC.

In a next presentation, Tim Jammer from TU Darmstadt talked about an automatic detection of MPI assertions. He showed a Clang/LLVM based static analysis to check whether the four MPI assertions defined in the 2019 standard draft specification hold for a given program.

Next, Van Man Nguyen from CEA described automatic code motion to extend MPI nonblocking overlap window. His solution to reduce overheads caused by network latencies or synchronizations between processes (i) transforms blocking MPI communications into their nonblocking counterparts and (ii) performs extensive code motion to increase the size of overlapping intervals between initialization and completion calls.

Finally, Adrian Munera Sanchez from BSC talked about a static analysis to enhance programmability and performance in OmpSs-2. He introduced a new algorithm to automatically and safely release OmpSs-2 task dependencies before a task has completed.

The workshop program information, including links to the talks and presentation slides is available under https://c3po-workshop.github.io/2020/program.

Acknowledgement. This work was performed under the auspices of the U.S. Department of Energy by Lawrence Livermore National Laboratory under Contract DE-AC52-07NA27344 (LLNL-MI-812627).

Compiler-Assisted Type-Safe Checkpointing

Jan-Patrick Lehr$^{(\boxtimes)}$, Alexander Hück, Moritz Fischer, and Christian Bischof

Scientific Computing, Technische Universität Darmstadt, Darmstadt, Germany
{jan-patrick.lehr,alexander.hueck,
christian.bischof}@tu-darmstadt.de,
moritz_friedrich.fischer@stud.tu-darmstadt.de

Abstract. TyCart is a tool for type-safe checkpoint/restart and extends the memory allocation sanitizer tool TypeART with type asserts. Type asserts let the developer specify type requirements on memory regions, and, in our example implementation, they are used to implement a type-safe interface for the existing checkpoint libraries FTI and VeloC. We evaluate our approach on a set of mini-apps, and an application from astrophysics. The approach shows runtime and memory overhead below 5% in smaller benchmarks. In the astrophysics application, the runtime overhead reaches 30% and the memory overhead 70%.

Keywords: Correctness · Checkpoint restart · Type mismatch · Sanitizer

1 Introduction

Application-level checkpointing is a technique to extend applications with the ability to periodically store their data to persistent storage, and to continue with that data in a later restart of the application. Two recent implementations are the Very-Low Overhead Checkpointing (VeloC) [17] library and the Fault Tolerance Interface (FTI) [2]. Both libraries enable Message Passing Interface (MPI)-parallel checkpoint/restart (CPR) mechanisms to provide distributed checkpointing while also exploiting the storage hierarchy for faster checkpoints.

To enable compatibility across different languages and applications, many libraries expose low-level C application programming interfaces (APIs) to the user. Low-level interfaces can be problematic, however, as they treat data as raw memory, leaving the particular specification to the user. This results in a variety of potential usage errors. For example, specifying the wrong type size results in a miscalculation of the memory region's extent, which causes the CPR library to illegally access memory outside the valid data allocation range. We use the terms *memory region* and *allocation* interchangeably.

The problem is not limited to CPR libraries, but generally applies to low-level, C-style, APIs that expose type-less pointer parameters (in $C/C{+}{+}$ **void**$*$)

© Springer Nature Switzerland AG 2020
H. Jagode et al. (Eds.): ISC High Performance 2020 Workshops, LNCS 12321, pp. 5–18, 2020.
https://doi.org/10.1007/978-3-030-59851-8_1

together with meta information, e.g., type sizes, to pass in data. Another well-known, and widely used, example for such an interface is the MPI library. To help developers implement correct applications, a mechanism to assert type and allocation-extent requirements at API boundaries is desirable.

```
1  double *pA = (double *) malloc(N * sizeof(double));
2  // memId: starts at pA, with size N*sizeof(double) bytes
3  VELOC_Mem_protect(memId, pA, N, sizeof(double));
4  VELOC_Checkpoint("CPLabel", CPVersion);
5  VELOC_Mem_unprotect(memId);
```

Listing 1.1: General scheme of checkpoint functionality using VeloC: (a) register an allocation for checkpointing, (b) perform the checkpoint, i.e., store all registered allocations to checkpoint "CPLabel" in version CPVersion, (c) de-register the allocation. Other APIs, e.g., FTI, work similarly.

For the MPI library, the MUST [9] tool was extended with the compiler-based tool TypeART [10]. TypeART instruments allocations and tracks the respective types and extents at runtime. MUST compares the tracked type information to the user-provided type information in MPI calls to check for correctness.

In this paper, we extend the approach of TypeART and propose the more general concept of *type asserts*. Type asserts allow to state requirements about allocated memory regions, i.e., pointers. Our tool TyCart provides general CPR-related type asserts. We provide example implementations for the two existing CPR libraries FTI and VeloC. The implementation guards calls to the CPR library against type- and extent-related usage errors by adding type asserts.

The paper is structured as follows: Sect. 2 explains the considered CPR APIs and potential usage errors. Sect. 3 introduces type asserts and explains how they address such errors. In Sect. 4, we evaluate the approach on a set of benchmarks before we discuss the results in Sect. 5. Related work is discussed in Sect. 6. Lastly, we conclude and give further research directions in Sect. 7.

2   Checkpoint Restart

Checkpoint/restart is a technique that enables a target software to periodically write out data, in order to continue the computation from the last stored data point in a subsequent restart. This is particularly relevant in large systems, in which the mean time between failure is relatively short, and applications have to be able to deal with system failure [2,3], or for longer runs on systems with schedulers that limit the time of a job. The mechanism can be implemented, e.g., as system-level or application-level CPR [6]. In this work, application-level CPR is considered, which is integrated into the target application by the developer, who, thus, can introduce usage errors.

The use of application-level CPR capability in a target application typically requires three steps, see Listing 1.1; excluding initialization and finalization.

Note that, the registration of allocations and the actual checkpoints can be placed at different locations in the target program. While the initial placement may have been obvious and known to all developers, checkpoint placement may be subject to tuning efforts and change over time. Splitting the interface into separate functions for registration, actual checkpoint, and deregistration is important for fine-grain control about which data is checkpointed at what point of the application. The placement of the calls to the actual checkpoint function is important for both checkpoint consistency and application performance. While this paper is not concerned with the challenge to generate a consistent checkpoint, many algorithms for general checkpoint consistency exist, for an overview see [8]. Identifying potential to minimize the performance impact on the target application has received considerable attention in high-performance computing [13,19], and more specifically in, e.g., adjoint algorithmic differentiation [3,14].

```
1  int *pi = (int *) malloc(N * sizeof(int));
2  // element count error
3  VELOC_Mem_protect(1, pi, X, sizeof(int));
4  // data type error
5  VELOC_Mem_protect(1, pi, N, sizeof(double));
```

Listing 1.2:(1)Erroneous argument X for the number of elements specification (line 3); the application may checkpoint too few, or too many elements. (2) Erroneous argument to the **sizeof** operator to determine the type's size (line 5).

2.1   Error Types

Both VeloC and FTI provide a *C*-API for compatibility across different languages. The allocation is provided as a type-less **void***, together with arguments that specify the size of the allocation's extent. Such interfaces allow for a variety of usage errors, yet only limited correctness checking can be provided. We distinguish three types of error that can occur.

(a) **Element Count Error**   The developer calculates the allocation's total extent using a wrong number of elements. Unfortunately, the library has a raw view of the memory, hence, no error checking can be performed. In the example in Listing 1.2, the memory region is allocated with size M * **sizeof**(**int**) bytes. However, when registering the allocation, the developer erroneously specifies X as the number of elements for it. This can lead to subtle bugs, i.e., if (1) X < N, a restart only partially restores the content of pi, leaving the remaining memory in an uninitialized state, and, (2) X > N, a checkpoint erroneously reads the memory out-of-bounds and a restart erroneously writes it out-of-bounds.

(b) **Data Type Error**   The developer uses a wrong type to calculate the allocation's total extent, i.e., passes the wrong type to the **sizeof** operator. In VeloC the data-type size in bytes is provided as **size_t** (see Listing 1.2 line 5), whereas in FTI, an FTI-type handle is created and used instead.

(c) **Change Allocation Before Checkpoint** The developer changes an already registered allocation, e.g., its extent, between its registration and the checkpoint. This is hard to catch, as the individual calls to the CPR library seem correct. With the outdated information from the time of registration, the CPR library copies the wrong number of elements.

All error types result in a miscalculation of the allocation's extent, and are not particular to the CPR use-case, but relevant for all C-style APIs.

3   Type Asserts for Checkpoint-Restart

To detect the illustrated errors, meta information for allocations registered for checkpointing is needed. The relevant information consists of the underlying data type and the number of elements allocated, i.e., the extent. Type asserts let the developer specify the expected type and extent for an allocation when registering it for checkpointing, hence, detect errors w.r.t. the usage of the CPR library.

   To that end, we use the type and memory allocation tracking sanitizer tool TypeART, see Fig. 1, which we briefly introduce in the next section. It is based on the LLVM framework and uses instrumentation and static analysis to provide, at runtime, the required allocation information. For a thorough discussion of TypeART, see [10]. To handle the particular semantics of the CPR libraries, we develop a specialized library called TyCart. It provides type asserts, implemented as marker functions that are handled by TypeART's LLVM passes, and, in addition, type safe API calls to the checkpoint libraries using the type information provided by TypeART. Marker functions are used to indicate that a particular variable should be tracked and checked at runtime. We distinguish regions marked (or registered) for tracking and those actually tracked at runtime.

3.1   TypeART

Analysis and Transformation Pass. The passes work on the LLVM intermediate representation[1] (IR) generated by the compiler. The analysis pass (1) finds all memory allocation instructions (i.e., stack, heap and globals), and, (2) filters stack and global variables that are not passed to marker functions. The transformation pass subsequently instruments each such allocation. The hook passes, (1) the memory address, (2) the extent, and, (3) a type id for the allocated type (see next paragraph). In Listing 1.3, an example of a heap allocation instrumentation is shown. Stack allocations are instrumented individually with the respective type information when entering their scope. They are freed as bulk operation, using a counter-based approach, when leaving the scope [10].

---

[1] https://llvm.org/docs/LangRef.html.

Runtime. The runtime library keeps track of the memory allocations during program execution based on the instrumentation callbacks. It associates the address with (1) a type id, identifying the type, and (2) the count of allocated elements, e.g., for an array. Its current implementation is not thread safe.

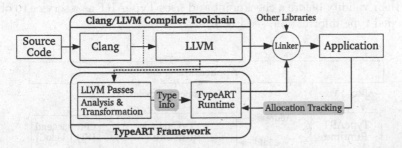

Fig. 1. TypeART framework, adapted from [10]. (1) The LLVM compiler is invoked with additional analysis and instrumentation passes to collect type information and instrument the relevant allocations. (2) The type information is serialized and later used by the runtime library. (3) The runtime library is linked with the target application. (4) During execution, the memory allocations are traced and combined with the previously extracted type information.

```
1    %1 = call i8* @malloc(i64 %0)  // %0 = n * sizeof(float)
2    %2 = udiv i64 %0, 4            // %2 = %0 / sizeof(float)
3    call void @__typeart_alloc( i8* %1,  i32 5,  i64 %2 )
4    %3 = bitcast i8* %1 to float*
```

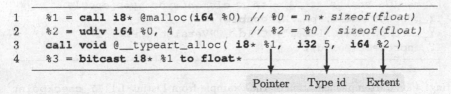

Listing 1.3: Instrumented LLVM IR (gray lines) for (**float***)malloc(n***sizeof** (**float**)). TypeART adds instructions to calculate the extent of the array dynamically. The type id is determined statically, here 5 for the built-in **float**.

Type Representation. A type id is added by the transformation pass to each instrumentation hook of the memory allocations. The runtime library uses the id for type-related bookkeeping. Built-in types have predetermined ids and layouts. For user-defined types, (1) a unique type id is generated, and (2) the type layout is serialized. When executing, the runtime library parses the serialized type information. Together with dynamically calculated extents, provided by the instrumentation, the runtime library is able to provide exact type information for any relevant allocation.

3.2   TyCart

TyCart implements *type asserts*, i.e., assert statements about the type and extent of an allocation. Since the tool specifically targets CPR libraries, it provides an interface similar to the targeted libraries VeloC and FTI. It reuses TypeART's analysis pass to find all relevant allocations, and to filter irrelevant allocations from instrumentation. It extends TypeART with a specialized transformation pass to process the TyCart interface functions and insert calls to its runtime library. The runtime library keeps track of registered memory regions, to re-assert their validity before a checkpoint and uses TypeART as a service to obtain the needed type information, see Fig. 2.

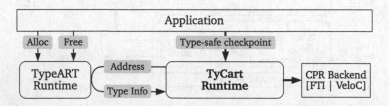

Fig. 2. Instead of direct calls to a CPR library, the equivalent type-safe API of TyCart is used. For each invocation, the type information of the memory pointer, provided by TypeART, is compared to the user-specified one of the type assert. A successful check passes the call to the respective CPR backend.

```
1   double *pA = (double *) malloc(N * sizeof(double));
2   // memId: starts at pA with N elements of type double
3   TY_protect(memId, pA, N, double);
4   TY_checkpoint("CPLabel", CPId, CPVersion, CPLevel);
5   TY_unprotect(memId);
```

Listing 1.4: TyCart implementation of the example from Listing 1.1. TY_checkpoint arguments: the label of the checkpoint, the id of the checkpoint, the version of the checkpoint and the level of the checkpoint. Label and version is used with VeloC, id and level with FTI.

Type Asserts. Type asserts allow specifying requirements about the data type and the extent of allocations. As outlined in Sect. 2, all introduced errors are the consequence of an inability to introspect allocations, given a type-less pointer. Using the proposed type asserts, TYPE_ASSERT(p, 100, double) introspects if the allocation p indeed points to 100 elements of type **double**. Hence, developers can explicitly state and check requirements on memory regions. However, two main limitations of this approach exist w.r.t. type-safe checkpointing. First, a single type assert only checks the allocation when it is executed, not with every checkpoint. Second, type asserts are decoupled from the CPR API and need to be maintained separately, introducing another source for error.

TyCart CPR Asserts. To address the drawbacks of single type asserts and better fit the CPR use-case, TyCart provides an interface that encapsulates both the type assert and the call to the CPR API. Different macros are provided to register a memory region, execute a checkpoint and deregister a memory region. Using FTI, a macro to register a type to FTI is also provided. Listing 1.4 reimplements the initial example (see Listing 1.1) using TyCart-provided macros.

The registration macro `TY_protect` expands to a TyCart marker function in the source code, which is subsequently handled by the LLVM transformation pass. The pass replaces the marker function with a call to the TyCart runtime library, and inserts the compiler-generated type id into the call. The type id is generated by TypeART during compilation, hence, cannot be substituted by the macro. TyCart's runtime library (1) executes the assert with the user-provided type and size, (2) inserts the assert into TyCart's assert-registration, and, (3) calls the CPR backend's registration function. The immediate check guards the CPR library against the error types *element count error* and *data type error*.

The `TY_checkpoint` macro iterates TyCart's assert-registration to re-assert all registered memory regions. Thereafter, the CPR backend's checkpoint function is called and performs the checkpoint. The re-assert guards against the *change allocation before checkpoint error*.

User-Defined Types. So far, only built-in types were discussed. In more complex codes, however, user-defined types are ubiquitous. Consider the example in Listing 1.5. In $C/C++$, the start address of a particular struct is identical to the address of its first member, here `size`. The TypeART runtime library, however, stores the most-outer type for a given address, i.e., **struct** `Vec` in the example. Thus, the address passed as argument to the type assert in line three is type ambiguous. In such cases, the TyCart runtime library recursively resolves user-defined types when passed a type-ambiguous address. It uses the static type-information to traverse the type layout, and check for a type match. If no matching type is encountered until further resolution is impossible, the assert fails. For cases in which it is desirable to only allow the specific type at an address, TyCart implements a *strict* check-mode, which does not recursively resolve types. The implementation of the strict mode is currently limited to the most-outer type.

Two interesting cases for user-defined types are sub-classes in $C++$ and unions in both C and $C++$. TypeART tracks the addresses and the type of a memory object, hence, the runtime library can determine the actual type of an object at a given address, independent of the type of the pointer that is used in the type assert. A **union** is tracked as a user-defined type by TypeART, and its size corresponds to the size of its largest possible type. TyCart, thus, can correctly determine the size of an allocation of a **union**, however, it leaves the correct determination of the current active type of the **union** to the user.

```
1  struct Vec {int size; double *data;} v;
2  // All values are initialized correctly, register v.size
3  TY_protect(memId, &v.size, 1, int);
```

Listing1.5:In strict mode, the assert in line 3 fails, as a **struct** Vec is tracked at that address, but **int** is specified. In weak mode, the struct is visited recursively, matching the **int** type as first member.

4 Evaluation

We apply TyCart to a set of benchmarks, i.e., serial C++ implementations of Conway's game of life [12] and a driven cavity problem ported from the MINPACK-2 collection [1] as well as the MPI-parallel applications LULESH [11], and a heat distribution code from the FTI repository [7]. Finally, we use TyCart to capture all relevant data to restart the compute kernel from a sequential version of the astrophysics simulation *eos-mbpt* [5] with ≈8.5M LoC. We also implemented both FTI and VeloC backend-specific versions for the targets. For the sequential applications, their *vanilla* baseline is run without MPI. All other applications are run using two MPI processes, and eight for LULESH, because FTI requires at least two MPI processes for its fault-tolerance scheme, and LULESH requires at least eight processes when executed MPI-parallel. TyCart's runtime checks are performed process-local and do not involve any communication, hence, neither runtime nor memory overhead scale with the number of processes. As a result, we only present benchmark results for these small process counts.

We collect *compile-time* statistics for (1) distinct instrumented heap allocation statements, and (2) filtering of global and stack variables. These statistics show the effectiveness of the employed translation-unit local filtering. However, the compile-time statistics are no indicator for the number of actual calls to instrumentation functions at runtime. Therefore, we collect *runtime* statistics for (1) number of regions registered for checkpointing, (2) size of an individual checkpoint, (3) maximum number of allocations tracked simultaneously, and, (4) total calls to instrumentation hooks at runtime. Finally, wall time and maximum memory usage of process 0 are also collected. In eos-mbpt, due to the use-case, one checkpoint is written, in the other benchmarks, ten are written. All checkpoints are written in synchronous mode to node-local disks, to exclude parallel file-system jitter from the measurements. The experiments are conducted on compute nodes of the Lichtenberg high-performance computer, each with two Intel Xeon 2680v3 processors, 64 GB of main memory, and HyperThreading and frequency scaling disabled. Results denote the median of ten consecutive runs on the same node and processor. The standard deviation for our measurements is 3%, except for the FTI & TyCart version of driven cavity (6%). We use the runtime of the vanilla version of the code as baseline. Of particular interest is the overhead TyCart introduces in addition to the CPR library.

Instrumentation and Registration. Table 1 lists the number of instrumented heap, global, and stack allocations and the corresponding percentage of variables excluded from the instrumentation. The table also lists the number of memory regions registered for checkpointing. Global variables, in contrast to stack allocations, are filtered effectively. In TypeART, no heap allocation filtering is performed to guarantee a consistent tracking of allocations and deallocations. In particular, the limited filtering in eos-mbpt results in many (unnecessarily) tracked allocations at runtime, see Table 2. The large number of individually registered regions in the case of driven cavity is due to registering the computed Jacobian matrix. It is not allocated as a contiguous block of memory, but each individual line of the matrix is registered separately. However, only very few additional allocations are tracked at all at runtime, see Table 2.

Table 1. Compile-time: number of instrumented heap allocations and frees; global and stack variables (percentage filtered). Checkpoint: allocations registered for checkpointing; file size per checkpoint per MPI process.

Benchmark	Compile time			Checkpoint	
	Heap	Globals (%)	Stack (%)	Regions	Size (MB)
driven cavity	15/32	1 (93)	17 (6)	10,003	764.0
eos-mbpt	482/160	203 (68)	549 (21)	7,845	6.7
game of life	12/28	1 (94)	7 (46)	4	48.0
heatdis	14/30	2 (89)	18 (0)	5	129.0
LULESH	14/30	6 (91)	39 (38)	57	7.0

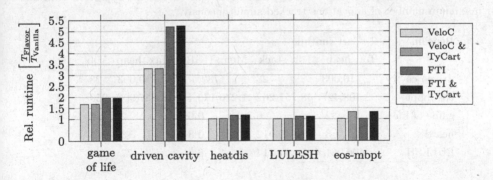

Fig. 3. Runtime overhead w.r.t. vanilla. Vanilla runtime: (1) game of life: 34.08 s, (2) driven cavity: 88.61 s, (3) heatdis: 206.30 s, (4) LULESH 2.0: 70.69 s, (5) eos-mbpt: 1,462.3 s.

Runtime and Memory Overhead. The naive introduction of a CPR library can substantially affect the runtime, see Fig. 3. Independent of TyCart, we see that FTI and VeloC have a noticeable impact on the runtime of the target, reported as (FTI/VeloC). Both libraries introduce significant overhead in the driven cavity (5.20x/3.30x) and the game of life (1.96x/1.78x) code, but only small overheads in heatdis (1.16x/1.01x) and LULESH (1.17x/1.00x). TyCart introduces an additional runtime overhead of approximately 1.01x over the CPR versions for all applications, except eos-mbpt (1.30x). The small runtime overhead is the result of compile-time filtering irrelevant allocations from instrumentation, thus, reducing the total number of instrumentation calls at runtime.

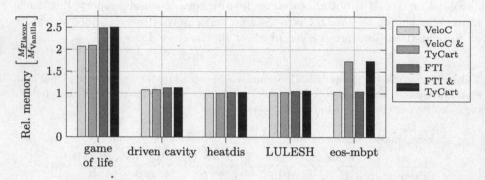

Fig. 4. Memory overhead w.r.t. vanilla. Vanilla RSS: (1) game of life: 52 MB, (2) driven cavity: 764 MB, (3) heatdis: 315 MB, (4) LULESH 2.0: 80 MB, (5) eos-mbpt: 1,827 MB.

Table 2. Total executed instrumentation calls for heap and stack allocations; information-tracking memory consumption as computed by the TypeART runtime; maximum number of allocations tracked simultaneously.

Benchmark	TyCart runtime				
	Tot. heap	Tot. stack	Mem. (KiB)	Max. heap	Max. stack
driven cavity	10,003	23	782.4	10,003	23
eos-mbpt	32,508,427	48,751,262	1,270,170.4	16,257,906	250
game of life	2	6	0.6	2	6
heatdis	3	30,012	0.8	3	15
LULESH	406,261	44,714	6.9	77	23

Comparing the CPR version to its TyCart version, the memory overhead is within 1.02x for all applications, and 1.67x for eos-mbpt, Fig. 4. Noticeable is the large memory overhead of the CPR version for game of life. In this application, almost its entire data is checkpointed. Using buffered I/O this is equivalent to doubling the memory footprint. For most of the applications, the typically modest number of concurrently tracked allocations, cf. Table 2, is a result of the application's small size, e.g., little call depth, in combination with the compile-time filtering.

On the other hand, the eos-mbpt code allocates most of its arrays on the heap, including function-local temporaries. All these allocations are instrumented, thus, many heap allocations are tracked, see Table 2. This is the primary reason for the comparably high runtime overhead. The peak memory overhead computed in the TypeART runtime library is a close estimate of the overhead observed in our benchmarks. In eos-mbpt, it can be accounted to (1) type information payload ($\approx$40%), (2) checkpoint registry ($\approx$1%), (3) GNU STL data structure bookkeeping ($\approx$59%). Also note the different characteristics that these codes exhibit w.r.t. their checkpointing behavior.

5 Discussion

Integrating TyCart into the project-specific version of eos-mbpt revealed uninitialized memory that was registered for checkpointing when running small data sets. The first level of indirection, **int***, in an array of **int**** was initialized correctly, but only a subset of these pointers was initialized to point to correct values. To assure no invalid pointer dereferences in the target code, previously uninitialized pointers are set to **NULL**, and only valid pointers are registered. Also, the use of heap allocations for function-local temporary arrays has been addressed by the developers. The higher runtime overhead in eos-mbpt is a result of the large number of allocations tracked at runtime.

Type ambiguity, as seen in Sect. 3.2 (User-Defined Types), occurs in the C++ game of life implementation and is solved using the default check-mode for type resolution. This is sufficient in the presented CPR use case, but introducing a *resolution level*, i.e., specifying the number of sub-type resolutions, for the strict mode may be desirable. As an alternative, allowing sets of types being specified would cover type ambiguity in a more controlled way.

The approach can be used with projects spanning across multiple translation units, however, four (current) limitations are inherited from TypeART. (1) The current implementation of compile-time filtering only considers the case when all uses of a variable are visible in a single translation unit. As a result, passing a mutable variable to a function from another translation unit, or a function pointer with undetermined call target, prevents TypeART from filtering. Employing more sophisticated program analysis techniques, e.g., whole-program value tracking, could help mitigate the limitation. (2) The LLVM IR does not distinguish signed and unsigned integer types, hence, type asserts do not work correctly in these instances. However, TyCart can still detect erroneously specified memory region sizes in all cases. (3) TyCart records an erroneous allocation type when the pointer-type cast is not in the same function as the initial allocation, e.g., the call to `malloc`. TypeART records these allocations to be of type **void***, thus, type asserts with the actual type fail. (4) The current implementation of the runtime library is not thread safe, thus, no thread-parallel programs can be considered.

Incremental checkpointing is currently unsupported, as TyCart asserts the registered number of elements for the checkpoint always to match the allocated number of elements. This prevents partial memory initialization at application restart, when TyCart is used for both checkpoint and restart. Also, restarting the application is not handled specifically, because data is restored into registered memory regions only. Thus, if the TyCart asserts succeed, it is assumed that the checkpoint data matches.

6   Related Work

In [15], the authors propose a directive-based approach to use FTI. Since the compiler introduces the calls to the FTI library, data type size computation is presumably correct. However, specifying the size of dynamically allocated data regions is left to the user and no mechanism is included to guard against element count errors. The source-level tool RTC [16] addresses memory-related bugs, such as type violations. The tool acts as a general memory sanitizer, whereas TyCart guards specific API functions to minimize overhead. This lightweight and API-specific design is also the reason for the comparably low overhead TyCart introduces. As a general, industry-grade tool to formulate and check requirements, Frama-C [4] with its specification language is well-known. The approach, as opposed to ours, works statically, thus inheriting all benefits and drawbacks of static analysis tools.

7   Conclusion and Future Work

This paper proposed the compiler-assisted type-safe checkpoint/restart tool TyCart. It uses the sanitizer tool TypeART to implement type asserts, a mechanism to specify type and extent requirements on memory regions. Using type asserts, TyCart provides a CPR-specific memory sanitizer tool that detects type-related usage errors of CPR libraries; our example implementation uses FTI and VeloC. The tool is based on the LLVM framework and applies a combination of static and dynamic analysis to implement allocation tracking and type checking.

Our evaluation on a set of benchmarks and a real-world application showed that TyCart's average runtime overhead is within 30%. The memory overhead is typically less than 5%, except for one application, where 67% memory overhead was measured. While we consider the tool already applicable for correctness checking, further improvements to reduce memory consumption seem beneficial.

The possibility for incremental checkpointing, as well as, the use of static analysis, e.g., symbolic execution, to detect (potentially) missing CPR calls is left as future work. Enabling the proposed approach to validate checkpoint metadata during application restart is of interest, however, this depends on the available metadata in the specific CPR library. Also, extending the proposed type asserts towards more expressiveness, e.g., no-alias requirements, or expose more introspection possibilities to developers [18], seem interesting research directions.

Acknowledgments. We thank Christian Drischler for providing the eos-mbpt application and appreciated discussion. This work was funded by the Hessian LOEWE initiative within the Software-Factory 4.0 project. Calculations for this research were conducted on the Lichtenberg high-performance computer of the TU Darmstadt. Funded by the Deutsche Forschungsgemeinschaft (DFG, German Research Foundation) – Project-ID 265191195 – SFB 1194.

References

1. Averick, B., Carter, R., Xue, G.L., More, J.: The MINPACK-2 test problem collection (1992). https://doi.org/10.2172/79972
2. Bautista-Gomez, L., Tsuboi, S., Komatitsch, D., Cappello, F., Maruyama, N., Matsuoka, S.: FTI: high performance fault tolerance interface for hybrid systems. In: Proceedings of 2011 International Conference for High Performance Computing, Networking, Storage and Analysis, SC 2011. ACM (2011). https://doi.org/10.1145/2063384.2063427
3. Bockhorn, A., Narayanan, S.H.K., Walther, A.: Checkpointing approaches for the computation of adjoints covering resilience issues. In: 2020 Proceedings of the SIAM Workshop on Combinatorial Scientific Computing, pp. 22–31. SIAM (2020). https://doi.org/10.1137/1.9781611976229.3
4. Cuoq, P., Kirchner, F., Kosmatov, N., Prevosto, V., Signoles, J., Yakobowski, B.: Frama-C. In: Eleftherakis, G., Hinchey, M., Holcombe, M. (eds.) SEFM 2012. LNCS, vol. 7504, pp. 233–247. Springer, Heidelberg (2012). https://doi.org/10.1007/978-3-642-33826-7_16
5. Drischler, C., Hebeler, K., Schwenk, A.: Chiral interactions up to next-to-next-to-next-to-leading order and nuclear saturation. Phys. Rev. Lett. **122**, 042501 (2019). https://doi.org/10.1103/PhysRevLett.122.042501
6. Egwutuoha, I.P., Levy, D., Selic, B., Chen, S.: A survey of fault tolerance mechanisms and checkpoint/restart implementations for high performance computing systems. J. Supercomput. **65**(3), 1302–1326 (2013). https://doi.org/10.1007/s11227-013-0884-0
7. FTI: FTI public GitHub examples (2017). https://github.com/leobago/fti/tree/master/examples. Accessed Mar 2020
8. Cao, G., Singhal, M.: On coordinated checkpointing in distributed systems. IEEE Trans. Parallel Distrib. Syst. **9**(12), 1213–1225 (1998). https://doi.org/10.1109/71.737697
9. Hilbrich, T., Protze, J., Schulz, M., de Supinski, B.R., Müller, M.S.: MPI runtime error detection with MUST: advances in deadlock detection. In: Proceedings of the International Conference on High Performance Computing, Networking, Storage and Analysis, SC 2012, pp. 1–10, November 2012. https://doi.org/10.1109/SC.2012.79
10. Hück, A., et al.: Compiler-aided type tracking for correctness checking of MPI applications. In: 2018 IEEE/ACM 2nd International Workshop on Software Correctness for HPC Applications (Correctness), pp. 51–58, November 2018. https://doi.org/10.1109/Correctness.2018.00011
11. Karlin, I., Keasler, J., Neely, R.: LULESH 2.0 updates and changes. Technical report LLNL-TR-641973, August 2013
12. Lehr, J.P.: Conway's game of life (2016). https://github.com/jplehr/GameOfLife/tree/master/serial_template. Accessed Mar 2020

13. Liu, Y., Nassar, R., Leangsuksun, C., Naksinehaboon, N., Paun, M., Scott, S.: A reliability-aware approach for an optimal checkpoint/restart model in HPC environments. In: 2007 IEEE International Conference on Cluster Computing, pp. 452–457 (2007). https://doi.org/10.1109/CLUSTR.2007.4629264
14. Lotz, J., Naumann, U., Mitra, S.: Mixed integer programming for call tree reversal. In: 2016 Proceedings of the SIAM Workshop on Combinatorial Scientific Computing, pp. 83–91. SIAM (2016). https://doi.org/10.1137/1.9781611974690.ch9
15. Maroñas, M., Mateo, S., Beltran, V., Ayguadé, E.: A directive-based approach to perform persistent checkpoint/restart. In: 2017 International Conference on High Performance Computing Simulation (HPCS), pp. 442–451 (2017). https://doi.org/10.1109/HPCS.2017.72
16. Milewicz, R., Vanka, R., Tuck, J., Quinlan, D., Pirkelbauer, P.: Runtime checking C programs. In: Proceedings of the 30th Annual ACM Symposium on Applied Computing, SAC 2015, 2107–2114. ACM (2015). https://doi.org/10.1145/2695664.2695906
17. Nicolae, B., Moody, A., Gonsiorowski, E., Mohror, K., Cappello, F.: VeloC: Towards high performance adaptive asynchronous checkpointing at large scale. In: 2019 IEEE International Parallel and Distributed Processing Symposium (IPDPS), pp. 911–920, May 2019. https://doi.org/10.1109/IPDPS.2019.00099
18. Rigger, M., Mayrhofer, R., Schatz, R., Grimmer, M., Mössenböck, H.: Introspection for C and its applications to library robustness. Art Sci. Eng. Program. **2**(2), 1–31 (2018). https://doi.org/10.22152/programming-journal.org/2018/2/4
19. Subasi, O., Kestor, G., Krishnamoorthy, S.: Toward a general theory of optimal checkpoint placement. In: 2017 IEEE International Conference on Cluster Computing (CLUSTER), pp. 464–474 (2017). https://doi.org/10.1109/CLUSTER.2017.127

Static Analysis to Enhance Programmability and Performance in OmpSs-2

Adrian Munera[✉], Sara Royuela, Roger Ferrer, Raul Peñacoba,
and Eduardo Quiñones

Barcelona Supercomputing Center, Barcelona, Spain
{adrian.munera, sara.royuela, roger.ferrer, raul.penacoba,
eduardo.quinones}@bsc.es

Abstract. Task-based parallel programming models based on compiler directives have proved their effectiveness at describing parallelism in High-Performance Computing (HPC) applications. Recent studies show that cutting-edge Real-Time applications, such as those for unmanned vehicles, can successfully exploit these models. In this scenario, OpenMP is a de facto standard for HPC, and is being studied for Real-Time systems due to its time-predictability and delimited functional safety. However, changes in OpenMP take time to be standardized because it sweeps along a large community. OmpSs, instead, is a task-based model for fast-prototyping that has been a forerunner of OpenMP since its inception. OmpSs-2, its successor, aims at the same goal, and defines several features that can be introduced in future versions of OpenMP. This work targets compiler-based optimizations to enhance the programmability and performance of OmpSs-2. Regarding the former, we present an algorithm to determine the data-sharing attributes of OmpSs-2 tasks. Regarding the latter, we introduce a new algorithm to automatically release OmpSs-2 task dependencies before a task has completed. This work evaluates both algorithms in a set of well-known benchmarks, and discusses their applicability to the current and future specifications of OpenMP.

Keywords: Programmability · Performance · Static analysis · OmpSs-2

1 Introduction

The growing demands of society regarding mobility, health, and industry, among others, have motivated the convergence of computer systems towards complex ecosystems. This affects dissimilar domains such as High-Performance Computing (HPC) and Real-Time systems, e.g., supercomputers combining shared memory computational nodes in a distributed memory environment targeting HPC, and Multi-Processing Systems-on-Chip (MPSoC), containing multiple and heterogeneous processing elements, targeting Real-Time applications.

© Springer Nature Switzerland AG 2020
H. Jagode et al. (Eds.): ISC High Performance 2020 Workshops, LNCS 12321, pp. 19–33, 2020.
https://doi.org/10.1007/978-3-030-59851-8_2

The need to exploit complex architectures effectively and efficiently has promoted the use of parallel programming models. As a result, several abstractions focusing on the *productivity* of parallel systems coexist [24]. A possible classification divides them in two groups: (1) *thread-based* models, which exploit data parallelism (i.e., distributing data), and (2) *task-based* models, which exploit task parallelism (i.e., distributing units of work, or *tasks*). The former force programmers to manage low-level details of the computation, such as data distribution and synchronization, while the latter typically offer a higher-level abstraction that simplifies these complexities. Task-based models also offer greater flexibility, making them more suitable for the parallelization of dynamic and unstructured applications. For these reasons, these have gained a broad acceptance.

Some representative task-based models are Intel Threading Building Blocks [27], CUDA graphs [23], OpenMP [13] and OmpSs [7]. The two former are *hardware-centric* models that expose the architectural features in the language, requiring programmers a considerable level of expertise to achieve productivity, while also preventing portability. The two latter are *parallelism-centric* approaches offering high-level APIs based on compiler directives that hide the complexities of the architecture, and focus on providing mechanisms to describe parallel units and the synchronizations among them. The simplicity of the latter, together with their productivity, makes them very appealing for programmers.

Among all parallel abstractions, OpenMP has become the de facto standard for shared-memory HPC [6] by virtue of its productivity [10,28], while it also supports heterogeneous computation through the acceleration model [2,12]. Moreover, it has an increasing interest in embedded computing [20,22] because of its delimited functional safety [18] and its proven time-predictability [21].

Introducing changes in OpenMP is a long-distance race that requires consensus of a large community, and prototype implementations of the involved vendors (e.g., Intel, IBM, and NVIDIA). Interestingly, OmpSs is a programming model, implemented on top of the Mercurium compiler [3] and the Nanos++ runtime [4]. The main goal of OmpSs has been fast-prototyping tasking features to include them in the OpenMP standard. Some of them, like task dependencies, task priorities, task loops, task reductions, taskwait dependencies, multi-dependencies and data affinity, are already included in OpenMP.

OmpSs-2 [5] is the second generation of OmpSs. It extends its predecessor with features covering dependencies across different task nesting levels and early release of dependencies, among others (see details in Sect. 3). The reason-to-be of OmpSs-2 is, as in OmpSs, to extend OpenMP with new features. For this reason, the novelties that OmpSs-2 introduces to tasking models, and the proved success of OmpSs to influence the OpenMP standard, motivates the interest of this work, which contributions are: (1) an algorithm to detect the correct data-sharing of OmpSs-2 tasks, targeting programmability and correctness, (2) an algorithm for the automatic release of task dependencies, targeting performance, and (3) an evaluation of both algorithms with LLVM in a set of benchmarks.

The remainder of the paper is organized as follows: Sect. 3 introduces OmpSs-2; Sect. 2 exposes the related work; Sect. 4 describes the proposed algorithms targeting performance, correctness and programmability in OmpSs-2 programs; Sect. 5 details of the implementation done in LLVM, and shows the evaluation of the proposed techniques; and Sect. 6 discusses the benefits of this work for OpenMP.

2   Related Work

Programmability is an important aspect of high-level programming models, as it is crucial for their adoption. Focusing on OpenMP, the scope of variables is a cumbersome and error-prone process that jeopardizes not only programmability, but also correctness. As a consequence, several works tackle the automatic scope of variables in OpenMP. Lin et al. [11] proposed the use of the default(AUTO) clause for such a purpose, and defined a set of rules to accomplish auto-scope in parallel regions. They showed that automatic and user-defined clauses can obtain the same performance. Voss et al. [25] evaluated the impact of the same clause for auto-parallelization purposes, concluding that several regions cannot be automatically parallelized because of the limitations of the technique: it only works for the OpenMP *thread model*, it offers limited inter-procedural analysis for arrays, and it lacks support for API functions calls. Later, Royuela et al. [17] proposed an algorithm to automatically scope variables in OpenMP 3.1 task regions. This work evaluates the algorithm using, among others, the BOTS benchmarks [8] and compares its results with those of the Oracle Solaris Studio 12.3 compiler mechanism with the same goal [15]. They exhibit an accuracy close to 85% compared to that of Solaris, close to 78%. Wang et al. [26] approached the same problem from a simplicity point of view, proposing an algorithm that uses taskwait directives to avoid the need for analyzing concurrency among tasks. Although this work presents better accuracy, it has an important negative impact on the performance of the resulting parallel code.

3   The OmpSs-2 Programming Model

OmpSs-2 [5] is a task-based parallel programming model built on top of a set of C/C++ and Fortran language directives and a runtime API. OmpSs-2 is similar to OpenMP [13] in which a sequential program is incrementally parallelized using annotations in the source code. In contrast, it is purely task-based, so the fundamental unit of concurrency, to exploit parallel execution, is the so-called *task*. Listing 1.1 shows the syntax of an OmpSs-2 task directive in C/C++.

When a thread of the program encounters a task construct, it *creates* a task. The execution of the structured block (in C/C++, this is the compound statement that follows the #pragma) of the task, is deferred until the task itself is *executed*. A task that has been created but not yet executed is called to be *ready*. A task is *complete* when it has finished its execution.

```
1 int x = 3, y = 4;
2 #pragma oss task \
3             shared(x) \
4             firstprivate(y) \
5             label(T)
6 {
7    x++;
8    y++;
9 }
10 #pragma oss taskwait
11 assert(x == 4);
12 assert(y == 4);
```

Listing 1.1. Basic task syntax.

```
1 #pragma oss task label(A)
2 {
3    #pragma oss task label(A1)
4    {}
5 }
6 #pragma oss task label(B)
7 {
8    #pragma oss task label(B1)
9    {}
10   #pragma oss taskwait
11   // B1 is complete
12   // A and A1 may not be complete
13 }
14 #pragma oss taskwait
15 // A, A1, B, and B1 are complete
```

Listing 1.2. Synchronization and nesting.

3.1   Data-Sharings

Variables used in the structured block that are declared inside the task region are local to the task, while those declared outside have an associated *data-sharing*. A *shared* data-sharing means that the task will capture the address of the variable, i.e. it will access the original variable. A *firstprivate* data-sharing means that the task will capture the value of the variable, i.e. it will access a copy of the variable. Shared variables are prone to data-races between the thread that executes the task and other threads, including the one that created the task.

3.2   Task Synchronization and Nesting

Tasks can be nestes in OmpSs-2: the execution of the enclosing task construct leads to the creation of the inner tasks, whose execution is also deferred. Parent tasks do not execute a taskwait at the end of their associated construct, so the enclosing task construct may complete before the nested tasks constructs do.

Synchronization is achieved using the taskwait directive, which waits for all tasks created in the current task context and those created in nested task contexts to complete, as shown in Listing 1.2. A wait clause attached to a task directive behaves as if a taskwait is inserted at the end of the task construct.

Applications may expose concurrency difficult to exploit due its dynamic nature. For these cases OmpSs-2 provides *dependency* clauses, like in, out or inout. When a thread of the program encounters a task construct, the runtime annotates the expressions denoting the memory referenced in those clauses. A task becomes ready when executing it would not violate its data dependencies respect to data dependencies of previous tasks created and not completed yet.

OmpSs-2 provides two more dependency clauses, concurrent and commutative, that are useful when several tasks participate in a reduction operation. The former is like inout, but allows parallelism across tasks with a concurrent dependency of the same object. The latter also acts as inout, but allows any ordering between tasks with the same commutative dependency. Unlike commutative, which is mutually exclusive, concurrent dependencies require explicit synchronization (e.g. locks) to avoid data races. Furthermore, dependency clauses can also be used in a taskwait directive, acting as a task with an empty construct.

Code in Listing 1.3 shows a program that creates 4 tasks. Tasks T1 and T2 can be executed concurrently. Task T3 will be ready once T1 completes. Task T4 will be ready once T1 and T2 complete. Task T5.1 will be completed after the taskwait with dependencies, W1. That taskwait would not wait for task T5.2.

```
1  int x, y, z1, z2;
2  #pragma oss task out(x) label(T1)
3  { x = 1; }
4  #pragma oss task out(y) label(T2)
5  { y = 1; }
6  #pragma oss task inout(x) label(T3)
7  {
8    assert(x == 1);
9    x++;
10 }
11 #pragma oss task in(x) in(y) label(T4)
12 {
13   assert(x == 2);
14   assert(y == 1);
15 }
16 #pragma oss taskwait
17 assert(x == 2);
18 assert(y == 1);
19 #pragma oss task out(z1) label(T5.1)
20 { z1 = 3; }
21 #pragma oss task out(z2) label(T5.2)
22 { z2 = 4; }
23 #pragma oss taskwait in(z1) // (W1)
24 assert(z1 == 3);
```

Listing 1.3. Tasks and dependencies.

```
1  int x = 1;
2  #pragma oss task weakinout(x) \
3                     label(A)
4  {
5    #pragma oss task inout(x) \
6                     label(A1)
7    {
8      assert(x == 1);
9      x++;
10   }
11 }
12 #pragma oss task weakinout(x) \
13                  label(B)
14 {
15 #pragma oss task inout(x) label(B1)
16   {
17     assert(x == 2);
18     x++;
19   }
20 }
21 #pragma oss taskwait
22 assert(x == 3);
```

Listing 1.4. Nested tasks and dependencies.

OmpSs-2 considers a unique domain for all the tasks of a program: tasks define the data they use as the regular dependency clauses, and the data used in nested tasks as a weaker form of dependency designated by the weakin, weakout and weakinout clauses. This links the dependency domains at all nesting levels while avoids unnecessary synchronizations between tasks.

Listing 1.4 shows an example of dependency between nested tasks A1 and B1 without synchronizing tasks A and B. Had the code used a regular inout dependency in tasks A and B, then task B would only be ready once A completes.

A created task becomes ready when all its dependencies have been *released* by its task predecessor set. Tasks release all their dependencies when they complete. OmpSs-2 allows executing tasks to early release their dependencies using the release directive. This provides fine-grained control for tasks that describe a large set of data-dependencies that are processed in chunks.

Listing 1.5 shows an example in which a task, T1, processes data in chunks. Such process is fast, so it may not be beneficial to create a task per chunk. Then, a slower process creates one task T2 per chunk. Without the release of dependencies, all T2 tasks would have to wait to the completion of T1. Because T1 releases dependencies earlier, T2 tasks may be ready even before T1 completes.

```
1  #pragma oss task out(data[0; size]) label(T1)
2  { // Task with an out dependency to all data[k], where 0 <= k < size
3    for (int i = 0; i < size; i += chunk_size) {
4      for (int j = i; j < chunk_size; j++)
5        fast_process(&data[j]);
6      #pragma oss release inout(data[i; chunk_size])
7      // The current task releases the inout dependency on all data[k],
8      // where i <= k < i + chunk_size
9    }
10 }
11 for (int i = 0; i < size; i += chunk_size) {
12   #pragma oss task in(data[i; chunk_size]) label(T2)
13   { // Task with an input dependency to all data[k],
14     // where i <= k < i + chunk_size
15     slow_process(&data[i], chunk_size);
16   }
17 }
```

Listing 1.5. Early release of dependencies.

4   Compiler Analysis Techniques for OmpSs-2

This section introduces two compiler analysis aiming at enhancing the programmability and performance of OmpSs-2 programs: (1) the automatic scope of variables in task constructs, and (2) the automatic release of task dependencies. Both techniques assume the input code is correct (e.g., dependencies are defined correctly), and that it keeps the sequential consistency property.

4.1   Automatic Definition of Task Data-Sharing Clauses, *Auto-sope*

The mechanism for automatically scoping variables in OmpSs-2 tasks we propose draws from a previous algorithm proposed for the same purpose in OpenMP 3.1 tasks [17]. That algorithm proceeds, for each task t, in two steps: (1) define the regions of code that can be concurrent with t, and (2) scope the variables based on their usage within t and its concurrent regions, and the liveness of the variables after the last point at which the task can be synchronized.

We have adapted the previously mentioned algorithm to the singularities of OmpSs-2, including (1) *nested tasks* and *weak dependencies*, (2) the concurrent and commutative dependency clauses, and (3) taskwait directives with dependency clauses. These features, missing in OpenMP 3.1 (some of them are included in OpenMP v5.0, as discussed in Sect. 6), have an impact in the first step of the algorithm, i.e., computing the regions of code concurrent with a task. These parts can be (a) other tasks, (b) portions of the parent task, and (c) different instances of the same task. Next we describe the first step of the *auto-scope* algorithm to adapt it to OmpSs-2:

1. Compute the points of the code delimiting the regions code that can be concurrent with a task t, which are:
   - *TSP(t)*, the task scheduling point (TSP) of the creation of t.
   - *Pre-sync(t)*, the last synchronization(s) before *TSP(t)*, which can be (a) taskwait directives, (b) the end of other task constructs with matching

dependencies, and (c) the beginning of the function enclosing t or the task scheduling point of the creation of the parent task.

- *Post-sync(t)*, the first synchronization(s) encountered after *TSP* where the task can be synchronized, which can be (a) taskwait directives, (b) the beginning of other task constructs with matching dependencies, and (c) the end of the function enclosing t or the end of the parent task.

  The pseudo-code that computes the *Pre-sync(t)* points is shown in Algorithm 1. The algorithm for computing the *Post-sync(t)* points is analogous to the one for the *Pre-sync(t)* points, but it traverses the paths starting from the successors of t, instead of searching in the predecessors.

2. Compute the regions of code that can be concurrent with t, which are:
   - Other tasks found between *Pre-sync*, and *Post-sync*, that are not synchronized yet by means of dependency clauses.
   - Different instances of t, if the task is within a loop, and *Post-sync* happens after the end of the loop.

Algorithm 1: Computation of the *Pre-sync(t)* set of a task t.

Data: Node containing task t
Result: Pre-sync(t): list of last synchronization points
foreach *path(p): possible path from t to the creation of its parent task, t', or the beginning of the enclosing function, f, whatever comes first* **do**

     list deps(p);   /* dependencies found in p */
     node n = path_deps(p).leaf;   /* node being traversed */
     while $n \mathrel{!=} NULL$ **do**
         if *n represents a* taskwait *directive without dependencies* **then**
             Pre-sync(t).insert(n);
             if *n dominates t* **then**
                 | return Pre-sync(t)
             else
                 | break;   /* stop searching this path */

         else if *(n represents a* task *construct*
                 ‖ *n represents a* taskwait *directive with dependencies)*
             && n synchronizes t **then**
             Pre-sync(t).insert(n);
             deps(p).insert(deps(n));
             if *deps(p) == deps(t)* **then**
                 | break;   /* stop searching this path */

         n = parent(n);   /* keep traversing ancestors */

- Code from the parent task found:
  - Between *TSP* and *Post-sync*.
  - Between the beginning of the loop and *TSP*, if *t* is enclosed within a loop and *Post-sync* occurs after the loop has ended.[1]

Figure 1 illustrates the points delimiting the concurrent regions of a task. There, Fig. 1a shows an OmpSs-2 sample code where a task T1: (1) creates task T2, which sets the value of *y*; (2) creates task T3, which updates the value of *y*; (3) updates the value of *y*; and (4) waits for the completion of tasks producing *y*. Additionally, Fig. 1b depicts a flow graph of the code, including the code in all tasks, the task scheduling points corresponding to the creation of the tasks (TxC), and the `taskwait`, as well as the *TSP*, *Pre-sync* and *Post-sync* points of task T3, represented with different symbols.

The rules that define the data-sharing attributes of a task remain the same as those defined in the original algorithm for OpenMP [17].

The adequate determination of the data-sharing attributes enhances the programmability of the model by freeing the programmer from the burden of manually defining these values. It also impacts correctness, for the algorithm can be used to check user-defined data-sharing attributes. Finally, it can also affect performance if variables unnecessarily privatized can be scoped as shared [19].

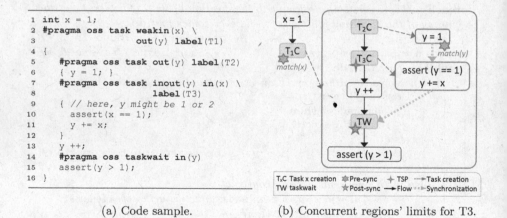

```
1  int x = 1;
2  #pragma oss task weakin(x) \
3                   out(y) label(T1)
4  {
5      #pragma oss task out(y) label(T2)
6      { y = 1; }
7      #pragma oss task inout(y) in(x) \
8                      label(T3)
9      { // here, y might be 1 or 2
10         assert(x == 1);
11         y += x;
12     }
13     y ++;
14     #pragma oss taskwait in(y)
15     assert(y > 1);
16 }
```

(a) Code sample.   (b) Concurrent regions' limits for T3.

Fig. 1. Example of concurrent regions in the OmpSs-2 *auto-scope* algorithm.

4.2 Automatic Release of Task Dependencies, *Auto-release*

OmpSs-2 allows releasing the dependencies of a task before the task has finished (see Sect. 3 for details). This feature may positively impact the performance of the application when a task uses certain data only at the beginning,

---

[1] A task t_2 synchronizes [19] a task t_1 if t_2 is created after t_1, and either (a) t_1 designates an out object that t_2 designates as in or out, or (b) t_1 designates an in object that t_2 designates as out, or (c) t_1 and t_2 designate the same commutative object.

and then performs other lengthy operations that delay the release of this data dependencies.

In order to enhance the performance of OmpSs-2 programs while reducing the work needed by the programmer, we present next a compiler analysis that automatically introduces `release` directives within tasks. The algorithm works, for each task t in the program with a set of variables included in dependency clauses, *dep_vars(t)*, as follows:

1. Compute liveness analysis [16] within t.
2. Traverse the statements of t in post-order and, for each statement s:
   (a) Gather the set of variables that are not live, *dead_vars(s)*.
   (b) Compute the set of variables to be released, *vars_to_release(s)*, as the intersection of *dead_vars(s)* and *dep_vars(t)*.
   (c) If *vars_to_release(s)* is not empty, introduce a `release` directive after s, including the variables in *vars_to_release(s)* as dependencies, as they were in the dependency clauses of t.
3. To reduce overhead, simplify the release directives as follows:
   (a) Remove the release directives if they are the last statement of the task, because the dependencies are going to be released at that point anyway.
   (b) Move release clauses outside loops to join the contiguous memory accesses of arrays and structures.

Figure 2 is an illustration of the liveness analysis. There, Fig. 2a shows the portion of the code in Listing 1.5 corresponding to task T1, and Fig. 2b shows a control-flow graph representation of that task with some nodes tagged with the information of liveness analysis. Overall, the analysis computes $live\_out(n)$, where n is a node of the control-flow graph, as the set of variables that can be used in any path reachable after n, taking into account the data-sharing attributes of nested tasks (i.e., if a variable is `private` in a nested task, then the original variable is not used at this point.) For example, after the call to $fast\_process$, the value of $data[j]$ will never be used again, so this variable is

```
1  #pragma oss task out(data[0; size])
2  for (int i = 0; i < size;
3         i += chunk_size) {
4      for (int j = i;
5             j < chunck_size; j++) {
6          // in the first iteration
7          // data[i;chunk_size] is used
8          fast_process(&data[j]);
9          // data[j] is never used again
10         // i and j are used in the
11         // respective loop increments
12     }
13 }
```

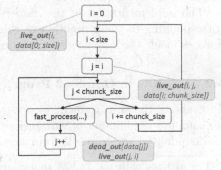

(a) Snippet of code in Listing 1.5.   (b) Control flow and liveness analysis.

Fig. 2. Example of liveness analysis.

dead. On the contrary, at the same point, the values of i and j are still live because the are used to update the next value of the same variables, respectively.

5 Evaluation

The algorithms described in Sect. 4 have been implemented in the LLVM compiler. Next subsections introduce some relevant details of the implementation, and show the evaluation of the two algorithms considering programmability (in the case of *auto-scope*) and performance (in the case of the *auto-release*).

5.1 LLVM Implementation

We have built the proposed techniques in LLVM, using a preliminary implementation of the OmpSs-2 model in Clang[2]. LLVM offers a stable and extensive tool-chain that includes several analysis, which simplifies the implementation task, while boosts the accuracy of the results. Particularly, we benefit from the following analysis already implemented: *dominator tree* (the LLVM DominatorTree class), used for detecting variable uses inside tasks and concurrent regions; *alias analysis* (the AAResults class), used to decide when different pointers and array accesses (may) point to the same memory location; and *scalar evolution* and other *loop analyses* (the ScalarEvolution, LoopInfo and IVUsers classes), used to recognize loops, analyze induction variables and recognize access patterns to arrays. Furthermore, we use two transformations required for the previous analysis to work: *loop-rotate*, which converts loops into do/while style loops, and *mem2reg*, which removes unnecessary *alloca* instructions. Finally, we take advantage of the *llvm-link* tool, which allows for linking several LLVM IR files into one, enhancing the possibilities for inter-procedural analysis, and hence the accuracy of our results.

Besides our algorithms, we have implemented *liveness* analysis in LLVM. This analysis uses the Value class, which gives information about the uses of a variable, while traverses the control-flow graph to search the paths that are reachable from a given node.

The implementation of the *auto-release* algorithm lacks its very last step, corresponding to the promotion of releases outside a loop when the individual releases inside the loop access contiguous memory. This remains as future work.

5.2 Benefits in OmpSs-2 Programmability: *Auto-scope*

To evaluate the enhancement in programmability of the auto-scope algorithm, we compute the number of variables automatically scoped for a series of benchmarks adapted to OmpSs-2 from the Barcelona OpenMP Task Suite [8], and

---

[2] The artifact with the LLVM tool-chain with the proposed algorithms, the Nanos runtime library, and the test-suit used for the evaluation is publicly available in https://gitlab.bsc.es/ppc-bsc/research/c3po-artifact/-/tags/v1.0. A stable version of Clang for OmpSs-2 and Nanos will be released in the next months.

other OmpSs-2 benchmarks (See Footnote 2). Table 1 shows the results. There, each row refers to a benchmark; the first block of columns describe relevant aspects of the benchmarks; and the second block shows the number of variables automatically scoped for each attribute; and the success ratio as the number of variables automatically scoped out of the number of variables used in the tasks of the program.

Table 1. Results of the *auto-scope* algorithm for OmpSs-2, implemented in LLVM, using different benchmarks.

	Description			LLVM results				
	#tasks	nested tasks	method	shared	private	firstprivate	undefined	(%)success
Alignment	1	no	iter	2	4	14	0	100%
FFT	41	no	rec	102	0	140	0	100%
Fib	2	no	rec	2	0	2	0	100%
Health	2	yes	iter&rec	1	1	2	0	100%
Floorplan	1	no	iter&rec	3	1	9	2	86.66%
NQueens	1	no	iter&rec	2	0	4	0	100%
Sort	9	yes	rec	27	0	10	0	100%
SparseLU	4	yes	iter	4	3	11	0	100%
UTS	2	no	iter&rec	2	1	3	0	100%
Cholesky	4	no	iter	4	0	12	0	100%
Saxpy	2	yes	iter	4	0	3	0	100%
Matmul	2	yes	iter	3	0	8	0	100%
TOTAL								98.88%

The results reveal the strengths of the algorithm combined with the capabilities of LLVM. For eleven out of twelve benchmarks we have been able to automatically scope all variables. Only for *floorplan*, there are two variables that have not been automatically scoped. This is because these variables are only used in functions which code is not reachable (i.e. *memcpy*), and hence their usage cannot be determined (although many benchmarks use functions from standard C libraries, if the variables are also written within the function, then what happens within those calls can be omitted; this is not the case when the variables are only read). Also composed variables (i.e. arrays) can be undefined if the *alias analysis* can not ensure there is no data race in any of the elements of the array, and it is used after the *Post-sync* points of the task.

The available mechanisms for the auto-scope of variables are not directly comparable with our technique because they target OpenMP, and do not support OmpSs-2 features. Nonetheless, a similar set of benchmarks was used to evaluate the algorithm we draw from [17], and we have improved the accuracy of the algorithm by virtue of the LLVM capabilities: the former offered an accuracy around the 85%, while our implementation is close to 100%. This, without losing performance, since we use the same rules for deciding the scope. Compared to other approaches [26] more conservative, we can advance that our approach will always perform equally or better because we do not use full-barriers (e.g., taskwait directives) to ease the algorithm, as they do.

5.3   Benefits in OmpSs-2 Performance: *Auto-release*

To evaluate the benefits in performance obtained with the *auto-release* algorithm, we have used two different configurations of the code shown in Listing 1.5: (1) the first one, called *Super fast process*, where *chunk_size* is set to 10000, *size* is set to 200000, and the call to *fast_process* takes $100\,\mu$s; and (2) the second one, called *Fast process*, where *chunk_size* is set to 1000, *size* is set to 20000, and the call to *fast_process* takes $1000\,\mu$s. For both configurations, the call to *slow_process* takes 5 s. For this evaluation, we have indeed removed the release directive from the original benchmark. Furthermore, we have evaluated the overhead of introducing a release call, which is around 200 ns.

Table 2 shows the execution time of the two configurations mentioned before, on an 8-core x86 2.60 GHz Intel processor, for three different versions: (1) original user's code without releasing any dependency; (2) user's code with the *auto-release* algorithm introducing individual releases inside the loop; and (3) user's code with manual release of a full array section. The numbers show that, when the execution time of the code where the release is introduced is fast enough, i.e., *Super fast process*, the benefits of automatically adding the release directive are not as good as they could be. This is due to the overhead of the release call, together with the need for modifying the regions a task depends on very often (i.e., runtime overhead). Nonetheless, there is still a significant benefit compared to not releasing any dependencies. On the other hand, when the execution time of the code where the release directive is not that short, i.e., *Fast process*, then there is not a significant difference between inserting individual releases or joining contiguous releases in a unique release directive.

Table 2. Results of the *auto-release* algorithm for OmpSs-2, implemented in LLVM, using different configurations of code in Listing 1.5.

	Execution time (us)	
	Super fast process	Fast process
No release	46747405	36233344
Release within loop	40607605	26570543
Release outside loop	35894357	26533354

Although the evaluation shows that the auto-release of dependencies does not achieve better performance than the manual version, it reveals two important aspects: (1) the algorithm enhances the programmability of OmpSs-2 by relieving the user from the need to release data dependencies manually; and (2) the performance gain obtained with the automatic pass is obvious compared to not using our technique. The fact that we do not obtain the same results as perfectly releasing dependencies manually is because the implementation lacks the last step: promoting release directives outside loops. However, the use of this algorithm allows for existing kernels to benefit from the mechanism without needing any modification in the source code.

6   Discussion

The algorithms presented in this work target the OmpSs-2 parallel programming model. Nonetheless, some features introduced in OmpSs-2 already exist in the OpenMP 5.0 specification. On the contrary, OpenMP 5.0 and the research lines being conducted for future specifications also include some features to be considered in these algorithms. Next we discuss all these features:

- The `commutative` clause in OmpSs-2 has been introduced in the OpenMP 5.0 specification as `mutexinoutset`. Both clauses has the same behavior. This feature affects the proposed auto-scope algorithm when determining the tasks that can be concurrent with a given task.
- The `concurrent` clause in OmpSs-2 has not yet been introduced in OpenMP. However, the first preview for the future OpenMP specification 5.1 [14] includes the `inoutset` clause, which has the same behavior. This clause affects the computation of concurrent tasks in the auto-scope algorithm.
- The `release` directive does not exist in OpenMP, so its behavior can not yet be applied. However, there are other models, such as DepSpawn [9], that also include this feature and could benefit from our analysis.
- OmpSs-2 forces parent tasks to cover the dependencies of children tasks with either regular dependencies or weak dependencies to fulfill compliance. This boosts the safety of OmpSs-2. For this reason, this restriction could be applied to OpenMP if this model is to be used in critical real-time systems.

Overall, this paper introduces a series of compiler analysis for OmpSs-2 that enhance its performance while improving its programmability. Furthermore, we have shown how other programming models, specially OpenMP, could benefit from this analysis. This work tackles the automatic scope of variables in task constructs and the automatic release of task dependencies once these variables are already computed. There are however other features that remain as a future work, including the automatic definition of task, taskwait and taskloop dependencies, and the analysis of *detached tasks*, i.e., tasks that detach the finalization of task from the completion of the code included in the task, while attach it to the occurrence of a given event. This feature, accomplished by means of the `detach` clause in OpenMP, exists also in other models like StarPU [1] (by means of the *starpu_task_end_dep_release* call), but is not included in OmpSs-2.

References

1. Augonnet, C., Thibault, S., Namyst, R., Wacrenier, P.A.: StarPU: a unified platform for task scheduling on heterogeneous multicore architectures. Concurr. Comput. Pract. Exp. **23**(2), 187–198 (2011)
2. Ayguadé, E., et al.: Extending OpenMP to survive the heterogeneous multi-core era. Int. J. Parallel Program. **38**(5–6), 440–459 (2010)
3. Barcelona Supercomputing Center: Mercurium. https://pm.bsc.es/mcxx
4. Barcelona Supercomputing Center: Nanos++. https://pm.bsc.es/nanox
5. Barcelona Supercomputing Center: Ompss-2. https://pm.bsc.es/ompss-2

6. Dagum, L., Menon, R.: OpenMP: an industry standard API for shared-memory programming. IEEE Comput. Sci. Eng. **5**(1), 46–55 (1998)
7. Duran, A., et al.: OmpSs: a proposal for programming heterogeneous multi-core architectures. Parallel Process. Lett. **21**(02), 173–193 (2011)
8. Duran, A., Teruel, X., Ferrer, R., Martorell, X., Ayguade, E.: Barcelona OpenMP tasks suite: a set of benchmarks targeting the exploitation of task parallelism in OpenMP. In: International Conference on Parallel Processing, pp. 124–131 (2009)
9. González, C.H., Fraguela, B.B.: A framework for argument-based task synchronization with automatic detection of dependencies. Parallel Comput. **39**(9), 475–489 (2013)
10. Kegel, P., Schellmann, M., Gorlatch, S.: Using OpenMP vs. threading building blocks for medical imaging on multi-cores. In: Europar, pp. 654–665 (2009)
11. Lin, Y., Terboven, C., Mey, D., Copty, N.: Automatic scoping of variables in parallel regions of an OpenMP program. In: Chapman, B.M. (ed.) WOMPAT 2004. LNCS, vol. 3349, pp. 83–97. Springer, Heidelberg (2005). https://doi.org/10.1007/978-3-540-31832-3_8
12. Martineau, M., McIntosh-Smith, S., Gaudin, W.: Evaluating OpenMP 4.0's effectiveness as a heterogeneous parallel programming model. In: International Parallel and Distributed Processing Symposium Workshops, pp. 338–347 (2016)
13. OpenMP ARB: OpenMP Application Program Interface, version 5.0 (2018)
14. OpenMP ARB: OpenMP Technical Report 8: version 5.1 preview (2019)
15. Oracle: Oracle Solaris Studio 12.2: OpenMP API User's Guide (2010). http://docs.oracle.com/cd/E18659_01/html/821-1381/toc.html
16. Royuela, S.: High-level compiler analysis for OpenMP. Ph.D. thesis (2018)
17. Royuela, S., Duran, A., Liao, C., Quinlan, D.J.: Auto-scoping for OpenMP tasks. In: Chapman, B.M., Massaioli, F., Müller, M.S., Rorro, M. (eds.) IWOMP 2012. LNCS, vol. 7312, pp. 29–43. Springer, Heidelberg (2012). https://doi.org/10.1007/978-3-642-30961-8_3
18. Royuela, S., Duran, A., Serrano, M.A., Quiñones, E., Martorell, X.: A functional safety OpenMP* for critical real-time embedded systems. In: de Supinski, B.R., Olivier, S.L., Terboven, C., Chapman, B.M., Müller, M.S. (eds.) IWOMP 2017. LNCS, vol. 10468, pp. 231–245. Springer, Cham (2017). https://doi.org/10.1007/978-3-319-65578-9_16
19. Royuela, S., Ferrer, R., Caballero, D., Martorell, X.: Compiler analysis for OpenMP tasks correctness. In: Computing Frontiers, pp. 1–8 (2015)
20. Royuela, S., Pinho, L.M., Quiñones, E.: Enabling Ada and OpenMP runtimes interoperability through template-based execution. J. Syst. Arch. **105**, 101702 (2020)
21. Serrano, M.A., Royuela, S., Quiñones, E.: Towards an OpenMP specification for critical real-time systems. In: International Workshop on OpenMP (2018)
22. Tagliavini, G., Cesarini, D., Marongiu, A.: Unleashing fine-grained parallelism on embedded many-core accelerators with lightweight OpenMP tasking. Trans. Parallel Distrib. Syst. **29**(9), 2150–2163 (2018)
23. Toledo, L., Peña, A.J., Catalán, S., Valero-Lara, P.: Tasking in accelerators: performance evaluation. In: 20th International Conference on Parallel and Distributed Computing, Applications and Technologies, pp. 127–132. IEEE (2019)
24. Varbanescu, A.L., Hijma, P., Van Nieuwpoort, R., Bal, H.: Towards an effective unified programming model for many-cores. In: IPDPS, pp. 681–692. IEEE (2011)
25. Voss, M., Chiu, E., Chow, P.M.Y., Wong, C., Yuen, K.: An evaluation of auto-scoping in OpenMP. In: Chapman, B.M. (ed.) WOMPAT 2004. LNCS, vol. 3349, pp. 98–109. Springer, Heidelberg (2005). https://doi.org/10.1007/978-3-540-31832-3_9

26. Wang, C.K., Chen, P.S.: Automatic scoping of task clauses for the OpenMP tasking model. J. Supercomput. **71**(3), 808–823 (2015)
27. Willhalm, T., Popovici, N.: Putting intel® threading building blocks to work. In: 1st International Workshop on Multicore Software Engineering, pp. 3–4 (2008)
28. Yu, C., Royuela, S., Quiñones, E.: OpenMP to CUDA graphs: a compiler-based transformation to enhance the programmability of NVIDIA devices. In: 23rd International Workshop on Software & Compilers for Embedded Systems (2020)

Automatic Detection of MPI Assertions

Tim Jammer[1,2]([✉]), Christian Iwainsky[1], and Christian Bischof[2]

[1] Hessian Competence Center for High Performance Computing (HKHLR),
Darmstadt, Germany
`{tim.jammer,christian.iwainsky}@tu-darmstadt.de`
[2] Department of Scientific Computing,
Technical University Darmstadt, 64283 Darmstadt, Germany
`christian.bischof@tu-darmstadt.de`

Abstract. The 2019 MPI standard draft specification includes the addition of defined communicator info hints. These hints are assertions that an application makes to an MPI implementation, so that a more optimized implementation is possible. The 2019 draft specifications defines four assertions: `mpi_assert_no_any_tag`, `mpi_assert_no_any_source`, `mpi_assert_exact_length` and `mpi_assert_allow_overtaking`. In this paper we will explore the capability of a Clang/LLVM based static analysis to check whether these assertions hold for a given program. With this tool, existing codebases can benefit from this new addition to the MPI standard without the need for costly human intervention.

Keywords: MPI 4.0 · Static analysis · MPI communicator info

1 Introduction

The upcoming version 4.0 of the MPI standard includes many changes. In particular, "the largest changes are the addition of persistent collectives, application info assertions, and improvements to the definitions of error handling" [10].

With the addition of defined application info assertions, it is possible to hint that MPI is used in a certain way enabling the possibility of a more optimized implementation; the `allow_overtaking` assertion is of particular interest. Using this assertion, an application can notify an MPI implementation that its correctness does not depend on the strict ordering of messages as described in section 3.5 of the standard [9]. If an application asserts that the overtaking of messages is allowed, or cannot happen due to the use of different tags and synchronization, an MPI implementation may entirely skip one of the costly phases of message matching ensuring the order of messages is preserved [12]. As Dang et al. point out [2], matching the messages in the correct order is especially costly in the case of multithreaded MPI.

The `no_any_tag` and `no_any_source` assertions quite straightforwardly tell an implementation that the `MPI_ANY_TAG` and `MPI_ANY_SOURCE` constants are not used in receiving operations. This would enable specific optimizations in the MPI library. The `exact_length` assertion tells that "the length [of] messages

© Springer Nature Switzerland AG 2020
H. Jagode et al. (Eds.): ISC High Performance 2020 Workshops, LNCS 12321, pp. 34–42, 2020.
https://doi.org/10.1007/978-3-030-59851-8_3

received by the process are equal to the lengths of the corresponding receive buffers" [10]. This does not mean the actual size of the buffer given to the receive operation contains exactly the space indicated by the arguments for count and datatype. This is already implied by the standard anyway and tools like MUST [5,6] already check if the programmer made this specific error. Rather the `exact_length` assertion tells an implementation that the size of the send messages match the size of the receive operations buffers. The MPI standard allows the sender to issue a send operation with less than the expected elements by the matching receive operation (e.g.., five integers being sent and matched by a receive operation for 20 integers). In this example, only the first 5 locations of the 20 integer long buffer will be filled. The program can then use the `MPI_Status` and `MPI_Get_count` to assess how many elements have actually been received. As the standard writes: "In the case of a message shorter than the receive buffer, MPI is quite strict in that it allows no modification of the other locations. A more lenient statement would allow for some optimizations" [10]. Therefore, the newly introduced assertion will allow for such optimizations.

As far as the MPI standard is concerned, it is up to the programmer to decide whether or not such an assertion to the MPI implementation can be used in a given program. In this paper, we present a compiler based tool that automatically detects whether one of these assertions can be made safely. Using this tool, an existing code base can benefit from the newly defined assertions, without a costly human analysis of the code base to check if it is safe to specify a given assertion.

Our work is not directly concerned with optimizing MPI applications. Therefore, we do not consider numerous works regarding the optimization of MPI applications (e.g., by overlapping computation and communication [1]) as related. As our approach is more related to other work on the usage of static analysis for MPI programs (like [4,7,8,11]). These work is mostly focused on detecting programming errors made by an application engineer and therefore facilitate a correct usage of MPI. In contrast, our work does not focus on correct MPI usage by the programmer[1], but support developers in the possibility to utilize a more optimized MPI implementation by specifying additional optional assertions.

Apart from that there is lots of work to optimize MPI Applications, for example by overlapping computation and communication (like [1]). But in our work, we do not change the application. Rather we check if a certain condition hold for a given application. An applications for which these assertions hold may then utilize a more optimized implementation.

In the next section, we will explain our tool's static analysis approach for deciding if the newly defined assertions hold. In Sect. 3, we discuss the feasibility and shortcomings of our approach, summarize in Sect. 4 and provide an outlook on possible future work.

---

[1] We assume the use of MPI in an application to be correct.

2   Analysis Approach

To analyze whether or not an application can be augmented with an assertion to the MPI library, we developed an LLVM compiler pass to statically analyze the program at compile time. Currently we restrict ourselves to C and C++ applications using the Clang compiler. As the analysis operates on the LLVM intermediate representation, our approach should be transferable to other LLVM input languages. This explicitly includes Fortran, once a stable version of flang is available in later LLVM versions.

Our analysis assumes that the input program is fully standard compliant and deadlock-free. Otherwise, the assumptions made during the analysis might not hold.

Section 2.1 covers the analysis of the `allow_overtaking` assertion, while Sect. 2.2 covers the `exact_length` assertion.

We skip a detailed description of the analysis for the `no_any_tag` and `no_any_source` assertions. It is quite trivial to check for constant values during compilation. Hence, if the analysis does not detect any `MPI_ANY_SOURCE` and `MPI_ANY_TAG` used in MPI operations, the corresponding assertion can be used.

Our Analysis is interprocedural, but currently limited to the scope of one object file[2]. Therefore, if a function from another object file is called that is neither part of the standard library nor MPI itself, our pass will state that it is not safe to use any of the assertions.

2.1   `allow_overtaking` Assertion

To detect if the `allow_overtaking` assertion can be specified, our pass analyzes all occasions where a message is sent and checks if it could conflict with other sent messages in regards to these messages not overtaking each other.

Conflicting Send Operations. A send operation is considered conflict-free, if there is no other send operation (a) with the same communicator and (b) message tag (c) to the same target. Furthermore, it is considered conflict free, if a send operation with matching communicator, tag and target is (d) not on the same codepath or (e) separated by a synchronization of the processes.

Conditions a, b and c can in many cases be checked statically (e.g., the used message tag is different). In order to get the best results for this analysis, it is important to use an optimization level that includes constant propagation. Hence, the analysis pass we developed should be executed after all other LLVM optimization passes. Our tool will only consider the message tag, target process or the used communicator to be different, if a difference can be statically proven. For this purpose it is not necessary, that the exact value can be computed statically in a particular case. In many cases a data-flow- and dependency-analysis can show that there will be a difference in the value at any time during the

---

[2] Refer to Sect. 4 for ideas on how to overcome this shortcoming.

program's execution. For example, it is sometimes possible to prove that the message tag of a send operation is different in each loop iteration and this operation can therefore not conflict with itself. This analysis, which is the base for several well known compiler optimizations like loop transformations, is done by the LLVM tool-chain through the `ScalarEvolution` analysis pass.

If a unique message envelope cannot be detected statically, two send operations will be marked as conflicting, although in the actual execution of the program they might still be conflict free. We will discuss an example of this case in Sect. 3.

For condition d, our pass will check if there exist any code path (i.e. a path in the control-flow graph) between the two operations.

Synchronization. Finally, our LLVM pass tries to prove that on *all* possible codepaths between two send operations there is a process synchronization (condition e). In the case of a `barrier`, i.e. when a sending process exits the barrier, the analysis can assume that the target has successfully posted a matching receive operation; otherwise, the program is erroneous, due to the possibility of a deadlock. Therefore, the analysis can assume due to our requirement of deadlock-freeness that a matching receive has completed on the target process. As the other process also reached the synchronization point, all other open receive operation have been completed up to that point, unless it is implemented as a non-blocking operation, which we discuss in the next paragraph. By assuming the receive operation has completed at the synchronization point, the analysis can safely assure that no overtaking is possible between a message sent before the synchronization and after the synchronization.

The MPI standard mandates that we may not draw any conclusion about the execution state of another processes from other collective operations apart from the completion of the barrier. (see section 5.13 of the MPI standard [9]) However, the use of an `MPI_Allreduce` implies a barrier-like synchronization. This implicit barrier is not implied by the MPI standard in any way, rather it results of the required data flow for the `allreduce` operation. A program cannot have the result of an `allreduce` operation available, unless all processes have entered it.

Of course, a synchronization as explained above only prevents a conflict, if it uses the same communicator as the conflicting messages. Otherwise the analysis cannot draw any conclusion on the receiving processes status.

When considering `Rsend` or `Ssend`, we know by definition that the corresponding receive has started.[3] Therefore, it is not possible that the next message send will overtake and wrongfully match the receive operation currently active.

Non-blocking Operations. For `Isend` and `Bsend`, a synchronization only prevents a conflict if the operation completed locally using either `MPI_Wait` or

---

[3] The particular differences between `Rsend` and `Ssend` are not important for this consideration. Important is that when either of those operations successfully finishes, we can conclude that the matching receive has started on the target process.

`MPI_Buffer_detach`, respectively[4]. This holds, as our analysis only covers programs that are deadlock-free, according to the standard. If the receiving process has not posted the matching receive when all processes synchronize, a deadlock might occur.

For non-blocking collectives, at the point when the collective completes, as indicated by the use of `MPI_Wait`, the analysis can consider the processes synchronized, implying that the matching receive has to have been posted by that point.

If an application uses `MPI_Irecv`, we additionally have to check the assumption that a receive operation has finished when a synchronization takes place. To this end, we analyze if the scope where a non-blocking receive operation may be active does not cross a synchronization point. This means that we have to check if an `Irecv` operation is issued before a synchronization and if the matching `Wait` is issued after the synchronization. To take these cases into account, our tool also analyzes whether the receive operations are conflict free in the same manner as explained earlier for the send operations (conditions `a-e`).

There is no need for special considerations when applying our tool to a multithreaded program. If two threads send a message, the standard does not mandate that there is a defined order between these messages. (see Sect. 3.5 of the MPI standard [9]) Hence, if the assertion allows for messages to overtake each other, this does not have an effect on a correct program, as the order of these two operations was not defined in the first place. The standard only guarantees that messages sent by one thread will be received in that order by the other process. Therefore the considerations taken for the single-threaded program are also sufficient for a multi-threaded program.

2.2 `exact_length` Assertion

In our opinion it is a good programming practice to distinguish messages with different length by the use of different message tags, in order to avoid programming mistakes that may accidentally match a longer message to a shorter receive buffer. Hence, we group the communication operations by the used message tag for our analysis. All messages with a non-constant message tag will be grouped in the same group. If a receive specifies `MPI_ANY_TAG` it matches to all message tags, meaning that it is considered part of every group.

The `exact_length` assertion can safely be specified, if the length of all sending and all receiving operation is identical within each group. Otherwise the assertion still could hold, but this is not assertable by our approach using only static analysis. We implemented this analysis as a proof of concept in our LLVM pass, knowing that its use is currently limited and that a more refined approach is desirable. Such an approach could leverage synchronization points and code

---

[4] Currently we have not implemented coverage for the `Ibsend` operation, but the implementation would in principle be the same with the difference that both an `MPI_Wait` and a following `MPI_Buffer_detach` is required for the operation to be considered locally complete.

structure to further segregate the message-size groups into fine grained groupings. Messages split by a synchronization point, are not required to have the same size when using the same message tag.

3 Evaluation

We have tested our developed Clang pass using 48 different small MPI programs[5] designed for this purpose. As the detection for no_any_tag and no_any_source is trivial constant-matching extensive tests are not necessary - the compiler with its pre-implemented analyzes does the work here. For the exact_length assertion, we validated using our test suite and did not observe any issues. As this analysis is conservative, we might miss opportunities where this assertion might be used, but the correctness of the implementation was shown to be ok. As the analysis of the allow_overtaking assertion required more program logic and is more complex, we will focus the evaluation on this aspect.

The test cases where written in order to test the design aspects of our analysis. This means we designed them from scratch as white box tests for our implementation. We also included several different implementations of a mini-app alike 2D-stencil code calculating heat dispersion. This more elaborate example originated from teaching of MPI programming. In order to meaningfully evaluate our implementation with other mini-apps, one has to manually do extensive and rigorous checking if the assertions can be specified for the respective code. As this can be error-prone and comes with a huge effort, we stick to this well known teaching example. Nevertheless, this example will illustrate the feasibility and shortcomings of our approach.

For roughly 60% of the test cases, it is not safe to specify the allow_overtaking assertion. Of these cases, our tool detected all cases where it was not safe to use the assertion.

```
1  switch (rank) {
2  case 0:
3      MPI_Recv(/*from rank 1*/);
4      MPI_Ibarrier(MPI_COMM_WORLD, &bar_req);
5      MPI_Wait(&bar_req, MPI_STATUS_IGNORE);
6      MPI_Recv(/*from rank 1*/);
7  break;
8  case 1:
9      MPI_Ibarrier(MPI_COMM_WORLD, &bar_req);
10     MPI_Send(/*to rank 0*/);
11     MPI_Wait(&bar_req, MPI_STATUS_IGNORE);
12     MPI_Send(/*to rank 0*/);
13 break;
14 }
```

Listing 1.1. Exemplary test case with the Ibarrier, where our pass could not prove, that no overtaking of the messages is possible.

---

[5] Available together with the source code of the analysis tool.

There were, however, some similar cases involving an overlap of communication and synchronization, where our approach could not detect that there is no possibility for the involved messages to overtake. One example is shown in Listing 1.1. The messages sent by rank 1 can never overtake each other in this case, but our approach cannot show at compile time that the send operation in line 10 can never overtake the message sent in line 12. This is due to the use of blocking send/receive in the time between an asynchronous barrier and its corresponding wait. With logical inference, we can conclude that the receive of rank 0 must have completed, for the barrier to complete. However, our current implementation cannot draw such conclusions. It must, according to our current design, consider the send of rank 1 to be part of both the pre-barrier and post-barrier communication region. And, as it conflicts in the post-barrier region, it must consider a potential overtaking and advice against using the `allow_overtaking` assertion. Further research may enable to draw such conclusions, but currently we accept the conservative limitation of our current approach.

Another case, where our tool could not detect that the `allow_overtaking` assertion could be specified, occurs when each process communicates with its predecessor and successor in a ring-like fashion. This means, that for this communication scheme rank 0 is the successor of rank $n-1$. In this case, the shortcoming of our static approach cannot prove at compile time, that the predecessor and successor are different. After all, the program could be called with only two MPI ranks. This is not a shortcoming of our implementation, as with only two ranks the predecessor and successor are the same, meaning that it is indeed possible that the message sent to the next rank will overtake the message to the previous rank in this case. Using different message tags for forward and backward communication mitigates this problem.

In the more complex example of a 2D-stencil code, our tool detects that all assertions could be specified, if different message tags are used for the different iterations. If the same message tag is used for all iterations, our tool rightfully concludes that the `allow_overtaking` assertion could indeed not be specified, because the order of messages must match the order of iterations as a message from one iteration should not match to a receive in the next iteration.[6] This is a classic case of a loop driven dependency [3].

Besides the functional aspects, we tested the overhead our analysis contributes to the compilation time with our elaborate mini-app alike example with about 400 lines of code using Clang's `-ftime-report` option. As Clang reports that our analysis pass requires only 0.3% (0.0014 s) of the total execution time for all LLVM passes executed on optimization level `-O2`, we consider the overhead of our pass to be negligible when other optimizations are applied.

---

[6] Splitting the iteration with a synchronization is also possible but only introduces unnecessary synchronization overhead in this case.

4   Conclusion

MPI 4.0 offers (in its current draft [10]) new assertions enabling aggressive optimizations by the MPI library: the `allow_overtaking` and `no_any_tag` as well
as `no_any_source` and `exact_length` assertions. However, in order to specify
those users must analyze their code to ascertain if the requirements for those
are met. We present an LLVM compiler-pass that can statically check program
properties and provide feedback to the user for those assertions. While our analysis can provide perfect feedback for `no_any_tag` and `no_any_source`, feedback
for `allow_overtaking` and `exact_length` depends on the properties of the program. With `allow_overtaking` and `exact_length` our analysis does not detect
all cases where it is possible, but when it infers that the use of those assertions is
possible, this is correct. Especially the analysis for overtaking messages is complex and relies on detailed understanding of the semantics of MPI send, receive
and collective operations. Evaluating the resulting tool, available at https://
github.com/tudasc/mach, on a custom set of test-codes showed no observable
deficiencies. In summary, we provided a first step to lower the burden of manual
analysis and therefore facilitate the usage of those assertions.

Using a Clang optimization pass, we will extend the analysis pass to automatically insert the assertions into the code. Therefore, our tool can be viewed
as a compiler optimization that in some cases can optimize the use of the MPI
library.

In the future we plan to address the main drawback of our current implementation, i.e. its limitation to a single object file. Besides the usage of a whole
program representation, an annotation whether an assertion holds for a function
will facilitate such an analysis with multiple object files. Additionally, one can
also limit the scope of the assertion to one object file, by duplicating the used
MPI communicator[7] and only specify the assertions to the duplicated communicator, while replacing all uses of the original communicator with its duplicate. In
the future, we also want to further refine our analysis (e.g., to also incorporate
the usage of `MPI_Probe`).

An empirical analysis of the performance gained in real applications is
planned, once MPI implementations have incorporated the usage of the proposed assertions and exploited the expected performance benefits. When we
know about the actual performance gain, it is possible to determine if there is
a trade-off in performance, if one changes the application in order to allow the
specification of an assertion (e.g., use different message tags), or if such a change
would lead to less overall performance. With these data we plan to extend our
tool to give the programmer guidance on how to change an application so that
the assertions hold, in order to facilitate the expected performance gains.

Acknowledgements. This work was supported by the Hessian Ministry for Higher
Education, Research and the Arts through the Hessian Competence Center for High-
Performance Computing. We want to thank the anonymous reviewer for their sugges-
tion to address the current limitation of our tool by duplicating the MPI communicator.

---

[7] Using `MPI_Comm_dup_with_info`.

References

1. Danalis, A., Pollock, L., Swany, M., Cavazos, J.: MPI-aware compiler optimizations for improving communication-computation overlap. In: Proceedings of the 23rd International Conference on Supercomputing, pp. 316–325 (2009)
2. Dang, H.V., Snir, M., Gropp, W.: Towards millions of communicating threads. In: Proceedings of the 23rd European MPI Users' Group Meeting, pp. 1–14 (2016)
3. Dowd, K., Severance, C.: High performance computing (2010). http://cnx.org/content/col11136/1.5
4. Droste, A., Kuhn, M., Ludwig, T.: MPI-checker: static analysis for MPI. In: Proceedings of the Second Workshop on the LLVM Compiler Infrastructure in HPC, pp. 1–10 (2015)
5. Hilbrich, T., Schulz, M., de Supinski, B.R., Müller, M.S.: MUST: a scalable approach to runtime error detection in MPI programs. In: Müller, M., Resch, M., Schulz, A., Nagel, W. (eds.) Tools for High Performance Computing 2009, pp. 53–66. Springer, Heidelberg (2010). https://doi.org/10.1007/978-3-642-11261-4_5
6. Hück, A., et al.: Compiler-aided type tracking for correctness checking of MPI applications. In: 2018 IEEE/ACM 2nd International Workshop on Software Correctness for HPC Applications (Correctness), pp. 51–58. IEEE (2018)
7. Jaeger, J., Saillard, E., Carribault, P., Barthou, D.: Correctness analysis of MPI-3 Non-blocking communications in PARCOACH. In: Proceedings of the 22nd European MPI Users' Group Meeting, pp. 1–2 (2015)
8. Luecke, G., Chen, H., Coyle, J., Hoekstra, J., Kraeva, M., Zou, Y.: MPI-CHECK: a tool for checking Fortran 90 MPI programs. Concurr. Comput. Pract. Exp. **15**(2), 93–100 (2003)
9. Message Passing Interface Forum: MPI: A Message-Passing Interface Standard Version 3.1 (2015). https://www.mpi-forum.org/docs/mpi-3.1/mpi31-report.pdf
10. Message Passing Interface Forum: MPI: A Message-Passing Interface Standard 2019 Draft Specification (2019). https://www.mpi-forum.org/docs/drafts/mpi-2019-draft-report.pdf
11. Saillard, E., Carribault, P., Barthou, D.: PARCOACH: combining static and dynamic validation of MPI collective communications. Int. J. High Perform. Comput. Appl. **28**(4), 425–434 (2014)
12. Schonbein, W., Dosanjh, M.G.F., Grant, R.E., Bridges, P.G.: Measuring multi-threaded message matching misery. In: Aldinucci, M., Padovani, L., Torquati, M. (eds.) Euro-Par 2018. LNCS, vol. 11014, pp. 480–491. Springer, Cham (2018). https://doi.org/10.1007/978-3-319-96983-1_34

Automatic Code Motion to Extend MPI Nonblocking Overlap Window

Van Man Nguyen[1,2,3,4]([✉]), Emmanuelle Saillard[2], Julien Jaeger[1,3],
Denis Barthou[2,4], and Patrick Carribault[1,3]

[1] CEA, DAM, DIF, 91297 Arpajon, France
{van-man.nguyen.ocre,julien.jaeger,patrick.carribault}@cea.fr
[2] Inria, Bordeaux, France
{van-man.nguyen,emmanuelle.saillard,denis.barthou}@inria.fr
[3] Laboratoire en Informatique Haute Performance pour le Calcul et la simulation, Bruyères-le-Châtel, France
[4] Bordeaux Institute of Technology, University of Bordeaux, LaBRI, Bordeaux, France

Abstract. HPC applications rely on a distributed-memory parallel programming model to improve the overall execution time. This leads to spawning multiple processes that need to communicate with each other to make the code progress. But these communications involve overheads caused by network latencies or synchronizations between processes. One possible approach to reduce those overheads is to overlap communications with computations. MPI allows this solution through its nonblocking communication mode: a nonblocking communication is composed of an initialization and a completion call. It is then possible to overlap the communication by inserting computations between these two calls. The use of nonblocking collective calls is however still marginal and adds a new layer of complexity. In this paper we propose an automatic static optimization that (i) transforms blocking MPI communications into their nonblocking counterparts and (ii) performs extensive code motion to increase the size of overlapping intervals between initialization and completion calls. Our method is implemented in LLVM as a compilation pass, and shows promising results on two mini applications.

Keywords: Static optimization · Message Passing Interface · Nonblocking communications

1 Introduction

HPC applications (e.g., simulations) run on clusters which sport a mix of shared- and distributed-memory architecture. In this context, the computations are spread over multiple NUMA (non-uniform memory access) nodes that are interconnected using a high speed network. Thus the application needs to perform communications between those nodes to carry out the simulation. However the communications can introduce overheads due to idle times, either because a

© Springer Nature Switzerland AG 2020
H. Jagode et al. (Eds.): ISC High Performance 2020 Workshops, LNCS 12321, pp. 43–54, 2020.
https://doi.org/10.1007/978-3-030-59851-8_4

process is waiting for data another process must send, or because processes not progressing at the same speed must synchronize. The time waiting on communications is not being spent on progressing the computation. A possible optimization would be to leverage these waiting times by performing computations independent of the communications.

The Message Passing Interface (MPI) defines multiple functions to perform communications over such distributed architectures. Among these operations, the nonblocking ones allow communications to asynchronously progress, thus enabling the overlap of communications by computations. Nonblocking communications are split into 2 distinct calls, one that initializes the exchange, and one that waits for its completion. To achieve overlapping, we have to insert computations, that are independent of the communications, between those calls so they can be performed while the communications are ongoing.

The use of nonblocking collective communications is however marginal. Many legacy codes still prefer blocking communications and the nonblocking form introduces a new complexity: it is up to the developer to make sure that the code does not have any race condition. As statements can be inserted and executed while the communication is ongoing, they can have an influence on the communication buffers. Many prior works proposed techniques to increase overlapping time by looking for specific patterns of code architecture such as producer-consumer loops or by performing basic code motion. In this paper we propose an automatic optimization that transforms blocking MPI calls into their nonblocking counterparts and that optimizes their overlapping potential through extensive code motion. Our contributions are the following:

- Automatic transformation of blocking MPI calls into their nonblocking mode.
- Increase of overlapping possibilities by performing extensive code motion to move apart data dependencies.
- Implementation using a state-of-the-art and widespread compilation framework (LLVM).

Section 2 presents related work on the use of nonblocking communications in optimizing HPC applications. Section 3 introduces a simple motivating example. Section 4 describes the optimization pass and finally, its implementation and the results are the subject of Sect. 5.

2 Related Work

2.1 Asynchronous Communications in Scientific Applications

Many applications rely on nonblocking communications to improve performance on large-scale clusters. But code developers usually perform manual transformations and major redesign of widely-used algorithms to demonstrate the advantages of such nonblocking calls by reducing communication overheads.

Clement *et al.* proposed a sorting algorithm suited for distributed architectures [2]. The algorithm is an adaptation of a partition-based sorting algorithm that leverages nonblocking calls in order to overlap communications with computations. Although their solution shows potential, it requires balance between the read and write, network, and computing times.

Similarly Kandalla *et al.* implemented the Breadth First Search algorithm with nonblocking neighborhood MPI collective communications [11]. Even if they show a communication overhead improvement up to 70%, the execution time does not improve and sometimes degrades. This might be caused by the additional operations that are needed to partition the problem.

Manually inserting testing points inside the overlapping window, such as calls to the MPI_Test function, is an approach taken by some developers to enforce the progression of asynchronous communications. Hoefler *et al.* used this solution to propose an optimization of a conjugate gradient solver [9] using LibNBC [10], a custom library which implements MPI nonblocking collective communications. Song *et al.* developed an algorithm for the 3D Fast Fourier Transform using nonblocking MPI collectives, and pushed this approach further by automatically determining a set of parameters, including the frequency of calls to MPI_Test, in order to achieve performance [14].

2.2   Automatic Transformation of MPI Codes

On the topic of automatic transformations for MPI, Danalis *et al.* described communication-computation overlapping possibilities including the transformation of blocking calls into their nonblocking counterparts, the decomposition of collective calls into point-to-point ones, the application of code motion, variable cloning, and loop tiling and fission to increase the overlapping window [4]. ASPhALT implements a subset of those optimizations using the open64 source-to-source compiler [3]. It aims at optimizing producer-consumer loops by performing prepush transformations, meaning that it will try to send the data as soon as it is generated so that consumer computation can be performed while the next chunk of data is being produced. The producer-consumer loop is partitioned with an arbitrary size to control the amount of data that is generated, shared and computed.

Guo *et al.* showed how to improve this approach by adding a performance analytical model of the application [7]. With the help of user-added annotations, it predicts performance and decides when the transformation of blocking calls into nonblocking ones becomes worthy. The transformation itself and the code motion are still manually done.

Das *et al.* proposed an approach based on a Wait Graph to sink the completion call of nonblocking communications [5], that is to move it at a later point in the execution. This graph contains information about the control and data flow, enabling them to sink the wait call to the nearest statement that uses a communication buffer.

Petal [1] is a compiler pass implemented within the ROSE [13] compiler that also sinks completion calls to the nearest dependency point. Ahmed *et al.* used an alias analysis to detect whether a statement uses a communication buffer. Their method transforms nonblocking communications into persistent communications when they are nested inside a loop.

Prior work on the transformation of MPI codes to expose communication-computation overlap possibilities has been mostly focused on a specific scenario such as producer-consumer loops. The attempts at widening the overlap frame have been limited by the nearest sensitive statement. In this paper we propose a solution that performs extensive code transformation and motion so that the size of the overlapping window can be significantly increased.

3   Motivating Example

This section illustrates how our work transforms MPI codes to increase the possibilities of overlapping communications with computations.

```
1    MPI_Alltoall(d1, sendcount, MPI_BYTE, d2,
2        recvcount, MPI_BYTE, MPI_COMM_WORLD);
3    matrix_multiply(a, b, res, matrix_size);
4    touch(d1);
5    matrix_multiply(a2, b2, res2, matrix_size);
```

Listing 1.1: Basic example

The *alltoall* communication at line 1 in Listing 1.1 is blocking. Every MPI process that is involved in the communication has to wait at that statement until their input communication buffers (d1) become available again, and until their output communication buffers (d2) have received the data from other MPI processes. A possible improvement in this context would be to translate that blocking *alltoall* call into nonblocking calls with an initialization (MPI_Ialltoall) and a completion (MPI_Wait). We can now move the completion call beyond the first matrix computation, as it is not involved in the communication, and before the function call that accesses the d1 communication buffer.

```
1    MPI_Request req;
2    MPI_Ialltoall(d1, sendcount, MPI_BYTE, d2,
3        recvcount, MPI_BYTE, MPI_COMM_WORLD, &req);
4    matrix_multiply(a, b, res, matrix_size);
5    MPI_Wait(&req, MPI_STATUS_IGNORE)
6    touch(d1);
7    matrix_multiply(a2, b2, res2, matrix_size);
```

Listing 1.2: Optimized version of Listing 1.1

In prior work, the calls would be hoisted or sunk to the first statement that reads or writes to a communication buffer, depending on the call, as presented in Listing 1.2. However there are statements beyond the first dependency that are independent of the MPI call. Moving those statements along with the nonblocking call will further increase the overlapping window. Applied to the previous example, it results in the code in Listing 1.3. In this paper we propose a method to perform such code motion to increase the possibilities of overlapping communications with computations by identifying such boundaries and by displacing them further. In the previous code snippet, the completion and the touch calls are moved beyond the second matrix computation as well, leading to a wider overlapping window.

```
1   MPI_Request req;
2   MPI_Ialltoall(d1, sendcount, MPI_BYTE, d2,
3           recvcount, MPI_BYTE, MPI_COMM_WORLD, &req);
4   matrix_multiply(a, b, res, matrix_size);
5   matrix_multiply(a2, b2, res2, matrix_size);
6   MPI_Wait(&req, MPI_STATUS_IGNORE)
7   touch(d1);
```
Listing 1.3: Optimized version of Listing 1.1 with extensive code motion

4   Maximizing Communication-Computation Overlap

As defined in the standard, a nonblocking MPI communication is composed of two calls: an initialization and a completion call. This form enables the overlap of communications with computations by inserting statements between these two calls. In order to avoid race conditions, those statements should not modify the communication buffers. As suggested by prior work, it is possible to perform multiple code transformations such as loop fission or sinking the wait to the nearest dependent statement to enlarge the overlapping frame. To go one step further, we propose to move not only the initialization call but also the statements that contribute to the values used in this call, and the same for the completion call and the statements that depend on it. Defining these backward and forward slices [15] of computations associated to the MPI calls, and their insertion points, is the heart of our contribution in order to increase the size of the overlapping window.

4.1   Finding Slices and Insertion Point

The principle of the method is to automatically determine for any data-exchange based point-to-point and collective MPI call all statements that it depends on (the backward slice for that call) and all statements that depend on it (the forward slice). These slices correspond to a sequence of statements connected by dependencies. In this work, the scope of these slices is limited to statements that are in the same control-flow structure: same function, same loop and same if-then-else construct. To find the slices and the insertion points, we specifically rely on the Control-Flow Graph (CFG) of the function. It is a directed graph where the vertices are basic blocks (BB). A basic block is a sequence of instructions (or statements) that have to be executed in a specific order. When the first instruction of a given BB has been executed, then the following instructions in that BB must be executed in that order. One can only enter a BB through its first instruction, and leave it through its last. The edges are the execution paths between the basic blocks.

For every point-to-point and collective communication, we consider their communication buffers and we iteratively build their backward slice. Starting from the MPI call, the CFG is backwardly visited and each statement that belongs to the use-def or def-use chains of the MPI call is collected. Each statement that uses or defines a communication buffer and all statements that it depends on are taken into account. Thus, those chains are iteratively scanned, allowing the slice to capture indirect dependencies as well. The iterative method stops when leaving the if-then-else, for loop, or function, surrounding the MPI call, or when the next statement to put in the list is in another control structure. The collected sequence of statements correspond to the backward slice, and the place in the CFG where the iterative method stops to the insertion point for this slice and for the initialization call. The same applies for the forward slice, moving forward in the CFG from the MPI call.

Algorithm 1 describes this code transformation for MPI communications, for the specific case of the initialization call insertion.

First, we build the backward slice of the call. In order to walk through the CFG from statement to statement, we extend the notion of dominance and post-dominance from BB to statements. A statement s_1 dominates a statement s_2 if s_1 belongs to a BB dominating the BB of s_2, or if s_1 precedes s_2 in the sequence of a BB.

We stop iterating over the statements once a suitable insertion point has been found for the initialization call. If needed, we allocate a new MPI_Request and create a new call site that will initialize the communication. That new nonblocking call site will use the same argument list as the blocking version, at which we append the request. Those newly created instructions are added at the insertion point. The correctness of an insertion point for the initialization call is defined by the function STMT_IMMOVABLE_INIT, and described in Sect. 4.2.

We operate the same way for the completion call by visiting the subsequent statements, starting at the MPI call site. Once we find a suitable insertion point for the completion call, we insert the MPI_Wait() call, using the MPI_-Request that has been created for the corresponding initialization call, or the MPI_Request from the pre-existing nonblocking communication, as its argument.

Finally, the original blocking call is removed from the function. If the communication was already nonblocking, then the original call is simply moved to the first insertion point.

Algorithm 1. Finding an insertion point for the initialization call

---

    procedure INSERT_MPI_INIT_CALL(function)
Require: List of MPI communications called in function
Ensure: MPI nonblocking init calls are inserted along with their dependencies at valid
    locations.
        for all mpi_call $\in$ function **do**
            list_stmt_init $\leftarrow \emptyset$
            V $\leftarrow$ get_dependencies(mpi_call)   ▷ *Build the list of statements upon which*
the MPI call depends using use-def and def-use chains.
            stmt $\leftarrow$ mpi_call.get_stmt()
            while stmt_immovable_init(stmt, mpi_call.get_stmt(), V) = false **do**
                stmt $\leftarrow$ immediate dominator(stmt)
                if stmt $\in V$ **then**
                    list_stmt_init $\leftarrow$ list_stmt_init $\cup$ {stmt}
            insert_init $\leftarrow$ stmt
            Move statements from list_stmt_init to the point of the code where stmt is
    the immediate dominator, and insert the init call

    procedure STMT_IMMOVABLE_INIT(stmt, call_stmt, V)
Ensure: True if stmt is a valid insertion point
        if stmt is the first statement of the function **then return** true
        for all tstmt between stmt and its immediate dominator **do**
            if tstmt $\in V$ **then return** true
        if call_stmt is between stmt and its immediate post-dominator **then return** true
        if stmt is a MPI procedure **and** stmt $\neq$ call_stmt **then return** true
        return false

4.2 Defining a Suitable Insertion Point

For each MPI communication, the insertion point for the initialization or the
completion call is the statement after which we will move the initialization,
or before which we will move the completion call. The specific case for the
initialization is displayed in the STMT_IMMOVABLE_INIT function of Algorithm 1.
    A statement is an insertion point if:

- The statement is the first statement of the current function.
- There is a control flow dependency.
- The statement is an MPI call. This constraint prevents from undoing previous
  transformations and from having different sequences of MPI collective calls,
  while allowing multiple pending nonblocking calls. Moreover according to the
  standard, it is not allowed to execute MPI functions beyond the boundaries
  defined by calls such as `MPI_Init` and `MPI_Finalize`.

In the literature another condition would also be a suitable insertion point:

- There is a data dependency between the call and the current statement.

    This condition is limiting the size of the overlapping interval. While it is
necessary to not overlap such data dependencies to keep the correctness of the

program, other statements beyond this first dependency might be completely independent of the MPI call. In such case it can be useful to not stop at this first data dependency, and to add it to the list of statements that will be moved around, along with the insertion of the initialization or the completion calls when a stronger condition is reached.

This limitation is the reason why this condition is not taken into account in our work. In the following section, we will describe how we deal with such data dependencies.

4.3   Displacing the Dependencies to Achieve Overlap

While traversing the CFG, we visit every statement until a valid insertion point, defined in Sect. 4.2, is found either by going from immediate dominator to immediate dominator as shown in Algorithm 1 for the initialization, or by going from immediate postdominator to immediate postdominator for the completion call. In the meantime, every visited statement that belongs to the slice, thus every visited statement that use or define an argument of the MPI call, will be enqueued rather than being considered as an insertion point, as explained in the previous section. Those statements will need to be moved to the insertion location to keep the dependencies and to prevent race conditions that could be caused by the introduction of nonblocking communications. A queue is used to store those statements to ensure that the order in which they were visited can be reproduced.

When a suitable insertion point has been found for the initialization or completion call, we dequeue the instructions at that location while ensuring that the execution order of those statements is kept. In the case of the initialization call, the newly created MPI_Request (if necessary), and the nonblocking call are inserted after dequeuing all the dependent statements. In the case of the completion call, the call is inserted before dequeuing the other statements. This way, the order between the dependencies is kept.

5   Implementation and Experimental Results

5.1   Implementation Using LLVM

Algorithm 1 is implemented as a compilation pass in the LLVM compiler [12]: the code is represented as an intermediate representation (IR) which allows us to be completely independent of the source language. The only language-related information we need to consider is the representation of the MPI calls in the parsed language, to be able to correctly capture them. LLVM defines many analysis passes whose results can be reused in other optimizations and user-defined passes. These passes provide us the list of loops, the dominator and post-dominator trees for a given function, and the use-def and def-use chains of each value. The pass is applied on selected files of an MPI application using the LLVM opt tool.

5.2   Experimental Results

All measurements are performed on a supercomputer based on Intel Sandybridge processors. This partition is composed of 3,360 cores, each one having 4,000 Mo of memory, distributed over 210 nodes. The nodes are interconnected using infiniBand. We used the OpenMPI installed by default on this environment, which is based on version 2.0.4.

Our method is evaluated by measuring the duration of each newly created overlapping window for the motivating example presented in Listing 1.1 and for two mini applications from the Mantevo project [8]: miniMD and miniFE. For blocking calls that have been transformed into their nonblocking form we insert the time measurement functions immediately below the initialization and above its associated completion call: we measure the execution time of the statements that are inside the overlapping window. For example in Listing 1.3, the first reading would be placed after the MPI_Ialltoall between lines 3 and 4, and the second before the MPI_Wait between lines 5 and 6, thus measuring the duration taken by the two matrix computations that makes the overlapping window up.

All results are collected per process and averaged. We measure the effectiveness of our method by comparing non-iterative transformations (related work, denoted as basic) with extensive code motion (our method, denoted as extended). A wide overlapping window means a communication–computation overlap possibility.

Each version of all the codes was run to ensure numerical results remained valid with each transformation.

The example in Listing 1.1 is a slightly modified version of a benchmark designed to measure the performance of nonblocking MPI calls, specifically their ability to asynchronously progress communications [6]. This example helps verify the correctness and performance of the transformations. The matrix size in the matrix_multiply call is set so that the function takes a user-defined duration to complete, $2,500\,\mu s$ in our runs.

Our optimization pass successfully translated the blocking *alltoall* call into its nonblocking counterparts and the completion call was sunk below the second matrix computation. Table 1 shows the duration of the overlapping window measured for Listings 1.2 and 1.3. The result confirms what we statically observed on the IR with an overlapping window of $4,803\,\mu s$, which roughly corresponds to the overlapping of both matrix computations when performing extensive code motion. Similarly when using a basic code motion technique the observed duration of the overlapping interval is at $2,406\,\mu s$, corresponding to the execution of one matrix operation.

Table 1. Overlapping window duration for the motivating example

MPI call	File	Line	Interval duration basic (μs)	Interval duration extended (μs)
MPI_Alltoall	bench.c	28	2,406.57	4,803.15

MiniMD simulates molecular dynamics using the Lennard-Jones potential or the Embedded Atom Model (EAM). It is a simpler version of LAMMPS and is written in about 5000 lines of C++ code. We used version 1.2, the EAM force and a problem of size 128^3. The benchmark is deployed over 8 nodes, using 15 cores on each node. Applied to each file of the benchmark, our pass transformed 57 MPI calls. Out of those 57 calls, 30 were executed during the run. The most significant transformations are shown in Table 2, the 24 remaining transformations have an overlapping window that is too narrow to expose any potential gain for asynchronous progression. The `MPI_Allreduce` called in thermo.cpp shows the bigger overlapping interval when applying extensive code motion.

Table 2. Most significant overlapping window duration for miniMD

MPI call	File	Line	Interval duration basic (μs)	Interval duration extended (μs)
MPI_Allreduce	thermo.cpp	133	0.05	65.84
MPI_Bcast	force_eam.cpp	524	41.59	54.34
MPI_Bcast	force_eam.cpp	525	32.53	42.51
MPI_Bcast	force_eam.cpp	526	25.66	35.37
MPI_Bcast	force_eam.cpp	527	16.71	18.31
MPI_Bcast	force_eam.cpp	528	9.40	10.09
Max. MPI call overlap			**125.94**	**226.46**

MiniFE aims at approximating an unstructured implicit finite element application using fewer than 8000 lines of code in C++. We used version 2.0 and as with miniMD, measurements use the reference benchmark and a problem of size 1024^3. It is also run on 8 sandy nodes using 15 cores on each. Our pass found and transformed 37 MPI calls. Out of those 37 calls, 22 were detected at runtime and only 3 of them had a significant overlapping window in either the basic or the extensive case. The duration of their overlapping interval is shown in Table 3. The basic approach is unable to expose any overlapping potential. Using extensive code motion, we successfully created an overlapping window of 4 ms.

Table 3. Most significant overlapping window duration for miniFE

MPI call	File	Line	Interval duration basic (μs)	Interval duration extended (μs)
MPI_Allreduce	SparseMatrix_functions.hpp	313	0.11	4193
MPI_Bcast	utils.cpp	92	0.51	166
MPI_Allreduce	make_local_matrix.cpp	216	0.22	1.41
Max. MPI call overlap			**0.84**	**4360.41**

5.3 Discussion

In this section we chose to display the duration of the overlap windows instead of the actual execution time of each program. Success in hiding the communication times of MPI nonblocking calls heavily depends on the MPI runtime implementation and on how efficient it is in conducting asynchronous progression. Nonblocking MPI communications are also often more time consuming than their blocking counterparts, mainly due to the progression mechanism. For these reasons the performance gain one can achieve depends more on the quality of the MPI implementation than on the quality of the transformation method.

As our work focuses on increasing the size of the overlap windows, it is clearer to display the duration of these intervals. Their duration does not depend on the quality of the MPI implementation, and allows to clearly show the benefits of our method when compared to state-of-art.

It is also necessary to note that our optimization pass only detects dependencies that can be resolved through the semantics of the code. As a consequence, it is not able to properly capture statements or calls that have no data dependencies, yet that have an implicit relationship with the communication, such as probes to measure the communication time.

6 Conclusion

In this paper we propose a method to automatically perform extensive code motion in order to increase overlapping opportunities for nonblocking MPI communications. Our algorithm builds on and improves state-of-the-art methods to transform all blocking communications of a program into nonblocking operations. While previous work only moves apart the nonblocking calls to the first instruction they depend on, we use code motion to further extend computation-communication overlaps. Our method was implemented as a pass in the LLVM compiler and successfully tested on two miniapplications.

In future work, we will aim at improving the support for already existing nonblocking communications. In the current implementation, only initialization calls are moved, because we did not yet succeed in matching existing completion calls (`MPI_Test*()` and `MPI_Wait*()`) to their corresponding initialization calls. Thus, the code motion misses information to capture all necessary data dependencies to ensure the validity of the insertion point. Being able to link the completion calls to their respective initialization calls will allow moving both calls to increase overlap possibilities. Another limitation of our approach is the analysis being intraprocedual. Pushing the boundaries of the analysis beyond the current function would further improve overlap possibilities.

References

1. Ahmed, H., Skjellum, A., Bangalore, P., Pirkelbauer, P.: Transforming blocking MPI collectives to non-blocking and persistent operations. In: Proceedings of the 24th European MPI Users' Group Meeting, pp. 1–11 (2017)

2. Clement, M.J., Quinn, M.J.: Overlapping computations, communications and I/O in parallel sorting. J. Parallel Distrib. Comput. **28**(2), 162–172 (1995)
3. Danalis, A., Pollock, L., Swany, M.: Automatic MPI application transformation with ASPhALT. In: 2007 IEEE International Parallel and Distributed Processing Symposium, pp. 1–8. IEEE (2007)
4. Danalis, A., Pollock, L., Swany, M., Cavazos, J.: MPI-aware compiler optimizations for improving communication-computation overlap. In: Proceedings of the 23rd International Conference on Supercomputing, pp. 316–325 (2009)
5. Das, D., Gupta, M., Ravindran, R., Shivani, W., Sivakeshava, P., Uppal, R.: Compiler-controlled extraction of computation-communication overlap in MPI applications. In: 2008 IEEE International Symposium on Parallel and Distributed Processing, pp. 1–8. IEEE (2008)
6. Denis, A., Trahay, F.: MPI overlap: benchmark and analysis. In: 2016 45th International Conference on Parallel Processing (ICPP), pp. 258–267 (2016)
7. Guo, J., Yi, Q., Meng, J., Zhang, J., Balaji, P.: Compiler-assisted overlapping of communication and computation in MPI applications. In: 2016 IEEE International Conference on Cluster Computing (CLUSTER), pp. 60–69. IEEE (2016)
8. Heroux, M.A., et al.: Improving performance via mini-applications. Sandia National Laboratories, Technical report SAND2009-5574 3 (2009)
9. Hoefler, T., Gottschling, P., Rehm, W., Lumsdaine, A.: Optimizing a conjugate gradient solver with non-blocking collective operations. In: Mohr, B., Träff, J.L., Worringen, J., Dongarra, J. (eds.) EuroPVM/MPI 2006. LNCS, vol. 4192, pp. 374–382. Springer, Heidelberg (2006). https://doi.org/10.1007/11846802_52
10. Hoefler, T., Lumsdaine, A.: Design, Implementation, and Usage of LibNBC. Technical report, Open Systems Lab, Indiana University, August 2006
11. Kandalla, et al.: Can network-offload based non-blocking neighborhood MPI collectives improve communication overheads of irregular graph algorithms? In: 2012 IEEE International Conference on Cluster Computing Workshops, pp. 222–230. IEEE (2012)
12. Lattner, C., Adve, V.: LLVM: a compilation framework for lifelong program analysis & transformation. In: International Symposium on Code Generation and Optimization, CGO 2004, pp. 75–86. IEEE (2004)
13. Quinlan, D.: ROSE: compiler support for object-oriented frameworks. Parallel Process. Lett. **10**(02n03), 215–226 (2000)
14. Song, S., Hollingsworth, J.K.: Computation-communication overlap and parameter auto-tuning for scalable Pparallel 3-D FFT. J. Comput. Sci. **14**, 38–50 (2016)
15. Weiser, M.: Program slicing. In: Proceedings of the 5th International Conference on Software Engineering, ICSE 1981, pp. 439–449. IEEE Press (1981)

First International Workshop on the Application of Machine Learning Techniques to Computational Fluid Dynamics Simulations and Analysis (CFDML)

First International Workshop on the Application of Machine Learning Techniques to Computational Fluid Dynamics Simulations and Analysis

1 Background and Description

The First International Workshop on the Application of Machine Learning Techniques to Computational Fluid Dynamics Simulations and Analysis (CFDML), co-located with ISC 2020 Digital, was held on-line on June 25th, 2020. The event was designed to stimulate research at the confluence of computational fluid dynamics (CFD) and machine learning (ML), by providing a venue to exchange new ideas and discuss challenges and opportunities. The workshop was also an opportunity to expose a rapidly emerging field to a broader research community. It brought together researchers and industrial practitioners working on various aspects of applying ML to CFD and related domains, in order to provide a venue for discussion, knowledge transfer, and collaboration among the research community.

The combination of CFD with ML is a recently emerging research direction with the potential to enable the solution of so far unsolved problems in many application domains. ML is already applied to a number of problems in CFD, such as the identification and extraction of hidden features in large-scale flow computations, finding undetected correlations between dynamical features of the flow, generating synthetic CFD datasets through high-fidelity simulations, and predicting simulation results with physics-informed learning techniques. These approaches are forming a paradigm shift, changing the focus of CFD from, e.g., time-consuming feature detection to in-depth examinations of such features or from expensive simulations on high-performance computers to fast predictions on small desktop computers using reduced order and surrogate models trained on simulation generated data. These methods, thereby, enable deeper insight into the physics involved in complex natural processes and accelerate predictions for design processes in various fields in industry and research.

The workshop solicited papers on all aspects of CFD where ML plays a significant role or enables the solution of complex problems in CFD and related fields. Topics of interest included physics-based modeling with the main focus on fluid physics, such as reduced modeling for dimensionality reduction and the Reynolds-averaged Navier-Stokes (RANS) turbulence modeling, shape and topology optimization in solids, prediction of aeroacoustics, uncertainty quantification and reliability analysis, reinforcement learning for the design of active/passive flow control, and ML approaches that enable or enhance any of the above techniques. All submitted manuscripts were peer reviewed by three program committee members using a single-blind process. Submissions were evaluated on originality, technical strength, significance, quality of presentation, and interest and relevance to the workshop. Six papers were selected for workshop presentation and inclusion in the proceedings. Authors were asked to revise their papers based on the feedback of the program committee members.

2 Workshop Summary

Authors of all accepted papers were asked to record videos of their presentations, which were posted together with PowerPoint slides on the workshop's website1[1] prior to the event. On the day of the workshop, all presenters and attendees connected to a Zoom channel for an on-line two-hour long panel and Q&A session. Paper presenters gave a brief summary of their work and the attendees asked questions and discussed the results. This session was attended by 30 participants. The recording of this session was distributed to the organizing committee and all the participants.

2.1 Research Papers

In the first research presentation, Zhang and Piggott discussed their paper "Unsupervised Learning of Particle Image Velocimetry". The authors proposed a novel unsupervised deep learning approach to infer velocity fields from Particle Image Velocimetry (PIV) measurements. The proposed approach makes use of a loss function inspired by classical optical flow methods, in order to remove the need for ground truth data. The approach shows significant promise, with competitive results compared to recently proposed supervised deep learning methods, and the potential to generalize to complex real-world flow scenarios where the ground truth is effectively unknowable.

Next, Harel et al., in their paper "Complete Deep Computer-Vision Methodology for Investigating Hydrodynamic Instabilities", explored the application of a variety of deep computer-vision techniques to hydrodynamic instability problems. The authors investigated the use image retrieval, template matching, parameter regression and spatiotemporal prediction, focusing on an important canonical flow, the Rayleigh-Taylor instability. The proposed models and data are made publicly available, and the authors noted that many of the models can be easily applied to existing simulation results, or to new more complex problems via transfer learning.

The next three presentations discussed the use of neural networks as a surrogate model to provide flow field predictions. Such techniques have the potential to replace or augment expensive computational simulations early on in the design process. Rüttgers et al., in their paper "Prediction of Acoustic Fields using a Lat-tice-Boltzmann Method and Deep Learning", trained a novel deep convolution neural network (CNN) on a dataset obtained from 20,000 lattice-Boltzmann simulations. The CNN showed considerable success in predicting the acoustic fields in a 2D square domain, and the authors discussed plans to extend the framework to three dimensional. Meanwhile, in their paper "Data-Driven Techniques to Enhance and Supplement Computational Fluid Dynamics Prediction Capabilities", Bekemeyer et al. used a fully connected three-layer neural network to predict the surface pressure on the NASA common research model. Afterwards, Nogueira et al. presented their paper "Reduced Order Modelling of Dynamical Systems using Artificial Neural Networks Applied to Water Circulation". They discussed the development of two low-dimensional surrogate models to produce a 36-hour forecast of the depth-averaged hydrodynamics at Lake

---

[1] http://www.ncsa.illinois.edu/enabling/data/deep_learning/news/cfdml20.

George in the USA. Their models involved the use of fully connected and long short-term memory neural networks, combined with proper orthogonal decomposition to reduce the dimensionality of the input data. The models were found to achieve promising accuracy levels (within 6% of the prediction range).

Finally, Luo et al. presented their research on "Parameter Identification of RANS Turbulence Model using Physics-Embedded Neural Network". Instead of seeking to replace the computational simulations, this work advocates for the use of a neural network to augment the turbulence model in an existing CFD framework. Loss functions are proposed to explicitly encode information about the turbulent transport physics within the neural network. An inverse problem is then solved by treating the five parameters in the turbulence model as random variables, with the turbulent kinetic energy and dissipation rate as known quantities from DNS simulation. The authors hypothesize that using the neural network to provide only turbulence model parameters (rather than the full turbulence stress field), aids with solver convergence as well as making the model more generalizable.

2.2 Panel Discussion

The workshop was concluded by a panel discussion on the topics covered in the presentations as well as important future research directions. A recurring discussion point was how to generalize the presented ML techniques to be also applicable to flows outside the training dataset. For example, how well does a neural-network-based sur-rogate model perform when predicting flows at higher Reynolds numbers than those encountered during training? A common talking point here was that there is a pressing need for more high-quality datasets in or-der to explore this. Additionally, some participants felt that in order for ML-based techniques to be adopted in industry, there is a need for uncertainty quantification and interpretation of the ML methods.

Organizing Committee

Volodymyr Kindratenko	National Center for Supercomputing Applications, USA
Andreas Lintermann	Jülich Supercomputing Centre, Forschungszentrum Jülich GmbH, Germany
Charalambos Chrysostomou	The Cyprus Institute, Cyprus
Jiahuan Cui	Zhejiang University, China
Eloisa Bentivegna	IBM Research, UK
Ashley Scillitoe	The Alan Turing Institute, UK
Morris Riedel	University of Iceland, Iceland
Jenia Jitsev	Jülich Supercomputing Centre, Forschungszentrum Jülich GmbH, Germany
Seid Koric	National Center for Supercomputing Applications, USA
Shirui Luo	National Center for Supercomputing Applications, USA

Madhu Vellakal   National Center for Supercomputing Applications,
                             USA
Jeyan Thiyagalingam   Science and Technology Facilities Council, UK

Complete Deep Computer-Vision Methodology for Investigating Hydrodynamic Instabilities

Re'em Harel[1,2], Matan Rusanovsky[2,3], Yehonatan Fridman[2,3], Assaf Shimony[4], and Gal Oren[3,4(✉)]

[1] Department of Physics, Bar-Ilan University, Ramat-Gan, Israel
reemharel22@gmail.com
[2] Israel Atomic Energy Commission, P.O.B. 7061, Tel Aviv, Israel
[3] Department of Computer Science, Ben-Gurion University of the Negev,
P.O.B. 653, Be'er-Sheva, Israel
{matanru,fridyeh,orenw}@post.bgu.ac.il
[4] Department of Physics, Nuclear Research Center-Negev,
P.O.B. 9001, Be'er-Sheva, Israel
shimonya@gmail.com

Abstract. In fluid dynamics, one of the most important research fields is hydrodynamic instabilities and their evolution in different flow regimes. The investigation of said instabilities is concerned with highly non-linear dynamics. Currently, three main methods are used for understanding of such phenomena – namely analytical and statistical models, experiments, and simulations – and all of them are primarily investigated and correlated using human expertise. This work demonstrates how a major portion of this research effort could and should be analysed using recent breakthrough advancements in the field of Computer Vision with Deep Learning (CVDL, or Deep Computer-Vision). Specifically, this work targets and evaluates specific state-of-the-art techniques – such as Image Retrieval, Template Matching, Parameters Regression and Spatiotemporal Prediction – for the quantitative and qualitative benefits they provide. In order to do so, this research focuses mainly on one of the most representative instabilities, the Rayleigh-Taylor instability (RTI). We include an annotated database of images returned from simulations of RTI (*RayleAI*). Finally, adjusted experimental results and novel *physical loss* methodologies were used to validate the correspondence of the predicted results to actual physical reality to evaluate the model efficiency. The techniques which were developed and proved in this work can serve as essential tools for physicists in the field of hydrodynamics for investigating a variety of physical systems. Some of them can be easily applied on already existing simulation results, while others could be used via Transfer Learning to other instabilities research. All models as well as the dataset that was created for this work, are publicly available at: https://github.com/scientific-computing-nrcn/SimulAI.

© Springer Nature Switzerland AG 2020
H. Jagode et al. (Eds.): ISC High Performance 2020 Workshops, LNCS 12321, pp. 61–80, 2020.
https://doi.org/10.1007/978-3-030-59851-8_5

Keywords: Fluid Dynamics · Hydrodynamic instabilities ·
Rayleigh-Taylor instability · Computer Vision · Deep learning · Image
retrieval · Template matching · Regressive convolutional neural
networks · Spatiotemporal prediction

1   Introduction

The Rayleigh-Taylor instability occurs in an interface between two fluids with
different densities in which the lighter fluid pushes the heavier fluid [1]. RTI is
found in many hydrodynamic experiments and natural phenomena such as water
suspended in oil in earth's gravity, Inertial Confinement Fusion (ICF), astrophysical systems, and many more [2]. Due to its importance, numerous experiments
studying the growth of the instability and its effects on other phenomena are
performed constantly all over the world [3–6]. Generally speaking, there are two
types of experimental platforms for investigating the evolution of RTI: Liquid
or gas systems (for example [3–5]) and High-Energy-Density Physics (HEDP)
systems, in which the fluids are in plasma state after being heated by powerful
lasers (for example [7,8]). In the former systems, it is difficult to control the initial
perturbation, but due to the fact that between consecutive frames (2D images,
the main diagnostics in the experiments) the time difference is short (compared
to the duration of the experiment), namely it typically varies from milliseconds
to seconds. Therefore, it is feasible to obtain with a fast camera tens or more
frames per experimental shot. In the latter systems, the initial perturbation can
be machined precisely prior to the laser drive – while the materials are in a solid
state – but the time scales are much shorter (about tens of nanoseconds) and
only one or at most few frames can be obtained from a single experimental shot.
Therefore, the experimental data from both types of experimental systems contain a partial reflection of the instability – either the exact initial perturbation
or the detailed temporal evolution of the instability is missing, while both are
crucial for understanding the phenomenon. The growth of the perturbation in
RTI depends on numerous variables such as viscosity, ablation, surface tension,
small density gradients, and more. These variables are of different importance in
different physical and experimental systems. In this work the case of two incompressible and immiscible fluids and a single-mode sinusoidal initial perturbation
is considered. In this case, the early growth is exponential in time (T) and is
proportional to (via linear stability theory):

$$e^{\sqrt{\mathcal{A}kg}T} \tag{1}$$

where k is the wave number $k = 2\pi/\lambda$, λ is the wavelength, g is earth's gravity
(and in the general case the acceleration of the system), and $\mathcal{A}$ is the well known
Atwood number, given by:

$$\mathcal{A} = \frac{\rho_1 - \rho_2}{\rho_1 + \rho_2} \tag{2}$$

where ρ_1 is the density of the heavier fluid and ρ_2 of the lighter one. In the
late non-linear growth of such a single-mode perturbation, bubbles of the lighter

fluid penetrate into the heavy fluid and spikes of heavy fluid penetrate into the light fluid at constant velocities, given by [9]:

$$u_{b/s} = \sqrt{\frac{2\mathcal{A}g\lambda}{c_d \left(1 \pm \mathcal{A}\right)}} \qquad (3)$$

where u_b and u_s are the velocities of the bubble and the spike, respectively. The quantity c_d is the drag coefficient, which equals to 6π and 3π for 2D and 3D, respectively. As the perturbation grows, the shear velocities on the sides of the bubbles and the spikes create vortices due to the Kelvin-Helmholtz instability (KHI), in which the two materials mix in small length scales. Needless to say that in reality (experiments), knowing the exact conditions of the density and the viscosity of the two fluids is unrealistic. A possible way to bridge this gap is via simulations [10] (which are much cheaper than performing additional experiments): Given the correct initial parameters one can simulate the experiment and extract the missing time frames. However, initiating the simulation with the exact initial parameters is impossible due to experimental uncertainties. Nevertheless, it is still a viable solution as one can run parameter-sweep and select the most similar simulation in comparison to the experiment. However, this solution might be difficult as there are many different parameters (both physical parameters with uncertainties and parameters in the analysis of the experimental results), which makes this process hard for a human. Nowadays, the usage of different deep learning techniques in this scientific area is growing [11–19], and as it progresses, the above problem might also be solved using Computer Vision with Deep Learning (CVDL, or Deep Computer-Vision), since the introduction of deep learning techniques to the Computational Fluid Dynamics (CFDs) field proved to yield excellent results [20–26]. Therefore, we first define and devise several key Computer Vision (CV) problems, which collaboratively will enhance the understanding of RTI and other physical phenomena as follows:

1. Given a diagnostic *image* from a simulation/experiment, *sort* a database in accordance with an image similarity score to the input.
2. Given a diagnostic *image* from simulation/experiment, *extract the parameters* of the simulation that yields a best match to an image in a database.
3. Given a *partial template* of a phenomena from a simulation/experiment, *find* matches in a database and *sort* them in accordance with an image similarity score to the input.
4. Given a *set of images* that correspond to a set of time steps, and a time parameter T, *predict* future non-existing time steps images.

Table 1. Quantitative and qualitative advantages for defined problems using CVDL.

#	Task	Quantitative & Qualitative advantages
I.	Database sorting by an image similarity score	• Meaningful order • Extraction of non-regressive parameters
II.	Regressive parameter extraction	• Physical parameters that fit the experimental data • Uncertainty margins of the model training
III.	Find and sort partial templates by an image similarity score	• Meaningful order • An extensive and reliable matching survey which decrease the uncertainty margins for the template assumption compared to full images analysis only
IV.	Temporal inter/extrapolation of experiments	• Data augmentation for low-data experiments • Assurance and extension of a model

The completion of the tasks above using CVDL techniques have both quantitative and qualitative advantages over classical optimization techniques, as summarized in Table 1:

I. **Image Retrieval**: A database (in this case, images) is sorted by an image similarity score, that corresponds to a meaningful physical similarity ordering score. In addition, the physical simulation parameters that yield the maximal image similarity (for example, with the experimental results) can be used as a non-regressive optimization. Similarly, uncertainty margins for the physical parameters can be calculated by defining a minimal required similarity factor.

II. **Parameter Regression**: Given experimental results and corresponding simulations with a set of free parameters, the technique provides the values of the free parameters for a best fit to the experimental results *iff* the model training and validation loss converges to approximately the same (small) value (thus, it successfully generalized the problem). The advantage over the parameter extraction in the first technique results from the regression process, which is significant when the simulation database is incomplete.

III. **Partial Template Matching**: Generally, it is valuable for physical problems in which there is a measurable pattern that is sensitive to any of the physical parameters. For example, in [27], the evolution of vortices, created by supersonic KHI, was measured and compared with hydrodynamic simulations. The analysis in [27] was based on the large-scale structures (i.e. the widths of the vortices). The medium-scale structures (i.e. the roll-ups within the vortices) were measured in the experiment and were compared to the simulations qualitatively. A more detailed analysis of the templates of the roll-ups could provide additional physical insights such as the effect of viscosity in the experimental conditions. Another example, that is relevant to the evolution of RTI, is originated from morphology differences between experiments in HEDP platforms and simulations of them. A detailed analysis of the morphology of the bubbles and the spikes can provide insights on magnetic effects due to the plasma conditions in these experiments [28] or perhaps other physical effects. A third example is the measurement of ablative RTI [29, 30] that is relevant to astrophysical systems. Similar to the KHI example, The ablation effects were analyzed by the width of the mixing zone. The morphology of the spikes was affected by the ablation as clearly seen from the experimental images and simulations. A detailed analysis of the structure of the spikes can provide further insights on the ablation effects. In each of the examples above, the Partial Template Matching technique might provide a meaningful image similarity order between the sub-patterns within the simulation images to the template input of the experimental image. In addition, this technique provides a more extensive and more reliable matching survey, which can decrease the uncertainty margins for the physical parameters, compared to analyses of the full images only. Therefore, it can serve as a convenient method for analyzing the physical effects and their significance.

IV. **Spatiotemporal Prediction**: Provides a temporal interpolation/ extrapolation of experimental results. First, it can be useful especially when the time-step ranges of the simulation and the experiment differs and when a prediction of experimental results at additional times are needed. Moreover, It can be used as a data augmentation methodology, by predicting images from some already known time-steps. This technique can also be used for self assurance: In cases of series of experimental images, one can provide images from a reduced range of time-steps. One possible way to evaluate the model is by predicting the images from time-steps outside the given range, and comparing them to the ones at hand.

We note that the techniques above can be applied on existing simulations databases, since physicists usually perform parameter surveys in order to analyze experimental data using simulations. In other words, it can be applied on previous works without running any additional simulation.

The rest of the paper is organized as follows: First, in Sect. 2 the state-of-the-art RTI database – *RayleAI* – that contains images with different parameters of a RTI simulation is introduced. Then, the different CVDL methods that are used in order to solve the key problems presented in Sect. 1 – specifically Information maximizing Generative Adversarial Network (InfoGAN), Parameters Regression (pReg), Quality-Aware Template Matching (QATM) and Predictive Recurrent Neural Network (PredRNN) – are covered with correspondence to the tasks above. Afterwards, a new evaluation methodology for the tasks above, named *physical loss* is introduced in Sect. 4. Next, the results of the different CVDL methods and evaluations are presented. Finally, future directions are proposed.

2   *RayleAI* – Database Characteristics

In order to implement the CVDL techniques described above, a state-of-the-art annotated simulation images database named *RayleAI* [31] was formed. The simulations were performed using the DAFNA hydrodynamic code [32], a multi-material Eulerian code with interface tracking and Adaptive Mesh Refinement (AMR) capabilities, which was validated for hydrodynamic instabilities [27,33]. The code solves the Euler equations, which are relevant to the turbulent flow in the simulated experimental system (Reynolds number of ∼6000 [6]). The initial perturbation is in the shape of a sinusoidal single-mode given by $y = h\cos(2\pi x/\lambda)$ where h is the initial amplitude height. The simulated domain is $x = 2.7$ cm (half of the wavelength, i.e. $\lambda = 5.4$ cm) and $y = 5.4$ cm (h varies between simulations as detailed below), with reflected walls boundary conditions on all edges. The spatial resolution is 64×128 cells, which was found converged and yields the smallest experimentally measured patterns. Each fluid follows the equation of state of an ideal gas (with adiabatic index $\gamma = 5/3$) and a hydrostatic equilibrium was set adiabatically with a pressure of 1 bar on the interface. The simulation input consists of three free parameters: Atwood number, gravitational acceleration and the amplitude of the perturbation (as well as additional time parameter). The database contains 101,250 images produced by 1350 different simulations, 75 time steps for each simulation, where the stride is 0.01 s, with unique set of the free parameters per each simulation. The format of the repository is built upon directories, each represents a simulation performance

Table 2. Diagnostic of RTI in different T and h values from *RayleAI*.

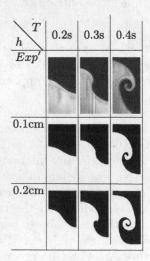

h \ T	0.2s	0.3s	0.4s
Exp'			
0.1cm			
0.2cm			

Table 3. Simulation parameters.

Parameter	From	To	Stride
Atwood number ($\mathcal{A}$)	0.02	0.5	0.02
Gravity (g) [cm/s²]	600	800	25
Amplitude (h) [cm]	0.1	0.5	0.1
X [cm]	2.7	2.7	0.0
Y [cm]	5.4	5.4	0.0

Fig. 1. The full image from the experiment ($T = 0.4$ s).

with the directory name indicating the parameters of the specific simulation, and each directory holds several images corresponding to each relevant time step. For example, the directory *gravity_750_amplitude_0.5_atwood_0.16* is a simulation with $g = 750$ cm/s^2, initial amplitude of 0.5 cm, and $\mathcal{A} = 0.16$. The ranges of the Atwood number, gravity and initial perturbation are presented in Table 3. Table 2 shows the simulation images from DAFNA compared to the experimental images, with $g = 750$ cm/s^2 and $\mathcal{A} = 0.16$.

The choice of these exact parameters were derived from the well known experimental results [6]. The physical parameters in the experiment were $\mathcal{A} = 0.155$, $g = 740$ cm/s^2 and $h = 0.54$ cm. The initial amplitude is not given but can be estimated from the first image by about $h = 0.1$ cm. Thus, one can deduce that the simulation in the database with $\mathcal{A} = 0.16$, $g = 750$ cm/s^2 and $h = 0.1$ cm should produce the closet result to the experimental one (as shown in Table 2). An example of an experimental image is shown in Fig. 1. The experiment images were originally taken in grayscale. For optimal results, each image was processed with two methods (Erode-Dilate vs. Histogram Equalization), and the most fitting result that resembles the interface between the two fluids (by expert opinion) was selected, cropped and resized, and then binarized by a threshold. Those images are also included in the database under the *experiment* folder.

3 Deep Computer-Vision Methods

3.1 Task I: Image Retrieval Using InfoGAN

Generative Advreserial Network (GAN) [34] is a framework capable of learning a *generator* network G that transforms noise variable z from some noise distribution into a generated sample $G(z)$, while the training of the generator is optimized against a *discriminator* network D, which targets to distinguish between real samples with generated ones. The fruitful competition of both G and D, allows G to generate samples such that D will have difficulty with distinguishing real samples from them. In the context of game theory, this competition might be referred as a variation of a MinMax game in which each player tries to maximize the minimum gain. In this game for example, G maximizes its minimum gain by generating images with higher resemblance to real images, while D improves its distinguishing capabilities, thus hardening the generation process of G. The ability to generate indistinguishable new data in an unsupervised manner is one example of a machine learning approach that is able to understand an underlying deep, abstract and generative representation of the data. InfoGAN [35] utilizes latent code variables c_i, which are added to the noise variable. These noise variables are randomly generated from a user-specified domain. The latent variables impose an information theory regularization term to the optimization problem, which forces G to preserve the information stored in c_i through the generation process. This allows learning interpretative and meaningful representations of the data, with a negligible computation cost, on top of a GAN. The high-abstract-level representation can be extracted from the discriminator (e.g.

the last layer before the classification) into a feature vector. These features can be used in order to measure the similarity between some input image to any other image, by applying some distance function (e.g. l_2 norm) on the features of the input to the features of the other image. This methodology provides the ability to order images similarity to a given input image [36].

In order to evaluate InfoGAN performances over *RayleAI*, the classic CV technique of LIRE [37] is used for comparison. LIRE is a library that provides image retrieval based on image characteristics among other classic features. LIRE is built on top of the open-source text search engine *Lucene* [38]. LIRE takes numeric images descriptors, which are mainly vectors or sets of vectors, and stores them inside a *Lucene* index as text along with the image path within a *Lucene* document. For the evaluation of the similarity of two images, one can calculate their distance in the space they were indexed to. Many state-of-the-art methods for extracting features can be used, such as Gabor Texture Features [39], Tamura Features [40], or FCTH [41]. For the purposes of this work, the Tamura Features method is the most suitable method that LIRE provides, as it indexes *RayleAI* images in a more dispersed fashion. The Tamura feature vector of an image is an 18 double values descriptor that represents texture features in the image that correspond to human visual perception.

3.2   Task II: Parameters Regression Using Convolutional Neural Networks – *pReg*

Many Deep Learning techniques obtain state-of-the-art results for regression tasks, in a wide range of CV applications [42] such as Pose Estimation, Facial Landmark Detection, Age Estimation, Image Registration and Image Orientation [43,44]. Most of the deep learning architectures used for regression tasks on images are Convolutional Neural Networks (ConvNets), which are usually composed of blocks of Convolutional layers followed by a Pooling layer, and finally Fully-Connected layers. The dimension of the output layer depends on the task and its activation function is usually linear or sigmoid.

ConvNets can be used for retrieving the parameters of an experiment image, via regression. The presented model (henceforth *pReg*) (Fig. 2) consists of 3 Convolutional layers with 64 filters, with a kernel size 5×5, and with l_2 regularization, each followed by a Max-Pooling layer, a Dropout of 0.1 rate, and finally Batch Normalization. Then, there are two Fully-Connected layers of 250 and 200 features, which are separated again by a Batch Normalization layer. Finally, the Output layer of the network has 2 features (as will described next), and is activated by sigmoid which maps the values to $[0, 1]$, to prevent the exploding gradients problem. This is important, as in regression tasks gradients might grow rapidly and eventually explode, if there are no regularizations on the output features. Since the most significant parameters for describing each image frame are Atwood number and time – which *pReg* is trained to predict – only a subset of *RayleAI* was used for the training set, namely images with the following parameters: $\mathcal{A} \in [0.08, 0.5]$ (with a stride of 0.02), $g \in \{625, 700, 750, 800\}$ cm/s^2, $h \in [0.1, 0.5]$ cm (with a stride of 0.1 cm) and $T \in [0.1, 0.6]$ s (with a stride

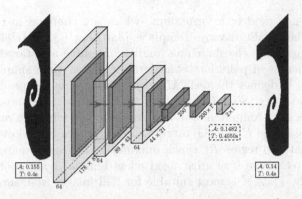

Fig. 2. ConvNet model, named *pReg*, for $\mathcal{A}$ and T parameters regression. Yellow layers are convolutional layers (5×5, with ReLU activation), orange are pooling layers, purple are dense layers with ReLU activation and the green layer is the output layer, activated by sigmoid. Green connections with arrows indicate connections with batch normalization, and the blue dashed connection is a regular connection. The left image is an example of an experimental input, with the real parameters of $\mathcal{A}$: 0.155, T: 0.4 s, which the model predicts for the values $\mathcal{A}$: 0.1482, T: 0.4050 s as can be seen under the green layer. The red dotted trend indicates the similarity search operation that quantifies the distance of images from *RayleAI*, based on the l_2 distance over $\mathcal{A}$ and T. (Color figure online)

of 0.01 s). A small amount of values for gravity and for amplitude was fixed, so that the network will not try to learn the variance that these parameters impose while expanding the database with as minimal noise as possible. The value ranges of Atwood number and time were chosen in order to expose the model to images with both small and big perturbations such that the amount of the latter case ones will not be negligible. The reduced training set consists of ~16K images and the validation set consists of ~4K images. Nonetheless, for increasing generalization and for decreasing model overfitting, data augmentation was employed. Since there is high significance for the perspective from which each image is taken, the methods of data augmentation should be carefully chosen: Rotation, shifting and flipping methods may generate images such that the labels of the original parameters do not fit for them. Therefore, the training set was augmented with only zooming in/out (zoom range = 0.1) via TensorFlow [45] preprocessing.

3.3 Task III: Quality-Aware Template Matching Using QATM

One variation of the Template Matching problem is defined as follows: Given an exemplar image E, find the most similar region of interest in a target image S [46]. Classical template matching methods often use Sum-of-Squared Differences (SSD) and Normalized Cross-Correlation (NCC) [47] to asses the similarity score between a template and an underlying image. These approaches work well when the transformation between the template and the target search image is simple.

However, with non-rigid transformations, which are common in real-life, they tend to fail. The Quality-Aware Template Matching (QATM) [48] algorithm is inspired by assessing the matching quality of source and target patches. It takes the uniqueness of pairs into consideration rather than simply evaluating matching score. It defines the $QATM(e, s)$ - measure as the product of likelihoods that a patch $s \in S$ is matched in E and a patch $e \in E$ is matched in S. Once $QATM(e, s)$ is computed, one can compute the template matching map for the template image E and the target searched image S, and eventually, can find the best-matched region R^* which maximizes the overall matching quality. Therefore, the technique is of great need when templates are complicated and targets are noisy. Thus, it is most suitable for RTI images from simulations and experiments.

3.4   Task IV: Time Series Prediction Using PredRNN

Learning the evolution of the RTI in order to predict future time or gap frames requires both understanding of the spatial aspects of each time frame (e.g. the interface between the fluids), and understanding of temporal development: As the time progresses, the simulation tends to be more and more chaotic. Convolutional Long Short Term Memory networks (CLSTMs) [49] is a class of algorithms which are able to predict future image states by past and present image states based on training sequences of images. The architecture of this network is based on a two-dimensional grid of units that pass spatial information vertically (upwards), and temporal information horizontally (rightwards). However, the standard CLSTMs architectures lack the capability of preserving the temporal information for long terms, since the spatial information that is learned via the top unit in a specific time step is not passed to the bottom unit in the next time step, leading to the loss of important information. PredRNN [50] is a state-of-the-art Long Short Term Memory (LSTM) Recurrent Neural Network (RNN) for predictive learning. PredRNN memorizes both spatial appearances and temporal variations in a unified memory pool. Unlike standard LSTMs, and in addition to the standard memory transition within them, memory in PredRNN can travel through the whole network in a zigzag direction, i.e, from the top unit of some time step to the bottom unit of the other. Thus, PredRNN is able to preserve the temporal as well as the spatial memory for long-term motions. In this work, PredRNN was used for predicting future time steps of simulations as well as experiments, based on a given sequence of time steps.

4   Evaluation Methodology

In order to test how the discussed above techniques perform on physical simulations as well as experiments, new task-specific test methods that quantify how well each technique operates on a concrete database are proposed. Novel evaluation methodologies are presented for the techniques discussed in Sects. 3.1, 3.2 and 3.3, based on a suitable corresponding loss measure for the first two tasks, and a sophisticated clustering-visualization method for the third (QATM). The evaluation of last technique presented in Sect. 3.4 will be discussed separately.

The first evaluation method, namely *physical loss*, quantifies *how meaningful the results of the technique are*, i.e., whether the results of the technique are reflected in the (physical) annotations of the data. For example, in the case of Image Retrieval, it is inconclusive to decide whether the results are sufficient solely based on visual examination, since it is a difficult task for humans to determine the correct ordering of lots of results. Thus, it is hard to establish whether the technique is satisfactory. Therefore, this work suggests to measure how each input image is *physically close* to each of the returned image outputs, based on some or all of their parameter labels. Thus, for Image Retrieval (and for Parameters Regression, explained later in Sect. 5.2) each output image gets two scores – one from the technique at hand, e.g. similarity score, and one from the difference between its parameters to the parameters of the input image. In the case of high correlations of these scores, one can infer that indeed the results of the technique are of a meaningful (physical) value. The Relative Error was chosen in this work as the parameter difference function, although it may be calculated via any desired error function. Note that since the ranges of the parameters are scaled differently, it is suggested to normalize them beforehand.

Furthermore, one important aspect that results from *physical loss* is the ability to identify the parameters which are likely to produce a small impact on the simulation results (depending on time). For example, in the case of a small ratio between the amplitude and the wavelength of the perturbation (up to a few percent), RTI grows linearly according to Eq. 1 and approximately preserves its initial shape. Therefore, two simulations that differ only by their initial small amplitudes will practically result in the same late evolution up to a constant time shift. As a result, it is expected from physical considerations that if one produces an amplitude-based *physical loss* methodology for later time steps, the CVDL techniques will generate semi-random values of error as the amplitude hardly affects the simulation in later time steps, or in other words, once the two fluids are mixed and form a chaotic mixture of the two. A similar result is also expected for the gravity parameter since for incompressible fluids (a good approximation in this case), two simulations that differ only by the gravity parameter will practically result in the same evolution as a function of the normalized time. A useful definition of the normalized time is $\tilde{T} = \sqrt{Ag/\lambda}T$ as also reflected from Eq. 1. Concluding the above physical influence of the initial amplitude and the gravity parameters, only the Atwood number and time parameters should have a significant impact on the results and are expected to be identified using the *physical loss* methodology.

Another new evaluation method was developed for cases where there are no meaningful (physical) annotations. Specifically in the case of Template Matching, where some partial template is searched through a database. Unlike the *physical loss* case, the physical parameters of the returned partial region of interest have no unique physical labels, since it might be expected to find this template in images from a wide range of different parameters. To this end, a relaxed-evaluation method, that quantifies how well the technique at hand separates similar images from dissimilar images is presented. Similarly to the *physical loss* methodology, two values for each output are used: The score from the technique, and a cluster number – returned from some unsupervised clustering algorithm. Scenarios in which continuous sequences from the results of the technique are from the same cluster might indicate the ability of the technique to perform a proper distinction between classes of similarity to a given input template. Alternatively, cases of sequences of results from mixed clusters, especially in the first and most similar regions, might prove that the technique did not succeed in separating the most similar images from the rest. K-Means was used as the clustering algorithm, after extracting the main features from each image using Principal Component Analysis (PCA) in order to achieve more precise results [51]. Section 5 presents the evaluation results of the techniques from Sect. 3.

5 Results and Discussion

5.1 Task I: Image Retrieval

In order to test the performance of InfoGAN against LIRE, two separate test cases were studied: *Random* and *Complex*. In the first general test case, 13K random input test images were chosen from *RayleAI*. In the latter, approximately 10K input images with $T > 0.25$ s were chosen in order to pick the most complex images, as the RTI is more chaotic and dominant in this regime. Then, InfoGAN and LIRE were performed on the entire *RayleAI* dataset for both test cases. Then, for each tested image and for each tool, the results were sorted according to the similarity scores that were given by the model. To evaluate the results and quantify how well the tools performed, the *physical loss* methodology, introduced in Sect. 4, was employed over the Atwood number parameter. Then, for each tool and test case, the average *physical loss* was calculated.

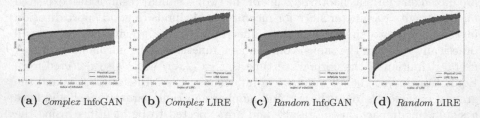

(a) *Complex* InfoGAN   (b) *Complex* LIRE   (c) *Random* InfoGAN   (d) *Random* LIRE

Fig. 3. LIRE and InfoGAN averaged *physical loss* methodology over Atwood number. (Color figure online)

Figure 3 presents the *physical loss* using a comparison between the technique score [in blue] and the *physical loss* [in red] per each index. A thin blue line is drawn to correlate them. We present only the Atwood number parameter, as it is the most significant parameter. Figures 3a and b, show that InfoGAN outperformed LIRE on the complex images test, as the averaged *physical loss* of the first – and most important – indices of InfoGAN is ∼0.25, in contrast to ∼0.4 of LIRE. Furthermore, InfoGAN outperforms LIRE along the entire 2K first examined indices, showing many powerful capabilities in the complex data case. Figures 3c and d, presents that InfoGAN and LIRE perform quite the same in the first indices, with averaged *physical loss* of ∼0.4. Yet, when focusing on the entire 2K first indices, it can be seen that InfoGAN starts to outperform LIRE with smaller *physical loss* values. Additionally, it seems that there is a higher correlation between the scores of InfoGAN to their corresponding *physical loss* values (blue and red lines act accordingly) in each of the test cases, which indicates again the InfoGAN has a better ability to learn the underlying physical pattern of the data. Another important aspect in which InfoGAN outperforms LIRE in both test-cases is the width of the *physical loss* trend: As the red trend is thinner, there is less noise and therefore the results have more physical sense. As one can notice, the red lines of InfoGAN are thinner than the red lines of LIRE. Note, that in all figures, the blue lines are normalized by the min-max normalization method, contrary to the red lines which are presented as raw values. The overwhelming superiority of InfoGAN is somehow expected and can be explained as the ability of a deep learning model to learn complex patterns from the new tailor-made and trained database. Although LIRE provides decent results without requiring to be trained on a specific organized database (which obtaining is not always an easy task), it is still a classical image processing tool, which lacks the learning capabilities that will allow it to understand deep patterns from the data. Therefore, for image retrieval applications with suitable databases, InfoGAN should be used.

5.2   Task II: Parameters Regression

In order to test the performances of the *pReg* network, evaluation tests that are similar to the tests presented in Sect. 4 were employed. *pReg* was used to predict the – activated by the sigmoid – parameters: $\mathcal{A}$ and T for 2K random images. Then, for each image a search was performed through *RayleAI* for the 2K images with the lowest scores, based on their l_2 distance between their $\mathcal{A}$ and T activated by sigmoid parameters, to that of the input image.

As can be seen in Fig. 4a, the model explains the dependence on time well, especially in the lowest (≤ 500) and highest (≥ 1500) indices, since the red dots of the normalized *physical loss* over the time, and the blue dots of the normalized l_2 distance from the predicted parameters, act similarly. The slightly higher difference between the dots in the middle of the scale ($500 < $ indices $ < 1500$) is somehow expected, as it is harder for models to predict the parameters accurately in cases where there is a 'mild' physical difference. Yet, in cases where there is a high resemblance or significant difference with respect to the *physical loss*, it is more likely that the model will predict similar parameters or dissimilar parameters, respectively. Figure 4b shows that the model explains dependence on the Atwood number parameter even better, as the graphs are almost the same

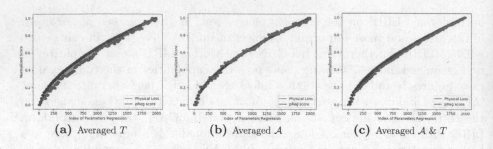

(a) Averaged T (b) Averaged $\mathcal{A}$ (c) Averaged $\mathcal{A}$ & T

Fig. 4. *pReg* averaged *physical loss* over the Atwood number and the time.

with some small noise. This can be explained by the significance and importance of the Atwood number parameter. Figure 4c shows that the combination
of Atwood number and time greatly outperforms the former two cases, since
the red trend almost converges to the blue trend. Note that as the predicted
parameters in *pReg* are only $\mathcal{A}$ and T, and the difference is calculated only over
them, for each input image there are lots of images in *RayleAI* with the same
calculated distance – same $\mathcal{A}$ and T, but different g or h. Therefore the trends
in Figs. 4b, a, c might have dense blocks of dots – with almost the same scores.
Finally, since images with the same $\mathcal{A}$ and T but different g or h have the same
loss (over $\mathcal{A}$ and T), they are ordered arbitrarily. Therefore, the *physical loss*
over all parameters does not explain the similarity order of *pReg*, because of the
arbitrariness that g and h impose.

5.3   Task III: Template Matching

For the evaluation of the QATM algorithm 16 meaningful templates were
cropped from the experimental images. For each template, the following procedure was employed: The QATM algorithm was performed on each image in
RayleAI and a matched sub-figure was found. Then, the results were sorted
in accordance to the QATM matching scores. For results evaluation, the loss
methodology of PCA and K-Means was employed as described in Sect. 4.

Figure 5 presents the results of three representative templates, while in each
the normalized score results of the algorithm are sorted in an increasing order.
The color of every point represents the cluster of the corresponding template,
achieved by the K-Means algorithm. The triangles and the circles lying above
the curves represent the median and the average of the indices of each cluster,
respectively. To keep the trends readable, only one of each 30 dots is presented.
As can be seen in Fig. 5a, the clustering algorithm divides the indices into four
separate and distinct areas: There is pure congestion of blue dots in the first
thousands of indices, without any rogue non-blue dots. This indicates that the
algorithm understood the template successfully and found lots of significantly
similar sub-figures. This powerful result might be explained because the searched
template is of a 'unique' shape, which helps QATM extract lots of uncommon
features and correlate them to *RayleAI*. Figure 5b, shows a pure congestion of

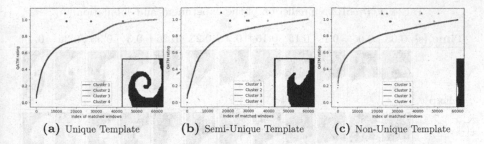

Fig. 5. PCA and K-Means clustering methodology made on QATM results. (Color figure online)

blue dots in the first hundreds of indices, and a mixture of blue and red dots, with the unignorable presence of green dots in the right following indices. This mixture of clusters that appears in relatively small indices indicates that the algorithm's results start to be less meaningful after a couple of hundreds of indices. This can be explained by the search template that is less unique than the previous template. Finally, in Fig. 5c the blue and red clusters seem to be inseparable all along the index axis. This indicates that the algorithm did not understand well the template and has difficulties to bring quality matched templates, as expected from the lack of uniqueness of the input template.

5.4 Task IV: Spatiotemporal Prediction

The PredRNN model was trained on *RayleAI* sequences of 0.01 s time steps. However, RTI experiment's parameters are the following: $g = 740$ cm/s^2, estimated amplitude, and $\mathcal{A} = 0.155$ and it contains 12 black and white images with an interval of ~0.033 s between each couple of consecutive frames, while the time steps of *RayleAI*'s simulation are of 0.01 s. In order to fill the missing time steps, PredRNN was used to predict the missing time intervals of the experiment. The missing time steps were filled in an iterative manner, by predicting a single future time step at a time. Furthermore, the quality of the prediction of a simulation was tested with the following parameters: $g = 725$ cm/s^2, $\mathcal{A} = 0.14$ and $h = 0.3$ cm. As an input, the first 10 images of the simulation were given, while predicting a total of 49 time steps.

The results of PredRNN prediction are shown in Table 4. The columns represent time steps ranging from the initial time of $T_{init} = 0.03$ s to the final time of $T_{fin} = 0.4$ s. The first and third rows of images represent the images of the corresponding time steps of the experiment and the simulation respectively, and as such can be considered to be Ground Truths (GTs). The second and the fourth rows of images represent the prediction of PredRNN on the corresponding time steps of the *filled* experiment and the simulation, respectively. As one can see, PredRNN produces almost identical predictions to the GT images. To evaluate the quality of the image produced by PredRNN, Peak Signal-to-Noise Ratio score was used. PSNR measures the quality of reconstruction of loss

Table 4. PredRNN prediction of the experiment and simulation.

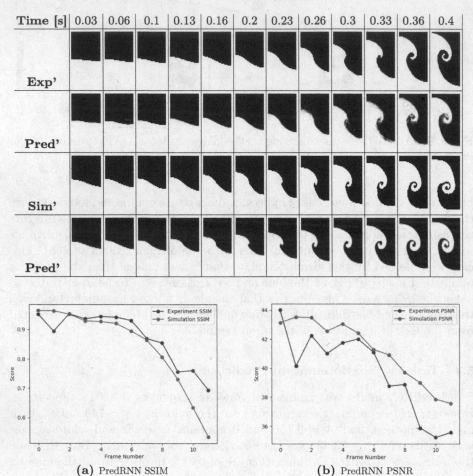

Time [s]	0.03	0.06	0.1	0.13	0.16	0.2	0.23	0.26	0.3	0.33	0.36	0.4
Exp'												
Pred'												
Sim'												
Pred'												

(a) PredRNN SSIM (b) PredRNN PSNR

Fig. 6. Structural Similarity Index Measure (SSIM) and Peak Signal-to-Noise Ratio (PSNR) scores of the predicted experimental and simulated results.

compression codecs. When comparing the different images, PSNR is an approximation to human perception of reconstruction quality. Complementary, Structural Similarity Index Measure (SSIM) that predicts the perceived quality of the images [52] was used. In Fig. 6 quantifies the quality of the predicted images using PSNR and SSIM evaluation tests between the produced PredRNN images to their corresponding GT images, similarly to [50]. Both scores measure the similarity between the predicted frame and its corresponding GT frame. These scores decrease as time progresses, due to the expected difficulty of the model to predict the distant future. However, its worth noting that a simple image sharpening on the predicted results can dramatically increase both SSIM and PSNR scores.

6 Conclusions and Future Work

This work presents a state-of-the-art complete CVDL methodology for investigating hydrodynamic instabilities. First, the problems were defined and their significance was emphasised. Second, a new comprehensive tagged database, which contains simulated diagnostics for training, and experimental ones for testing, was created for the needed learning process. Third, it was shown how the novel methodology targets the main acute problems in which CVDL can aid in the current analysis process, namely using deep image retrieval; regressive deep convolutional neural networks; quality aware deep template matching; and deep spatiotemporal prediction. Fourth, a new *physical loss* and evaluation methodology was formed. This methodology enables to compare the performances of the model against the physical reality, and by such to validate its predictions. At last, the usage of the methods on the trained models was exemplified and their performances were exemplified using the new *physical loss* methodology. In all of the four tasks, excellent results, which prove the methodology suitability to the problem domain were achieved. Thus, it is stressed that the proposed methodology can and should be an essential part of the hydrodynamic instabilities investigation toolkit, along with analytical and statistical models, experiments and simulations.

In regard to future work, an extension of the methodology might be useful for solving the discrepancy between simulations and experiments when it is clear that the initial parameters of the simulation does not cover the *entire* physical scope. Since in many cases a classical parameter sweep does not yield the desired results, an extension of the model – in the form of unmodelled parameters regression – should be used. For example, it might be useful for the physical problem presented in [29, 30], in which the simulation results do not cope with the experimental ones. Thus, an extended deep regressive parameter extraction model should be applied in a new form such that unknown parameters – i.e. parameters which are not part of the simulation initiation – could be discovered and formulated. This is crucial, as numerous current efforts suggest that often there is a missing part in the understanding of the simulated results. Thus, preventing any traditional method to match the simulated results to the experimental ones. Once discovered, in order to understand and formulate said unknown parameters, an extensive Explainable AI (XAI) methodology [53] should be performed.

Another strength of the presented methodology is that it can be applied on an already existing data in case that parameter sweep was previously performed on other physical data. Therefore, it might yield physical insights without running any additional simulation. In addition, the toolkit can be easily suited to the physical problem. For example, if the width of vortices was investigated in a previous research [27, 33, 54], template matching would be useful for investigating the inner structure of the vortices; With series of experimental images from different times at hand, the spatiotemporal prediction can be used for prediction of results at unmeasured times. Finally, the models presented in this work might be invaluable for learning physical problems with less training data and a more complex form, using Transfer Learning [55].

Acknowledgments. This work was supported by the Lynn and William Frankel Center for Computer Science. Computational support was provided by the NegevHPC project [56].

References

1. Sharp, D.H.: Overview of Rayleigh-Taylor instability. Technical report, Los Alamos National Lab., NM (USA) (1983)
2. Drazin, P.G.: Introduction to Hydrodynamic Stability, vol. 32. Cambridge University Press, Cambridge (2002)
3. Read, K.I.: Experimental investigation of turbulent mixing by Rayleigh-Taylor instability. Phys. D Nonlinear Phenom. **12**, 45–58 (1984)
4. Dalziel, S.B.: Rayleigh-Taylor instability: experiments with image analysis. Dyn. Atmos. Ocean. **20**(1–2), 127–153 (1993)
5. Dimonte, G., Schneider, M.: Turbulent Rayleigh-Taylor instability experiments with variable acceleration. Phys. Rev. E **54**(4), 3740 (1996)
6. Waddell, J.T., Niederhaus, C.E., Jacobs, J.W.: Experimental study of Rayleigh-Taylor instability: low Atwood number liquid systems with single-mode initial perturbations. Phys. Fluids **13**(5), 1263–1273 (2001)
7. Knauer, J.P., et al.: Single-mode, Rayleigh-Taylor growth-rate measurements on the omega laser system. Phys. Plasmas **7**(1), 338–345 (2000)
8. Remington, B.A., et al.: Rayleigh-Taylor instabilities in high-energy density settings on the national ignition facility. Proc. Natl. Acad. Sci. **116**(37), 18233–18238 (2019)
9. Goncharov, V.N.: Analytical model of nonlinear, single-mode, classical Rayleigh-Taylor instability at arbitrary Atwood numbers. Phys. Rev. Lett. **88**(13), 134502 (2002)
10. Youngs, D.L.: Numerical simulation of turbulent mixing by Rayleigh-Taylor instability. Phys. D Nonlinear Phenom. **12**(1–3), 32–44 (1984)
11. Spears, B.K., et al.: Deep learning: a guide for practitioners in the physical sciences. Phys. Plasmas **25**(8), 080901 (2018)
12. Humbird, K.D., Peterson, J.L., Spears, B.K., McClarren, R.G.: Transfer learning to model inertial confinement fusion experiments. IEEE Trans. Plasma Sci. **48**, 61–70 (2019)
13. Gonoskov, A., Wallin, E., Polovinkin, A., Meyerov, I.: Employing machine learning for theory validation and identification of experimental conditions in laser-plasma physics. Sci. Rep. **9**(1), 7043 (2019)
14. Avaria, G., et al.: Hard X-ray emission detection using deep learning analysis of the radiated UHF electromagnetic signal from a plasma focus discharge. IEEE Access **7**, 74899–74908 (2019)
15. Humbird, K.D.: Machine learning guided discovery and design for inertial confinement fusion. PhD thesis (2019)
16. Gaffney, J.A., et al.: Making inertial confinement fusion models more predictive. Phys. Plasmas **26**(8), 082704 (2019)
17. Kustowski, B., Gaffney, J.A., Spears, B.K., Anderson, G.J., Thiagarajan, J.J., Anirudh, R.: Transfer learning as a tool for reducing simulation bias: application to inertial confinement fusion. IEEE Trans. Plasma Sci. **48**, 46–53 (2019)
18. Kim, Y.J., Lee, M., Lee, H.J.: Machine learning analysis for the soliton formation in resonant nonlinear three-wave interactions. J. Korean Phys. Soc. **75**(11), 909–916 (2019). https://doi.org/10.3938/jkps.75.909

19. Gonoskov, A.: Employing machine learning in theoretical and experimental studies of high-intensity laser-plasma interactions (2019)
20. Raissi, M., Perdikaris, P., Karniadakis, G.E.: Physics-informed neural networks: a deep learning framework for solving forward and inverse problems involving nonlinear partial differential equations. J. Comput. Phys. **378**, 686–707 (2019)
21. Raissi, M., Wang, Z., Triantafyllou, M.S., Karniadakis, G.E.: Deep learning of vortex-induced vibrations. J. Fluid Mech. **861**, 119–137 (2019)
22. Mohan, A.T., Gaitonde, D.V.: A deep learning based approach to reduced order modeling for turbulent flow control using lstm neural networks. arXiv preprint arXiv:1804.09269 (2018)
23. Wang, Z., et al.: Model identification of reduced order fluid dynamics systems using deep learning. Int. J. Numer. Methods Fluids **86**(4), 255–268 (2018)
24. Lye, K.O., Mishra, S., Ray, D.: Deep learning observables in computational fluid dynamics. J. Comput. Phys. **410**, 109339 (2020)
25. Nathan Kutz, J.: Deep learning in fluid dynamics. J. Fluid Mech. **814**, 1–4 (2017)
26. Huang, H., Xiao, B., Xiong, H., Zeming, W., Yadong, M., Song, H.: Applications of deep learning to relativistic hydrodynamics. Nucl. Phys. A **982**, 927–930 (2019)
27. Wan, W.C., et al.: Observation of single-mode, Kelvin-Helmholtz instability in a supersonic flow. Phys. Rev. Lett. **115**(14), 145001 (2015)
28. Fryxell, B., et al.: The possible effects of magnetic fields on laser experiments of Rayleigh-Taylor instabilities. High Energy Density Phys. **6**(2), 162–165 (2010)
29. Kuranz, C.C., et al.: How high energy fluxes may affect Rayleigh-Taylor instability growth in young supernova remnants. Nat. Commun. **9**(1), 1–6 (2018)
30. Huntington, C.M., et al.: Ablative stabilization of Rayleigh-Taylor instabilities resulting from a laser-driven radiative shock. Phys. Plasmas **25**(5), 052118 (2018)
31. RayleAI Database. https://github.com/scientific-computing-nrcn/RayleAI
32. Klein, Y.: Construction of a multidimensional parallel adaptive mesh refinement special relativistic hydrodynamics code for astrophysical applications. Master's Thesis (2010)
33. Wan, W.C., et al.: Observation of dual-mode, Kelvin-Helmholtz instability vortex merger in a compressible flow. Phys. Plasmas **24**(5), 055705 (2017)
34. Goodfellow, I., et al.: Generative adversarial nets. In: Advances in Neural Information Processing Systems, pp. 2672–2680 (2014)
35. Chen, X., Duan, Y., Houthooft, R., Schulman, J., Sutskever, I., Abbeel, P.: InfoGAN: interpretable representation learning by information maximizing generative adversarial nets. In: Advances in Neural Information Processing Systems, pp. 2172–2180 (2016)
36. Gan-Image-Similarity code repository. https://github.com/marcbelmont/gan-image-similarity
37. Chatzichristofis, S.A., Lux, M.: Lire: Lucene image retrieval - an extensible Java CBIR library (2008)
38. The Apache Lucene project. https://lucene.apache.org
39. Zhang, D., Wong, A., Indrawan, M., Lu, G.: Content-based image retrieval using Gabor texture features. IEEE Trans. Pami **13**, 13–15 (2000)
40. Thanamani, A.S., Haridas, K.: Well-organized content based image retrieval system in RGB color histogram, Tamura texture and Gabor feature (2014)
41. Chatzichristofis, S.A., Boutalis, Y.S.: FCTH: fuzzy color and texture histogram-a low level feature for accurate image retrieval. In: 2008 Ninth International Workshop on Image Analysis for Multimedia Interactive Services, pp. 191–196. IEEE (2008)

42. Lathuilière, S., Mesejo, P., Alameda-Pineda, X., Horaud, R.: A comprehensive analysis of deep regression. IEEE Trans. Pattern Anal. Mach. Intell. **42**(9), 2065–2081 (2019)

43. Fischer, P., Dosovitskiy, A., Brox, T.: Image orientation estimation with convolutional networks. In: Gall, J., Gehler, P., Leibe, B. (eds.) GCPR 2015. LNCS, vol. 9358, pp. 368–378. Springer, Cham (2015). https://doi.org/10.1007/978-3-319-24947-6_30

44. Mahendran, S., Ali, H., Vidal, R.: 3D pose regression using convolutional neural networks. In: Proceedings of the IEEE International Conference on Computer Vision Workshops, pp. 2174–2182 (2017)

45. Abadi, M., et al.: TensorFlow: a system for large-scale machine learning. In: 12th USENIX Symposium on Operating Systems Design and Implementation (OSDI 2016), pp. 265–283 (2016)

46. Brunelli, R.: Template Matching Techniques in Computer Vision: Theory and Practice. Wiley, Hoboken (2009)

47. Raof, R.A.A., Nazren , A.B.A., Wafi, N.M., Hisham, M.B., Yaakob, S.N.: Template matching using sum of squared difference and normalized cross correlation. In: 2015 IEEE Student Conference on Research and Development (SCOReD). IEEE (2015)

48. Abd-Almageed, W., Natarajan, P., Cheng, J., Wu, Y.: QATM: quality-aware template matching for deep learning. In: 2019 IEEE/CVF Conference on Computer Vision and Pattern Recognition (CVPR). IEEE (2019)

49. Shi, X., et al.: Convolutional LSTM network: a machine learning approach for precipitation nowcasting. In: Advances in Neural Information Processing Systems, pp. 802–810 (2015)

50. Wang, Y., Long, M., Wang, J., Gao, Z., Philip, S.Y.: PredRNN: recurrent neural networks for predictive learning using spatiotemporal Lstms. In: Advances in Neural Information Processing Systems, pp. 879–888 (2017)

51. Ding, C., He, X.: K-means clustering via principal component analysis. In: Proceedings of the Twenty-First International Conference on Machine Learning, p. 29 (2004)

52. Hore, A., Ziou, D.: Image quality metrics: PSNR vs. SSIM. In: 2010 20th International Conference on Pattern Recognition, pp. 2366–2369. IEEE (2010)

53. Ribeiro, M.T., Singh, S., Guestrin, C.: "Why should i trust you?" explaining the predictions of any classifier. In: Proceedings of the 22nd ACM SIGKDD International Conference on Knowledge Discovery and Data Mining, pp. 1135–1144 (2016)

54. Shimony, A., et al.: Construction and validation of a statistical model for the nonlinear Kelvin-Helmholtz instability under compressible, multimode conditions. Phys. Plasmas **25**(12), 122112 (2018)

55. Tan, C., Sun, F., Kong, T., Zhang, W., Yang, C., Liu, C.: A survey on deep transfer learning. In: Kůrková, V., Manolopoulos, Y., Hammer, B., Iliadis, L., Maglogiannis, I. (eds.) ICANN 2018. LNCS, vol. 11141, pp. 270–279. Springer, Cham (2018). https://doi.org/10.1007/978-3-030-01424-7_27

56. NegevHPC Project. http://www.negevhpc.com

Prediction of Acoustic Fields Using a Lattice-Boltzmann Method and Deep Learning

Mario Rüttgers[1,2,3(✉)] ⑩, Seong-Ryong Koh[2] ⑩, Jenia Jitsev[2] ⑩,
Wolfgang Schröder[1,3] ⑩, and Andreas Lintermann[2,3] ⑩

[1] Institute of Aerodynamics and Chair of Fluid Mechanics,
RWTH Aachen University, Wüllnerstraße 5a, 52062 Aachen, Germany
m.ruettgers@aia.rwth-aachen.de
[2] Jülich Supercomputing Centre, Forschungszentrum Jülich GmbH,
Wilhelm-Johnen-Straße, 52425 Jülich, Germany
[3] Jülich Aachen Research Alliance Center for Simulation and Data Science,
Seffenter Weg 23, 52074 Aachen, Germany

Abstract. Using traditional computational fluid dynamics and aeroacoustics methods, the accurate simulation of aeroacoustic sources requires high compute resources to resolve all necessary physical phenomena. In contrast, once trained, artificial neural networks such as deep encoder-decoder convolutional networks allow to predict aeroacoustics at lower cost and, depending on the quality of the employed network, also at high accuracy. The architecture for such a neural network is developed to predict the sound pressure level in a 2D square domain. It is trained by numerical results from up to 20,000 GPU-based lattice-Boltzmann simulations that include randomly distributed rectangular and circular objects, and monopole sources. Types of boundary conditions, the monopole locations, and cell distances for objects and monopoles serve as input to the network. Parameters are studied to tune the predictions and to increase their accuracy. The complexity of the setup is successively increased along three cases and the impact of the number of feature maps, the type of loss function, and the number of training data on the prediction accuracy is investigated. An optimal choice of the parameters leads to network-predicted results that are in good agreement with the simulated findings. This is corroborated by negligible differences of the sound pressure level between the simulated and the network-predicted results along characteristic lines and by small mean errors.

Keywords: Deep convolutional neural networks · Aeroacoustic predictions · Lattice-boltzmann method

1 Introduction

State-of-the-art machine learning (ML), e.g., deep learning (DL) techniques that require very large datasets for successful training, can greatly benefit from high-performance computing (HPC) simulations. Such simulations can be used to

© The Author(s) 2020
H. Jagode et al. (Eds.): ISC High Performance 2020 Workshops, LNCS 12321, pp. 81–101, 2020.
https://doi.org/10.1007/978-3-030-59851-8_6

generate lots of training data. They come with the flexibility to obtain datasets corresponding to various task setting parameterizations, which can be used to train ML models. In contrast, obtaining data from experiments can be costly, less flexible, and sometimes even impossible. Trained ML models are capable of performing different forms of predictions on variables of interest if novel input is provided. Their knowledge is based on observations of phenomena acquired from the training on simulated data. Such data-driven models are often used as surrogate models to accelerate predictions compared to classical computationally demanding simulators, given the accuracy provided is sufficient.

Especially in the field of computational fluid dynamics (CFD), DL models trained on simulated data are capable of accelerating the prediction of flow fields. Conventional flow solvers need time to reach solutions at which the impact of initial conditions vanishes. Then, they can be used to compute, e.g., averaged results of the flow. In this case, the period of averaging needs to be bridged before the results can be analyzed. To overcome this issue, methods to accelerate the prediction of steady flow fields using convolutional neural networks (CNNs) are studied [3,7]. In [7], the flow over simplified vehicle bodies is predicted with CNNs. The corresponding surrogate model is considerably faster than traditional flow solvers. In [3], CNNs are successfully applied to predict flow fields around airfoils with varying angles of attack and REYNOLDS numbers. Lee and You [16] predict the unsteady flow over a circular cylinder using DL methods. They reveal large-scale vortex dynamics to be well predictable by their models. In [17], CNNs to predict unsteady three-dimensional turbulent flows are investigated. The CNNs correctly learn to transport and integrate wave number information contained in feature maps. Additionally, a method that can optimize the number of feature maps is proposed. Unsteady flow and force coefficients are the main focus of the investigations in [22], in which a data-driven method using a CNN for model reduction of the Navier-Stokes equations is presented. In [27], a generative adversarial network (GAN) to forecast movements of typhoons is used and satellite images along with velocity information from numerical simulations are incorporated. This allows for 6-hour predictions of typhoons with an averaged error <95.6 km. Unlike numerical predictions on HPC systems, the GAN-based method takes only seconds. Bode et al. [4] propose a physics-informed GAN and successfully model flow on subgrid scales in turbulent reactive flows.

To improve quality and robustness of DL models, training is frequently performed on very large data sets obtained from simulations run on HPC systems. In aerodynamic problems, small-scale structures and/or fluid mechanics based perturbations can strongly influence the acoustic field although they might contain only a small amount of total energy. In many engineering applications, modeling flow-induced sound requires interdisciplinary knowledge about fluid mechanics, acoustics, and applied mathematics. Furthermore, the numerical analysis demands high-resolution numerical simulations to accurately determine the various flow phenomena, e.g., turbulent shear layers [24], fluid-structure interactions [6], and combustion processes [29], that determine the acoustic field.

The sheer quantity and often high dimensionality of the parameters describing such flow fields complicate post-processing of the simulated data. This poses a challenge to derive new control models and to make progress in design optimizations [13,33]. The turn-around time between prototyping and manufacturing depends on the complexity of fundamental physical mechanisms. A recent effort to enhance the efficiency of design development employs an ML framework to predict acoustic fields of a variety of fan nozzle and jet configurations [21]. Although the concept has not yet been realized, this ML-based approach illustrates a prospective possibility to reduce design cycle times of new engine configurations.

The main objective of the present study is the prediction of acoustic fields via a robust ML model based on a deep encoder-decoder CNN. The CNN is trained by acoustic fields containing noise sources surrounded by multiple objects. The numerical results are obtained from simulations using a lattice-Boltzmann (LB) method. They include the simulation of wave propagation, reflection, and scattering due to the interaction with sound-hard surfaces.

In the following, the numerical methods to predict room aeroacoustics with CNNs are described in Sect. 2. Subsequently, results from the sound fields predicted by CNNs are presented and juxtaposed to results of LB simulations in Sect. 3. Finally, a summary is given, conclusions are drawn, and an outlook is presented in Sect. 4.

2   Numerical Methods

To generate training data for the CNN, aeroacoustic simulations are run with an LB method on two-dimensional rectangular meshes. The LB method is described in Sect. 2.1, followed by a presentation of the geometrical setup, and the computational meshes in Sect. 2.2. Section 2.3 explains the imposed boundary and initial conditions. Section 2.4 describes how the acoustic fields are analyzed. Finally, the network architecture for the prediction of aeroacoustic fields is presented in Sect. 2.5.

2.1   Lattice-Boltzmann Method

To compute the aeroacoustic pressure field, an LB method is employed. The governing equation is the Boltzmann equation with the simplified right-hand side (RHS) Bhatnagar-Gross-Krook (BGK) collision term [2]

$$\frac{\partial f}{\partial t} + \xi_k \frac{\partial f}{\partial x_k} = -\frac{1}{\tau}(f - f^{eq}). \tag{1}$$

The particle probability density functions (PPDFs) $f = f(\vec{x}, \vec{\xi}, t)$ describe the probability to find a particle of a fluid around a location $\vec{x}$ with a particle velocity $\vec{\xi}$ at time t [1,8]. The left-hand side (LHS) of Eq. (1) describes the evolution of fluid particles in space and time, while the RHS describes the collision of

Table 1. Physical quantities of the setup and the non-dimensional viscosity ν.

Mesh	$\Delta\tilde{x}$ [m]	$\Delta\tilde{t}$ [s]	$\tilde{\omega}$ [Hz]	$\tilde{\nu}$ [m^2/s]	ν
$\mathcal{M}_c$	0.2	$3.4 \cdot 10^{-4}$	58.8	$1.551717 \cdot 10^{-5}$	$1.318959 \cdot 10^{-7}$
$\mathcal{M}_f$	0.1	$1.7 \cdot 10^{-4}$	117.6	$1.551717 \cdot 10^{-5}$	$2.637920 \cdot 10^{-7}$

particles. The collision process is governed by the relaxation parameter $1/\tau$ with relaxation time τ to reach the Maxwellian equilibrium state f^{eq}. The discretized form of Eq. (1) yields the lattice-BGK equation

$$f_k(\vec{x} + \xi_k \Delta t, t + \Delta t) = f_k(\vec{x}, t) - \frac{1}{\tau}(f_k(\vec{x}, t) - f_k^{eq}(\vec{x}, t)). \tag{2}$$

The quantity Δt is the time increment and τ is a function of the kinematic viscosity ν and the speed of sound c_s, i.e.,

$$\tau = \frac{\nu + \Delta t c_s^2/2}{c_s^2}. \tag{3}$$

In the LB context, the spatial and temporal spacing are set to $\Delta x = \Delta t = 1.0$ such that $c_s = 1/\sqrt{3}$. Table 1 exemplarily lists the LB viscosity for two meshes $\mathcal{M}_c$ and $\mathcal{M}_f$ with different resolutions. Note that these values are derived in Sect. 2.3. The LB viscosity is an artificial parameter simply influencing the time step, i.e., how much physical time $\tilde{t}$ is covered by a single Δt in the simulation. Using the viscosities listed in Table 1 would lead to extremely small time steps. For this reason and in order to conduct numerically stable simulations, ν is set to a feasible value according to [28]. The indices k in Eq. (2) depend on the discretization scheme and represent the different directions of the PPDFs. In this work, the two-dimensional discretization scheme with 9 PPDFS, i.e., the D2Q9 model [25] is used. The discretized equilibrium PPDF is given by

$$f_k^{eq} = w_k \rho \left(1 + \frac{\xi_k \vec{u}}{c_s^2} + \frac{(\xi_k \vec{u})^2}{2c_s^4} - \frac{\vec{u}^2}{2c_s^2} \right), \tag{4}$$

where the quantities w_k are weighting factors for the D2Q9 scheme given by $4/9$ for $k \in \{0\}$, $1/9$ for $k \in \{1, \ldots, 4\}$, and $1/36$ for $k \in \{5, \ldots, 8\}$, and $\vec{u}$ is the fluid velocity. The macroscopic variables can be obtained from the moments of the PPDFs, i.e., the density $\rho = \sum_k f_k$. The pressure can be computed using the ideal gas law by $p = c_s^2 \rho = (1/3)\rho$.

The LB method has been chosen for several reasons [18]: (i) the computations can be performed efficiently in parallel, (ii) it is straightforward to parallelize the code, (iii) boundary conditions can easily be applied in contrast to, e.g., cut-cell methods, and (iv) there is no need to solve a pressure Poisson-equation for quasi-incompressible flow as the pressure and hence the acoustic field is an explicit result of the lattice-BGK algorithm. Furthermore, the LB method can be applied for low to high KNUDSEN numbers Kn. In the continuum limit, i.e. for small Kn, the Navier-Stokes and Euler equations can directly be derived from the Boltzmann equation and the BGK model [8].

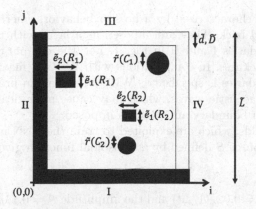

Fig. 1. Computational domain.

2.2 Geometrical Setup and Computational Meshes

The computational domain has a square shape containing randomly distributed objects. In physical space, denoted in the following by $<\tilde{}>$, the domain has an edge length of $\tilde{L} = 25.6$ m. Throughout this study, the number of objects varies depending on the complexity of a computation. The domain of the most complex case is shown in Fig. 1. It has two rectangular objects R_1 and R_2 and two circular objects C_1 and C_2. Their size is a function of the characteristic length $\tilde{C} = \tilde{L}/16$, i.e., R_1 and R_2 have edge lengths $\tilde{e}_1(R_1), \tilde{e}_2(R_1), \tilde{e}_1(R_2), \tilde{e}_2(R_2) \in [\tilde{C}, 2\tilde{C}]$, and C_1 and C_2 have radii $\tilde{r}(C_1), \tilde{r}(C_2) \in [\tilde{C}, 2\tilde{C}]$. All objects have a minimum distance of $\tilde{d} = \tilde{C}$ from the domain boundaries and may overlap.

Two-dimensional uniformly refined meshes $\mathcal{M}_f$ and $\mathcal{M}_c$ with two distinct resolutions are generated in Cartesian coordinates. In the fine mesh $\mathcal{M}_f$ each cell has an edge length of $\Delta \tilde{x}_f = (1/16)\tilde{C} = 0.1$ m resulting in 256×256 cells. The coarse mesh $\mathcal{M}_c$ has a cell length of $\Delta \tilde{x}_c = (1/8)\tilde{C} = 0.2$ m and a total of 128×128 cells.

2.3 Boundary and Initial Conditions

Two types of boundary conditions are imposed at the four domain boundaries according to [11], i.e., non-reflecting (NRBCs) and wall boundary conditions (WBCs) are prescribed. As shown for boundaries III and IV in Fig. 1, the NRBCs have a buffer layer thickness of $\tilde{D} = \tilde{C}$ to ensure a complete dissipation of acoustic waves and to avoid reflective phenomena at the domain boundaries. In the buffer layer, an absorption term [11]

$$F_{ad} = -\sigma(f_k^{eq}(\vec{x}, t) - f_a), \tag{5}$$

with weighting factor f_a and $\sigma = \sigma_m(\tilde{\delta}/\tilde{D})^2$ is added to Eq. (2). The quantity $\tilde{\delta}$ is the distance to the buffer layer and σ_m is a constant specified as 0.1.

The WBCs are characterized by a no-slip behavior, where the PPDFs are reflectively bounced back. They are imposed as a layer with thickness $\tilde{D} = \tilde{C}$ as shown for boundaries I and II in Fig. 1, i.e., the computational domain is reduced by this thickness. In computations with WBC, a maximum number of three domain boundaries is specified as WBC in a random process. To prevent strong overlaps of acoustic waves, which may cause numerical instabilities, at least at one domain boundary an NRBC is imposed.

The acoustic fields, which are exploited to train the CNN model, are configured by a simple source S defined by a sinusoidal function given by

$$S(t) = A \cdot \sin(2\pi\omega t), \tag{6}$$

with a frequency $\omega = 0.02 \cdot (1/\Delta t)$ and the amplitude $A = 0.1 \cdot \rho_\infty$ and $\rho_\infty = 1.0$ in the LB context. A set of the training data is generated by the computational domains with a noise source restricted by a geometry, i.e., the minimum distance $\tilde{C}$ between the noise source and the sound-hard objects satisfies the condition $L < 2\tilde{C}$ where L is a distance between monopoles and domain boundaries. With $\omega = 1/T$, this yields a non-dimensionalized harmonic period of $T = 50\Delta t$. One wavelength λ is computed from $\lambda = u_w/\omega$, with $u_w = \Delta x/\Delta t$ being the velocity with which information is transported in the LB context. This results in $\lambda = 50\Delta x$ for computations in this study, if not stated otherwise.

The relationship between ω in LB context and the frequency $\tilde{\omega}$ in physical space is obtained by inserting

$$\Delta \tilde{t} = \Delta \tilde{x} \frac{c_s}{\tilde{c}_s}, \tag{7}$$

with the physical speed of sound $\tilde{c}_s = 340\,\text{m/s}$ at reference temperature $T_\infty = 298.15K$ into the equation for the frequency $\tilde{\omega} = 0.02(1/\Delta\tilde{t})$. The relationship between ν in the LB context and the kinematic viscosity $\tilde{\nu}$ in physical space is given by

$$\nu = \tilde{\nu} \cdot \frac{\Delta\tilde{t}}{(\Delta\tilde{x})^2} \qquad \text{with} \qquad \tilde{\nu} = \frac{1}{\tilde{\rho}_\infty} \cdot \frac{K_1 \cdot T_\infty^{\frac{3}{2}}}{T_\infty + K_2}. \tag{8}$$

The latter equation is Sutherland's law [32] with $\tilde{\rho}_\infty = 1.184\,\text{kg/m}^3$, $K_1 = 1.458 \cdot 10^{-6}\,\text{kg/(ms·K}^{1/2})$, and $K_2 = 110.4K$. Table 1 lists all necessary variables in their dimensional and non-dimensional form for $\mathcal{M}_f$ and $\mathcal{M}_c$.

2.4   Evaluation of Acoustic Fields

The acoustic fields are determined by a set of the computational domains which include at least one noise source and randomized solid surfaces. For fluid cells at location $(i,j), i,j \in \{1,\ldots,m\}$, the sound pressure level SPL is defined by

$$SPL(i,j) = 20\log_{10}(p'_{\text{rms}}(i,j)), \tag{9}$$

where the maximum number of mesh points m is $m = 128$ for the coarse grid and $m = 256$ for the fine grid configurations. The root-mean-square (rms) values of pressure fluctuations p' are calculated by

$$p'_{\text{rms}}(i,j) = \sqrt{\frac{\sum_{n=1}^{N}(p_n(i,j) - p_{\text{avg}}(i,j))^2}{N}}, \tag{10}$$

where $p_{\text{avg}}(i,j)$ is the mean pressure averaged over the time period N, and $p_n(i,j)$ is the instantaneous pressure resulting from the simulation at a time step n within that period. Simulations are carried out for $3,000$ time steps. The averaging period $N = 2,000$ starts after $1,000$ time steps when the acoustic field is fully developed.

2.5 Machine Learning Techniques

An encoder-decoder CNN is trained to predict the SPL in a supervised manner using results of the aforementioned LB simulations. The CNN is fed with four types of input data:

(i) types of boundary condition;
(ii) location of monopoles;
(iii) cell distances for objects;
(iv) cell distances for monopoles.

To correctly predict aeroacoustic fields, the CNN needs to learn the impact of the various boundary conditions and the location of monopoles on the acoustic field. Therefore, considering inputs (i) and (ii), cells at location (i,j) are assigned segmentation values

$$\Upsilon(i,j) = \begin{cases} 0, & \text{empty or NRBC cell} \\ \frac{1}{2}, & \text{WBC or object cell} \\ 1, & \text{monopole cell} \end{cases}. \tag{11}$$

A sensitivity analysis of the input data has been performed before the training. This analysis revealed that solely using boundary parameters leads to poor predictions of the network, i.e., it is not effective for CNNs learning from flow simulations. This is in line with findings in [7]. Since acoustic signals propagate with a certain wavelength and amplitude at a certain sound speed, distances are also important parameters for learning. For this purpose, inputs (iii) and (iv) are provided to the CNN in the form of distance functions Φ_o for objects and Φ_m for monopoles. Such an approach has previously been used for CNNs to predict steady-state flow fields [3,7]. The distance functions are defined by

$$\Phi_o(\mathbf{x}) = \begin{cases} d(\mathbf{x}, \partial\Omega) & \mathbf{x} \notin \Omega \\ 0 & \mathbf{x} \in \{\partial\Omega, \Omega\} \end{cases} \quad \text{and} \quad \Phi_m(\mathbf{x}) = d(\mathbf{x}, M), \tag{12}$$

i.e., for each cell $\mathbf{x}$ with location (i, j) in a domain the minimal distances $d(\mathbf{x}, \partial \Omega)$ and $d(\mathbf{x}, M)$ to the boundary $\partial \Omega$ of an object Ω and to a monopole M are determined. Obviously, it is $\Phi_o(\mathbf{x}) = \Phi_m(\mathbf{x}) = 0$ on the boundary and exactly at the monopole source. For Φ_o, an assignment of negative distances for cells inside of an object, as it is usually used by signed-distance functions, turned out to have a negative impact on predictions, which is why $\forall(\mathbf{x} \in \Omega : \Phi_o = 0)$. The distances are computed by the fast marching method [30] and are normalized by $\tilde{L}$. Learning from distances like inputs (iii) and (iv) alone results in mispredictions near domain boundaries. A combination of all presented types of inputs has been found to favorably affect predictions.

In the following, the CNN used for predicting the SPL fields is referred to as acoustics field predictor (AFP). The corresponding network architecture is shown in Fig. 2 for a case that uses arrays with the size of $\mathcal{M}_f$ as inputs. Inputs (i) and (ii) are combined to one array. Together with fields (iii) and (iv) they are stacked to form channels of the input. It should be noted that physical quantities such as the pressure distribution are a solution of the acoustic fields computation and constitute the ground truth. They are not known a priori and hence cannot be used for training.

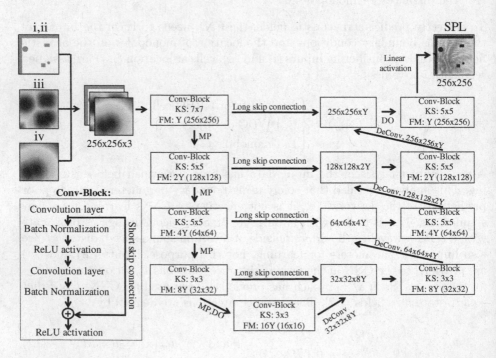

Fig. 2. Network architecture of the AFP including size and number of feature maps (FMs) as a multiple of Y, kernel size (KS), 2×2 maximum pooling layers (MP), dropout layers (DO), convolutional blocks, and deconvolutional layers.

The architecture is inspired by distinct architectures that employ long skip connections between encoder and decoder layers [19,26,34], like for instance U-net architectures, which have been successfully used for medical image segmentation [26]. Skip connections between encoding and decoding paths allow the re-use and fusion of features on different scales. To preserve information from features on all scales, the activity of each encoder layer is directly fed to the corresponding decoder layer via long skip connections. These connections are chosen to have residual form, adding the activity of encoder layers to the output of decoder layers. This setup is similar to [19], however, different from the original U-net architecture, where long skip connections have dense form and concatenate layers on the same scale. As depicted in Fig. 2, the residual long skip connections perform identity mapping by adding source encoder layer outputs to target decoder layer outputs [9,19]. This kind of connectivity allows for direct gradient flow from higher to lower layers across all hierarchy stages during the backward pass, which prevents common issues with vanishing gradients in deep architectures. In contrast to dense long skip connections, residual skip connections lead to smaller numbers of activations to be handled in the decoding path during the forward and backward passes. As a consequence, they decreased memory consumption and are more efficient and faster in training without sacrificing prediction accuracy. Short skip residual connections are also used in so called convolutional residual blocks (Conv-Blocks). Here, convolutional layers, batch normalization (BN), and rectified linear unit (ReLU) activation functions are employed. BN acts as a regularizer, shifting activity of the layers to zero mean, unit variance. This leads to faster and more reliable network convergence [10]. The number of feature maps (FMs) is a multiple of a given factor Y. The output of the first convolutional layer is added to the input of the last ReLU activation, see Fig. 2, which defines residual short skip connections in Conv-Blocks. A combination of long and short skip connections leads to faster convergence and stronger loss reduction [5]. In the encoder path, downscaling is performed by 2×2 maximum pooling layers (MP). To further avoid overfitting, yet another regularization method, dropout (DO) [31] is used during training, with a DO probability of $P = 0.5$. The final layer is fully connected with a linear activation function, which is frequently used for regression outputs [15]. Weights and biases are initialized from a truncated normal distribution centered around the origin with a standard deviation of $\sigma_{std} = \sqrt{2/f}$, where f is the number of connections at a layer [9]. They are updated by an adaptive moments (ADAM) optimizer [12]. The ADAM optimizer adjusts the learning rate (LR) by considering an exponentially decaying average of gradients computed in previous update steps. The initial learning rate is set to $LR = 0.001$. The batch size BS represents the number of training data passed to the network in a single training iteration. In Sect. 3 it will be shown that in this context a batch size of $BS = 5$ achieves the best results. Therefore, it is used throughout this study, if not stated otherwise. The ground truth GT distribution SPL_{GT} is obtained from

$$SPL_{GT} = \frac{SPL - SPL_{mean}}{SPL_{std}}, \tag{13}$$

where SPL_{mean} and SPL_{std} are the mean and the standard deviation of the complete training dataset of the a priori simulations. The predictions need to be denormalized before the SPL can be analyzed.

Data augmentation is used to increase training data diversity and to encourage learning of useful invariances. Therefore, the coordinate axes i and j are transposed randomly. Furthermore, for inputs (i) and (ii), the segmentation values $\Upsilon(i,j)$ are changed to augmented inputs $\Upsilon_{augm}(i,j)$ according to

$$\Upsilon_{augm}(i,j) = \begin{cases} \Upsilon(i,j) & i=j \\ \Upsilon(j,i) & i \neq j. \end{cases} \tag{14}$$

The total loss L_{tot} between simulated (superscript "sim") and predicted (superscript "$pred$") SPL values is defined by

$$L_{tot} = L_{MSE} + 2 \cdot \underbrace{(L_{GDL}^{I} + L_{GDL}^{II} + L_{GDL}^{III} + L_{GDL}^{IV})}_{L_{GDL}}, \tag{15}$$

which is a combination of the mean squared error MSE

$$L_{MSE} = \frac{1}{m^2} \sum_{i=1}^{m} \sum_{j=1}^{m} \left(SPL(i,j)^{sim} - SPL(i,j)^{pred} \right)^2 \tag{16}$$

with $1 \leq i,j \leq m$ and a gradient difference loss L_{GDL}. Gradient losses GDL in i- and j-directions are considered by L_{GDL_I} and $L_{GDL_{II}}$, and diagonal gradients by $L_{GDL_{III}}$ and $L_{GDL_{IV}}$.

Three types of gradient losses are addressed in this work. The four directions indicated by roman numbers I–IV in Eq. (15) are defined by introducing integer variables k and l, i.e., the four directions are denoted by $I : (k=1, l=1)$, $II : (k=2, l=2)$, $III : (k=1, l=2)$, and $IV : (k=2, l=1)$. In the first type, L_{GDL_A}, the difference between two neighboring cells is considered, inspired by the gradient loss in the work of Mathieu et al. [20]

$$L_{GDL_A} = \frac{1}{(m-1)(m - \mathrm{mod}(p,2))} \cdot$$
$$\sum_i \sum_j [SPL_{i+s,j+t}^{sim} - SPL_{i,j}^{sim} - SPL_{i+s,j+t}^{pred} + SPL_{i,j}^{pred}]^2. \tag{17}$$

In Eq. (17) the gradient losses of four neighboring points are defined by the notations $p = \mathrm{mod}(k,2) + \mathrm{mod}(l,2)$, $s = 1 - \mathrm{mod}(k+1,2) \cdot \mathrm{mod}(l+1,2)$, and $t = (-1)^{k+1} \cdot \mathrm{mod}(p,2) + 1 - s$. The gradient loss terms of the first type have a 1st-order accuracy in terms of a forward difference (FD) formulation [23]. To integrate radial propagation of a point source into the loss function, central difference (CD) schemes are added. The gradient loss L_{GDL_B} uses a 2nd-order accurate CD formulation that incorporates two neighboring cells. The 2nd-order accurate gradient loss terms in a two-dimensional domain read

$$L_{GDL_B} = \frac{1}{4 \bmod(k+l+1,2) + 8 \bmod(k+l,2)(m-2)(m-2 \cdot \bmod(p,2))} \cdot$$

$$\sum_i \sum_j \left[SPL^{sim}_{i+s,j+t} - SPL^{sim}_{i-s,j-t} - SPL^{pred}_{i+s,j+t} + SPL^{pred}_{i-s,j-t} \right]^2 \qquad (18)$$

The third type of gradient loss, L_{GDL_C}, is formulated with a 4th-order accurate CD scheme and includes four neighboring cells, i.e., two cells in each direction

$$L_{GDL_C} = \frac{1}{144 \bmod(k+l+1,2) + 32 \bmod(k+l,2)(m-4)(m-4 \cdot \bmod(p,2))} \cdot$$

$$\sum_i \sum_j \left[-SPL^{sim}_{i+2s,j+2t} + 8SPL^{sim}_{i+s,j+t} - 8SPL^{sim}_{i-s,j-t} + SPL^{sim}_{i-2s,j-2t} \right.$$

$$\left. + SPL^{pred}_{i+2s,j+2t} - 8SPL^{pred}_{i+s,j+t} + 8SPL^{pred}_{i-s,j-t} - SPL^{pred}_{i-2s,j-2t} \right]^2 . \qquad (19)$$

The cell-wise prediction accuracy is evaluated by the absolute error

$$\Xi(i,j) = \frac{\left| SPL^{pred}(i,j) - SPL^{sim}(i,j) \right|}{\left| SPL^{sim}_{max} - SPL^{sim}_{min} \right|}. \qquad (20)$$

between SPL^{pred} and SPL^{sim} with $SPL^{sim}_{max} = \max(SPL^{sim})$ and $SPL^{sim}_{min} = \min(SPL^{sim})$. From the Ξ distribution of each simulation a mean absolute error

$$\Gamma = \frac{1}{m^2} \sum_{i=1}^{m} \sum_{j=1}^{m} \Xi(i,j) \qquad (21)$$

is calculated to evaluate the prediction quality.

3   Results

In the following, findings of a grid convergence study are discussed in Sect. 3.1. Results of network-predicted acoustic fields are presented for three cases 1–3 in Sects. 3.2, 3.3, and 3.4. The complexity of the cases is continuously increased.

The acoustic simulations are conducted on multiple graphics processing units (GPUs). At average, a solution on $\mathcal{M}_f$ is obtained in ≈ 120 s on a single GPU. Up to ten GPUs are employed to accelerate the process. Once trained, the network predictions take only a fraction of a second on a single modern GPU and only a few seconds on any low end computer such as a laptop. For all computations the GPU partition of the JURECA system [14], Forschungszentrum Jülich, is employed. Each GPU node is equipped with two NVIDIA K80 GPUs.

3.1   Grid Convergence Study

A grid convergence study is conducted in a free-field domain containing only a single monopole at the center and no walls. The impact of doubling the number

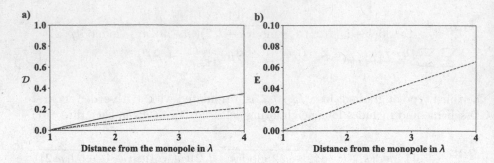

Fig. 3. a) $\mathcal{D} = (SPL - SPL_{max})/SPL_{max}$ at a distance from up to 4λ in radial direction from a monopole placed in the center of a free field. Three resolutions for one wavelength are juxtaposed: $\mathcal{D}(\lambda = 100\Delta x) \cdots$, $\mathcal{D}(\lambda = 50\Delta x)$ - - -, $\mathcal{D}(\lambda = 25\Delta x)$ —. b) Error E between $\mathcal{D}(\lambda = 50\Delta x)$ and $\mathcal{D}(\lambda = 100\Delta x)$.

of cells used to resolve one wavelength λ on the SPL accuracy is investigated. Therefore, the wavelength resolutions at a distance of up to 4 wavelengths in radial direction from the source, which corresponds to the maximum appearing distance considered in the subsequently discussed cases 1–3, is analyzed. In order to obtain results in a farfield from the center for $\lambda = 100\Delta x$, the domain is extended to $1,024 \times 1,024$ cells. Figure 3a) shows the divergence $\mathcal{D} = (SPL - SPL_{max})/SPL_{max}$ from the maximum SPL value SPL_{max}, which appears at a distance of one wavelength from the monopole location, for $\lambda = 25\Delta x$, $50\Delta x$, and $100\Delta x$. From this figure, it is evident, that the divergence increases with increasing distance from the monopole. Furthermore, Fig. 3b) shows the error for $\lambda = 50\Delta x$ compared to $\lambda = 100\Delta x$, i.e., $E = \mathcal{D}(\lambda = 50\Delta x) - \mathcal{D}(\lambda = 100\Delta x)$. Throughout this work a wavelength of $\lambda = 50\Delta x$ is used, which covers distances up to 2λ in cases 1–2, and up to 4λ in case 3. At distances 2λ and 4λ, errors of $E = 0.0239$ and $E = 0.0657$ are obtained. It should be noted that using $\lambda = 100\Delta x$ would massively increase the computational effort and hence, as the corresponding error is acceptable, meshes with $\lambda = 50\Delta x$ are employed in all cases.

3.2   Case 1: Simple Setup and Parameter Study

The domain in case 1 contains one monopole M_1 at the center $(8C, 8C)$ and one randomly positioned circular object C_1. Each computational domain consists of 128×128 cells in the two dimensions. The acoustic solutions of $3,000$ simulations are split into $2,600$ training data, 200 validation data, and 200 test data. Three sub-cases 1A, 1B, and 1C listed in Table 2 are configured by one noise source and one solid object. In case 1A, the number of FMs is investigated by varying the factor Y as shown in Fig. 2. Variations of $Y = 8$, $Y = 16$ and $Y = 32$ lead to $517,867$, $2,066,001$ and $8,253,089$ trainable parameters. It is evident from comparing Figs. 4b), 4c), and 4d) with the simulation results in Fig. 4a) that $Y = 32$ qualitatively reproduces the simulation best. For $Y = 8$, the AFP

Table 2. Simulation configurations defined by objects, the number of noise sources (no. noise) and simulations (no. sim) generated by randomized distributions of objects. The number of feature maps (FMs) is defined by Y. The gradient losses GDL are calculated by FD, 2nd-order-accurate, and 4th-order-accurate CD schemes. The quantities BS and Γ are the batch size and the mean acoustic error.

Case	Object(s)	No. noise	No. sim	Y	GDL method	BS	Γ
1A	C_1	1	3,000	8	FD	5	0.17506
	C_1	1	3,000	16	FD	5	0.03312
	C_1	1	3,000	32	FD	5	0.00887
1B	C_1	1	3,000	32	FD	5	0.00887
	C_1	1	3,000	32	2nd order CD	5	0.00671
	C_1	1	3,000	32	4th order CD	5	0.00222
1C	C_1	1	3,000	32	2nd order CD	5	0.00671
	C_1	1	3,000	32	2nd order CD	10	0.00626
	C_1	1	3,000	32	2nd order CD	20	0.00413
2	R_1, C_1	1	3,000	32	2nd order CD	5	0.00359
	R_1, C_1	1	6,000	32	2nd order CD	5	0.00280
3	R_1, R_2, C_1, C_2	2	6,000	32	2nd order CD	5	0.02581
	R_1, R_2, C_1, C_2	2	10,000	32	2nd order CD	5	0.02268
	R_1, R_2, C_1, C_2	2	20,000	32	2nd order CD	5	0.01937

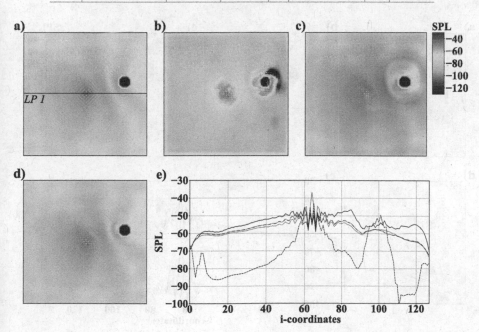

Fig. 4. Example of SPL fields of case 1A: a) simulation result, b) network prediction with $Y = 8$, c) $Y = 16$, and d) $Y = 32$; e) SPL distribution at $j = 64$ along $LP1$: simulation result $\cdots$, network prediction with $Y = 8$ - - -, $Y = 16$ —, and $Y = 32$ - · -.

94   M. Rüttgers et al.

completely fails to generate a physically meaningful SPL field. In case of $Y = 16$, acoustic waves distant from the object are reproduced well, but superpositions of acoustic waves in the vicinity of the object are too strong, see Fig. 4c). The SPL distribution shown in Fig. 4e) along the characteristic line $LP1$, see Fig. 4a), substantiates these findings. The valley between M_1 and C_1, and the decrease of the SPL value in the shadow of C_1 are only captured well for $Y = 32$. Furthermore, the CNN has problems capturing fluctuations at the center of M_1 as non-physical SPL values are found at isolated locations close to the object. The mean error Γ listed in Table 2 shows $Y = 32$ to have the lowest deviation among the three computations. The training time to reach a convergence of the loss function increased from approximately one hour for $Y = 8$ up to two and four hours for $Y = 16$ and $Y = 32$.

To overcome inaccurate predictions close to monopoles, the nature of a noise source is incorporated into the loss function of the AFP. A simple FD gradient loss does not consider that monopoles are point sources spreading waves into all directions. In case 1B, two variations of losses are investigated that are based on the CD formulations provided in Sect. 2.5. From Fig. 5 it is obvious that thereby non-physical SPL values vanish near objects. Furthermore, Fig. 5(c) shows an improvement of the SPL distribution at the center and surroundings of M_1 predicted by a 2nd-order accurate CD gradient loss. In contrast, using a

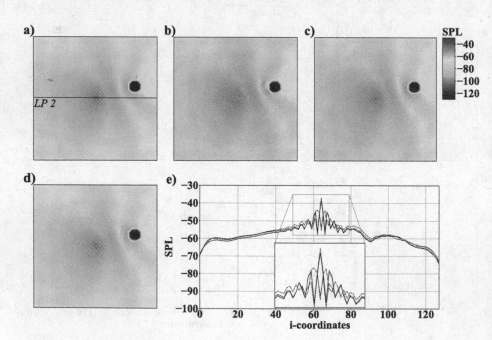

Fig. 5. Example of SPL fields of case 1B: a) simulation result, b) network prediction with FD, c) a 2nd-order accurate CD , and d) a 4th-order accurate CD gradient loss; e) SPL at $j = 64$ along $LP2$: simulation result $\cdots$, network prediction with FD - - -, 2nd-order accurate CD —, and 4th-order accurate CD gradient losses - $\cdot$ -.

4th-order accurate CD formulation lowers the accuracy of the predictions near M_1, see Fig. 5(d). It is, however, evident from Table 2 that a slightly lower Γ is achieved than using a 2nd-order formulation. This is due to the 4th-order accurate CD gradient loss computations reproducing simulations slightly better at locations distant from monopoles and objects, see Fig. 5(e). SPL fluctuations at the center of M_1 are by far closer to the ground truth using the 2nd-order accurate formulation. Since this study focuses on the prediction of complex acoustic fields with multiple noise sources, the advantages of the 2nd-order accurate formulation are considered more valuable, i.e., in the following this type of loss is employed.

The impact of BS is investigated in Fig. 6. Figure 6e) plots the SPL distribution along line $LP3$, see Fig. 6a). Although predictions with $BS = 10$ and $BS = 20$ show a slight decrease of Γ, see Table 2, several shortcomings are recognizable in predicted SPL fields. Figures 6c) and e) show that with $BS = 10$ non-physical fluctuations near the objects are introduced. These fluctuations are also present for $BS = 20$ and are superimposed by inaccuracies appearing in the vicinity of M_1 and at the domain boundaries, i.e., $BS = 5$ delivers the best results.

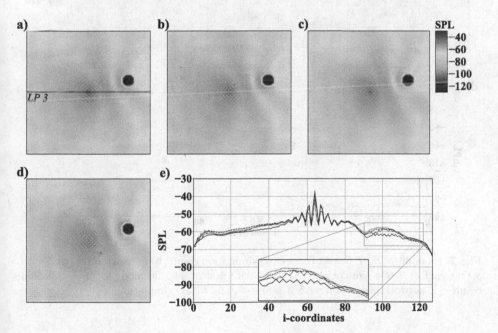

Fig. 6. Example for SPL fields of case 1C: a) simulation result, b) network prediction with $BS = 5$, c) $BS = 10$, and d) $BS = 20$; e) SPL distribution at $j = 64$ along line $LP3$: simulation result $\cdots$, network prediction with $BS = 5$ - - -, $BS = 10$ —, and $BS = 20$ - · -.

3.3 Case 2: Influence of the Number of Training Data

In case 2, the number of training, validation, and test data is analyzed. Compared to case 1, the complexity is increased by adding a rectangular object R_1 to the domain. The training, validation, and test data are composed of $2,600, 200$ and 200 simulations for a total of $3,000$, and of $5,200, 400$, and 400 for a total of $6,000$ simulations. The setups for these cases are summarized in Table 2.

Figure 7 compares the results of an LB simulation qualitatively and quantitatively along line $LP4$, see Fig. 7a), with predictions generated by using $3,000$ and $6,000$ simulations for learning. When the amount of data is increased, nonphysical fluctuations disappear in regions, where sound waves propagate towards the surface of R_1. Furthermore, the predictions of the acoustic field in the vicinity of C_1 improve from $3,000$ to $6,000$ training datasets.

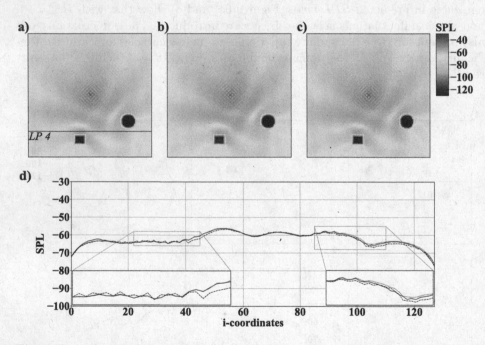

Fig. 7. Example of SPL fields of case 2: a) simulation result, b) network prediction with $3,000$, and c) $6,000$ simulations; SPL distribution at $j = 30$ along $LP4$: simulation result $\cdots$, network prediction with $3,000$ - - -, and $6,000$ simulations —.

3.4 Case 3: Complex Setup and Impact of Increasing Training Data

Case 3 ties on to the findings from the previous cases to predict SPL fields in a domain containing objects C_1, C_2, R_1, and R_2, see Fig. 1, on $\mathcal{M}_f$. From $\mathcal{M}_c$ to $\mathcal{M}_f$ the number of trainable parameters increases from $8,253,089$ to $8,256,225$. NRBC and WBC boundary conditions are imposed randomly at the domain

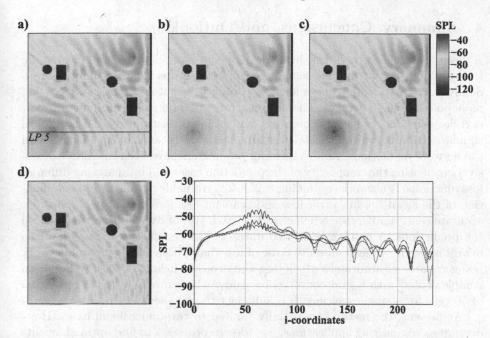

Fig. 8. Example of SPL fields of case 3: a) simulation result, b) network prediction with 6,000, c) 10,000, and d) 20,000 simulations; SPL distribution at $j = 80$ along $LP5$: simulation result $\cdots$, network prediction with 6,000 - - -, 10,000 —, and 20,000 simulations - $\cdot$ -.

boundaries. Two monopoles M_1 and M_2 are placed inside of the domain. M_1 is located at $(5C, 5C)$ and M_2 is positioned randomly. For the training, validation, and testing of the AFP, a total number of 20,000 simulations is used. Results of computations with different simulation inputs are compared to the ground truth in Fig. 8. Note that the WBC is imposed at domain boundary IV, however, the complete thickness $\tilde{D}$ is not visualized in the figure. The first case uses 6,000 simulations with a distribution of 5,200, 400, and 400 for training, validation, and testing. The second case employs 10,000 simulations with a distribution of 8,800, 600, and 600 for training, validation, and testing. The last case employs all 20,000 simulations with a distribution of 18,000, 1,000, and 1,000 for training, validation, and testing. For reference, the different setups and the corresponding results are listed in Table 2. Obviously, the error Γ decreases when the number of training data is increased. From Figs. 8(c) and (e) it is evident that the AFP trained with 8,800 datasets overpredicts the SPL near M_1. In general, it can be stated that with an increasing complexity the SPL is more difficult to predict compared to cases 1 and 2. To be more specific, from case 1 to case 3 the error Γ increases by one order of magnitude, i.e., it is at $\Gamma = 0.01937$ in case 3. However, complex acoustic fields are reproduced. For a number of 18,000 simulation, training took 96 hours to reach a convergence of the loss function.

4   Summary, Conclusions, and Outlook

A deep learning method has been developed to predict the sound pressure level distribution in two-dimensional aeroacoustic setups including multiple randomly distributed rectangular and circular objects as hard reflective surfaces and monopoles as sound sources. The deep learning method is based on an encoder-decoder convolutional neural network, which has been trained with numerical simulations based on a lattice-Boltzmann method. To analyze the accuracy of the network predictions, various learning parameters have been tuned by successively increasing the complexity of the prediction cases and by analyzing different loss functions. A network containing $8, 256, 225$ trainable parameters, a combination of the mean-squared error loss and gradient loss formulated by a 2nd-order accurate central difference scheme, and a batch size of five positively influenced the predictions. A number of $18, 000$ datasets has been used to train the deep neural network. A mean absolute error of less than 2% shows the neural network being capable of accurately predicting the acoustic fields. The study has been complemented with a grid convergence study, which revealed that a resolution of 50 cells for a single wavelength is sufficient to yield accurate results.

At present, the method is spatially limited to two-dimensional cases. However, most engineering applications, e.g., design processes to find optimal layouts for low-noise turbojet engines, feature three-dimensional phenomena. Extending the presented deep learning method to learn from three-dimensional simulations will lead to accelerated predictions of three-dimensional aeroacoustic problems. Furthermore, realistic acoustic fields are frequently characterized by interactions of multiple noise sources with various frequencies and amplitudes. Therefore, it is necessary to extend the current setup to monopoles with multiple frequencies and amplitudes. Apart from increasing the domain's complexity, the level of generalization will be increased. The presented acoustic field predictor has been trained and tested on similar situations. Its capabilities to generalize will be enhanced by testing on situations that have not been part of the training process, e.g., training with four objects and testing with five. Instead of strictly separating different gradient losses, the impact of combining them in a single loss and employing individual weights will be analyzed. In addition, physics-informed losses that allow the network to comply with physical laws of aeroacoustics will be integrated. Furthermore, adversarial training will be investigated by adding a discriminator with an adversarial loss to the current architecture. Such GAN type architectures have the potential to help finding a suitable loss from the training data. It is also worth mentioning that the method presented in this study has the potential to support solving noise control problems. It remains to investigate if a dedicated acoustic field predictor that can quickly give feedback on the arrangement of multiple monopoles is capable of finding optimal acoustic setups. Therefore, the presented acoustic field predictor will be integrated into a reinforcement learning loop.

Acknowledgments. The authors gratefully acknowledge the computing time granted through the Jülich Aachen Research Alliance (JARA) on the supercomputer

JURECA [14] at Forschungszentrum Jülich. Furthermore, the authors would like to thank Forschungszentrum Jülich GmbH, RWTH Aachen University, and the JARA Center for Simulation and Data Science (JARA-CSD) for research funding. This work was performed as part of the Helmholtz School for Data Science in Life, Earth and Energy (HDS-LEE).

References

1. Benzi, R., Succi, S., Vergassola, M.: The lattice Boltzmann equation: theory and applications. Phys. Rep. **222**(3), 145–197 (1992). https://doi.org/10.1016/0370-1573(92)90090-M
2. Bhatnagar, P.L., Gross, E.P., Krook, M.: A Model for collision processes in gases. I. Small amplitude processes in charged and neutral one-component systems. Phys. Rev. **94**(3), 511–525 (1954). https://doi.org/10.1103/PhysRev.94.511
3. Bhatnagar, S., Afshar, Y., Pan, S., Duraisamy, K., Kaushik, S.: Prediction of aerodynamic flow fields using convolutional neural networks. Comput. Mech. **64**(2), 525–545 (2019). https://doi.org/10.1007/s00466-019-01740-0
4. Bode, M., et al.: Using Physics-Informed Super-Resolution Generative Adversarial Networks for Subgrid Modeling in Turbulent Reactive Flows (2019)
5. Drozdzal, M., Vorontsov, E., Chartrand, G., Kadoury, S., Pal, C.: The importance of skip connections in biomedical image segmentation. In: Carneiro, G., et al. (eds.) LABELS/DLMIA -2016. LNCS, vol. 10008, pp. 179–187. Springer, Cham (2016). https://doi.org/10.1007/978-3-319-46976-8_19
6. Ewert, R., Schröder, W.: On the simulation of trailing edge noise with a hybrid LES/APE method. J. Sound Vib. **270**, 509–524 (2004). https://doi.org/10.1016/j.jsv.2003.09.047
7. Guo, X., Li, W., Iorio, F.: Convolutional neural networks for steady flow approximation. In: Proceedings of the 22nd ACM SIGKDD International Conference on Knowledge Discovery and Data Mining - KDD 2016, pp. 481–490. ACM Press, New York (2016). https://doi.org/10.1145/2939672.2939738
8. Hänel, D.: Molekulare Gasdynamik, Einführung in die kinetische Theorie der Gase und Lattice-Boltzmann-Methoden. Springer, Heidelberg (2004). https://doi.org/10.1007/3-540-35047-0
9. He, K., Zhang, X., Ren, S., Sun, J.: Delving deep into rectifiers: surpassing human-level performance on ImageNet classification. In: 2015 IEEE International Conference on Computer Vision (ICCV), pp. 1026–1034. IEEE (2015). https://doi.org/10.1109/ICCV.2015.123
10. Ioffe, S., Szegedy, C.: Batch normalization: accelerating deep network training by reducing internal covariate shift. In: ICML 2015: Proceedings of the 32nd International Conference on International Conference on Machine Learning, Lille, France, pp. 448–456. W&CP (2015). https://doi.org/10.5555/3045118.3045167
11. Kam, E.W.S., So, R.M.C., Leung, R.C.K.: Lattice Boltzman method simulation of aeroacoustics and nonreflecting boundary conditions. AIAA J. **45**(7), 1703–1712 (2007). https://doi.org/10.2514/1.27632
12. Kingma, D.P., Ba, J.: Adam: A Method for Stochastic Optimization (2014)
13. Koh, S.R., Meinke, M., Schröder, W.: Numerical analysis of the impact of permeability on trailing-edge noise. J. Sound Vib. **421**, 348–376 (2018). https://doi.org/10.1016/j.jsv.2018.02.017
14. Krause, D., Thörnig, P.: JURECA: modular supercomputer at Jülich supercomputing centre. JLSRF **4**, A132 (2018). https://doi.org/10.17815/jlsrf-4-121-1

15. Lathuilière, S., Mesejo, P., Alameda-Pineda, X., Horaud, R.: A comprehensive analysis of deep regression (2018)
16. Lee, S., You, D.: Data-driven prediction of unsteady flow over a circular cylinder using deep learning. J. Fluid Mech. **879**, 217–254 (2019). https://doi.org/10.1017/jfm.2019.700
17. Lee, S., You, D.: Mechanisms of a convolutional neural network for learning three-dimensional unsteady wake flow (2019)
18. Lintermann, A., Meinke, M., Schröder, W.: Zonal Flow Solver (ZFS): a highly efficient multi-physics simulation framework. Int. J. Comut. Fluid Dyn. 1–28 (2020). https://doi.org/10.1080/10618562.2020.1742328
19. Mao, X., Shen, C., Yang, Y.B.: Image restoration using very deep convolutional encoder-decoder networks with symmetric skip connections. In: Advances in Neural Information Processing Systems, pp. 2802–2810 (2016)
20. Mathieu, M., Couprie, C., LeCun, Y.: Deep multi-scale video prediction beyond mean square error (2015)
21. McKee, C., Harmanto, D., Whitbrook, A.: A conceptual framework for combining artificial neural networks with computational aeroacoustics for design development. In: Proceedings of the International Conference on Industrial Engineering and Operations Management (2018)
22. Miyanawala, T.P., Jaiman, R.K.: An efficient deep learning technique for the navier-stokes equations: application to unsteady wake flow dynamics (2017)
23. Moin, P.: Fundamentals of Engineering Numerical Analysis. Cambridge University Press, London (2001)
24. Niemöller, A., Schlottke-Lakemper, M., Meinke, M., Schröder, W.: Dynamic load balancing for direct-coupled multiphysics simulations. Comput. Fluids **199**, 104437 (2020). https://doi.org/10.1016/j.compfluid.2020.104437
25. Qian, Y.H., D'Humières, D., Lallemand, P.: Lattice BGK Models for Navier-Stokes Equation. EPL **17**(6), 479–484 (1992). https://doi.org/10.1209/0295-5075/17/6/001
26. Ronneberger, O., Fischer, P., Brox, T.: U-net: Convolutional networks for biomedical image segmentation (2015)
27. Rüttgers, M., Lee, S., Jeon, S., You, D.: Prediction of a typhoon trackusing a generative adversarial network and satellite images. Sci. Rep. **9** (2019). https://doi.org/10.1038/s41598-019-42339-y
28. Salomons, E.M., Lohman, W.J.A., Zhou, H.: Simulation of sound waves using the lattice Boltzmann method for fluid flow: benchmark cases for outdoor sound propagation. PLoS ONE **11**(1), e0147206 (2016). https://doi.org/10.1371/journal.pone.0147206
29. Schlimpert, S., Koh, S.R., Pausch, K., Meinke, M., Schröder, W.: Analysis of combustion noise of a turbulent premixed slot jet flame. Combust. Flame **175**, 292–306 (2017). https://doi.org/10.1016/j.combustflame.2016.08.001
30. Sethian, J.: Level Set Methods and Fast Marching Methods: Evolving Interfaces in Computational Geometry, Fluid Mechanics, Computer Vision, and Materials Science. Cambridge Monographs on Applied and Computational Mathematics. Cambridge University Press, Cambridge (1999)
31. Srivastava, N., Hinton, G., Krizhevsky, A., Sutskever, I., Salakhutdinov, R.: Dropout: a simple way to prevent neural networks from overfitting. J. Mach. Learn. Res. **15**(56), 1929–1958 (2014)
32. Sutherland, W.: The viscosity of gases and molecular force. Philos. Mag. **36**(5), 507–531 (1893)

33. Zhou, B.Y., Koh, S.R., Gauger, N., Meinke, M., Schröder, W.: A discrete adjoint framework for trailing-edge noise minimization via porous material. Comput. Fluids **172**, 97–108 (2018). https://doi.org/10.1016/j.compfluid.2018.06.017
34. Zhou, Z., Siddiquee, M.M.R., Tajbakhsh, N., Liang, J.: Unet++: redesigning skip connections to exploit multiscale features in image segmentation. IEEE Trans. Med. Imaging **39**(6), 1856–1867 (2019)

Unsupervised Learning of Particle Image Velocimetry

Mingrui Zhang[✉] and Matthew D. Piggott

Department of Earth Science and Engineering,
Imperial College London, South Kensington Campus, London, UK
mingrui.zhang18@imperial.ac.uk

Abstract. Particle Image Velocimetry (PIV) is a classical flow estimation problem which is widely considered and utilised, especially as a diagnostic tool in experimental fluid dynamics and the remote sensing of environmental flows. Recently, the development of deep learning based methods has inspired new approaches to tackle the PIV problem. These supervised learning based methods are driven by large volumes of data with ground truth training information. However, it is difficult to collect reliable ground truth data in large-scale, real-world scenarios. Although synthetic datasets can be used as alternatives, the gap between the training set-ups and real-world scenarios limits applicability. We present here what we believe to be the first work which takes an unsupervised learning based approach to tackle PIV problems. The proposed approach is inspired by classic optical flow methods. Instead of using ground truth data, we make use of photometric loss between two consecutive image frames, consistency loss in bidirectional flow estimates and spatial smoothness loss to construct the total unsupervised loss function. The approach shows significant potential and advantages for fluid flow estimation. Results presented here demonstrate that our method outputs competitive results compared with classical PIV methods as well as supervised learning based methods for a broad PIV dataset, and even outperforms these existing approaches in some difficult flow cases. Codes and trained models are available at https://github.com/erizmr/UnLiteFlowNet-PIV.

Keywords: Particle Image Velocimetry (PIV) · Velocity field diagnostics · Deep learning · Unsupervised learning

1 Introduction

Particle Image Velocimetry (PIV) is one of the most popular measurement techniques in experimental fluid dynamics, and is also used to diagnose flow information from the remote sensing of large-scale environmental flows. The method provides quantitative measurements of velocity fields in fluids that can be used to explore complex flow phenomena. When conducting the PIV technique, the fluid

© Springer Nature Switzerland AG 2020
H. Jagode et al. (Eds.): ISC High Performance 2020 Workshops, LNCS 12321, pp. 102–115, 2020.
https://doi.org/10.1007/978-3-030-59851-8_7

under investigation is seeded with sufficiently small tracer particles (or the presence of naturally occurring features is exploited). These particles are assumed to follow the flow dynamics. With illumination (in the laboratory often through the use of lasers to capture image information over a two-dimensional plane), the particles in the fluid are visible. By comparing resulting flow images between time levels, velocity field information can be inferred [1]. There are two main techniques used for performing classical PIV: cross-correlation and variational optical flow methods.

The development of deep learning techniques has inspired a new direction for tackling PIV-like problems. Several authors have in the literature proposed and demonstrated the use of supervised learning based methods for PIV. However, due to the unavailability of a broad range of reliable ground truth training data, supervised learning methods have limitations, especially when seeking to generalise to real-world problems. On the other hand, unsupervised learning is a type of machine learning approach that looks for previously undetected patterns in a dataset with no pre-existing labels and with minimum human supervision [2].

In this paper we propose a new fluid velocity estimation method using an unsupervised learning strategy based upon particle images.

1.1 Cross-correlation and Variational Optical Flow Methods

There are two main standard approaches for performing particle image velocimetry: cross-correlation and optical flow methods. The cross-correlation method calculates a displacement by searching for the maximum cross-correlation between two interrogation windows from an image pair [3], e.g., such as in the *WIDIM* (window deformation iterative multi-grid) method. The cross-correlation method is efficient and relatively easy to implement. However, it only outputs a spatially sparse (compared to the resolution of the seed particles in the fluid) displacement field and requires post-processing. The variational optical flow method was proposed by Horn and Schunck (HS) [4]. It is a motion estimation approach that has been applied to PIV problems [5]. It treats the PIV problem through the solution of an optimisation problem, seeking the minimisation of an objective function. The method can output a dense displacement field, but the optimisation process is time-consuming.

1.2 Deep Learning Methods

Machine learning methods, especially deep learning, have made great progress in applications to many real-world problems in recent years. In the PIV community, deep learning has been introduced recently. In [6], the authors provided a proof-of-concept on this topic, where artificial neural networks are designed to perform end-to-end PIV for the first time in this work.

PIV techniques are closely related to computational photography, a subdomain of computer vision. In this community, there are several important works related to the motion estimation problem using deep learning. The *FlowNetS* and *FlowNetC* networks [7] were the first proposed for dense optical flow estimation.

FlowNet2 [8], an extension of *FlowNet*, improves the optical flow estimation to a state-of-the-art level. In addition, a lighter-weight network *LiteFlowNet* [9] has also been proposed. It achieves a similar level accuracy compared to *FlowNet2*, using less trainable parameters. Although the networks mentioned above have achieved excellent performance for estimating motion fields from consecutive image pairs, their applications is generally limited to rigid or quasi-rigid motion.

Therefore, it is of interest to explore the performance of these existing networks on particle image velocimetry problems.

2 Related Work

Supervised and unsupervised learning are two different learning approaches. The key difference is that supervised learning requires ground truth data while unsupervised learning does not.

2.1 Supervised Learning Methods

End-to-end supervised learning using neural networks for PIV was first introduced by Rabault et al. in [6]. A convolutional neural network and a fully-connected neural network were trained to perform PIV on several test cases. That work provided a proof-of-concept for the research community. However, the trained model did not achieve the ultimate quality of result compared with traditional PIV methods, and the application scenarios considered were limited to relatively simple cases. Lee et al. [10] proposed a cascaded network architecture. The network was verified to produce results comparable to standard PIV methods (one-pass cross-correlation method, three-pass window deformation). However, it had larger computational costs and lower efficiency. Another deep architecture approach based on supervised learning was proposed by Cai et al. in [11]. In that work the author developed a motion estimator *PIV-FlowNetS-en* based upon *FlowNet*. The estimator is able to extract features from particle images and output dense displacement fields. The model was evaluated both on synthetic and experimental data, and was shown to achieve good accuracy with high efficiency compared to correlation-based PIV methods such as the *WIDIM* method. Follow-up work introduced a more complex but lighter-weight network *PIV-LiteFlowNet-en* [12], based on *LiteFlowNet* [9]. The model was shown to have the same level of performance as variational optical flow methods in terms of estimation accuracy, while showing advantages in terms of efficiency.

The supervised learning approach relies heavily on large volumes of training data. However, in most real-world scenarios, especially in fluid dynamics, there is no easily available ground truth data and/or it is extremely difficult to annotate the data accurately through human means. Although the use of synthetic data (e.g.. based upon computational fluid dynamics studies) can help construct large annotated datasets, the gap between synthetic and real-world scenarios limits the generalisation abilities of the constructed networks. This can mean that supervised learning based approaches may struggle when confronted with data from real-world problems.

2.2   Unsupervised Learning Methods

Unsupervised learning is a type of machine learning that, in contrast, looks for previously undetected patterns in a dataset with no pre-existing labels and with minimum human supervision.

To the best of our knowledge, there are no previous examples of approaches that tackle the PIV problem based on unsupervised learning. In the computer vision community, there is some previous work related to the use of unsupervised learning for optical flow estimation. Yu et al. [13] suggested an unsupervised method based on *FlowNet* in order to sidestep the limitations of synthetic datasets. They use a loss function that combines a data term (photometric loss) measuring photometric constancy over time with a spatial term (smoothness loss) modelling the expected variation of flow across the image. In [14], Meister et al. extended the work using a symmetric, occlusion-aware loss based on both forward and backward optical flow estimates. They also made use of iterative refinement by stacking multiple *FlowNet* networks. The model showed advantages and outperformed supervised learning on challenging realistic benchmarks.

Our work is inspired in part by Meister et al. [14]; we extend the unsupervised learning strategy to PIV problems, building our model based on *LiteFlowNet* instead of *FlowNet*. We trained our model on a synthetic PIV dataset generated by Cai et al. in [11]. Unlike the supervised strategy, we only use the particle images pairs in the dataset, and leave the ground truth motion data (which is used to generate the image pairs) for benchmarking purposes.

3   Method

Given a grayscale image pair $I_1, I_2 : P \rightarrow \mathbb{R}^1$ as input, our goal is to estimate the forward flow field from I_1 to I_2, $\mathbf{F}^f \equiv (u^f, v^f)^T$, where u_f and v_f are scalar velocity fields in two orthogonal directions. As we take the bidirectional estimate into consideration, the backward flow field is defined as $\mathbf{F}^b \equiv (u^b, v^b)^T$. In Sect. 3.1 we will introduce the unsupervised loss and how the loss is integrated for training. The network architecture will be described in Sect. 3.2.

3.1   Unsupervised Loss

In the training process, the input only contains image pairs I_1, I_2, without the velocity field ground truth. Therefore, we use traditional optical flow measurements to evaluate our results. The total unsupervised loss is a combination of photometric loss, estimate flow smoothness loss and consistency loss between forward and backward fields.

Photometric Loss. The photometric loss is defined in terms of the difference between the first image and the warped second image using the forward flow field estimate, and the difference between the second image and the warped first image using the backward estimate. The bidirectional photometric loss is thus defined as the sum of two parts:

$$L_P(I_1, I_2, \mathbf{F}^f, \mathbf{F}^b) = \sum_{\mathbf{x} \in P} \rho \left(I_1(\mathbf{x}) - I_2(\mathbf{x} + \mathbf{F}^f(\mathbf{x})) \right) \tag{1}$$
$$+ \rho \left(I_2(\mathbf{x}) - I_1(\mathbf{x} + \mathbf{F}^b(\mathbf{x})) \right),$$

where $\rho(\cdot)$ is the generalized Charbonnier penalty function, $\rho = (x^2 + \epsilon^2)^\gamma$, which is a differentiable, robust convex function [15]. We use the values $\gamma = 0.45, \epsilon = 10^{-3}$ in this work.

Image 'backwarping' is the key step when computing the photometric loss. In order to make the loss backpropagation possible during the training process, we use the differentiable bilinear sampling scheme proposed in [16]. The basic idea is first to generate a sampling coordinate in target image I_2, using I_1 and the flow field estimate $\mathbf{F}^f$. The coordinate can be described as: $\mathbf{x_s} = \mathbf{x} + \mathbf{F}^f(\mathbf{x}) = (x_1 + F_u^f, y_1 + F_v^f)$, here $\mathbf{x}$ is the coordinate field for image I_1. A bilinear sampler is then used to construct the warped image in terms of coordinate $\mathbf{x}$:

$$I_{\text{warp}}(\mathbf{x}) = \sum_{x_s^i, y_s^i \in \mathbf{x_s}} I_2(\mathbf{x_s}) \max(0, 1 - |x_s - x_s^i|) \max(0, 1 - |y_s - y_s^i|). \tag{2}$$

Smoothness Loss. There are regions in the images that lack necessary information. For example, there may be insufficient particles near image boundaries, as the particles move out of the image area in the second frame or the particles have not entered the image in the first frame. Therefore, to tackle resulting ambiguities, a smoothness loss is included into our total unsupervised loss. To enhance the regularisation effects, we use a second-order smooth constraint [17]:

$$L_S(\mathbf{F}^f, \mathbf{F}^b) = \sum_{(\mathbf{s}, \mathbf{r}) \in \mathbf{N}(\mathbf{x})} \sum_{\mathbf{x} \in P} \rho \left(\mathbf{F}^f(\mathbf{s}) - 2\mathbf{F}^f(\mathbf{x}) + \mathbf{F}^f(\mathbf{r}) \right) \tag{3}$$
$$+ \rho \left(\mathbf{F}^b(\mathbf{s}) - 2\mathbf{F}^b(\mathbf{x}) + \mathbf{F}^b(\mathbf{r}) \right),$$

where $\mathbf{N}$ represents a four channel filter (x, y and two diagonals, see Fig. 1). Therefore, the process here is first to compute the convolution of the two flow components (u in the x and v in the y directions) with the four channel filter respectively, then compute their Charbonnier loss.

Consistency Loss. The forward and backward flow estimates should be consistent, i.e. the forward flow $\mathbf{F}^f$ is expected to be the inverse of the backward flow $\mathbf{F}^b(\mathbf{x} + \mathbf{F}^f)$ at the corresponding pixel in the second image. The sum of this pair of flow fields should therefore be zero, and similarly for the backward flow estimate. The consistency loss function can thus be defined as:

$$L_C(\mathbf{F}^f, \mathbf{F}^b) = \sum_{\mathbf{x} \in P} \rho \left(\mathbf{F}^f + \mathbf{F}^b(\mathbf{x} + \mathbf{F}^f) \right) \tag{4}$$
$$+ \rho \left(\mathbf{F}^b + \mathbf{F}^f(\mathbf{x} + \mathbf{F}^b) \right).$$

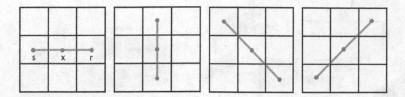

Fig. 1. Four channel filter used in the smoothness loss: in the directions x, y and the two diagonals, shown in the frames above from left to right respectively. s, x, r indicate the three neighboring pixels considered for each direction.

Final Integrated Loss. The final integrated loss, L, combines the above loss terms using weighted (with scalar weights λ_P, λ_S, λ_C) summation:

$$L(I_1, I_2, \mathbf{F}^f, \mathbf{F}^b) = \lambda_P L_P + \lambda_S L_S + \lambda_C L_C. \tag{5}$$

3.2   Network Architecture

UnLiteFlowNet-PIV. Our network, named *UnLiteFlowNet-PIV*, is based on *LiteFlowNet* [9]. It extracts two images' features using a two-stream convolution neural network (NetC) with shared weights. NetC has a pyramidal structure and encodes the image from full resolution to a sixth of that of the original. Then a decoder (NetE) performs cascaded flow inference (convolutionally upsampling) with flow regularisation. The final flow estimate is upsampled to the original resolution using bilinear interpolation. In our work, we compute both the forward and backward flow in one estimation. The input for the forward flow estimation is (I_1, I_2), and it is (I_2, I_1) for the backward flow (Fig. 2).

Training Loss. The training loss function's design is similar to that in *FlowNet* [7] and *LiteFlowNet* [9], and uses a multi-scale resolution loss. It is the weighted sum of the estimation losses from each of the intermediate layers:

$$L_T = \sum_i w_i L_i, \tag{6}$$

where L_i is the loss function (5). At each layer, the image pair (I_1, I_2) is downsampled to compute the current layer's loss. As the distance between pixels effectively changes after downsampling, the flow estimate is multiplied by the appropriate scaling factor, which is the fraction between the current and the full image resolution. Here, $i_{\max} = 6$, and L_6 indicates the loss at full resolution.

4   Evaluation

4.1   PIV Dataset

The dataset considered in this work was generated by Cai et al. [11]. The dataset contains 15,050 particle image pairs with the originating flow field ground truth

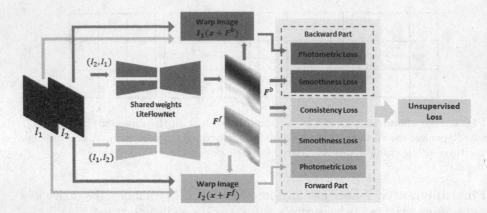

Fig. 2. Data flow for *UnLiteFlowNet-PIV*, from inputs to unsupervised loss. Due to taking bidirectional flows into consideration, the red components represent the forward part, with the image pair (I_1, I_2) as input. The blue components indicate the backward part. Although there are two networks shown for clarity, since shared weights are used there is only one in the implementation. (Color figure online)

data obtained from computational fluid dynamics simulations. There are eight different types of flow contained in the dataset, including 'uniform' flow, flow past a backward facing step ('back-step') and past a 'cylinder', both at a variety of Reynolds numbers, 'DNS-turbulence', sea surface flow driven by a quasi-geostrophic model ('SQG'), etc. Detailed information on the dataset is provided in Table 3. In our work we use half of the dataset for training and the other half for testing.

4.2   Training Details

We train the model for 40,000 iterations with a batch size of four image pairs using the Adam optimiser. The learning rate is kept at 10^{-4}. The smoothness loss weight is $\lambda_C = 3.0$, the consistency loss weight $\lambda_C = 0.2$, photometric loss weight $\lambda_P = 1.0$. The weights for different layers are set to [12.7, 5.5, 4.35, 3.9, 3.4, 1.1] as in [14], from the full resolution to the lowest level. The image pair are normalized from value ranges of 0–255 to 0–1 before feeding into the network.

4.3   Results

Table 1 compares the accuracy of our model with previous work and different approaches, including classical PIV and state-of-the-art deep learning based methods. The results are evaluated on the PIV dataset, with the Averaged End-point Error (AEE) calculated for different flow types. In order to compare the results easier, we set the units of the AEE to pixel per 100 pixels. The AEE can be described as the L^2-norm of the difference in flow estimation $\mathbf{F}^e$ and the flow ground truth $\mathbf{F}^g$:

$$\text{AEE} = \|\mathbf{F}^e - \mathbf{F}^g\|_2 . \tag{7}$$

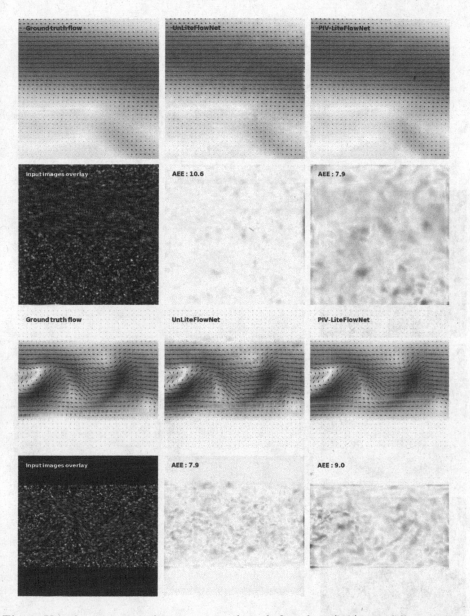

Fig. 3. Visual comparisons between ground truth flow data (left), our fully unsupervised model *UnLiteFlowNet-PIV* (middle) and *PIV-LiteFlowNet* (right) shown on the first and third rows for respectively the 'Back-step' and 'Cylinder' flow cases. The flow field colour is coded in HSV [18]. The second and fourth rows show the input images overlays (left), along with the errors and corresponding Averaged Endpoint Error (AEE) values for the two networks and image pairs considered. In the error plots the white colour indicates zero error, and pixel colour with higher saturation represents larger errors. It can be observed that even though our new unsupervised model never has access to the ground truth during training, it still tends to outperform the supervised model. See also Figs. 4 and 5 for further cases.

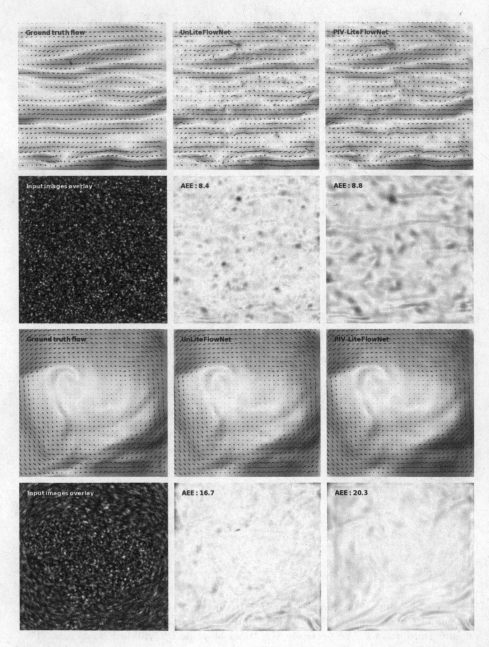

Fig. 4. Caption as for Fig. 3 but now for the flow cases 'JHTDB-channel' (first two rows) and 'DNS-turbulence' (final two rows). It can be observed that errors are distributed along the vortex boundaries in both models. However, our *UnLiteFlowNet-PIV* model does tend to demonstrate lower errors in the interior, e.g.. around the regions with strong internal vortices.

Comparison to Classical PIV. It can be observed that our unsupervised model outperforms classical correlation-based PIV WIDIM methods in almost all flow cases, especially for the challenging cases of DNS-turbulence and SQG. Although the unsupervised model does not outperform the Horn–Schunck (HS) optical flow method [4], the differences are relatively small. In addition, as mentioned above, the HS optical flow method requires a large amount of computational time in order to conduct the optimisation process, which results in low efficiency especially when multiple image pairs need to be processed. Without considering the time to load images from disk, the computational time for 500 image (256×256) pairs using our *UnLiteFlowNet-PIV* is 10.17 s on an Nvidia Tesla P100 GPU, while the HS optical method requires roughly 556.5 s and WIDIM (with a window size of 29×29) requires 211.5 s on an Intel Core I7-7700 CPU [12]. Although the classical PIV methods are tested on a CPU, as shown in the [6,11] the speed improvements for them running on GPUs are limited. Therefore, efficiency is a great advantage for learning based methods compared to the classical approaches.

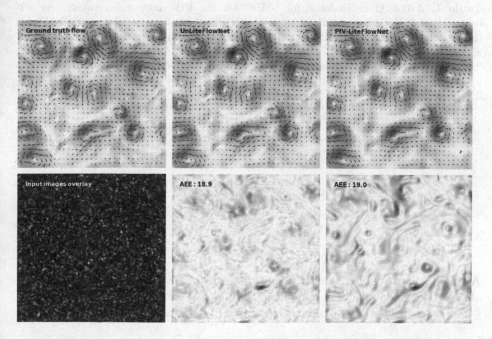

Fig. 5. Caption similar to Fig. 3, but now only showing the 'SQG' case. The *UnLiteFlowNet-PIV* model again shows more than competitive performance on this challenging flow case.

Comparison to Deep Learning PIV. The unsupervised learning approach shows potentially significant advantages compared to state-of-the-art supervised learning methods. Figures 3, 4 and 5 demonstrate comparisons between our fully unsupervised model *UnLiteFlowNet-PIV* and *PIV-LiteFlowNet*. *PIV-LiteFlowNet* [12] uses a similar network architecture to our *UnLiteFlowNet-PIV*, but is trained using a supervised learning strategy with ground truth data. Although the unsupervised *UnLiteFlowNet-PIV* never has access to the ground truth data during the training process, it still outperforms most supervised learning methods (*PIV-NetS-noRef*, *PIV-NetS*, *PIV-LiteFlowNet*), especially on difficult cases. Therefore, the unsupervised learning method with an accurate loss function shows competitive capabilities and often better performance compared to supervised methods.

PIV-LiteFlowNet-en [12] is an enhanced version of *PIV-LiteFlowNet*, it adds one additional layer at the end of the NetE, which improves its inference ability but makes the network more complicate and heavier. We did not try to construct deeper networks in our work for brevity. There are ideas for improving the performance by stacking networks [8], which would also be an interesting avenue to explore in further work.

Table 1. Averaged Endpoint Error (AEE) for the PIV dataset (averaged over all impage pairs), the error unit is set to pixel per 100 pixels for easier comparison. From top to bottom, WIDIM and HS optical flow are the classical PIV methods described in Sect. 1.1, the next four rows are state-of-the-art supervised learning methods described in Sect. 2.1. The final row shows results of our unsupervised method introduced in this work.

Methods	Back-step		Cylinder		JHTDB channel		DNS turbulence		SQG	
	Train	Test	Train	Test	Train	Test	Train	Test	Train	Test
WIDIM [12]	–	3.4	–	8.3	–	8.4	–	30.4	–	45.7
HS optical flow [12]	–	4.5	–	7.0	–	6.9	–	13.5	–	15.6
PIV-NetS-noRef [11]	13.6	13.9	19.8	19.4	24.6	24.7	50.6	52.5	51.9	52.5
PIV-NetS [11]	5.8	5.9	6.9	7.2	16.3	15.5	27.1	28.2	28.9	29.4
PIV-LiteFlowNet [12]	5.5	5.6	8.7	8.3	10.9/	10.4	18.8	19.6	19.8	20.2
PIV-LiteFlowNet-en [12]	3.2	3.3	5.2	4.9	7.9	7.5	11.6	12.2	12.4	12.6
UnLiteFlowNet-PIV	–	10.1	–	7.8	–	9.6	–	13.5	–	19.7

Ablation Study. There are three components to the loss function as mentioned above. The contributions to model performance of each component are investigated here. Results are summarize in Table 2. The model is trained for 40,000

Table 2. Averaged Endpoint Error (AEE) on test dataset for models trained by different loss functions. The error unit is set to pixel per 100 pixels for easier comparison.

Loss function	Back-Step	Cylinder	JHTDB channel	DNS turbulence	SQG
$L_P + L_S + L_C$	10.1	7.8	9.6	13.5	19.7
$L_P + L_S$	11.6	10.5	15.3	21.4	22.5
$L_P + L_C$	14.1	38.4	18.1	23.6	25.5

Table 3. Detailed description of the PIV dataset considered, from [11]. dx refers to the particle displacements considered between two image frames in units of number of pixels. Re refers to the Reynolds numbers considered. 'JHTDB' implies that the data was taken from the Johns Hopkins turbulence databases [19]. Refer to [11] for further details.

Metric name	Description	Condition	Quantity
Uniform	Uniform flow	$|dx| \in [0, 5]$	1000
Back-step	Flow past a backward facing step	Re = 800	600
		Re = 1000	600
		Re = 1200	1000
		Re = 1500	1000
Cylinder	Flow past a circular cylinder	Re = 40	50
		Re = 150	500
		Re = 200	500
		Re = 300	500
		Re = 400	500
DNS-turbulence	Homogeneous and isotropic turbulent flow	–	2000
SQG	Sea surface flow driven by SQG model	–	1500
Channel flow	Channel flow provided by JHTDB	–	1600
JHTDB-mhd1024	Forced MHD turbulence provided by JHTDB	–	800
JHTDB-isotropic1024	Forced isotropic turbulence provided by JHTDB	–	2000

iterations with three different loss functions: $L_P + L_S + L_C$ (i.e. the full loss function), $L_P + L_S$ (no consistency loss), and $L_P + L_C$ (no smoothness loss). The model trained using the full loss performs the best among the three on the test dataset. Removing either smoothness or consistency loss leads to a worse performance on the test dataset considered here.

5   Conclusion

We present here the first work using an unsupervised learning approach for solving Particle Image Velocimetry (PIV) problems. The proposed unsupervised learning approach shows significant promise and potential advantages for fluid flow estimation. It yields competitive results compared with classical PIV methods as well as existing supervised learning based methods, and even outperforms them on some difficult flow cases. Furthermore, the unsupervised learning method does not rely on any ground truth data in order to train, which makes it extremely promising to generalize to complex real-world flow scenarios where ground truth is effectively unknowable, and thus represents a key advantage over supervised methods.

Acknowledgements. The authors would like to acknowledge funding from the Chinese Scholarship Council and Imperial College London (a pump priming research award from the Energy Futures Lab, Data Science Institute and Gratham Institute – Climate Change and the Environment) that supported this work.

References

1. Adrian, R., Westerweed, J.: Particle Image Velocimetry. Cambridge University Press, Cambridge (2011)
2. Hinton, G., Sejnowski, T.: Unsupervised Learning: Foundations of Neural Computation. MIT Press, Cambridge (1999)
3. Westerweel, J.: Fundamentals of digital particle image velocimetry. Exp. Fluids 23(12), 1379–1392 (1997)
4. Horn, B., Schunck, B.: Determining optical flow. Artif. Intell. 17(1–3), 185–203 (1981)
5. Ruhnau, P., Kohlberger, T., Schnorr, C., Nobach, H.: Variational optical flow estimation for particle image velocimetry. Exp. Fluids 38(1), 21–32 (2005)
6. Rabault, J., Kolaas, J., Jensen, A.: Performing particle image velocimetry using artificial neural networks: a proof-of-concept. Meas. Sci. Technol. 28(12), 125301 (2017)
7. Dosovitskiy, A., et al.: Flownet: learning optical flow with convolutional networks. In: Proceedings of the IEEE International Conference on Computer Vision, pp. 2758–2766 (2015)
8. Ilg, E., Mayer, N., Saikia, T., Keuper, M., Dosovitskiy, A., Brox, T.: Flownet 2.0: evolution of optical flow estimation with deep networks. In: Proceedings of the IEEE Conference on Computer Vision and Pattern Recognition, vol. 2 (2017)
9. Hui, T., Tang, X., Loy, C.: LiteFlowNet: a lightweight convolutional neural network for optical flow estimation. In: Proceedings of IEEE Conference on Computer Vision and Pattern Recognition, pp. 8981–8989 (2018)
10. Lee, Y., Yang, H., Yin, Z.: PIV-DCNN: cascaded deep convolutional neural networks for particle image velocimetry. Exp. Fluids 58(12), 1–10 (2017). https://doi.org/10.1007/s00348-017-2456-1
11. Cai, S., Zhou, S., Xu, C., Gao, Q.: Dense motion estimation of particle images via a convolutional neural network. Exp. Fluids 60(4), 1–16 (2019). https://doi.org/10.1007/s00348-019-2717-2
12. Cai, S., Liang, J., Gao, Q., Xu, C., Wei, R.: Particle image velocimetry based on a deep learning motion estimator. IEEE Trans. Instrum. Meas. 69(6), 3538–3554 (2019)
13. Yu, J.J., Harley, A.W., Derpanis, K.G.: Back to basics: unsupervised learning of optical flow via brightness constancy and motion smoothness. In: Hua, G., Jégou, H. (eds.) ECCV 2016. LNCS, vol. 9915, pp. 3–10. Springer, Cham (2016). https://doi.org/10.1007/978-3-319-49409-8_1
14. Meister, S., Hur, J., Roth, S.: UnFlow: unsupervised learning of optical flow with a bidirectional census loss. In: The Thirty-Second AAAI Conference on Artificial Intelligence (2018)
15. Sun, D., Roth, S., Black, M.: A quantitative analysis of current practices in optical flow estimation and the principles behind them. Int. J. Comput. Vis. 106(2), 115–137 (2014)
16. Jaderberg, M., Simonyan, K., Zisserman, A., Kavukcuoglu, K.: Spatial transformer networks. In: NIPS'15: Proceedings of the 28th International Conference on Neural Information Processing Systems, vol. 2, pp. 2017–2025 (2015)
17. Zhang, C., Li, Z., Cai, R., Chao, H., Rui, Y.: As-rigid-as-possible stereo under second order smoothness priors. In: Fleet, D., Pajdla, T., Schiele, B., Tuytelaars, T. (eds.) ECCV 2014. LNCS, vol. 8690, pp. 112–126. Springer, Cham (2014). https://doi.org/10.1007/978-3-319-10605-2_8

18. Baker, S., Scharstein, D., Lewis, J., Roth, S., Black, M., Szeliski, R.: A database and evaluation methodology for optical flow. Int. J. Comput. Vis. **92**(1), 1–31 (2011)

19. Li, Y., et al.: A public turbulence database cluster and applications to study Lagrangian evolution of velocity increments in turbulence. J. Turbul. **9**(9), N31 (2008)

Reduced Order Modeling of Dynamical Systems Using Artificial Neural Networks Applied to Water Circulation

Alberto Costa Nogueira Jr.[1]([✉]), João Lucas de Sousa Almeida[1],
Guillaume Auger[2], and Campbell D. Watson[2]

[1] IBM Research, Hortolandia, SP 13186-900, Brazil
albercn@br.ibm.com
[2] IBM Research, Yorktown Heights, NY 10598, USA
cwatson@us.ibm.com
https://www.research.ibm.com/labs/brazil/

Abstract. General circulation models are essential tools in weather and hydrodynamic simulation. They solve discretized, complex physical equations in order to compute evolutionary states of dynamical systems, such as the hydrodynamics of a lake. However, high-resolution numerical solutions using such models are extremely computational and time consuming, often requiring a high performance computing architecture to be executed satisfactorily. Machine learning (ML)-based low-dimensional surrogate models are a promising alternative to speed up these simulations without undermining the quality of predictions. In this work, we develop two examples of fast, reliable, low-dimensional surrogate models to produce a 36 h forecast of the depth-averaged hydrodynamics at Lake George NY, USA. Our ML approach uses two widespread artificial neural network (ANN) architectures: fully connected neural networks and long short-term memory. These ANN architectures are first validated in the deterministic and chaotic regimes of the Lorenz system and then combined with proper orthogonal decomposition (to reduce the dimensionality of the incoming input data) to emulate the depth-averaged hydrodynamics of a flow simulator called SUNTANS. Results show the ANN-based reduced order models have promising accuracy levels (within 6% of the prediction range) and advocate for further investigation into hydrodynamic applications.

Keywords: Model reduction · Dynamical systems · Artificial neural networks · Water circulation

1 Introduction

Dynamical systems are mathematical descriptions for the evolution of many complex and sophisticated real-world processes. General circulation models simulate

Supported by The Jefferson Project at Lake George, which is a collaboration of Rensselaer Polytechnic Institute, IBM, and The FUND for Lake George.

H. Jagode et al. (Eds.): ISC High Performance 2020 Workshops, LNCS 12321, pp. 116–136, 2020.
https://doi.org/10.1007/978-3-030-59851-8_8

a class of dynamical systems that have well suited features for environmental applications, including weather and hydrodynamic prediction. These physics-based predictions are commonly used to make time-critical decisions in response to, for example, occurrences of extreme weather [1] or harmful algal blooms in water bodies [23]. However, a drawback of general circulation models is the time duration for execution, often taking hours to complete. Reducing this execution time would be of benefit to many users.

Machine learning has emerged as a promising technique to significantly reduce the simulation time of dynamical systems. Artificial neural networks (ANNs) have been successfully developed as surrogate models of their more computationally-demanding counterparts. In essence, ANNs "learn" to perform tasks through examples without the need to be programmed with rigid rules to execute specific tasks. For example, [12] replaced a reservoir simulator with ANNs trained on the input and the output of the model, making the surrogate model agnostic to the origin of the inputs and substantially decreasing the compute time. [18] used a method based on LSTM networks to simulate reduced order chaotic dynamical systems, including a barotropic climate model. Their method outperforms other techniques in short-term predictions, but long-term predictions experience a cumulative error, leading to erroneous long-term forecasts.

Other machine learning methods used in fluid dynamics simulations include [20], who used a physics-informed machine learning approach to improve prediction of Reynolds stress in fluids from an estimation in a Reynolds averaged framework. They used the Random Forest method to build the regression functions and an available direct numerical simulation (DNS) data-set served as training for their framework. Their methodology improved the estimation of Reynolds stress, but generated spurious changes in some cases. [7] used a convolutional neural network to accurately reconstructed the velocity field in a fluid, with a 700 times speedup, including the divergence-free condition for the fluid in their loss function.

A recent review of machine learning for fluid mechanics [2] highlighted that combining data driven methods (e.g., ANNs) with reduced order models (ROMs) is a compelling technique that can outperform each of its components. [2] highlighted encouraging results by [19], who used a type of recurrent neural network with long-short term memory (LSTM) to create data-driven predictions of extreme events in a complex dynamical system.

With this in mind, we hereby develop two low-dimensional ANN-based ROMs to simulate the hydrodynamics of a freshwater lake in New York, USA. ROMs represent a technique for reducing the computational complexity of mathematical models in numerical simulations. A common technique for order reduction is proper orthogonal decomposition (POD), which is a numerical scheme that compresses data and preserves the essence of the original information in the form of an orthonormal basis matrix (which is optimal in the least-squares sense) [21]. The POD method can decouple the approximate solution of a dynamical system (e.g., water circulation in a lake) into spatial and temporal components; the spatial components can then be computed offline while an ANN can predict the temporal coefficients of the ROM.

Hence, the objective of this work is to investigate the feasibility of using ANN-based ROMs to simulate the hydrodynamics of a freshwater lake. Specifically, we task ourselves with generating a 36 h hydrodynamic forecast and compare its skill to the full-order approximate solution given by a high-resolution, hydrostatic model.

The paper is arranged as follows. First, the dimensionality reduction to produce the ROM is described, followed by the philosophy and workflow for two ANN-based ROMs. We then demonstrate the effectiveness of an ANN at predicting the deterministic and chaotic regimes of a discrete system called the Lorenz system, followed by results from the ANN-based ROMs predicting the depth-averaged hydrodynamics of a freshwater lake.

2   Dimensionality Reduction

Consider the full order well-posed dynamical system given by

$$\frac{\partial Q(\mathbf{x}, t)}{\partial t} + \mathcal{N}(Q(\mathbf{x}, t)) = S(\mathbf{x}, t), \quad (\mathbf{x}, t) \in \Omega \times \mathcal{T} \tag{1}$$

with suitable initial and boundary conditions. Above, $\Omega \subset \mathbb{R}^d (d = 1, 2, 3)$ and $\mathcal{T} \subset [0, T]$ refer to the space domain and time, respectively. $Q, S : \Omega \times \mathcal{T} \longrightarrow \mathbb{R}^n$ denote the space-time solution and source term, respectively, with n being the number of dependent variables in the system. $\mathcal{N}$ is a general nonlinear operator associated to the dynamical system of interest.

After spatial discretization by any suitable numerical technique, the full order system is reduced to a system of ordinary differential equations (ODE) as

$$\frac{dQ_h(t)}{dt} + \mathcal{N}_h(Q_h(t)) = S_h(t), \quad t \in \mathcal{T} \tag{2}$$

where $Q_h : \mathcal{T} \longrightarrow \mathbb{R}^M$ is the discrete solution, M is the number of degrees of freedom (DOFs) of the discrete dynamical system, $\mathcal{N}_h$ and $S_h : \mathcal{T} \longrightarrow \mathbb{R}^M$ are the corresponding discrete nonlinear operator and source term, respectively.

Repeatedly solving the discrete system of ODEs, which is the case in many forecasting applications, is a hard working and time consuming task. It motivates us to seek an approximate solution of the full-order problem based on a linear combination of reduced basis functions $\{\psi_l\}_{1 \leq l \leq L} \subset \mathbb{R}^L$ with $L \ll M$. Thus, the reduced space spanned by the reduced basis functions is

$$\mathbb{V}_{rb} = span\{\psi_1, \ldots, \psi_L\} \subset \mathbb{V}_h \tag{3}$$

where $\mathbb{V}_h$ is a finite dimensional subspace of a Hilbert space $\mathbb{V}$ defined over the domain Ω.

An approximation of the full-order system can be expressed by the ansatz

$$Q(\mathbf{x}, t) \approx Q_{rb}(\mathbf{x}, t) = \overline{q}(\mathbf{x}) + q'(\mathbf{x}, t) = \overline{q}(\mathbf{x}) + \sum_{i=1}^{L} a_i(t)\psi_i(\mathbf{x}) \tag{4}$$

where $\mathbf{a}(t) = [a_1(t), \ldots, a_L(t)]^T \in \mathbb{R}^L$ is defined as the vector of coefficients of the approximate solution and, $\overline{q}$ and q' are mean and fluctuating quantities that split the approximation Q_{rb}. According to [21], such splitting prevents the first reduced coefficient from containing most of the energy of the original system and therefore adds stability to the reduced system. It is worth noting that we only expand the term q' since it depends on both time and space.

For the sake of conciseness, we denote $\Psi_i = \psi_i(\mathbf{x})$, and define the following reduced basis matrix $\Phi = [\Psi_1, \ldots, \Psi_L] \in \mathbb{R}^{M \times L}$ which will be used later on.

2.1   Proper Orthogonal Decomposition

A sharp definition of the POD method can be found in [21] where the authors state that it is a numerical technique that compresses data preserving the essence of the original information through an orthonormal basis matrix. Such matrix is built to be the optimal solution of a least-squares problem.

To construct a reduced basis using the POD, we start by arranging a collection of N snapshots of the fluctuating quantities introduced in Eq. (4) column-wise as $\mathcal{Q}' = [q'(\mathbf{x}, t_1), \ldots, q'(\mathbf{x}, t_N)] \in \mathbb{R}^{M \times N}$, which is called the snapshot matrix. At this stage, we consider that q' is evaluated as a uniform lattice or a set of randomly distributed points. However, the fluctuation values still depend on $\mathbf{x}$ since these variables must be integrated with respect to the space coordinates to form a correlation matrix (as we shall see later in the solution of the maximization step of the POD method).

Based on the expansion defined in Eq. (4) and using the reduced basis matrix definition, we can write $\mathcal{Q}'$ as

$$\mathcal{Q}' = \Phi \mathcal{A} \quad \text{with} \quad \Phi \in \mathbb{R}^{M \times L}, \ \mathcal{A} \in \mathbb{R}^{L \times N}, \tag{5}$$

where we used the matrix of temporal coefficients defined as $\mathcal{A} = [\mathbf{a}(t_1), \ldots, \mathbf{a}(t_N)]$.

It is straightforward to show that each Ψ_i basis function satisfies the following equation

$$\Psi_i = \lambda_i^{-1/2} \mathcal{Q}' v_i \tag{6}$$

with $\lambda_1 \geq \lambda_2 \geq \ldots \geq \lambda_L$, where $\lambda_i^{-1/2}$ is the normalization factor and v_i are the eigenvectors of the following eigen problem

$$\mathbf{C} v_i = \lambda_i v_i, \tag{7}$$

where $\mathbf{C} = \int_\Omega \mathcal{Q}'^T \mathcal{Q}' \, d\Omega$ is the correlation matrix[1]

---

[1] Writing the correlation matrix as an integral over the domain Ω means that we are weighting each variable in the vector q' associated to a lattice point $\mathbf{x}_i$ with the corresponding volume V_i of a fictitious control volume enclosing that lattice point. For fluctuation data q' collected from unstructured finite element-like grids, the enclosing volume of a point $\mathbf{x}_i$ taken at the centroid of a mesh cell is the cell's own volume.

A standard way to estimate the dimension L of the reduced basis Φ is the following criterion

$$\frac{\sum_{i=1}^{L} \lambda_i}{\sum_{i=1}^{M} \lambda_i} \geq \gamma, \tag{8}$$

where $0 < \gamma < 1$ is a threshold that indicates the amount of energy of the original full order system being preserved by the reduced order system.

A simple projection operation is sufficient to recover the temporal coefficients associated to the spatial basis functions

$$a_j\left(t_i\right) = \left(\mathcal{Q}'\left(\mathbf{x}, t_i\right)\right)^T \Psi_j. \tag{9}$$

It provides the necessary inputs for training the artificial neural networks which compose the reduced order models proposed in this work.

3   Artificial Neural Networks

As the name suggests, an ANN is a computational system inspired by brain functioning [13]. An ANN consists of a collection of units called artificial neurons and virtual wired connections between neurons called edges that mimic synapses in a biological brain. Information is transmitted from input neurons towards output neurons according to the paths imposed by the connections forming a directed graph. Neurons are typically arranged into layers and a sequence of such interconnected layers creates the ANN itself. Usually, weights and biases are associated with edges and neurons, respectively, to adjust the learning process of the network for any specific application. In this work, we consider two types of ANNs: the traditional fully connected neural network (FCNN) [15] and a specific recurrent neural network (RNN) [10] called the LSTM neural network [5]. The code implementation was written in Python using Numpy and Keras together with the TensorFlow AI library.

4   ANN-Based Reduced Order Models

The POD method produces a separation of variables of the original dynamical system (cf. Eq. 4). The spatial basis can be computed offline from the snapshot matrix and remains fixed for each simulation data set. The projection of the fluctuating quantities onto the spatial basis provides the input for training the ANN-based ROM that we seek. Such an approach gives us an approximation of the temporal coefficients such that

$$\mathcal{C} \approx \mathcal{A} = \Phi^T \mathcal{Q}', \tag{10}$$

where $\mathcal{C} = [\mathbf{c}(t_1), \ldots, \mathbf{c}(t_N)]$, $\mathcal{C} \in \mathbb{R}^{L \times N}$, analogous to the definition of matrix $\mathcal{A}$. It is woth noting from Eq. (5) that we can easily recover $\mathcal{A}$ since Φ is an orthonormal matrix. Once the approximation of the temporal coefficients is obtained, we can write the desired reduced basis approximate solution of the original dynamical system as

$$Q_{rb} = \overline{q} + \Phi\, C. \tag{11}$$

This result accomplishes our goal of having a ROM that works as a proxy model of the original full order system. In the following, we show how to build two types of ANN-based ROMs.

4.1   FCNN ROM

After performing the POD method, we can rewrite Eq. (4) as an exclusive time dependent set of equations

$$Q_{rb}(t) = \overline{q} + q'(t) = \overline{q} + \sum_{i=1}^{L} a_i(t)\Psi_i, \tag{12}$$

and we can differentiate them with respect to time to obtain

$$\frac{dQ_{rb}(t)}{dt} = \sum_{i=1}^{L} \Psi_i \frac{da_i(t)}{dt} = \Phi\dot{\mathbf{a}}(t). \tag{13}$$

Noting that Eq. (2) can be recast as

$$\frac{dQ_h(t)}{dt} = S_h(t) - \mathcal{N}_h(Q_h(t)), \tag{14}$$

we can combine both equations in such a way that we isolate the time derivative of the reduced basis coefficients on the left and keep all the nonlinearities and sources of the dynamical system on the right; that is,

$$\dot{\mathbf{a}}(t) \approx \Phi^T \left(S_h(t) - \mathcal{N}_h(Q_h(t)) \right). \tag{15}$$

It suggests that all the complexity of the dynamical system under analysis can be described by the evolution of the temporal coefficients $\mathbf{a}(t)$. Given that, we set up a FCNN as a regression tool to estimate $\dot{\mathbf{a}}(t)$ as follows

$$\dot{\mathbf{a}}(t) \approx \frac{d\mathbf{c}(t)}{dt} = \mathbf{W}^{[l]}\mathbf{G}^{[l-1]} + \mathbf{b}^{[l]}, \tag{16}$$

where $\mathbf{W}^{[l]}$ is the weight matrix of the last layer of the FCNN, $\mathbf{G}^{[l-1]}$ is the activation matrix of the penultimate layer and $\mathbf{b}^{[l]}$ is the bias vector of the last layer.

Figure 1 shows a schematic representation of the operations performed to construct the FCNN ROM. The FCNN is designed to receive the temporal coefficients $\mathbf{a}(t)$ as input from the (lake circulation) flow field variables and the atmospheric forcing terms (cf. input vectors $\mathbf{a}_c$ and $\mathbf{a}_f$ on the bottom left of Fig. 1, respectively) and to return an approximation of the time derivative of the flow field coefficients as output. Such an approach is inspired by the work of

[9] which focused on computational fluid dynamics applications, though it did not depend on external atmospheric forcing terms.

The FCNN's loss function is minimized with respect to the time derivative of the temporal coefficients $\mathbf{a}(t)$, computed with a high resolution finite difference scheme. To recover the approximate time coefficients $\mathbf{c}(t)$ computed by the FCNN, we use a 5-stage 4th order strong stability preserving Runge-Kutta (RK) scheme. Such an approach allows us to predict the field variables of the dynamical system beyond the training window because $\bar{q}(\mathbf{x})$ and $\Psi_i(\mathbf{x})$ depend only on the spatial coordinates. Furthermore, RK time-steps used to reconstruct field variables don't need to be the same size as those used for training the FCNN, ensuring great flexibility for the FCNN ROM.

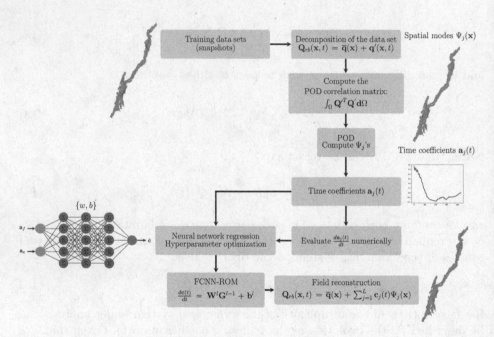

Fig. 1. Schematic of the FCNN ROM workflow. On the bottom left, the inputs of the ANN $\mathbf{a}_c$ and $\mathbf{a}_f$ are the time coefficients associated with the lake circulation flow fields and the atmospheric forcing variables, respectively. The output $\dot{\mathbf{c}}$ is the approximation of the time derivative of the time coefficients associated to the water circulation.

4.2   LSTM ROM

The LSTM neural network is a type of Recurrent Neural Network (RNN) which has been primarily utilized in speech modeling [14] and language translation [17]. However, some authors have applied it successfully in forecasting problems including turbulent flows [11], weather prediction [6], and runoff applications [24].

For a given time series $a_i(t)$, the LSTM uses a double-leaf moving window with input and output time lengths Δt_{in} and Δt_{out}, respectively, to create a set of training sequences. Upon minimization of the loss function, given a section of the time series with length Δt_{in} on the left leaf of the moving window, the LSTM learns how to predict the adjacent section of the time series with length Δt_{out} on the right leaf of the moving window. Once trained, the LSTM can perform a forecast of length Δt_{out} using the last Δt_{in} section of the time series. If we want to stretch the forecast length for multiple time lengths Δt_{out}, we feedback the trained LSTM with each predicted extrapolation.

Looking at the time coefficients $a_i(t)$ in Eq. (4), we can interpret them as a set of L time series of length N associated with each spatial mode Ψ_i. Given that, we use an LSTM neural network with a suitable moving window to estimate the temporal coefficients $\mathbf{a}(t)$ directly so that we can forecast the dynamical system under analysis by extrapolating those time series. Equation (9) provides the necessary input for training the LSTM ROM.

We should remark that the LSTM ROM workflow is nearly identical to that of the FCNN ROM except that the LSTM neural network does not rely on the derivative of temporal coefficients $(\dot{\mathbf{a}}(t))$ to minimize the loss function. The FCNN box in Fig. 1, which computes weights and biases to estimate $\dot{\mathbf{a}}(t)$, can therefore be replaced by an LSTM neural network that outputs the temporal coefficients $\mathbf{a}(t)$ themselves.

5   Numerical Results

This section demonstrates the effectiveness of the proposed ANN-based ROMs via two examples: predicting the state of a discrete system called a Lorenz attractor, and the movement of water in a freshwater lake. Note that while the Lorenz attractor is a discrete system and does not require dimensionality reduction, it is, from a theoretical standpoint, a suitable case study for evaluating the ability of ANNs to forecast deterministic and chaotic physical behavior.

5.1   Lorenz Attractor

The Lorenz attractor is a set of chaotic solutions of the Lorenz system which consists of the following set of three ODEs:

$$\frac{\mathrm{d}x}{\mathrm{d}t} = \sigma(y - x), \tag{17}$$

$$\frac{\mathrm{d}y}{\mathrm{d}t} = x(\rho - z) - y, \tag{18}$$

$$\frac{\mathrm{d}z}{\mathrm{d}t} = xy - \beta z. \tag{19}$$

This system, originally developed by Edward Lorenz in the early 1960s, was an attempt to represent atmospheric convection through a two dimensional fluid flow of uniform depth with an imposed temperature difference in the vertical direction. Thus, in the system above, x is a quantity describing the rate of convection, y is the horizontal temperature variation, and z is the vertical temperature variation. Parameters σ, ρ and β are the Prandtl number, a number proportional to the Rayleigh number and a geometric factor, respectively.

The time derivatives of the coordinates x, y and z can be interpreted as three separate time series. Once this system of three ODEs is numerically integrated along a period T using a time step dt, we have the necessary dataset to train and test the ANN which models the Lorenz system behavior. As noted above, a dimensionality reduction is not required.

In this numerical example, we trained a FCNN to predict the deterministic and chaotic regimes of the Lorenz system. As the chaotic regime was supposed to be much harder to predict than the deterministic one, we performed a hyperparameter optimization using the library Optuna (https://optuna.org/) to find the best neural network architecture for predicting the chaotic case. Then we used the same FCNN to predict both system behaviors. The best hyperparameters configuration is shown in Table 1.

Table 1. Best FCNN hyperparameters configuration.

Neurons per layer	Learning rate	L^2 regularization	Activation function	Loss function	Optimizer
$\{3, 24, 25, 33, 22, 26, 3\}$	$5.2e{-}06$	$2.3e{-}05$	ELU	Mean Squared Error	ADAM/L-BFGS-B

The ANN's weights and biases were optimized by two algorithms applied successively. First, the ADAM algorithm iterates 2000 cycles and then the L-BFGS-B scheme completes the optimization process until the convergence is reached. ADAM is a variant of the classical Stochastic Gradient Descent (SGD) method which is an iterative method for optimizing an objective function. Similarly, L-BFGS-B is a second order quasi-Newton algorithm that performs the same task with the advantage of showing greater accuracy. As the former method is computationally more efficient, it gives a quick enhanced initial guess to the latter. The physical parameters of the deterministic Lorenz system were set as: $\rho = 14.0$, $\sigma = 10.0$, $\beta = 8/3$, $T = 12.0\,\mathrm{s}$, $dt = 0.001\,\mathrm{s}$.

Figure 2 shows plots of the discrete variables and their time derivatives compared to the true solutions over time, along with the absolute errors[2]. We observe that the FCNN can predict variables x, y and z with moderate accuracy only for a short period (about two seconds) since the errors of the time derivatives of the discrete variables are one order of magnitude smaller than the derivative values themselves. However, all time derivatives reach the system steady state with some positive or negative bias resulting in a clear discrepancy between predicted and reference solutions for x, y and z. As the architecture of the FCNN was optimized to predict persistent unsteady behavior, typical of chaotic regimes, it

---

[2] Relative errors are not suited for the analysis because the time derivative of the reference solution has many values close to zero.

was expected that only the oscillatory patterns would be captured by the ANN in the deterministic case.

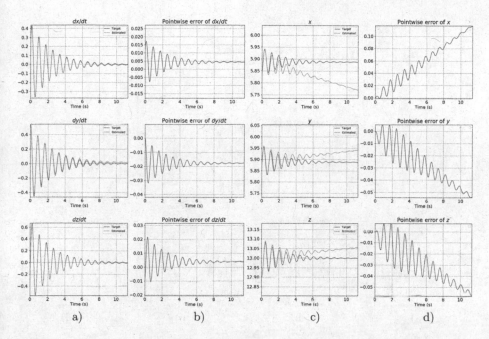

Fig. 2. Deterministic Lorenz system: a) $\dot{x}, \dot{y}, \dot{z}$ true and predicted; b) $error_{\dot{x}} = \dot{x}_{true} - \dot{x}_{pred}$, $error_{\dot{y}} = \dot{y}_{true} - \dot{y}_{pred}$, $error_{\dot{z}} = \dot{z}_{true} - \dot{z}_{pred}$; c) x, y, z true and predicted; d) $error_x = x_{true} - x_{pred}$, $error_y = y_{true} - y_{pred}$, $error_z = z_{true} - z_{pred}$.

Figure 3 shows the same distribution of plots for the chaotic regime, which has the same physical parameters as in the deterministic system except for $\rho = 28.0$. In this case, we report time in terms of Lyapunov timescale which mirrors the limits of the predictability of the system: counting the number of Lyapunov units over which the ANN matches the dynamical system's patterns provides a threshold beyond which the ANN will fail to predict the system's behavior. In the numerical experiments, we computed the Lyapunov unit as $\approx 1/\lambda_{max} = 1.06s.$, where λ_{max} is the system's largest positive Lyapunov exponent (LLE). We observe that the errors of the predicted time derivatives of the discrete variables are two orders of magnitude smaller than the maximum values reached by the derivatives themselves (Figs. 3a and 3b). Such performance is sufficient to provide a remarkable correspondence between predicted and reference time series for all discrete variables x, y and z for nearly 9 Lyapunov units, as shown in Fig. 3c. It is clear that hyperparameter optimization tuned for the chaotic regime increased the quality of the FCNN prediction substantially. However, it is not obvious how to extend such predictability limits to realistic hydrodynamics systems since the LLE are not readily available for such complex systems.

For the sake of brevity, we omitted the results of the LSTM approach for the Lorenz system as they are quite similar to the FCNN ones.

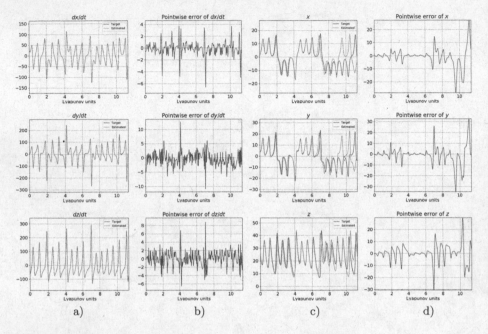

a)   b)   c)   d)

Fig. 3. Chaotic Lorenz system: a) $\dot{x}, \dot{y}, \dot{z}$ true and predicted; b) $error_{\dot{x}} = \dot{x}_{true} - \dot{x}_{pred}$, $error_{\dot{y}} = \dot{y}_{true} - \dot{y}_{pred}$, $error_{\dot{z}} = \dot{z}_{true} - \dot{z}_{pred}$; c) x, y, z true and predicted; d) $error_x = x_{true} - x_{pred}$, $error_y = y_{true} - y_{pred}$, $error_z = z_{true} - z_{pred}$.

5.2   Hydrodynamics at Lake George

Lake George is a freshwater lake in upstate New York, USA. It is considered of medium size (51.5 km × 2.15 km) with a total surface area of 117.4 km^2. It is the subject of a multiyear research effort called The Jefferson Project that has a goal of understanding the impact of human activity on fresh water, and how to mitigate those effects. A operational prediction system has developed as part of The Jefferson Project to perform short-term (1–7 day) forecasts of the weather, hydrology and hydrodynamics (*viz.* water circulation) at Lake George [22].

Currently, hydrodynamic predictions are performed daily using the Stanford unstructured-grid, nonhydrostatic, parallel coastal ocean model (SUNTANS). SUNTANS solves the three dimensional Reynolds-averaged Navier-Stokes (RANS) equations on an unstructured, horizontal grid and fixed z-level vertical domain using a finite-volume (FV) discretization. SUNTANS has been extensively used in a variety of hydrodynamic applications with good results [3]. For Lake George, the SUNTANS grid has a varying horizontal resolution of

10–50 m and a vertical resolution of 0.5 m close to the surface and 1.6 m at the deepest point of the lake. Its configuration for daily forecasts at Lake George contains over 40,000 grid cells and takes around $11/2$ h to complete a 36 h forecast using 30 high-end processing cores.

To simulate realistic conditions, SUNTANS requires a realistic atmospheric forcing. For Lake George, this is provided by the Weather Research and Forecasting (WRF) model v3.9.1 [16], which has been configured to generate daily, 36 h forecasts for Lake George at 0.33 km horizontal resolution. More details about the model setup can be seen in [22]. WRF is said to be one-way coupled to SUNTANS (i.e., the forecasted state of SUNTANS does not feedback into WRF).

The time duration and obvious energy requirements demanded by SUNTANS motivates us to develop a hydrodynamic surrogate model using ANN-based ROMs. In the following, we discuss the numerical experiments made with the FCNN and LSTM ROMs. Note that we are not attempting to reconstruct the full 3D hydrodynamic state of Lake George; rather, we focus on reconstructing the 2D depth-averaged values of four variables: temperature, density, and northward and eastward water velocity. With such a simplified reconstruction, a ML-based surrogate takes only a couple of seconds to perform a 36 h water circulation forecast. Compared with the 1 1/2 h of a regular forecast made by SUNTANS, it demonstrates a significant prediction speed up. While a time complexity analysis for the forward propagation of feed forward neural networks results in $O(N^4)$, such an analysis seems to be virtually unattainable given the huge complexity of a PDE solver based on a FV discretization method like SUNTANS.

Training data was provided by daily WRF and SUNTANS forecasts with 10 min output resolution for the period from April 1st to 20th, 2019. Each forecast overlaps by 12 h and was included in the training. Data from a single 36 h forecast by WRF and SUNTANS on April 21st, 2019 was used for testing. The data contained four atmospheric variables from WRF: surface air temperature and pressure, and northward and eastward surface wind velocity; and four depth-averaged hydrodynamic variables from SUNTANS: density, temperature and northward and eastward water velocity. All data was collected from the centroid of each SUNTANS cell (including the WRF data which was projected onto the SUNTANS grid).

The aim is to generate a 36 h depth-averaged hydrodynamics forecast of Lake George starting from April 21st, with a 5% error in the L2-norm with respect to the full order approximate solution (given by SUNTANS across the same forecast interval).

FCNN ROM for Hydrodynamics. To find the best performance models, we applied a hyperparameter optimization on the FCNN architecture of 600 configurations randomly chosen with different numbers of hidden layers, neurons per layer and optimizer iterations, and dropout values and learning rates. Empirical tests revealed that 5 spatial modes Ψ_j represent the main circulation features over the entire lake (see Fig. 4), preserving 96% of the total energy of the full order system. Table 2 shows the percentage preservation by each spatial mode, indicating how representative each mode is at explaining the variance in each circulation variable (e.g., density, temperature and velocity components). It is worth noting that the preserved energy of each spatial mode is the same regardless of the circulation variable as the eigenvalues of the correlation matrix are the same for each circulation variable.

Table 2. Percentage of preserved energy in each spatial mode.

$\Psi_1(\mathbf{x})$	$\Psi_2(\mathbf{x})$	$\Psi_3(\mathbf{x})$	$\Psi_4(\mathbf{x})$	$\Psi_5(\mathbf{x})$	Total preserved energy
91.4%	2.4%	1.1%	0.6%	0.5%	96.0%

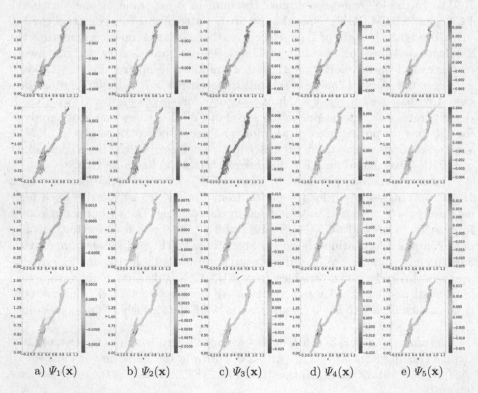

a) $\Psi_1(\mathbf{x})$ b) $\Psi_2(\mathbf{x})$ c) $\Psi_3(\mathbf{x})$ d) $\Psi_4(\mathbf{x})$ e) $\Psi_5(\mathbf{x})$

Fig. 4. From top to bottom: Spatial modes relative to Density, Temperature, East and North velocity components.

Figure 5 shows the time series of the 5 temporal coefficients for each spatial mode. In these plots, blue lines correspond to input used for training the machine learning model, green lines represent the "true" values simulated by SUNTANS for testing, and the orange lines represent predicted values by the

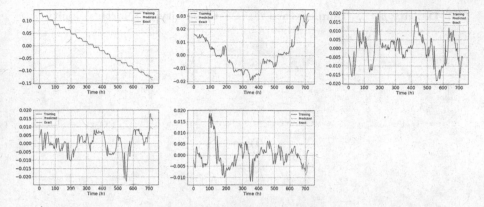

Fig. 5. Temporal coefficients of the FCNN ROM corresponding to the 5 spatial modes. From left to right, first row: $a_1(t), a_2(t)$ and $a_3(t)$; second row: $a_4(t)$ and $a_5(t)$.

FCNN ROM. The time series corresponding to the FCNN ROM temporal coefficients are predicted fairly well. It suggests that the numerical differentiation of the temporal coefficients recovered from the full order model are quite consistent and reliable, ensuring an accurate reconstruction of the ROM coefficients through the RK time integration procedure. Although the error of the predicted time series corresponding to the fourth and fifth modes had been relatively large, their contributions to the approximating capacity of the surrogate model is quite insignificant as shown in Table 2.

When the time coefficients are multiplied by the spatial modes according to Eq. (11), the FCNN ROM produces the desired 36 h hydrodynamic forecast for Lake George. Figure 6 shows the comparison between the predicted physical state of Lake George at the end of the 36 h forecast, and its "true" physical state from SUNTANS. In these plots, the physical variables (temperature, density and velocity) have been normalized (their values are restricted to the range $[0, 1]$).

It is evident that variables which change slowly with time, such as density and temperature, are better approximated by the FCNN ROM than water velocity. The water velocity is acutely sensitive to surface winds which can change rapidly with time. The error plots in Fig. 7b shows the impact of a strong wind event between 12 and 23 h that significantly increases the error of the water velocity components, degrading the performance of the whole model. Such high frequency fluctuations are difficult for the neural network to capture because the correlation matrix **C** takes into consideration all physical variables at once.

Figure 7a shows the 3 best FCNN ROMs, ranked according to the relative error of the averaged water velocity components ($\frac{u+v}{2}$). This choice was made considering evidence of the difficulty in approximating fast-changing variables. The hyperparameter optimization strategy generates a set of candidates labeled with arbitrary numerical indices such as 1617, 1561 and 1100 (cf. Fig. 7) to identify each individual model that was trained. The water velocity components were expected to influence the choice of the best ROMs because they are harder

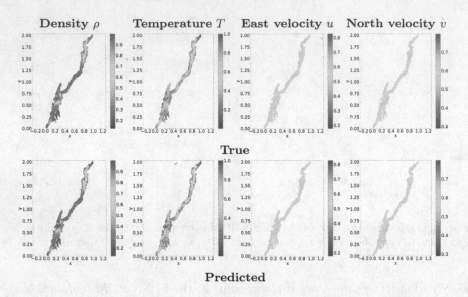

Fig. 6. Full order model solution vs. FCNN ROM approximation for density, temperature and velocity components.

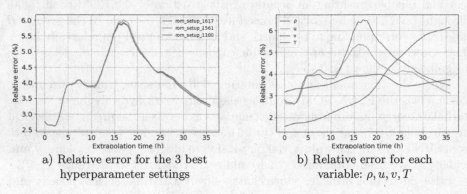

a) Relative error for the 3 best
hyperparameter settings

b) Relative error for each
variable: ρ, u, v, T

Fig. 7. a) Best performances based on the average $\frac{u+v}{2}$ error; b) Best configuration: model 1617.

to approximate, as noted previously. Figure 7b shows the L^2-norm relative error of each variable for the best FCNN ROM setup.

The relative error of all variables is kept below 7% for the duration of the 36 h forecast, which is quite remarkable. At the end of the forecast, only the density relative error is above the target of 5%, although a visual comparison between the predicted and true density distributions shows very small differences. The error levels achieved are even more impressive if we consider that SUNTANS uses an internal 3 second time step to reach its solution, while the surrogate model has an effective timestep of 10 min (the frequency of data output from SUNTANS and WRF). We should also highlight that deep neural networks performed much better than shallow ones, none of which were selected in the top three FCNN ROM setups.

Table 3 shows the optimum hyperparameters selection for FCNN ROM number 1617.

Table 3. FCNN ROM best hyperparameters configuration.

Hidden layers	Neurons/Layer	Dropout/Layer	Learning rate	Adam iter
8	$\{83, 65, 67, 145, 59, 103, 81, 129\}$	0.3	1e$-$05	5040

For the sake of completeness, we also investigated the ability of the FCNN ROM to provide accurate predictions of flow velocities at specific touristic regions at Lake George. We identified two places of interest using lat-long coordinates: Million Dollar beach in the south and City of Bolton in the middle west. Circular areas with 1.0 km of radius centered at those points delimit the regions of interest where we evaluated the 36 h time averaged error of the best surrogate model (labeled 1617) to predict eastward and northward flow velocities.

Table 4 shows the time averaged error of the flow velocity components for the two specific regions of interest.

Table 4. Time averaged percentage error of flow velocities at two regions of interest.

Placement	u error (%)	v error (%)
Million Dollar beach	0.6	0.5
City of Bolton	3.0	2.4

LSTM ROM for Hydrodynamics. The LSTM learning process used an asymmetrical sliding window with 200 min input and 10 min output. As before, hyperparameter optimization was performed using a very simple strategy of randomly generating different neural network architectures. Such a strategy was essential to create a competitive model compared with the FCNN ROM.

Figure 8 shows the time series of the 5 temporal coefficients for each spatial model of the LSTM. The spatial modes are the same as those used by the FCNN ROM and have already been depicted in the previous subsection. Remarkably, the LSTM ROM can adequately predict the time series associated with the temporal coefficients without needing to (directly) compute the time derivatives of the temporal coefficients, nor integrate the time derivative approximation with an RK scheme.

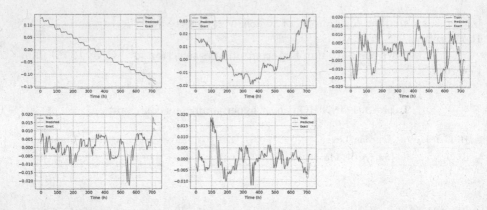

Fig. 8. Temporal coefficients of the LSTM ROM corresponding to the 5 spatial modes. From left to right, first row: $a_1(t), a_2(t)$ and $a_3(t)$; second row: $a_4(t)$ and $a_5(t)$.

Figure 9 shows the comparison of the predicted physical state of Lake George with the assumed true physical state. As with the FCNN ROM, the depth-averaged temperature and density variables are better approximated than velocity due to their large inertial trends. Only the main patterns of the velocity components can be described by the LSTM ROM. However, as with the FCNN ROM, there is a monotonic increasing relative error of the density variable. This is in part because the model performance ranking was based on the relative error of the average velocity components. The increasing error of the density variable was not observed when the performance criterion was changed to include other metrics, such as the error based on the average of all physical variables.

From the error plots of the 3 best performing LSTM ROMs (Fig. 10), the relative error remains below 6% (and below 7% for each variable) for the duration of the forecast, which again is a remarkable result. As with the FCNN ROM, we observe a similar increase in the relative error from 12 to 23 h when the surface wind strengthened. At the end of the 36 h forecast, only the density relative error is slightly above the target of 5%, demonstrating the strong ability of the LSTM architecture to deal with time-evolving sequences. Table 5 shows the optimum hyperparameters selection for LSTM ROM number 230.

However, such improved results comes with a price: the LSTM ROM needs 4.8 times more degrees of freedom (i.e weights and biases) than the FCNN ROM to perform equivalently[3].

---

[3] The LSTM minimization algorithm finds 264,690 optimal weights and biases while FCNN requires only 55,101.

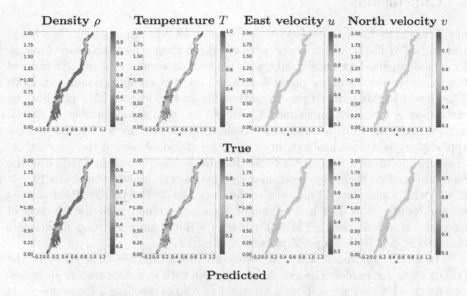

Fig. 9. Full order model solution vs. LSTM ROM approximation for density, temperature and velocity components.

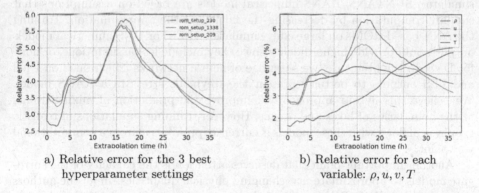

a) Relative error for the 3 best hyperparameter settings

b) Relative error for each variable: ρ, u, v, T

Fig. 10. a) Best performances based on the average $\frac{u+v}{2}$ error; b) Best configuration: model 230.

Table 5. LSTM ROM best hyperparameters configuration.

Hidden layers	LSTM cells per layer	Dropout	Learning rate	Adam iterations
3	$\{133, 92, 129\}$	$\{0.2, 0.3, 0.3\}$	0.01	1000

6   Conclusions

In this work, we have developed two ANN-based ROMs, namely an FCNN ROM and an LSTM ROM, which are capable of reproducing a hydrodynamic forecast for a medium-sized freshwater lake with reasonable accuracy (a relative error of less than 6% over the entire prediction range) and low computational cost. Both ANN-based ROMs reduced the dimensionality of the original data provided by the full-order hydrodynamics model, SUNTANS, to a small number of spatial basis through the POD technique. POD shows great promise for hydrodynamics applications as it drastically reduced the computational cost of the forecasting.

More specifically, both ANN-based ROMs performed well at predicting the temporal coefficients of the depth-averaged hydrodynamic variables. The FCNN ROM (with a deep neural network configuration) and the LSTM ROM showed similar results for a 36 h hydrodynamic forecast, trained with the 19 days of forecasts. However, the LSTM ROM used 4.8 times more learning parameters than the FCNN ROM to perform equivalently.

The FCNN approach was also tested on predicting the time series of the Lorenz attractor model. The validation example with hyperparameter optimization for the chaotic regime showed outstanding results reaching 9 Lyapunov units until failing to represent the system's trends. FCNN also described relatively well the unsteady section of the deterministic case although with a clear bias in all discrete variables for the final steady state pattern.

We applied machine learning techniques to data generated by the RANS simulator, SUNTANS. RANS numerical models are based on assumptions that simplify computation by decreasing the fidelity of the approximation. Training the ANN-based ROMs on large eddy simulation (LES) or DNS numerical models output would provide higher fidelity since they include less assumptions, or none for DNS. In the literature, we see usage of neural networks [20] trained on DNS and LES outputs to better represent the Reynolds stress in a RANS model. We believe this hybrid approach will improve the prediction of mixing events at the boundaries of lakes and oceans. However, running simulations of realistic geophysical flows with these models is currently prohibitive from a computational viewpoint.

Another important point that deserves attention is the capacity of the surrogate models to approximate fast changing physical quantities. In [8] the authors point out that POD-ROMs can produce accurate results only if the problem of interest admits a fast decaying Kolmogorov n-width which corresponds to the class of diffusion-dominant problems. Circulation is mostly a convection-dominant problem with strong variability in velocity components. Another factor influencing the accuracy of ROMs is the chaotic/turbulent behavior.

As a next step, we want to test the ability of nonlinear dimensionality reduction [4,8] techniques to describe the circulation features with higher fidelity.

References

1. Benjamin, S.G., et al.: A north American hourly assimilation and model forecast cycle: the rapid refresh. Mon. Weather Rev. **144**(4), 1669–1694 (2016). https://doi.org/10.1175/MWR-D-15-0242.1
2. Brunton, S.L., Noack, B.R., Koumoutsakos, P.: Machine learning for fluid mechanics. Annu. Rev. Fluid Mech. **52**(1), 477–508 (2020). https://doi.org/10.1146/annurev-fluid-010719-060214
3. Fringer, O., Gerritsen, M., Street, R.: An unstructured-grid, finite-volumne, non-hydrostatic, parallel coastal ocean simulator. Ocean Model. **14**, 139–173 (2006)
4. Gonzalez, F., Balajewicz, M.: Deep convolutional recurrent autoencoders for learning low-dimensional feature dynamics of fluid systems (2018)
5. Hochreiter, S., Schmidhuber, J.: Long short-term memory. Neural Comput. **9**, 1735–1780 (1997). https://doi.org/10.1162/neco.1997.9.8.1735
6. Karevan, Z., Suykens, J.: Transductive LSTM for time-series prediction: an application to weather forecasting. Neural Netw. (2020). https://doi.org/10.1016/j.neunet.2019.12.030
7. Kim, B., Azevedo, V.C., Thuerey, N., Kim, T., Gross, M., Solenthaler, B.: Deep fluids: a generative network for parameterized fluid simulations. Comput. Graph. Forum (Proc. Eurographics) **38**(2) (2019)
8. Lee, K., Carlberg, K.: Model reduction of dynamical systems on nonlinear manifolds using deep convolutional autoencoders. J. Comput. Phys. (2019). https://doi.org/10.1016/j.jcp.2019.108973
9. Lui, H.F.S.: Construction of reduced order models for fluid flows using deep neural networks. Master's thesis, State University of Campinas (2019)
10. Miljanovic, M.: Comparative analysis of recurrent and finite impulse response neural networks in time series prediction. Indian J. Comput. Sci. Eng. **3** (2012). http://www.ijcse.com/docs/INDJCSE12-03-01-028.pdf
11. Mohan, A., Gaitonde, D.: A deep learning based approach to reduced order modeling for turbulent flow control using LSTM neural networks (2018)
12. Navrátil, J., King, A., Rios, J., Kollias, G., Torrado, R., Codas, A.: Accelerating physics-based simulations using end-to-end neural network proxies: an application in oil reservoir modeling. Front. Big Data **2** (2019). https://doi.org/10.3389/fdata.2019.00033
13. Nielsen, M.: Neural Networks and Deep Learning. Determination Press (2015). https://books.google.com.br/books?id=STDBswEACAAJ
14. Sak, H., Senior, A., Beaufays, F.: Long short-term memory recurrent neural network architectures for large scale acoustic modeling (2014)
15. Schmidhuber, J.: Deep learning in neural networks: an overview. Neural Netw. **61**, 85–117 (2015)
16. Skamarock, W.C., et al.: A description of the advanced research WRF version 3. NCAR technical note -475+STR (2008)
17. Sutskever, I., Vinyals, O., Le, Q.V.: Sequence to sequence learning with neural networks. In: Ghahramani, Z., Welling, M., Cortes, C., Lawrence, N.D., Weinberger, K.Q. (eds.) Advances in Neural Information Processing Systems 27, pp. 3104–3112. Curran Associates, Inc. (2014). http://papers.nips.cc/paper/5346-sequence-to-sequence-learning-with-neural-networks.pdf
18. Vlachas, P., Byeon, W., Wan, Z., Sapsis, T., Koumoutsakos, P.: Data-driven forecasting of high-dimensional chaotic systems with long short-term memory networks. Proc. Roy. Soc. A: Math. Phys. Eng. Sci. **474**(2213), 20170844 (2018)

19. Wan, Z.Y., Vlachas, P., Koumoutsakos, P., Sapsis, T.: Data-assisted reduced-order modeling of extreme events in complex dynamical systems. PLoS ONE **13** (2018). https://doi.org/10.1371/fdata.2018.0197704
20. Wang, J.X., Wu, J.L., Xiao, H.: Physics-informed machine learning approach for reconstructing Reynolds stress modeling discrepancies based on DNS data. Phys. Rev. Fluids **2**, 034603 (2017). https://doi.org/10.1103/PhysRevFluids.2.034603
21. Wang, Q., Ripamonti, N., Hesthaven, J.: Recurrent neural network closure of parametric POD-Galerkin reduced-order models based on the Mori-Zwanzig formalism (2019)
22. Watson, C.D., et al.: The application of an internet of things cyber-infrastructure for the study of ecology of lake George in the Jefferson project (2018)
23. Wynne, T., et al.: Evolution of a cyanobacterial bloom forecast system in western lake Erie: development and initial evaluation. J. Great Lakes Res. **39**, 90–99 (2013). Remote Sensing of the Great Lakes and Other Inland Waters
24. Xiang, Z., Yan, J., Demir, I.: A rainfall-runoff model with LSTM-based sequence-to-sequence learning. Water Resour. Rese. **56** (2020). https://doi.org/10.1029/2019WR025326

Parameter Identification of RANS Turbulence Model Using Physics-Embedded Neural Network

Shirui Luo[1]([⊠]), Madhu Vellakal[1], Seid Koric[1], Volodymyr Kindratenko[1], and Jiahuan Cui[2]

[1] University of Illinois at Urbana-Champaign, Urbana, IL 61801, USA
{shirui,vcmadhu,koric,kindrtnk}@illinois.edu
[2] Zhejiang University-University of Illinois at Urbana-Champaign Institute,
Haining 314400, Zhejiang, China
jiahuancui@intl.zju.edu.cn

Abstract. Identifying the appropriate parameters of a turbulence model for a class of flow usually requires extensive experimentation and numerical simulations. Therefore even a modest improvement of the turbulence model can significantly reduce the overall cost of a three-dimensional, time-dependent simulation. In this paper we demonstrate a novel method to find the optimal parameters in the Reynolds-averaged Navier–Stokes (RANS) turbulence model using high-fidelity direct numerical simulation (DNS) data. A physics informed neural network (PINN) that is embedded with the turbulent transport equations is studied, physical loss functions are proposed to explicitly impose information of the transport equations to neural networks. This approach solves an inverse problem by treating the five parameters in turbulence model as random variables, with the turbulent kinetic energy and dissipation rate as known quantities from DNS simulation. The objective is to optimize the five parameters in turbulence closures using the PINN leveraging limited data available from costly high-fidelity DNS data. We validated this method on two test cases of flow over bump. The recommended values were found to be $C_{\epsilon 1} = 1.302$, $C_{\epsilon 2} = 1.862$, $C_\mu = 0.09$, $\sigma_K = 0.75$, $\sigma_\epsilon = 0.273$; the mean absolute error of the velocity profile between RANS and DNS decreased by 22% when using these neural network inferred parameters.

Keywords: Turbulence modeling · Neural network · Physics embedded machine learning

1 Introduction

Reynolds-averaged Navier–Stokes (RANS) simulation remains the workhorse computational fluid dynamics (CFD) method for industrial enterprises due to its computational efficiency and easy implementation. However, many flows are difficult to simulate accurately using RANS models, for example, flow with strong

© Springer Nature Switzerland AG 2020
H. Jagode et al. (Eds.): ISC High Performance 2020 Workshops, LNCS 12321, pp. 137–149, 2020.
https://doi.org/10.1007/978-3-030-59851-8_9

adverse pressure and separation, jet-in-crossflow interactions. The inaccuracy could be due to RANS inherent simplifications or, more often the case, the use of inappropriate RANS constants which are usually estimated by fitting to experimental results of simple flows [1]. The closure model in RANS equations has traditionally evolved through a combined efforts of mathematics, flow theory, empiricism, and rudimentary data-driven techniques such as single or two-variable curve-fitting. These tunable parameters have been determined from experiments with air and water for fundamental turbulent boundary layers and free shear flows [2]. Table 1 lists some of the most commonly used constants in many CFD solvers as the default parameter values (we will refer to them as the "default" values). They have been found to work well for a wide range of wall-bounded and free shear flows. However, there is ample empirical evidence that these parameters are far from being universal [3–5] and the optimal parameter values can vary substantially for different flow configurations. Thus, it is unlikely that the default values of $\kappa - \epsilon$ model parameters should yield accurate simulations for all cases, and calibration (either by experimental or high-fidelity simulation data) for each specific flow configuration should be a pre-requisite [6].

Compared to experimental data, high-fidelity simulation data can provide a more comprehensive view of the flow than when used for RANS models calibration, as simulation data can provide flow quantities which cannot be measured in experiments. If high-fidelity simulation data is provided, the calibration process is then an inverse problem that given the abundant observable flow field data from simulation, we need to infer the unknown parameters in the RANS model transport equations. Solving these inverse problems with differential equations, however, is typically computationally prohibitive and often requires the solution of ill-posed problems. Early works on optimizing RANS closure parameters include schemes like adjoint-based method [7], ensemble Kalman filter [8], and evolution methods such as the covariance matrix adaption evolution strategy. Instead of minimizing the error of the whole flow fields, the loss functions in these previous efforts usually are some aerodynamic coefficients, for example, the drag coefficient, lift coefficient, and the pitching moment coefficient when designing an airfoil.

In this work we use a physics-informed neural network (PINN) to calibrate the five parameters in turbulence model using the whole flow fields from high-fidelity simulations. The principal idea behind PINN is that: there are some principal physical laws that govern the time-dependent dynamics of a system (e.g. RANS turbulence model) and thus this prior information can act as a regularization agent that constrains the space of admissible solutions to a manageable size. For example, in incompressible fluid dynamics, we can discard any non-realistic flow solutions that violate the conservation of mass principle. In return, encoding such structured information into a learning algorithm results in amplifying the information content of the data that the algorithm sees, enabling it to quickly steer itself towards the right solution and generalize well even when only a few training examples are available. The PINN is then grounded in a principal physics model yet offers the flexibility of learned representations.

It is worth noting that our study is different from pure data-driven turbulence models, where researchers try to map a direct relationship between mean flow quantities with Reynolds stress. It is expected that a purely data-driven turbulence model is substantially more challenging than a physics-based model since a turbulence model requires to discover both the model form and model parameters whereas a purely data-driven model will abandon the abundant physics in the RANS turbulence model by only relying on the neural network to map the non-linear relationships. As such, the drawback of purely data-driven models is that training datasets play pivoting roles and thus this approach suffers from lack of extrapolation ability or poor generalization. Even though the model fits very well to training data, it cannot generalize well to unobserved test data. To overcome this drawback, the datasets are required to be sufficiently rich with great variability, which are generally not available. Despite recent efforts for efficient creation of datasets with encouraging results, generating the required training dataset size still requires substantial computational effort. Rather than improving the model-form error, our work only focuses on calibrating the uncertain parameters in the RANS model, that is, whether RANS simulations could be improved by using better parameters. This work has a similar concept of data assimilation, which involves combining observations (high-fidelity simulation data) with "prior knowledge" (mathematical representations of RANS turbulence model) to obtain an estimate of the true state (optimal parameters in RANS model). By exploiting inside the neural network training the underlying physical laws described by turbulence models, the PINN requires substantially less training data to achieve high accuracy. This work unlocks a range of opportunities in parameters tuning for fluid simulations.

The paper is organized as follows: Sect. 2 reviews the RANS $\kappa - \epsilon$ turbulence model, including two transport equations. Section 3 introduces the physics informed neural network and its specific application for RANS turbulence modeling. Section 4 runs a study case with the "flow over the bump" datasets. Section 5 concludes the paper.

2   RANS $\kappa - \epsilon$ Turbulence Model

The flow of a viscous incompressible fluid with constant properties is governed by the Navier-Stokes equations:

$$\frac{\partial u_i}{\partial t} + \frac{\partial (u_i u_j)}{\partial x_j} = -\frac{\partial p}{\partial x_i} + \nu \frac{\partial^2 u_i}{\partial x_j \partial x_j} \tag{1}$$

$$\frac{\partial u_i}{\partial x_j} = 0 \tag{2}$$

where u_i is the fluid velocity, p is the pressure (divided by the density ρ), ν is the fluid kinematic viscosity. In RANS, the Reynolds decomposition will decompose the dependent variables into mean and fluctuating parts:

$$u_i = \overline{u_i} + u_i', \; p = \overline{p} + p' \tag{3}$$

where $\overline{u_i}$ and $\overline{p}$ are ensemble averages of u_i and p, respectively, and u_i' and p' are the random fluctuations about the mean field. By substituting the decomposed terms into NS equation and taking an ensemble average, one obtains the system of partial differential equations that governs the mean-velocity and pressure fields of incompressible turbulence flow:

$$\frac{\partial \overline{u_i}}{\partial t} + \overline{u_j}\frac{\partial \overline{u_i}}{\partial x_j} = \frac{\partial \overline{p}}{\partial x_i} + \nu\frac{\partial^2 \overline{u_i}}{\partial x_j \partial x_j} - \frac{\partial \tau_{ij}}{\partial x_j} \tag{4}$$

$$\frac{\partial \overline{u_i}}{\partial x_j} = 0 \tag{5}$$

where $\tau_{ij} = \overline{u_i'u_j'}$ is the unclosed Reynolds-stress term that incorporates the effects of turbulence motions on the mean stresses. The Reynolds stress tensor contains six independent unknowns and solving equations requires approximating the Reynolds stress in terms of $u, \nabla u$, or other computable quantities. In the RANS $\kappa - \epsilon$ turbulence model, this term is approximated by the eddy-viscosity model as:

$$\tau_{ij} = \overline{u_i'u_j'} \approx \frac{2}{3}\kappa\delta_{ij} - 2\nu_T \overline{S_{ij}} \tag{6}$$

where κ is the average kinetic energy of the velocity fluctuations:

$$\kappa = \frac{1}{2}\overline{u_i'u_i'} \tag{7}$$

$\overline{S_{ij}}$ is the strain-rate tensor of the mean field:

$$\overline{S_{ij}} = \frac{1}{2}(\frac{\partial \overline{u_i}}{\partial x_j} + \frac{\partial \overline{u_j}}{\partial x_i}) \tag{8}$$

ν_T is the turbulent eddy viscosity, in the $\kappa - \epsilon$ turbulence model, this term is modeled as:

$$\nu_T = C_\mu\frac{\kappa^2}{\epsilon} \tag{9}$$

where ϵ is the rate of dissipation of turbulent kinetic energy as:

$$\epsilon = \nu\overline{\frac{\partial u_i'}{\partial x_j}\frac{\partial u_i'}{\partial x_j}} \tag{10}$$

The transport equations of turbulent kinetic energy and dissipation rate are:

$$\frac{\partial \kappa}{\partial t} + \overline{u_i}\frac{\partial \kappa}{\partial x_i} = -\tau_{ij}\frac{\partial \overline{u_i}}{\partial x_j} - \epsilon + \frac{\partial}{\partial x_i}(\frac{\nu_T}{\sigma_\kappa}\frac{\partial \kappa}{\partial x_i}) + \nu\frac{\partial^2 \kappa}{\partial x_i \partial x_i} \tag{11}$$

$$\frac{\partial \epsilon}{\partial t} + \overline{u_i}\frac{\partial \epsilon}{\partial x_i} = -C_{\epsilon 1}\frac{\epsilon}{\kappa}\tau_{ij}\frac{\partial \overline{u_i}}{\partial x_j} + \frac{\partial}{\partial x_i}(\frac{\nu_T}{\sigma_\epsilon}\frac{\partial \epsilon}{\partial x_i}) - C_{\epsilon 2}\frac{\epsilon^2}{\kappa} + \nu\frac{\partial^2 \kappa}{\partial x_i \partial x_i} \tag{12}$$

The two transport equations represent the turbulent properties of flow, they can account for history effects like convection and diffusion of turbulent energy.

Here κ can be thought of as the variable that determines the energy in the turbulence and the ϵ determines the turbulence scale. The five tunable parameters in the above two transport equations are: C_μ, $C_{\epsilon 1}$, $C_{\epsilon 2}$, σ_κ, $\dot{\sigma}_\epsilon$. Table 1 shows the various model constants that largely are used in CFD community. In previous efforts [9,10], the parameters are determined by requiring the turbulence model to satisfy experimental data for certain simple standard flow cases. In Launder and Sharma model, for example, the C_μ coefficient is obtained by considering the log-law region of a turbulent boundary layer. The $C_{\epsilon 1}$ is usually fixed from calibrations with homogeneous shear flows, and $C_{\epsilon 2}$ is usually determined from the decay rate of homogeneous, isotropic turbulence. The last two constants, σ_κ and σ_ϵ, are optimized by applying the model to various fundamental flows such as flow in channel, pipes, jets, wakes [11].

Table 1. Various $\kappa - \epsilon$ turbulence model [3,9,12,13] constants that are typically used in CFD models.

Parameter	Launder and Sahrma	Jones and Launder	Chien	Yakhot and Orszag
$C_{\epsilon 1}$	1.44	1.55	1.35	1.063
$C_{\epsilon 2}$	1.92	2.0	1.8	1.7215
C_μ	0.09	0.09	0.09	0.0837
σ_κ	1.0	1.0	1.0	0.7179
σ_ϵ	1.3	1.3	1.3	0.7179

Previous efforts on clousure coefficient identification include schemes like adjoint-based method [7], ensemble Kalman filter [8], the Bayesian inference combined with some high dimensional model representation technique [14], and more recently the Isogeometric Analysis for solving PDE-constrained optimization problems. The RANS model then requires case-sensitive parameters in a sense that each category of flow should have their own most suitable parameters [6,15]. Once the high-fidelity data is available, a flexible and efficient scheme that can easily identify the optimal parameters for a specific category of flow is thus imperative.

3   Physics-Informed Neural Network

The first glimpses of promise for exploiting structured prior information to construct data-efficient and physics-informed learning machines have already been showcased in recent studies [16–22]. Based on these prior successes, the principal idea behind the PINN is that the principal physical laws (usually in the form of differential equations) that govern the time-dependent dynamic system are treated as the prior, this prior information is embedded in the network loss function and then can act as a regularization that constrains the space of admissible neural network solutions. The benefits of encoding such structured information is that it enables a learning algorithm to quickly steer itself towards the right solution. Such neural networks are constrained to respect any symmetries, invariances, or conservation principles originating from the physical laws that govern the observed data. In incompressible fluid dynamics problems, for example, we can constrain the solution space by discarding any non-realistic flow solutions that violate the conservation of mass principle.

Figure 1 shows the architecture of physics informed neural network for turbulence modeling application. A feedforward neural network is constructed to map the relationship between the coordinates, velocity with the turbulent kinetic energy and dissipation rate. The five tunable parameters in the RANS model are unknowns that we wish the PINN to optimize. The network's loss function combines the mean squared error loss with physical constraints as:

$$L = \frac{1}{N}\sum(\kappa^{real} - \kappa^{pred})^2 + \frac{1}{N}\sum(\epsilon^{real} - \epsilon^{pred})^2 + \omega_f * f + \omega_g * g \qquad (13)$$

where the MSE of κ and ϵ denote the mean squared error loss corresponding to the initial high-fidelity data, the f and g enforce the physics by penalizing any deviations of the predicted physical law. They are defined based on the two transport equations as:

$$f = \frac{\partial \kappa}{\partial t} + \overline{u_i}\frac{\partial \kappa}{\partial x_i} + \tau_{ij}\frac{\partial \overline{u_i}}{\partial x_j} + \epsilon - \frac{\partial}{\partial x_i}(\frac{\nu_T}{\sigma_\kappa}\frac{\partial \kappa}{\partial x_i}) - \nu\frac{\partial^2 \kappa}{\partial x_i \partial x_i} \qquad (14)$$

$$g = \frac{\partial \epsilon}{\partial t} + \overline{u_i}\frac{\partial \epsilon}{\partial x_i} + C_{\epsilon 1}\frac{\epsilon}{\kappa}\tau_{ij}\frac{\partial \overline{u_i}}{\partial x_j} - \frac{\partial}{\partial x_i}(\frac{\nu_T}{\sigma_\epsilon}\frac{\partial \epsilon}{\partial x_i}) + C_{\epsilon 2}\frac{\epsilon^2}{\kappa} - \nu\frac{\partial^2 \kappa}{\partial x_i \partial x_i} \qquad (15)$$

We did not need to specify the geometry or the boundary and initial conditions in the loss as other PINNs do. The parameters are calibrated not only by minimizing the squared residuals over specified collocation points, but the two transport equations are also embedded to constrain possible neural network solutions. The model parameters can be calibrated according to:

$$C_{\epsilon 1}, C_{\epsilon 2}, C_\mu, \sigma_\kappa, \sigma_\epsilon = argmin\ L \qquad (16)$$

Minimizing the loss function is usually performed using backpropagation in neural network models. In backpropagation, the gradients of an objective function with respect to the weights and biases of a deep neural network are calculated by starting off from the network output and propagating back towards the input layer using the chain rule. With the customized loss, the neural network is optimized under partial differential equation constraints. While it seems that the loss function (embedded with transport equations) is too sophisticated to quickly get the gradient, the truth is that the differential operations in the transport equations are easily adapted and implemented in the deep learning platform, as the backpropagation in TensorFlow and the derivatives computation are implemented in automatic differentiation. The differential operations in the transport equations can be easily embedded in the computational graph by

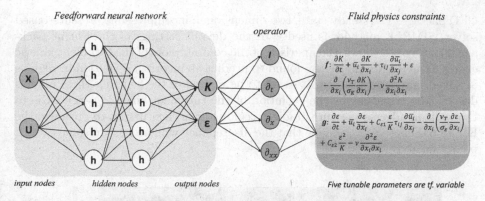

Fig. 1. The architecture of physics informed neural network for turbulence modeling application.

taking advantage of the chain rule in automatic differentiation. The loss function is then fully differentiable yet enforced with the PDE constraints.

Automatic differentiation in general, and the back-propagation algorithm is currently the dominant approach for training deep models by taking their derivatives with respect to the parameters (e.g., weights and biases) of the model. Here, we use the exact same automatic differentiation techniques, employed by the deep learning community, to physics-inform neural networks by taking their derivatives with respect to their input coordinates (i.e., space and time) where the physics is described by partial differential equations. It has been empirically observed that this structured approach introduces a regularization mechanism that allows us to use relatively simple feed-forward neural network architectures and train them with small amounts of data.

4   Case Study: Channel Flow with a Lower Curved Wall

The high-fidelity DNS dataset is composed of DNS of converging-diverging turbulent channel flows at two Reynolds numbers ($Re_\tau = 395$ and $Re_\tau = 617$) [23,24]. The dataset is from turbulent boundary layers (TBL) with strong adverse pressure gradient. It is critical to understand flow which undergoes separation and subsequent turbulent reattachment in the TBL to correctly predict the efficiency of many aerodynamic devices. Such turbulent flows have been regarded as being among the most challenging flow dynamics to predict using turbulence models [25]. It is thus of great interests to study whether turbulence models leveraging high-fidelity data can have a more satisfactory performance. The dataset includes 438 and 930 3D velocity and pressure fields for the two Reynolds respectively [26]. All the terms involved in the balance of each Reynolds stress component are provided. These DNS have been designed to test and validate turbulence model as flat channel flow data are used for inflow condition. The RANS calculations are performed using the Ansys Fluent v.14.0 commercial

CFD package. The steady-state, two-dimensional, incompressible pressure-based solver, SIMPLE method, is used with the default settings of the Fluent package [27]. Figure 2 shows a comparison of the contour plots of the turbulent kinetic energy. The RANS models are found to predict an incorrect evolution in regions of adverse pressure gradient. It seems to be related to the fact that these models do not correctly describe the evolution of the turbulent kinetic energy close to the walls in adverse pressure gradient regions. It is then urgent to optimize the RANS parameters in the hope that the discrepancy will, at least to some extent, be attenuated.

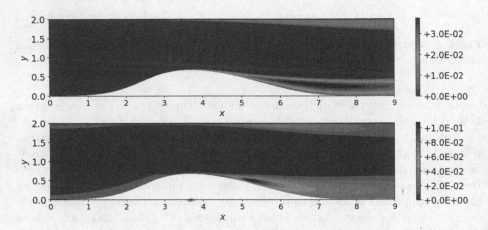

Fig. 2. A comparison of the contour plots of the time averaged turbulent kinetic energy (top) RANS (bottom) DNS when $Re_\tau = 395$.

To improve the RANS performance, we calibrate the five tunable parameters by the PINNs with the DNS data. The velocities, velocity gradients, pressure, along with other terms involved in the turbulent kinetic energy budgets are time and spanwise-averaged. The pre-processed DNS data are feed to the PINNs to optimize the five parameters by minimizing the customized loss function. The optimized parameters from the PINNs are:

$$C_{\epsilon 1} = 1.302, \ C_{\epsilon 2} = 1.862, \ C_\mu = 0.090, \ \sigma_\kappa = 0.750, \ \sigma_\epsilon = 0.273 \qquad (17)$$

Figures 3 and 4 show the comparison of the time averaged turbulent kinetic energy and dissipation rate from different simulations (top) DNS, (middle) Default RANS, (bottom) PINNs RANS. It is clear there is a big discrepancy between DNS with RANS, especially near the downstream wall region, where the adverse pressure gradient is most severe. While it is not very intuitive to tell from the contour plots, nevertheless, it is not hard to see that RANS with PINNs inferred parameters (bottom ones) are more closely agree to the DNS data than the RANS with default parameters (middle ones).

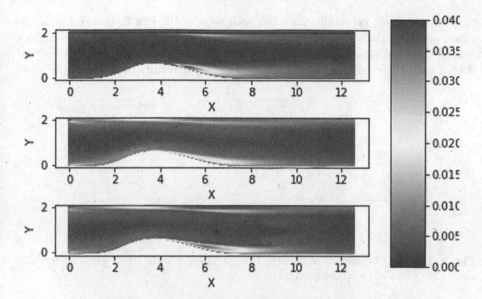

Fig. 3. A prior: Comparison of the time averaged turbulent kinetic energy from different simulations (top) DNS, (middle) Default RANS, (bottom) PINNs RANS.

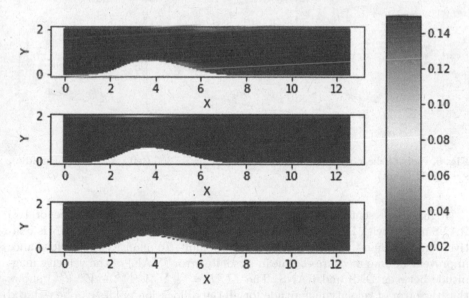

Fig. 4. A prior: Comparison of the time averaged dissipation rate from different simulations (top) DNS, (middle) Default RANS, (bottom) PINNs RANS.

To have a more straightforward understanding of the performance comparison, we plot the mean profiles of velocity and turbulence kinetic energy at three locations. These plots can allow us to more closely examine the difference of

146   S. Luo et al.

three simulations, especially near the wall region. Figures 5, 6 and 7 plot the mean profile of turbulent kinetic energy (TKE), x- and y- velocity along the y axis at three location when x = 5.7306, x = 6.1399, and x = 6.5493. It shows that RANS with PINN inferred parameters gives better results near the wall region.

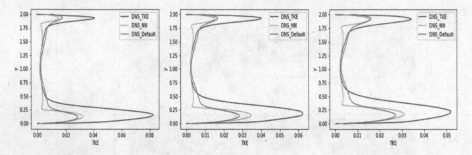

Fig. 5. Plots of the turbulent kinetic energy along y axis when x = 5.7306 (left), x = 6.1399 (middle), x = 6.5493 (right).

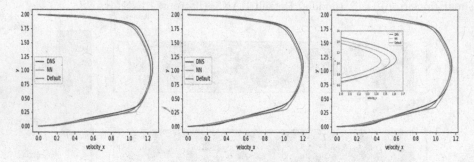

Fig. 6. Plots of the x-velocity along y axis when x = 5.7306 (left), x = 6.1399 (middle), x = 6.5493 (right).

Figure 8 presents the error contour plots showing the difference of two RANS models with DNS results. Apparently, the error between DNS-NN is relatively smaller than the error between DNS-Default. To quantify the performance improvements, we measure the mean absolute error (MAE) of the velocity magnitude between DNS and RANS. The $MAE = \frac{1}{N}\sum|V^{DNS} - V^{RANS}|$ shows that the error of velocity magnitude for all the collocation points can be reduced by 22% (from 0.069 to 0.054).

It is recognizable that while there is some improvement for the RANS with inferred parameters from PINNs, the error between RANS and DNS is still noteworthy. This inaccuracy is due to RANS's inherent simplifications rather than the inappropriate use of RANS constants which are usually estimated by fitting to experimental results of simple flows. If a more accurate result is required, switching to a more sophisticated model like LES is a more feasible option.

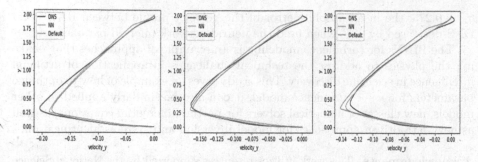

Fig. 7. Plots of the y-velocity along y axis when x = 5.7306 (left), x = 6.1399 (middle), x = 6.5493 (right).

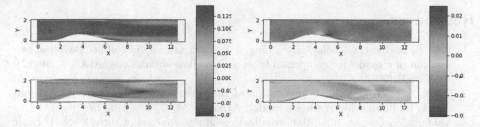

Fig. 8. A posteriori: Comparison of the error contour plots between RANS and DNS (left is the x-velocity, right is the y-velocity). (top) error between DNS-Default; (bottom) error between DNS-PINNs, apparently the error in the bottom is relatively smaller than the error in the top.

5   Conclusion

While high fidelity fluid simulations on high performance computing clusters have received great attention in recent years [28,29], RANS simulations remain the workhorse CFD method for industrial applications. In this paper we demonstrated an alternative method to calibrate the parameters in the RANS turbulence model with high-fidelity DNS data. We leveraged high-resolution DNS data to train a deep neural network to learn the mapping between the low-resolution flow and its high-resolution counterpart. We used a physics informed neural network that is embedded with the turbulent transport equations, physical loss functions are proposed to explicitly impose information of the transport equations to deep learning networks. This approach solves an inverse problem by treating the five parameters in turbulence model as random variables, with the turbulent kinetic energy and dissipation rate as known quantities from DNS simulation. The objective is to optimize the five parameters in turbulence closures using the PINN leveraging limited data available from costly high-fidelity DNS data. We validated this method on two test cases of flow over bump. The recommended values were found to be $C_{\epsilon 1} = 1.302$, $C_{\epsilon 2} = 1.862$, $C_{\mu} = 0.09$, $\sigma_K = 0.75$,

$\sigma_\epsilon = 0.273$, the mean absolute error of the velocity profile between RANS and DNS decreased by 22% when used the neural network inferred parameters.

The PINNs for turbulence modeling is an example of approaches that "bake in" the physics to address the technical challenges in application of artificial intelligence in scientific discovery. This study gives an example of how to optimize parameters for $\kappa - \epsilon$ turbulence model, it can also be similarly applied to other models, new classes of numerical solvers for partial differential equations, as well as new data-driven approaches for model inversion and systems identification.

Acknowledgments. This work utilizes resources supported by the National Science Foundation's Major Research Instrumentation program, grant #1725729, as well as the University of Illinois at Urbana-Champaign.

References

1. Ray, J., Dechant, L., Lefantzi, S., Ling, J., Arunajatesan, S.: Robust Bayesian calibration of a model for compressible jet-in-crossflow simulations. AIAA J. **56**(12), 4893–4909 (2018)
2. Thies, A.T., Tam, C.K.: Computation of turbulent axisymmetric and nonaxisymmetric jet flows using the $\kappa - \epsilon$ model. AIAA J. **34**(2), 309–316 (1996)
3. Yakhot, V., Orszag, S.A.: Renormalization group analysis of turbulence. I. Basic theory. J. Sci. Comput. **1**(1), 3–51 (1986)
4. Durbin, P.A.: Separated flow computations with the $\kappa - \epsilon$-v-squared model. AIAA J. **33**(4), 659–664 (1995)
5. Shih, T., Liou, W.W., Shabbir, A., Yang, Z., Zhu, J.: A new $\kappa - \epsilon$ eddy viscosity model for high reynolds number turbulent flows. Comput. Fluids **24**(3), 227–238 (1995)
6. Shirzadi, M., Mirzaei, P.A., Naghashzadegan, M.: Improvement of k-epsilon turbulence model for CFD simulation of atmospheric boundary layer around a high-rise building using stochastic optimization and monte carlo sampling technique. J. Wind Eng. Ind. Aerodyn. **171**, 366–379 (2017)
7. Dow, E., Wang, Q.: Quantification of structural uncertainties in the $\kappa - w$ turbulence model, p. 1762 (2011)
8. Kato, H., Obayashi, S.: Statistical approach for determining parameters of a turbulence model, pp. 2452–2457 (2012)
9. Launder, B.E., Sharma, B.: Application of the energy-dissipation model of turbulence to the calculation of flow near a spinning disc. Lett. Heat Mass Transf. **1**(2), 131–137 (1974)
10. Hanjalić, K., Launder, B.E.: A reynolds stress model of turbulence and its application to thin shear flows. J. Fluid Mech. **52**(4), 609–638 (1972)
11. Platteeuw, P., Loeven, G., Bijl, H.: Uncertainty quantification applied to the k-epsilon model of turbulence using the probabilistic collocation method, p. 2150 (2008)
12. Jones, W., Launder, B.E.: The prediction of laminarization with a two-equation model of turbulence. Int. J. Heat Mass Transf. **15**(2), 301–314 (1972)
13. Chien, K.: Predictions of channel and boundary-layer flows with a low-reynolds-number turbulence model. AIAA J. **20**(1), 33–38 (1982)
14. Zhang, J., Fu, S.: An efficient approach for quantifying parameter uncertainty in the SST turbulence model. Comput. Fluids **181**, 173–187 (2019)

15. Schaefer, J., Hosder, S., West, T., Rumsey, C., Carlson, J., Kleb, W.: Uncertainty quantification of turbulence model closure coefficients for transonic wall-bounded flows. AIAA J. **55**(1), 195–213 (2017)
16. Raissi, M., Perdikaris, P., Karniadakis, G.E.: Physics-informed neural networks: a deep learning framework for solving forward and inverse problems involving nonlinear partial differential equations. J. Comput. Phys. **378**, 686–707 (2019)
17. Raissi, M., Karniadakis, G.E.: Hidden physics models: machine learning of nonlinear partial differential equations. J. Comput. Phys. **357**, 125–141 (2018)
18. Lu, L., Meng, X., Mao, Z., Karniadakis, G.E.: DeepXDE: a deep learning library for solving differential equations. arXiv preprint arXiv:1907.04502 (2019)
19. Mao, Z., Jagtap, A.D., Karniadakis, G.E.: Physics-informed neural networks for high-speed flows. Comput. Methods Appl. Mech. Eng. **360**, 112789 (2020)
20. Nabian, M.A., Meidani, H.: A deep neural network surrogate for high-dimensional random partial differential equations. arXiv preprint 1806 (2018)
21. Nabian, M.A., Meidani, H.: Physics-driven regularization of deep neural networks for enhanced engineering design and analysis. J. Comput. Inf. Sci. Eng. **20**(1), 011006 (2020)
22. Sirignano, J., Spiliopoulos, K.: DGM: a deep learning algorithm for solving partial differential equations. J. Comput. Phys. **375**, 1339–1364 (2018)
23. Marquillie, M., Laval, J., Dolganov, R.: Direct numerical simulation of a separated channel flow with a smooth profile. J. Turbul. **9**, N1 (2008)
24. Marquillie, M., Ehrenstein, U., Laval, J.: Instability of streaks in wall turbulence with adverse pressure gradient. J. Fluid Mech. **681**, 205–240 (2011)
25. Wilcox, D.C.: Turbulence Modeling for CFD. DCW Industries, La Canada (1998)
26. Benzi, R., Biferale, L., Bonaccorso, F., et al.: TurBase: a software platform for research in experimental and numerical fluid dynamics, pp. 51–57 (2017)
27. Jesus, A., Azevedo, J.L., Laval, J.: Large eddy simulations and RANS computations of adverse pressure gradient flows, p. 267 (2013)
28. Borrell, R., et al.: Parallel mesh partitioning based on space filling curves. Comput. Fluids **173**, 264–2724 (2018)
29. Vazquez, M., et al.: Alya: multiphysics engineering simulation toward exascale. J. Comput. Sci. **14**, 15–27 (2016)

HPC I/O in the Data Center
Workshop (HPC-IODC)

HPC I/O in the Data Center Workshop (HPC-IODC)

Julian M. Kunkel[1], Jay Lofstead[2], and Jean-Thomas Acquaviva[3]

[1] University of Reading, Whiteknights, Reading RG6 6AY, UK
j.m.kunkel@reading.ac.uk
[2] Center for Computing Research, Sandia National Laboratories,
Albuquerque, USA
gflofst@sandia.gov
[3] Data Direct Networks, France
jtacquaviva@ddn.com

1 Introduction

Many public and privately funded data centers host supercomputers for running large scale simulations and analyzing experimental and observational data. These super-computers run usually tightly coupled parallel applications that require hardware components that deliver the best performance. In contrast, commercial data centers, such as Facebook and Google, execute loosely coupled workloads with a broad assumption of regular failures. The dimension of the data centers is enormous. A 2013 article summarizes commercial data centers' dimensions [4]. It estimates, for example, that Facebook hosts around 100 PB of storage, and Google and Microsoft manage around 1 million servers each – although the hardware is split among several physical data centers – a modus operandi not suitable for HPC centers. With the increasing importance of using machine learning to reveal underlying patterns in data, the data storage rates are accelerating to feed these additional use cases. Combining traditional modeling and simulation with ML workloads yields both a write and read-intensive workload for a single workflow.

Management of the huge amount of data is vital for the effective use of the con-tained information. However, with limited budgets, it is a daunting task for data center operators, especially as the design and storage system required hardware depends heavily on the executed workloads. A co-factor of the increasing difficulty is the increase in complexity of the storage hierarchy with the adoption of SSD and memory class storage technology. The US Department of Energy recognizes the importance of data management, listing it among the top 10 research challenges for Exascale [3].

There are several initiatives, consortia and special tracks in conferences that target RD&E audiences. Examples are the Storage Networking Industry Association (SNIA) for enterprises, the Big Data and Extreme-Scale Computing (BDEC) initiative[1], the Parallel Data Systems Workshop (PDSW) and the HEC FSIO workshop [1].

---

[1] http://www.exascale.org/bdec/.

There are many I/O workloads studies and performance analysis reports for parallel I/O available. Additionally, many surveys of enterprise technology usage include predictions of analysis for future storage technology and the storage market [2]. However, the analysis conducted for HPC typically focuses on applications and not on the data center perspective. Information about data center operational aspects is usually described in file system-specific user groups and meetings or described partially in research papers as part of the evaluation environment.

In the HPC IODC workshop, we bring together I/O experts from data centers and application workflows to share current practices for scientific workflows, issues, and obstacles for both hardware and the software stack, and RD&E to overcome these issues.

Due to the COVID-19 crisis, the ISC conference changed to a digital edition. We preserved the nature of the workshop and organized it as a virtual full-day meeting on the regular workshop day with minimal changes to the agenda.

2   Organization of the Workshop

The workshop was organized by

- Julian Kunkel (*University of Reading, UK*)
- Jay Lofstead (*Sandia National Labs, USA*)
- Jean-Thomas Acquaviva (*DDN*)

The workshop is supported by the Centre of Excellence in Simulation of Weather and Climate in Europe (ESiWACE), the Virtual Institute for I/O (VI4IO)[2] and the Journal of High-Performance Storage (JHPS)[3].

The workshop covered three tracks:

- **Research paper presentations** – authors needed to submit a paper regarding relevant state-of-the-practice or research for I/O in the datacenter.
- **Talks from I/O experts** – authors needed to submit a rough outline for the talk related to the operational aspects of the data center.
- A moderated **discussion** to identify key issues and potential solutions in the community.

The CFP has been issued at the beginning of January. Important deadlines were:

- Submission deadline: 2020-04-15 AoE
- Author notification: 2020-05-03
- Workshop: 2020-06-25
- Camera-ready papers: 2020-07-25

From all submissions, the program committee selected three talks from I/O experts and eleven research papers for presentation during the workshop.

---

[2] http://vi4io.org.

[3] https://jhps.vi4io.org/.

2.1 Program Committee

- Thomas Boenisch *(High-performance Computing Center Stuttgart)*
- Suren Byna *(Lawrence Berkeley National Laboratory)*
- Matthew Curry *(Sandia National Laboratories)*
- Sandro Fiore *(CMCC)*
- Wolfgang Frings *(Juelich Supercomputing Centre)*
- Javier Garcia Blas *(Carlos III University)*
- Adrian Jackson *(The University of Edinburgh)*
- Ivo Jimenez *(University of California, Santa Cruz)*
- Anthony Kougkas *(Illinois Institute of Technology)*
- Glenn Lockwood *(Lawrence Berkeley National Laboratory)*
- Jay Lofstead *(Sandia National Laboratories)*
- Carlos Maltzahn *(University of California, Santa Cruz)*
- Suzanne McIntosh *(New York University)*
- Maria Perez *(Technical University of Madrid)*
- Robert Ross *(Argonne National Laboratory)*
- George S. Markomanolis *(Oak Ridge National Laboratory)*
- Feiyi Wang *(Oak Ridge National Laboratory)*
- Bing Xie *(Oak Ridge National Lab)*

3 Workshop Summary

Over the full-day program, about 40 attendees were constantly connected to the virtual session. More than 100 participants expressed their interest to be informed about the workshop slides and presentations. In spite of the workshop being held online squarely on British Time making attending from North America more difficult. This is in line with the in-person attendance at previous instances and included many North American attendees, including some from the American west coast.

We had a good mix of talks from I/O experts, data center relevant research, and two discussion sessions. A short summary of the presentations is given in the following. The slides and video recordings of the presentations are available on the workshop's webpage: https://hps.vi4io.org/events/2020/iodc.

3.1 Research Papers

We have shifted our peer review process to be more community building oriented. Last year, we changed the review process to shepherd all papers with a solid core, but potentially presentation flaws, to help develop them so that they are acceptable for publication. If a paper cannot be successfully be revised in time for the workshop, it will be rejected. We find this approach is better for building an interactive community.

Our goal was to create a more open, fully interactive process for quickly developing research papers into quality publishable results.

To support this activity, we were excited to explore the open review process of the Journal of High-Performance Storage for the research track – the papers were publicly shared using GoogleDoc in the JHPS incubator and open for comments. We allowed authors to submit extended papers that may be potentially accepted on JHPS while the 12-page shorter workshop submissions will be published in this edition of Springer's Lecture Notes on Computer Science together with the other ISC workshops as was done previously.

Unfortunately, due to COVID-19, we received notes from various authors that they would not be able to make the deadline, hence the number of submissions this year was lower than usual.

In the first research papers session, HPC-IODC was presenting three different talks sharing the same interest for I/O performance characterization and analysis. Each of these talks brings its own originality, either with the usage of none HPC API for high-performance storage, or taking into account network considerations for I/O, or machine learning techniques applied to IO analysis. The following presentation try to capture the presentation itself as some elements of the discussion triggered. In more details, the research presentation covered the following topics:

- **Characterizing I/O Optimization Effect Through Holistic Log Data Analysis of Parallel File Systems and Interconnects**
  Yuichi Tsujita, Yoshitaka Furutani, Hajime Hida, Keiji Yamamoto, Atsuya Uno
  In his presentation, Dr. Tsujita discussed the value of observing not only file system metrics but also networks aspect in order to understand the I/O behavior of an application. Â Regarding the result of these analyses, Dr. Tsujita notes the difference between observation and resolution: as a different toolbox is needed to optimize user-level I/O patterns. For instance, at the K computer, experts were providing hints or training to improve I/O specifically for the complex MPI-IO. It remains that most users preferred POSIX-I/O. Therefore, POSIX is now the highest priority issue. Discussing further the weight of user choices, the author notes that despite the availability of optimized MPI-IO libraries as dynamically loadable shared libraries, most of the users keep the default MPI-IO implementation. One motivation of this work is to raise awareness among the user community, and that access to profiling information could push users to have interests in advanced I/O optimization.
- **Investigating the Overhead of the REST Protocol to Reveal the Potential for Using Cloud Services for HPC Storage**
  Frank Gadban, Julian Kunkel, Thomas Ludwig
  This work investigated the relevance of cloud APIs to address performance-oriented tasks. The authors observe that a correctly configured *REST* service can deliver high performance and match MPI in terms of bandwidth, thus making *REST* a relevant alternative to MPI based IO tools. Bandwidth was not the only investigated metric and the authors monitor as well the CPU cost of operating data movement. They observed that MPI can lead to a poor ratio in terms of bandwidth/cycle. However, the discussion arises and the point was made that in HPC and MPI in particular, CPU cycles can be used to decrease latency for instance. Therefore in terms of methodology, a higher rate of idle cycles is not always positive, such metric would

systematically penalize spin locking a classic usage of CPU resources to improve latency and time-critical performance. In the aspect of performance optimization, specifically for complex systems where performance can be capped by any of its components, reporting not raw performance but efficiency in respect of the network throughput and CPU utilization could an interesting way to extrapolate the results on the different architectures (e.g. HDR200 or faster CPUs).

– **Classifying Temporal Characteristics of Job I/O Patterns Using Machine Learning Techniques**
  Eugen Betke, Julian Kunkel
  In this talk, the authors present their results on the classification of HPC jobs based on collected information on their I/O pattern. I/O bottlenecks are a multi-factorial artifact due to a combination of I/O Patterns + IO Configuration System + I/O Workload. The processed data set covers an impressive 1.000.000 jobs. This work follows a previous and published study focused on the identification of IO-intensive jobs. However, their experience has shown that for large systems I/O intensive jobs could be numerous and the single job is not the right granularity to provide support and help to end-users. This has been the key motivation to pursue the research effort in order to classify and to cluster jobs. This is the purpose of the present paper. The resulting classification scheme is lightweight enough to be operated as soon as a job is over but can not be performed on-line (during job execution), so the method is near-line. The proposed methodology did not achieve the point where it can characterize I/O, for example, at the moment, it can not tell if jobs in this and these clusters can have a negative impact on the metadata server. This is work in progress, and at this stage understanding, I/O is still a manual task. It remains that classification is an important step toward the goal of automation. The benefit at the moment is the following: assuming a job is identified as slowing down of a file system (e.g. massive meta-data operations), with a simple lookup it is possible to find the whole cluster of jobs that can potentially cause the same issue to the file system. During the discussion, a point was made on conceptual constraints induced by an approach based on Machine Learning and Deep Learning. The authors conclude their talk on a long term objective of a learning model representative of the whole complexity of HPC-IO systems.

– **A Reinforcement Learning Strategy to Tune Request Scheduling at the I/O Forwarding Layer**
  Jean Luca Bez, Francieli Zanon Boito, Ramon Nou, Alberto Miranda, Toni Cortes, Philippe O. A. Navaux
  I/O optimization techniques can improve performance for the access patterns they were designed to target, but they often decrease for others. Moreover, these techniques usually depend on the precise tune of their parameters, which commonly falls back to the users. The authors propose an approach to tune parameters dynamically at runtime based on the I/O workload observed by the system. Our focusing is on the I/O forwarding layer as it is transparent to applications and file system independent. The approach uses a reinforcement learning technique to make the system capable of learning the best parameter value to each observed access pattern during its execution, eliminating the need for a complex and time-

consuming training phase. The authors evaluated the proposal for the TWINS scheduling algorithm designed for the I/O forwarding layer seeking to reduce contention and coordinate accesses to the data servers. They demonstrate the approach can reach a precision of 88% on the parameter selection in the first hundreds of observations of an access pattern, achieving 99% of the optimal performance. After the talk, it was noted that a baseline to optimal performance is necessary for comparison reason, as a naive approach may already lead to good performance numbers.

- **Data Systems at Scale in Climate and Weather: Activities in the ESiWACE Project**

  Julian Kunkel and the ESiWACE4 team.

  The ESiWACE project aims to enable global eddy-resolving weather and climate simulations on the upcoming (pre-)Exascale supercomputers. In this talk, a selection of efforts to mitigate the effects of the data deluge from such high-resolution simulations is introduced. In particular, the speaker described the advances in the Earth System Data Middleware (ESDM), which enables scalable data management and supports the inhomogeneous storage stack. ESDM provides a NetCDF compatible layer at a high-performance and portable-portable fashion. A selection of performance results was given and ongoing efforts for workflow support and active storage are discussed.

- **Phobos a scale-out object store implementing tape library support**

  Patrice Lucas, Philippe Deniel, Thomas Leibovici Phobos is an open-source scale-out distributed object store providing access to multiple backends from flash and hard drives to tape libraries. Very large datasets can be efficiently managed on inexpensive storage media without giving up performance, scalability or fault-tolerance. Phobos is designed to offer several data layouts, such as mirroring or erasure coding. IOs through tape drives are optimized by dedicated resource scheduling policies. Developed at CEA, Phobos is in production since 2016 to manage the France Genomique multi-petabyte dataset at TGCC.

3.2   Talks from Experts

The following talks from experts included some basic information about the site and typical application profiles but focus on information regarding I/O tools and strategies applied to mitigate the pressing issues. The first session of three experts talks are presenting aspect from production environments, the topics are rather diverse but the goal is shared: making a high-performance storage service to end-users available.

- **The ALICE data management pipeline**

  Massimo Lamanna

  ALICE is an experiment at CERN generating a large volume of data, in the range of 60PB. The data processing pipeline is complex starting with a very fast ingest phase in the range of 3.5 TB/sec. This phase is embarrassingly parallel and data can be compressed in the range x6. In the second phase, compressed data percolate through a compute-intensive process. The process refines and compresses further data, eventually leading to an additional factor x6 of compression. This later stage of compression is not completely lossless and is run on a large GPU farm. Previous experiments at CERN were relying on data replication as a protection scheme ALICE will be the first experiment using massively Erasure Code. The workload will be dominated by large files. Ceph would be a natural candidate for ALICE. In this respect, CERN has a dual policy toward Ceph: promotion and support. As an example, Ceph has been considered for OpenStack and Ceph is offered as a service in CERN alternatively to the homegrown file system EOS, but CERN tends to rely on EOS for extremely large configurations. EOS uses for some use cases Ceph as a back-end. The benefit of EOS is that CERN can shape the software to be exactly as needed and to satisfy specific requirements.

- **Accelerating your Application I/O with UnifyFS**
  Kathryn Mohror
  UnifyFS is an on-going effort initiated at Lawrence Livermore National Laboratory focuses on the development of a file system harnessing node-local storage resources. The motivation is the renewed importance of node-local storage with the emergence of Storage Class Memory. To limit the cost of synchronization and communication between peers of UnifyFS the system alleviates the POSIX constraints. Data are publicized when an explicit laminating process occurs. The lamination is quite similar to synchronization between the peer but the file is made immutable. Lamination is either implicit when a file is closed or explicit when *chmod()* is called. It should be noticed that lamination is about the content (file data) or not on the file path or metadata. The distance taken with the strict POSIX semantic is bringing performance improvements as illustrated by benchmark results or workload similar to checkpoint-restart.

- **How to recognise I/O bottlenecks and what to do about them**
  Rosemary Francis
  Rosemary Francis is the CEO of Ellexus company, a start-up specialized in I/O optimization and profiling. Ellexus develops two different products: Mistral and Breeze. Breeze allows an in-depth analysis of the I/O activity but generates a large amount of log information, in the range of *strace*. In order to integrate an I/O profiler within a job life-cycle, the second tool Mistral is more suitable. From her extensive operational knowledge of I/O management, Dr. Francis observes that AI applications are newer and cleaner: no legacy code or legacy libraries, consequently IO patterns tend to be much cleaner and saner. Furthermore, she observes that AI IO patterns are agnostic to parallelism, using a small size configuration it is easy to extrapolate the IO behavior on a larger system. For instance, insights collected on a single desktop have allowed the speaker to detect and fix an x3 performance issue on the whole cluster. The root cause of the performance issue was a misconfiguration in the Linux settings.

- **Managing Decades of Scientific Data in Practice at NERSC**
  Glenn Lockwood
  The National Energy Research Scientific Computing Center (NERSC) has been operating since 1974 and has been storing and preserving user data continuously for over 45 years as a result. This has resulted in NERSC building significant expertise in how to store and manage user data for long periods of time–a decade or more–

and the practical factors that must be considered when data must be retained for longer than the lifetime of the physical components of the data center, including the entire data center facility itself. As the relevance of HPC extends beyond modeling and simulation and the usable lifetime of data extends from months to years or decades, these best practices in long-term data stewardship are likely to become more important to more HPC facilities. To this end, the speaker presented some of the practical considerations, best practices, and lessons learned from managing the scientific data of NERSC's thousands of users over a period of four decades.

– **Portable Validations of Scientific Explorations with Container-native Workflows**
Ivo Jimenez

Researchers working in the computer, computational, or data science often find it difficult to reproduce experiments from artifacts like code, data, diagrams, and results which are left behind by previous researchers. The code developed on one machine often fails to run on other machines due to differences in hardware architecture, OS, software dependencies, among others. This is accompanied by the difficulty in understanding how artifacts are organized, as well as in using them in the correct order. Software container technology such as Docker, can solve most of the practical issues of portability, and in particular, container-native workflow engines can significantly aid experimenters in their work. In this talk, Popper was introduced, a container-native workflow engine that executes each step of a workflow in a separate dedicated container without assuming the presence of a Kubernetes cluster or any cloud-based Kubernetes service. With Popper, researchers can build and validate workflows easily in almost any environment of their choice including local machines, SLURM based HPC clusters, CI services, or Kubernetes based cloud computing environments. To exemplify the suitability of this workflow engine, three case studies with examples from Machine Learning and High-Performance Computing are turned into Popper workflows. It was also discussed how Popper can be used to aid in preparing artifacts associated with article submissions to conferences and journals, and in particular give an overview of the Journal of High-Performance Storage, a new eJournal that combines open reviews, living papers, digital reproducibility, and open access.

– **Tuning I/O Performance on Summit: HDF5 Write Use Case Study**
Xie Bing

The HDF5 I/O library is widely used in HPC across a variety of domain sciences for its simplicity, flexibility, and rich performance-tuning space. In this work, the authors addressed an observed HDF5 write performance issue on Summit at OLCF, which in particular is the poor write performance of HDF5 with the default configuration. To identify the performance issue, they developed an I/O benchmarking methodology to profile the HDF5 performance on Summit across scales, compute-node allocations, I/O configurations, and times. They developed a solution to the issue by altering the HDF5 alignment configuration which resulted in a 100x write performance improvement for the VPIC benchmark. The speaker expects the methodology and solution to be applicable to other platforms and technologies.

3.3 Discussion Sessions

The major distinguishing feature for this workshop compared to other venues is the discussion rounds. The opportunity for themed, open discussions about issues both pressing and relevant to the data center community facilitates sharing experiences, solutions, and problems.

Albeit the workshop was virtual, the discussion covered aspects around APIs, benchmarking, node-local IO vs. shared storage, setting defaults for users, storage, and code maintenance.

References

1. Bancroft, M., Bent, J., Felix, E., Grider, G., Nunez, J., Poole, S., Ross, R., Salmon, E., Ward, L.: Hec FSIO 2008 workshop report. In: High End Computing Interagency Working Group (HECIWG), Sponsored File Systems and I/O Workshop HEC FSIO (2009)
2. IDC: Enterprise storage services survey. http://www.idc.com/getdoc.jsp?containerId=254468
3. Lucas, R., committee members: Top ten exascale research challenges, February 2014. http://science.energy.gov/~/media/ascr/ascac/pdf/meetings/20140210/Top10reportFEB14.pdf
4. StorageServers Blog: Facts and stats of world's largest data centers, July 2013. https://storageservers.wordpress.com/2013/07/17/facts-and-stats-of-worlds-largest-data-centers/

Investigating the Overhead of the REST Protocol When Using Cloud Services for HPC Storage

Frank Gadban[1]([✉]), Julian Kunkel[2], and Thomas Ludwig[3]

[1] University of Hamburg, 20146 Hamburg, Germany
frank.gadban@studium.uni-hamburg.de
[2] Reading University, Reading, UK
[3] DKRZ, 20146 Hamburg, Germany

Abstract. With the significant advances in Cloud Computing, it is inevitable to explore the usage of Cloud technology in HPC workflows. While many Cloud vendors offer to move complete HPC workloads into the Cloud, this is limited by the massive demand of computing power alongside storage resources typically required by I/O intensive HPC applications. It is widely believed that HPC hardware and software protocols like MPI yield superior performance and lower resource consumption compared to the HTTP transfer protocol used by RESTful Web Services that are prominent in Cloud execution and Cloud storage. With the advent of enhanced versions of HTTP, it is time to reevaluate the effective usage of cloud-based storage in HPC and their ability to cope with various types of data-intensive workloads. In this paper, we investigate the overhead of the REST protocol via HTTP compared to the HPC-native communication protocol MPI when storing and retrieving objects. Albeit we compare the MPI for a communication use case, we can still evaluate the impact of data communication and, therewith, the efficiency of data transfer for data access patterns. We accomplish this by modeling the impact of data transfer using measurable performance metrics. Hence, our contribution is the creation of a performance model based on hardware counters that provide an analytical representation of data transfer over current and future protocols. We validate this model by comparing the results obtained for REST and MPI on two different cluster systems, one equipped with Infiniband and one with Gigabit Ethernet. The evaluation shows that REST can be a viable, performant, and resource-efficient solution, in particular for accessing large files.

Keywords: HPC · Cloud · Convergence · HTTP2 · RESTful APIs · HTTP3 · Storage

1 Introduction

High-Performance Computing (HPC) utilizes clusters of powerful and fast interconnected computers that can handle complex and data-intensive computational

© Springer Nature Switzerland AG 2020
H. Jagode et al. (Eds.): ISC High Performance 2020 Workshops, LNCS 12321, pp. 161–176, 2020.
https://doi.org/10.1007/978-3-030-59851-8_10

problems. These systems are managed by batch schedulers [29] where user jobs are queued to be served based on resource usage and availability and without any visibility or concerns on the costs of running jobs. Due to various factors, Cloud Computing [30] gained popularity over the last decade. This has led to the emergence of the *HPC Cloud*, where Cloud providers offer high-end hardware platforms and software environments to run HPC applications.

Due to its simplicity, reliability, flexibility, and consistency, HTTP is the de facto standard for accessing object storage like Amazon S3 [2], OpenStack Swift, and EMC Atmos. A wide adoption of cloud storage in HPC requires the evaluation of the suitability of using HTTP in the HPC environment as an alternative to HPC-native communication protocols like MPI.

In this work, we first provide a detailed examination of the HTTP protocol and its performance in terms of latency and throughput under different conditions for accessing remote data. Secondly, we elaborate on an analytic performance model for data transfer over several protocols, this model allows us to compare current and future protocols in a common framework and will help us predict protocol performance in different hardware environments. We perform several benchmarks comparing MPI to HTTP and use our model to validate the obtained results. Finally, and based on the evaluation, we pinpoint the cause of the HTTP overhead and find that TCP is not the ideal transport protocol for HTTP and that new versions of the HTTP protocol, like HTTP3 which uses UDP, might accelerate the usage of cloud storage in HPC. The structure of this paper is as follows: Sect. 2 represents the related work. Section 3 describes the test scenarios and defines the relevant metrics that will be addressed using our benchmarks. Section 4 describes the experimental procedure, the used systems, and the methodology of the evaluation conducted in this work. Section 5 analyzes the obtained results. The last section summarizes our findings.

2   Related Work

In the world of HPC, computational performance has long exceeded the performance of the traditional file-centric storage systems since the POSIX file system interface was hardly suitable for data management on supercomputers [41]. Many workarounds to address this issue were proposed, some of them tried to introduce evolved I/O algorithms in MPI, like Data aggregation/sieving in ROMIO [37] or to implement different data organizations on the back-end storage, like PLFS [3] or to introduce richer data formats for example HDF5, NetCDF [12]. Eventually and although a file represents a convenient way to store the data, the ideal concept for scientific computing/HPC would be rather the use of a data object model [26] where all levels of metadata are encapsulated. In object storage, data is exposed as objects instead of files or blocks. Each object typically includes the data itself, a globally unique identifier used to find the object over a distributed system and a variable amount of metadata that describes the data. Objects are often accessed directly from the client application, usually using a RESTful API [35]. As such, any comprehensive performance study of an object storage system should take into consideration the latency introduced by a RESTful system. Many researchers have tried to solve data transfer issues through HTTP; some [25] proposed encapsulating TCP data in UDP payloads, others [8] proposed a dynamic connection pool implemented by using the HTTP Keep-Alive feature to maximize the usage of open TCP connections and minimize the effect of the TCP slow start. Intel® is marketing DAOS [28] as the ultimate Open Source Object Store, nonetheless with a high vendor Lock-in potential since the promised performance can only be achieved on its own proprietary Optane [40] storage Hardware. Since Infiniband [1] is one of the most commonly used interconnects in HPC, the performance of IP over Infiniband [4,15] has been thoroughly studied, however, the performance of HTTP over IP over IB did not get much attention. Our approach to model and analyze the viability of HTTP over Infiniband using performance counters is explained in the next section.

3   Methodology

The two major efficiency indicators addressed in our study are latency and throughput. To our knowledge, few tried to assess the Performance of a REST Service inside HPC, i.e., within a high-performance network. This is why we introduce a modeling approach, based on performance counters, then we perform an evaluation on a testbed, consisting of a content server and a client application consuming the content. Our benchmark for storage access emulates a best-case scenario (HTTP GET Operation/Read Only Scenario from a "remote" Storage Server) because we only want to test the viability and base performance of REST/HTTP as an enabling technology for an object-store. The model with the performance counters can nevertheless be extended to assess and measure the resource consumption of different object storage implementations. The tools and the accomplished tests will be extensively described in Sect. 4. To identify the major factors impacting the performance, we vary the underlying hardware and the connection mechanism (Ethernet, Infiniband, RDMA) between the server and the client. Finally, to validate our model, we compare its predictions with the experimentally observed values.

3.1   Performance Model

To define our performance model, many metrics are considered, which depict the used hardware, the software stack, and the network protocol in use. Alongside the standard network metrics, we focus on hardware counters of the CPU namely the number of required CPU cycles to identify the processing cost of a data transfer and the L3 evicted memory, this can be used further to check the memory efficiency of the different implementations. In a first step, we consider TCP as a transport protocol, however, the model is later extended in Sect. 5 to cover MPI. The metrics involved can be summarized as follows. *Fixed system parameters:*

- R: CPU clock rate in Hz
- rtt: round trip time
- mtu: maximum transfer unit
- mss: maximum segment size, transmission protocol dependent (see Eq. (4))
- mem_tp: the memory throughput i.e. speed of data eviction from L3 to main memory.
- eBW [5]: is the effective bandwidth between client and server.

Experiment-specific configurations and results:

- Obj_size: file size transferred from the server to be read by the client.
- Nreq: number of requests achieved in 60 sec
- Ncon: number of open connections kept
- Nthr: number of CPU threads executing the benchmark on the client.

Observable metrics (e.g., using Likwid):

- CUC: number of unhalted cycles on each core
- L3EV: amount of data volume loaded and evicted from/to L3 from the perspective of CPU cores [16,21], L3EVs and L3EVc are for server and client respectively.
- PLR: the packet loss rate, proportional to the number of parallel connections.

In our preliminary model t(request) is the time starting from the sending of the first byte of the request to the time the complete response is received:

$$t(request) = t(client) + t(network) + t(server) \tag{1}$$

where t(client), t(network), t(server) are the time fractions needed by the client, network and server respectively to accomplish the request:

$$t(client) = t(compute) + t(memory) + t(cpu\_client\_busy) \tag{2}$$

$$t(server) = t(compute) + t(memory) + t(cpu\_server\_busy) + t(pending) \tag{3}$$

As a rough estimation of the network throughput when using the TCP protocol, and based on the Mathis et. al. formula [18], while presuming that the TCP window is optimally configured, we can safely assume that:

$$net\_tp = \min\{\frac{mss \cdot C}{RTT \cdot \sqrt{PLR}}, eBW\} \tag{4}$$

where $C = 1$ and $mss = mtu-40$ in case of Ethernet. From this we can calculate t_net:

$$t\_net = Obj\_size/net\_tp + t\_queuing \tag{5}$$

For the sake of simplicity, we suppose that the routing devices between the nodes don't add any latency and as such we can neglect t_queuing The execution time t(compute) can then be defined as:

$$t(compute) = CUC/R \tag{6}$$

t(memory) is the time to traverse the different memory caches, usually narrowed down to:

$$t(memory) = L3EV/mem\_tp \tag{7}$$

Putting it all together, and in the case of intra-node communication, we can safely assume that:

$$t(request) = \frac{CUCs}{Rs} + \frac{L3EVs}{mem\_tp} + \frac{CUCc}{Rc} + \frac{L3EVc}{mem\_tp} + \frac{Obj\_size}{net\_tp} \tag{8}$$

Generalizing a bit further, we end up with:

$$t(request) = \alpha \cdot rtt + \beta_1 \cdot \frac{CUCs}{Rs} + \beta_2 \cdot \frac{L3EVs}{mem\_tp} + \beta_3 \cdot \frac{CUCc}{Rc} + \beta_4 \cdot \frac{L3EVc}{mem\_tp} + \beta_5 \cdot \frac{Obj\_size}{net\_tp} \tag{9}$$

Where α is a weighting factor $(0 \leq \alpha < 1)$ [20], β_i are platform and protocol dependent factors to be evaluated in a later section. As such, many factors can influence the above starting from the application delivering the content which affects server CPU and memory usage, those metrics are also affected by the type of client consuming the data as well as by the networking protocol in use and the path traversed by the data. In the following sections, we validate this model while comparing the performance of HTTP over different types of hardware and connection protocols.

4   Experiments

The tests were performed on two different hardware platforms: the first is the WR Cluster, a small test system, equipped with Intel Xeon 5650 processors and Gbit Ethernet, the second is the Mistral supercomputer [9], the HPC system for earth-system research at the German Climate Computing Center (DKRZ), it provides 3000 compute nodes each equipped with an FDR Infiniband interconnect. The nodes used for the testing are equipped with two Intel Broadwell processors (E5-2680 @2.5 GHz) [23]

4.1   Benchmark and Analysis Tools

The RESTful API is the typical way to realize access to object storage, and as such the tools used in this article were preliminary developed to assess HTTP performance. The first experiment checks the latency introduced by a simple web server serving static files, the setup, shown in Fig. 1, consists of the lighttpd web server [24] hosting files of different sizes. These files contain randomly generated data, and are placed initially in the in-memory file system (tmpfs) to minimize any storage-related overhead such as disk drive access time. The tests are accomplished using the wrk2 tool [36]. In the following analysis, we vary the number of threads and the number of HTTP connections kept open while trying to keep a steady rate of 2000 requests/second for 60 s for each file size.

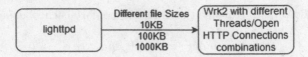

Fig. 1. A simplified overview of the benchmark setup

4.2 Latency

The diagrams in Figs. 2a and 2b show the obtained latency distributions.

Observations and interpretations:

- Latency linearly increases with the number of open connections (see Fig. 2a), especially true for small file sizes however when the file size grows beyond a certain limit, the number of connections will become irrelevant to the introduced latency (see Fig. 2b).
- As shown in Fig. 2c, for small file size, we observe a latency divergence in particular in the 99 percentile area for bigger file size, we noticed in the case of the 100 KB, the desired request rate of 2000 req/s is not met due to the limitation of the underlying network infrastructure (1 GB/s–125 MB/s)
- It is interesting to note that, in relation to file size (Fig. 2c) larger files lead to higher memory and network latencies in a way that they can saturate the server's network bandwidth, lowering throughput (see Fig. 2b). Therefore, for serving large files, high network bandwidth is more important than compute resources. On the other hand, increasing the number of open Connections (Fig. 2d) will trigger TCP's congestion mechanism and such they will be competing for the same bandwidth. Increasing the file size as well will cause the Open Connections to lose packets and get stuck waiting for retransmissions.

A similar latency distribution is observed when the tests are conducted on the same machine, thus using the optimized [10] loopback interface, where theoretically the network does not pose any throughput bottleneck (iperf [32] result 20 GBs). From these experiments, we learn that to optimize the throughput, the web requests should not be using different open connections but rather use one or a relatively small number of open Connections and label the web requests accordingly, which is commonly known as HTTP multiplexing [13], where, using the same TCP connection, multiple HTTP requests are divided into frames, assigned a unique ID called stream ID and then sent asynchronously, the server receives the frames and arranges them according to their stream ID and also responds asynchronously; same arrangement process happens at the client side allowing to achieve maximum parallelism.

4.3 Throughput

The network throughput of our system is calculated as follow:

$$Throughput = \frac{Nreq \cdot Obj\_size}{time}$$

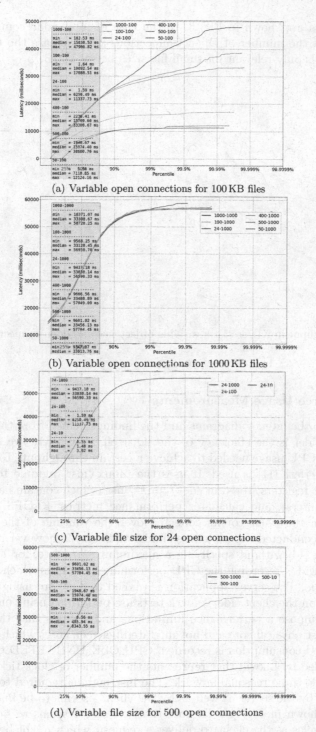

(a) Variable open connections for 100 KB files

(b) Variable open connections for 1000 KB files

(c) Variable file size for 24 open connections

(d) Variable file size for 500 open connections

Fig. 2. Measured latency for different experiments

The results are shown in Fig. 3. In the case of inter-node communication, an increase in the number of Open Connections will increase the throughput, however, this is only relevant for small file sizes below 1 MB.

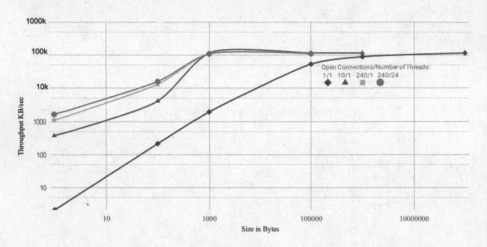

Fig. 3. Throughput in KB/sec for a variable object size and open connections/threads

4.4 Resource Usage Measurements

In addition to the latency diagrams and the findings gained from them, another point to consider is the efficiency of the IO itself, this is why we measure the Memory and CPU usage needed to achieve a certain throughput. To accomplish this, likwid-perfctr [11] is used. It uses the Linux 'msr' module to access the model specific registers stored in /dev/cpu/*/msr (which contain hardware performance counters), and calculates performance metrics, FLOPS, bandwidth, etc., based on the event counts collected over the runtime of the application process. The conducted experiment is similar to Sect. 4.2, however, this time we are using wrk [14] without specifying a maximum req/s rate, for 1 min, during this time Likwid is recording the CPU performance counters which are relevant in this scenario. The server application is pinned to one core using Likwid, the same is done on the client side, As wrk tests are performed using only 1 thread, this doesn't impose a performance limitations and ensures that the process is run on the first physical core and not migrated between cores which may lead to overhead. CPU consumption is recorded, CPU_CLK_UNHALTED_CORE is the metric provided by Likwid that represents the number of clock ticks needed by the CPU to do some reasonable work. The instructions required to accomplish one request - by the server as well as by the client - seems to be linear with the file size, as shown in Fig. 4a. To note that the server seems to be consuming more CPU cycles as the client to deliver a request, which might be because we are using the lighttpd web server without modifying the default configuration.

Note also that over a certain file size limit, the number of timeouts increases since we are approaching the maximum throughput achieved by the system.

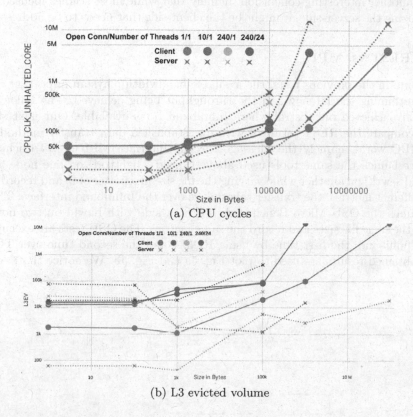

(a) CPU cycles

(b) L3 evicted volume

Fig. 4. Likwid metrics for the client and server with a variable size and open connections/threads combination

Regarding Memory Utilization: Basically, when reading a file (represented by HTTP response), the client needs to store the data received in memory. If the file size exceeds the size of the CPU cache, we expect that data is evicted to main memory, which is measured in L3 cache evictions. This metric is recorded using Likwid and shown in Fig. 4b. Basically, we can see that even for 100 MB files only 10 MB of data is evicted on the client. There is no eviction on the server because it sends the data directly to the client. This is an indication that zero-copy [39] is in use on the client and the network interface card offloads the processing of TCP/IP. This allows the network card to store the data directly into the target memory location. Generally, with zero-copy, the application requests the kernel to copy the data directly from a file descriptor to the socket bypassing the copy in user mode buffer and, therefore, reducing the number of context switches between kernel and user mode. Furthermore, when data does not fit in the processor L3 caches (12 MB), the evicted data, i.e., the data passed to memory increases significantly causing a performance drop, curiously the rate of increase of the client evicted memory is greater than on the server, leading us to another interesting conclusion, namely that while most studies focused on optimizing the server-side, it might be the client-side that needs to be addressed.

4.5   REST vs. MPI

As found in the previous tests, the available bandwidth plays an important role in determining the latency and the throughput being achieved. The following tests are achieved on Mistral where Infiniband [1] is available. Our next step is to compare the REST protocol with an established data transfer method in the HPC world, namely the Message Passing Interface MPI [38]. To achieve this we launch the same tools used above (likwid + lighttpd) on one node and (likwid + wrk) on another while varying the file size in a power of 2, and recording the different metrics, the transfer takes place over the Infiniband interface. Then we launch the OSU Micro Benchmark [27] alongside with likwid on two nodes using the same file sizes and record the same metrics. The OSU tests are executed over Infiniband, the first time by using RDMA and the second time over TCP. The obtained results are used to plot Fig. 5a and Fig. 5b. We notice that:

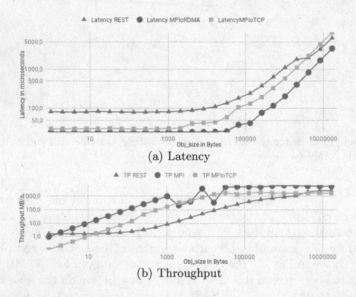

(a) Latency

(b) Throughput

Fig. 5. Results for the protocols for a variable file size

- For small object sizes, the latency of Rest is obviously higher than the one of MPI, as already mentioned in our latency tests, this is due to the HTTP overhead.

- The throughput achieved using MPI is better than the one using REST however when comparing MPI and REST both over TCP, we notice that this is not the case especially for very small and large files which leads to the conclusion that the overhead due to the TCP stack is the main factor slowing down the object storage implementation.
- The performance dip seen in the red line for a file size of above 1 KB is due to the MPI implementation that uses a combination of protocols for the same MPI routine, namely the use of the eager protocol [7] for small messages, and rendezvous protocol for larger messages.
- Another particular finding depicted by Fig. 6a is that the CPU cycles needed for the sender to push the data when using MPI is higher than by using REST, this becomes visible for file sizes above 100 KB.
- Fig. 6b shows that, as expected, the evicted data volume stays constant in the case of MPI over RDMAoIB because of the direct data transfer from server main memory to client main memory. Furthermore, the L3-evicted memory for both REST and MPI over TCPoIB is constant for files smaller than 100 KB but increases exponentially afterward. Presumably, because parts of the protocol such as network packets re/assembly is controlled by the kernel and not the network interface.

4.6   HTTP Overhead

For HTTP 1.1, knowing the amount of bytes read by the HTTP parser in wrk, and the number of request achieved: $overhead\_per\_request = \frac{bytes\_read}{Nreq} - objsize$

We find that the overhead is about 233 bytes per request, mainly due to the uncompressed, literally redundant, HTTP response headers.

5   Evaluation of the Performance Model

To validate the predictive model defined in Eq. (9), we use the values reported by the REST latency Benchmark on Mistral in Sect. 4.5; the hardware-specific parameters are calculated as follows: Data between sockets and memory is shipped via a 9.6 GT/s QPI interface [23]. According to the Intel QPI specification [22] 16 bit of data are transferred per cycle, thus the uni-directional speed is 19,6 GB/s. The communication protocol has an overhead of roughly 11 The compute nodes of Mistral are integrated in one FDR InfiniBand fabric, the measured bandwidth between two arbitrary compute nodes is 5.9 GByte/s, as such net_tp = 5,9 GByte/s, rtt measured using qperf and found = 0.06 ms and mtu = 65520 Bytes. We only need to get the values of the coefficients β_i in Eq. (9). This is done by using a regression analysis tool, in this case the one provided by Excel: the obtained R square and F values are examined, for each iteration, to check respectively the fitness and the statistically significant of our model. Finally we calculate the predicted values and we compare them to the

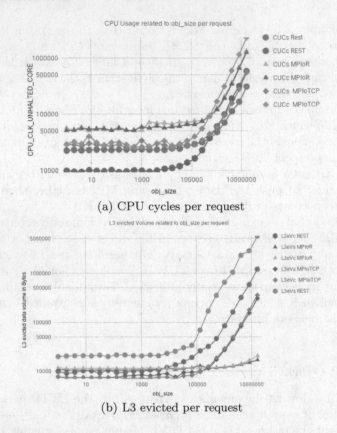

(a) CPU cycles per request

(b) L3 evicted per request

Fig. 6. Likwid metrics for the client and server for the different protocols

ones obtained in the benchmark by determining the error rate using Eq. (10). The tables can be found at: https://github.com/http-3/rest-overhead-paper.

$$error\% = (t\_req - t\_req\_calcul) \cdot 100/t\_req \qquad (10)$$

In case of RESToTCPoIB, we find that $(\alpha = 1)$, $\beta_1 = \beta_3 = \beta_4 \sim 1$, $\beta_2 = 6$ and $\beta_5 = 3/2$. The deviation (error rate) between the estimated value and the benchmark results is primarily below 10%, and indeed in the range of 1% for small and large file sizes. Equation (9) yields:

$$t(request) = rtt + \frac{CUCs}{Rs} + 6 \cdot \frac{L3EVs}{mem\_tp} + \frac{CUCc}{Rc} + \frac{L3EVc}{mem\_tp} + \frac{3}{2} \cdot \frac{Obj\_size}{net\_tp} \qquad (11)$$

In case of MPIoTCP, we obtain $(\alpha = 0.1)$, $\beta_1 = \beta_2 = \beta_3 = \beta_4 \sim 1$, and $\beta_5 = 2.7$. The error rate is less than 5% for small and large file sizes.

$$t(request) = 0.1 \cdot rtt + \frac{CUCs}{Rs} + \frac{L3EVs}{mem\_tp} + \frac{CUCc}{Rc} + \frac{L3EVc}{mem\_tp} + 2.7 \cdot \frac{Obj\_size}{net\_tp} \qquad (12)$$

In case of MPIoRDMA, we obtain ($\alpha = 0$), $\beta_1 = \beta_3 = 1/2$ and $\beta_2 = \beta_4 = \beta_5 \sim$ 1 . The error rate is primarily below 10%, and less than 5% for small and large file sizes.

$$t(request) = \frac{1}{2} \cdot \frac{CUCs}{Rs} + \frac{L3EVs}{mem\_tp} + \frac{1}{2} \cdot \frac{CUCc}{Rc} + \frac{L3EVc}{mem\_tp} + \frac{Obj\_size}{net\_tp} \quad (13)$$

By investigating the model terms, we can infer some general behavior and verify our expectations. The latency for MPIoRDMA is expected to be lower than the others, this is why α is close to 0 for this model. If β_5 is above 1, it is an indicator that we cannot achieve full network throughput. REST and MPIoTCP show otherwise similar performance characteristics while the MPIoRDMA model is approximated to use half the CUC, which actually means it needed twice as many compared to the TCP models - maybe due to busy waiting. These assumptions can be verified by looking at Fig. 6a and Fig. 6b. In conclusion, we notice that while TCP proved itself for end-to-end communications over long distances, it is however less suitable for data center networking, mainly because of its processing overhead, hence degrading the aspired performance. On the other side, CPU and Memory consumption for the REST over TCP Model remained adequate in comparison with MPI over TCP and MPI over RDMA.

5.1 Comparing the Protocols: HTTP1.1 vs. HTTP2 vs. HTTP3

The same setup described in Fig. 1 is used here, however the web server, in this case, should be able to deliver the three different protocols. Therefore, openlitespeed [33] is used and the suitable benchmark tool is h2load [17]. To note that we test here the ngtcp2 [31] implementation of HTTP3, because it's TLS library independent, not like other HTTP3 implementations like quiche [6] which requires boringssl. Since at the time of writing, the official OpenSSL Team doesn't support QUIC [34] we use a patched version of OpenSSL provided by the ngtcp2 team. Since HTTP3 didn't achieve the maturity phase yet, we are using the protocols as they are defined in the 27th Draft by the IETF QUIC Working group [19]. The latency and throughput results of the tests on Mistral over InfiniBand are shown in Fig. 7a and Fig. 7b

Although we are expecting HTTP2 and HTTP3 to perform better than HTTP 1.1, this is not the case. A closer look at the evolution of the parameters defined in our model reveals the cause: Despite the obvious traffic saving of HTTP2, it comes at a considerable memory consumption, which renders the gained advantages negligible. The chosen HTTP3 implementation is circa 10 times more CPU and memory consuming in comparison to the earlier versions, which indicates an implementation issue.

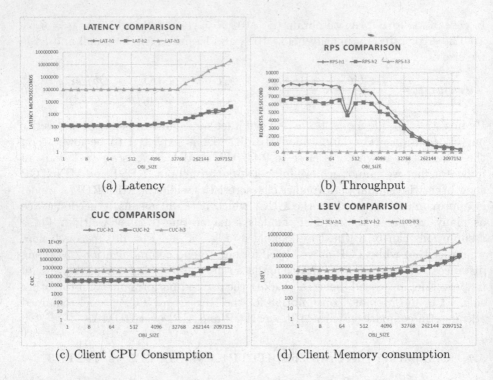

(a) Latency

(b) Throughput

(c) Client CPU Consumption

(d) Client Memory consumption

Fig. 7. Results for the different versions of the HTTP protocol

6   Summary

This paper provides a first assessment of using REST as a storage protocol in an HPC environment. A performance model for the relevant HTTP Get/Put operation based on hardware counters is provided and experimentally validated. Our results demonstrate that REST can provide, in many cases, similar latency and throughput to the HPC-specific implementations of MPI while enabling better portability. The developed model covered the general behavior of the different protocols well and was able to generalize and verify the expected behavior.

The new techniques introduced in HTTP (the use of a small number of connections, multiplexing the HTTP datagram, compressing the header and allowing the server to "push" data pro-actively to the client whilst eventually using UDP to accomplish these) bear the potential to improve performance and, thus, provide a perspective for using cloud storage inside HPC environments. However, in this evaluation, they couldn't show their benefit. As future work, we aim to validate that REST is a performant and efficient alternative to common HPC I/O protocols in an actual HPC scenario.

References

1. I.T. Association: About Infiniband. https://www.infinibandta.org/about-infiniband/. Accessed 29 July 2019
2. AWS: AWS S3. https://aws.amazon.com/de/s3/. Accessed 19 July 2019
3. Bent, J., et al.: PLFS: a checkpoint filesystem for parallel applications. In: Proceedings of the Conference on High Performance Computing Networking, Storage and Analysis, p. 21. ACM (2009)
4. Bortolotti, D., et al.: Comparison of UDP transmission performance between IP-over-InfiniBand and 10-Gigabit ethernet. IEEE Trans. Nucl. Sci. **58**(4), 1606–1612 (2011)
5. Chang, C.S., Thomas, J.A.: Effective bandwidth in high-speed digital networks. IEEE J. Sel. Areas Commun. **13**(6), 1091–1100 (1995)
6. Cloudflare: Implementation of the QUIC protocol. https://github.com/cloudflare/quiche. Accessed 01 Apr 2020
7. Denis, A., Trahay, F.: MPI overlap: benchmark and analysis. In: 45th International Conference on Parallel Processing (ICPP), pp. 258–267. IEEE (2016)
8. Devresse, A., Furano, F.: Efficient HTTP Based I/O on very large datasets for high performance computing with the Libdavix library. In: Zhan, J., Han, R., Weng, C. (eds.) BPOE 2014. LNCS, vol. 8807, pp. 194–205. Springer, Cham (2014). https://doi.org/10.1007/978-3-319-13021-7_15
9. DKRZ: Mistral. https://www.dkrz.de/up/systems/mistral/configuration. Accessed 19 July 2019
10. Dumazet, E.: Increase loopback MTU (2012). https://bit.ly/3c4PHVO. Accessed 24 Feb 2020
11. Eitzinger, J., Röhl, T., Hager, G., Wellein, G.: LIKWID 4 tools architecture
12. Folk, M., Heber, G., Koziol, Q., Pourmal, E., Robinson, D.: An overview of the HDF5 technology suite and its applications. In: Proceedings of the EDBT/ICDT 2011 Workshop on Array Databases, pp. 36–47. ACM (2011)
13. Gettys, J.: SMUX Protocol Specification. https://www.w3.org/TR/1998/WD-mux-19980710 (1998). Accessed 19 July 2019
14. Glozer, W.: wrk - a HTTP benchmarking tool. https://github.com/wg/wrk. Accessed 19 July 2019
15. Grant, R.E., Balaji, P., Afsahi, A.: A study of hardware assisted ip over InfiniBand and its impact on enterprise data center performance. In: IEEE International Symposium on Performance Analysis of Systems & Software (ISPASS), pp. 144–153. IEEE (2010)
16. Gruber, T.: Likwid:about L3 evict. https://github.com/RRZE-HPC/likwid/issues/213. Accessed 13 July 2019
17. h2load: benchmarking tool for HTTP/2 server. https://nghttp2.org/documentation/h2load.1.html. Accessed 19 Oct 2019
18. He, Q., Dovrolis, C., Ammar, M.: On the predictability of large transfer TCP throughput. Comput. Netw. **51**(14), 3959–3977 (2007)
19. IETF: QUIC Working Group. https://quicwg.org/. Accessed 01 April 2020
20. IETF: Request for Comments: 6298. https://tools.ietf.org/html/rfc6298 (2011). Accessed 19 Jan 2020
21. Intel: Address Translation on Intel X56xx. https://software.intel.com/en-us/forums/software-tuning-performance-optimization-platform-monitoring/topic/277182. Accessed 15 Sept 2019

22. Intel: An Introduction to the Intel® QuickPath Interconnect. https://www.intel.com/technology/quickpath/introduction.pdf. Accessed 15 Sept 2019
23. Intel: Intel® Xeon® Processor E5–2680. https://ark.intel.com/content/www/us/en/ark/products/81908/intel-xeon-processor-e5-2680-v3-30m-cache-2-50-ghz.html. Accessed 15 Sept 2019
24. Kneschke, J.: Lighttpd. https://www.lighttpd.net/. Accessed 29 July 2019
25. Ko, R.K., Kirchberg, M., Lee, B.S., Chew, E.: Overcoming large data transfer bottlenecks in restful service orchestrations. In: IEEE 19th International Conference on Web Services, pp. 654–656. IEEE (2012)
26. Liu, J., et al.: Evaluation of HPC application i/o on object storage systems. In: 2018 IEEE/ACM 3rd International Workshop on Parallel Data Storage & Data Intensive Scalable Computing Systems (PDSW-DISCS), pp. 24–34. IEEE (2018)
27. Liu, J., et al.: Microbenchmark performance comparison of high-speed cluster interconnects. IEEE Micro **24**(1), 42–51 (2004)
28. Lofstead, J., Jimenez, I., Maltzahn, C., Koziol, Q., Bent, J., Barton, E.: DAOS and friends: a proposal for an exascale storage system. In: Proceedings of the International Conference for High Performance Computing, Networking, Storage and Analysis, SC 2016, pp. 585–596. IEEE (2016)
29. Ma, D., Zhang, W., Li, Q.: Dynamic scheduling algorithm for parallel real-time jobs in heterogeneous system. In: The Fourth International Conference on Computer and Information Technology, CIT 2004, pp. 462–466. IEEE (2004)
30. Mell, P., Grance, T., et al.: The NIST definition of cloud computing (2011)
31. ngtcp2: Effort to implement IETF QUIC protocol. https://github.com/ngtcp2/ngtcp2. Accessed 01 Apr 2020
32. NLANR/DAST: Iperf. https://github.com/esnet/iperf. Accessed 11 July 2019
33. OpenLiteSpeed: OpenLiteSpeed Web Server. https://openlitespeed.org/. Accessed 19 Dec 2019
34. OpenSSL: QUIC and OpenSSL. https://www.openssl.org/blog/blog/2020/02/17/QUIC-and-OpenSSL/. Accessed 01 Apr 2020
35. Richardson, L., Ruby, S.: RESTful Web Services. O'Reilly Media Inc., Newton (2008)
36. Tene, G.: A constant throughput, correct latency recording variant of wrk. https://github.com/giltene/wrk2. Accessed 11 July 2019
37. Thakur, R., Gropp, W., Lusk, E.: Data sieving and collective i/o in ROMIO : In: Proceedings of the Seventh Symposium on the Frontiers of Massively Parallel Computation, Frontiers 1999, pp. 182–189. IEEE (1999)
38. The MPI Forum, C.: MPI: a message passing interface. In: Proceedings of the 1993 ACM/IEEE Conference on Supercomputing, Supercomputing 1993, pp. 878–883. ACM, New York (1993). https://doi.org/10.1145/169627.169855. http://doi.acm.org/10.1145/169627.169855
39. Tianhua, L., Hongfeng, Z., Guiran, C., Chuansheng, Z.: The design and implementation of zero-copy for Linux. In: Eighth International Conference on Intelligent Systems Design and Applications, vol. 1, pp. 121–126. IEEE (2008)
40. Wu, K., Arpaci-Dusseau, A., Arpaci-Dusseau, R.: Towards an unwritten contract of intel Optane SSD. In: 11th USENIX Workshop on Hot Topics in Storage and File Systems (HotStorage 19), Renton, WA. USENIX Association (2019)
41. Zadok, E., Hildebrand, D., Kuenning, G., Smith, K.A.: POSIX is dead! long live... errr... what exactly. In: Proceedings of the 9th USENIX Conference on Hot Topics in Storage and File Systems, p. 12. USENIX Association (2017)

Characterizing I/O Optimization Effect Through Holistic Log Data Analysis of Parallel File Systems and Interconnects

Yuichi Tsujita[1]([✉]), Yoshitaka Furutani[2], Hajime Hida[3], Keiji Yamamoto[1], and Atsuya Uno[1]

[1] RIKEN Center for Computational Science, Kobe, Japan
yuichi.tsujita@riken.jp
[2] Fujitsu Limited, Tokyo, Japan
[3] Fujitsu Social Science Laboratory Limited, Kawasaki, Japan

Abstract. Recent HPC systems utilize parallel file systems such as GPFS and Lustre to cope with the huge demand of data-intensive applications. Although most of the HPC systems provide performance tuning tools on compute nodes, there is not enough chance to tune I/O activities on parallel file systems including high-speed interconnects among compute nodes and file systems. We propose an I/O performance optimization framework using log data of parallel file systems and interconnects in a holistic way for improving performance of HPC systems including I/O nodes and parallel file systems. We demonstrate our framework at the K computer with two I/O benchmarks for the original and the enhanced MPI-IO implementations. Its I/O analysis has revealed that I/O performance improvements achieved by the enhanced MPI-IO implementation are due to effective utilization of parallel file systems and interconnects among I/O nodes compared with the original MPI-IO implementation.

Keywords: I/O characterization · Holistic log data analysis · K computer · FEFS · Lustre · Tofu · MPI-IO

1 Introduction

HPC systems have been facing the performance gaps between computing power and I/O performance. Parallel file systems such as GPFS [19] and Lustre [11] provide a large amount of storage capacity with high I/O bandwidth to bridge the gap. Most of the I/O optimization research works have addressed to improve I/O performance of their implementations in an empirical way using I/O benchmarks rather than analyzing I/O activities on target parallel file systems and data packet transfers through interconnects. With an increase in the number of compute nodes and target I/O nodes, it is quite difficult to tune an implementation only through such benchmark runs.

A profiling tool named Tofu PA [4] is provided at the K computer, which acquired statistical information called Tofu PA information representing packet

© Springer Nature Switzerland AG 2020
H. Jagode et al. (Eds.): ISC High Performance 2020 Workshops, LNCS 12321, pp. 177–190, 2020.
https://doi.org/10.1007/978-3-030-59851-8_11

transfer status in the Tofu interconnects [1] on used compute nodes, with the purpose to tune communications among compute nodes. However, there were no tools to get the Tofu PA information of Tofu interconnects among I/O nodes and I/O activities of its parallel file systems. A well-balanced I/O workload among compute nodes, I/O nodes, and parallel file systems is required to optimize I/O operations. Without knowing status of I/O nodes and parallel file systems, it is quite difficult to tune I/O operations in HPC applications.

It is expected that utilization of statistics log data of file system servers and interconnects provides quite useful metrics for I/O performance tuning by examining statistics of I/O request operations or data packet transfers through interconnects. In this context, we propose a framework that monitors data packet transfers on Tofu interconnects on I/O nodes and I/O activities of parallel file systems with the help of log data collected in the system administration. To our best knowledge, this is the first work to utilize data packet transfer information of Tofu interconnects on I/O nodes among the HPC systems using Tofu interconnects in tuning I/O operations. The framework consists of several components: log data collected by *fluentd* [3], a PostgreSQL database that keeps a large amount of executed job information (JOB-DB), compute-node information table, and analysis function.

Given a unique ID of each job (JOB-ID), the analysis function of the framework provides us data such as averaged values of essential I/O activities on used OSSes, bandwidth utilization of Tofu interconnects on I/O nodes, and heatmaps about I/O performance of used OSTs from the log data with the help of the JOB-DB. In this paper, we show how such analyzed data can be used for further performance improvements by examining I/O bottlenecks or unbalanced situations in I/O workload among I/O nodes.

2   Related Work

I/O bottlenecks in various applications were studied in [17,24]. These studies showed various characteristics in terms of I/O access patterns performed by applications on HPC systems using Lustre file systems. I/O monitoring at storage system level has been studied in [7,13,23]. Multi-platform study using system logs of file systems has been reported in [12].

Log data collection and analysis for performance tuning have been done in server-side analysis [8,9,25]. Detailed study in production runs has been done in [15] by analyzing server-side log data. Even sufficient logging of each server-side component did not provide causal relationships between client and server-side activities.

Interconnects are also one of the key components in HPC systems. Monitoring data transfers of interconnects has provided hot-spot of traffic congestion for instance, and such approaches have succeeded in analysis of application activities associated with the traffic condition [6,27]. However, it is not sufficient to characterize I/O activities on parallel file systems in HPC systems.

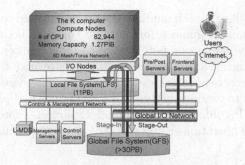

Fig. 1. System configuration of the K computer

Recently, holistic I/O monitoring has been proposed in several research works [10,26]. Lockwood et al. have proposed a holistic I/O monitoring framework named TOKIO [10]. It consisted of several components for monitoring, analysis and visualization for administrators and users. The work in [26] has proposed a monitoring framework named Beacon. This framework provides a collection of monitoring tools for Metadata Servers (MDSes) and Object Storage Servers (OSSes) and analysis functions including some visualization interface. These works are similar to our work regarding holistic approach in characterization of I/O activities.

In contrast, our work addresses examination of I/O activities through holistic log data analysis of Tofu interconnects and parallel file systems including associated I/O nodes. The uniqueness of this work is a holistic analysis framework using data packet transfer status on interconnects among I/O nodes and associated I/O activity traces at parallel file systems.

3   The K computer and Its File System Monitoring

3.1   Overview of the K Computer

The K computer finished its operation for about seven years in August 2019. The system had two-layered file systems, a single volume of a local file system (LFS) and eight volumes of a global file system (GFS) as shown in Fig. 1. The LFS was a scratch high-performance storage space which was used during computations, while the GFS was used to store programs and data with high redundancy. An enhanced Lustre named FEFS (Fujitsu Exabyte File System) [18] developed by Fujitsu based on the version 1.8 release was used to build both file systems. The K computer consisted of 82,944 compute nodes and 5,184 I/O nodes, where every system rack consisted of 96 compute nodes and six I/O nodes. Every compute node and I/O node were connected through the Tofu interconnects. The LFS is accessible from compute nodes through a subset of I/O nodes named local-I/O nodes (LIOs). Every node including I/O nodes consisted of Tofu network router (TNR) [1] where each TNR had 10 communication links (X+, X−, Y+, Y−, Z+, Z−, A, B+, B−, and C) to construct the 6D mesh/torus network.

Performance profiling tools including Tofu PA addressed to tune performance of compute nodes and communications among compute nodes. The tools have succeeded to leverage computing potential of the K computer, especially in tuning applications utilizing a large number of compute nodes. The only way to tune I/O operations is benchmark evaluations because there were no I/O profiling tools for users to examine activities of I/O nodes and parallel file systems including the Tofu PA information among I/O nodes. Therefore, it was quite difficult to tune I/O operations using only the existing profiling tools.

3.2   Log Collection for Monitoring the LFS

In the K computer operation, we have collected log data from servers associated with the LFS as shown in Fig. 2. We have deployed *fluentd* to collect performance metrics associated with I/O operations from 5,184 I/O nodes including 2,592 LIOs which also acted as OSSes for the LFS. The proposed analysis framework utilizes the following log data from a large amount of collected information by *fluentd* in the last few months of the K computer operation.

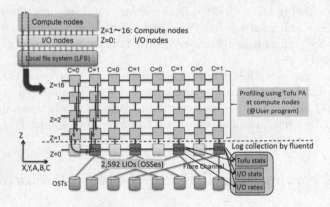

Fig. 2. Log collection from I/O nodes

- `Tofu stats`: Data packet transfer status metrics of I/O nodes on each Tofu interconnect link (the number of transferred packets, amount of transferred data size, and others)
- `I/O stats`: Statistics of I/O requests obtained from `/proc/fs/lustre/ost/ OSS/ost_io/stats` on every OSS
- `I/O rates`: Amount of size in read and write operations on every OST

Only the `I/O stats` have been collected at 1 min intervals, while the remainings have been collected at 10 min intervals as trial in a conservative manner due to limited storage space of the log-collection server and minimization in performance impact on I/O nodes during the K computer operation. More fine-grained log collection interval is our future work.

The Tofu stats consist of the following packet processing metrics of the 10 links, which are obtained from a TNR of each I/O node through the Tofu PA information:

- Cycle counts until target transfer buffer was available in packet transfers
- Amount of transferred data size

It is noted that the cycle counts in the Tofu stats correspond to congestion status since unavailability of transfer buffers in packet processing closely corresponds to packet transfer congestion. We enforced to retrieve those metrics from a TNR at every I/O node during the K computer operation for about a few months until the end of the K computer operation.

The I/O stats consist of the same statistics with those of a standard Lustre, where we especially focus on the three statistics; req_qdepth, req_active, and req_waittime. Such statistics give the status of I/O requests coming from compute nodes through I/O nodes. For instance, a large value in both req_qdepth and req_waittime indicates very busy status of OSSes or idle status of OSSes waiting for the next operation due to heavy load of an MDS before I/O accesses for instance. Such a situation is not suitable for effective I/O operations. req_active indicates the number of active threads for I/O operations. High numbers in only req_active indicate a very good condition in terms of I/O accesses.

The I/O rates give us I/O throughput status at each OST over time. Collected I/O throughput information is expected to show I/O behavior that happened on each OST.

3.3 Database for Executed Jobs

The PostgreSQL database server has collected information of executed jobs at the K computer on the JOB-DB database. The JOB-DB keeps used compute nodes, elapsed time, and start and finish times of job execution, for instance by associating with a JOB-ID. Therefore, we can refer to information of a target job from the JOB-DB by specifying a JOB-ID.

4   Analysis Framework for I/O Activities

Figure 3 depicts system overview of the implemented analysis framework, which is connected with associated log data collected by *fluentd* and the JOB-DB to analyze I/O activities on I/O nodes and the LFS. Given a target JOB-ID, the framework obtains information of the JOB-ID such as 6D mesh/torus network positions of used compute nodes and names of used system racks. Such information about used compute nodes and system racks is utilized to find used I/O nodes including LIOs from the I/O node table because the assigned I/O node layout is configured by the shape of assigned compute nodes. Besides, start and finish times of the target job obtained from the JOB-DB were used to pick up

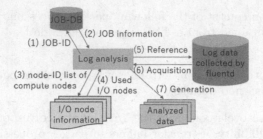

Fig. 3. Functional overview of implemented analysis framework

essential information associated with the JOB-ID from a large amount of log data collected by *fluentd*.

Once the framework collects all essential information, its log analysis function figures out and gives the following information for the given JOB-ID:

- Maximum waiting times of each interconnect at each used I/O node
- Bandwidth utilization ratio of the interconnects relative to the theoretical bandwidth
- I/O performance in both write and read operations on each used OST

The former two performance values are calculated by using the packet transfer metrics obtained from the TNR. The function converts the cycle counts into time value in the unit of second for the maximum waiting times. While the bandwidth utilization ratio during the job execution is obtained by dividing the peak bandwidth of the job by the theoretical bandwidth, where the peak bandwidth is obtained from throughput values collected in an elapsed time of the specified job. In the proposed framework, we use the maximum bandwidth utilization to examine effectiveness in packet transfers associated with I/O operations.

While the I/O performance values were obtained by dividing an amount of data size in read and write operations by a monitoring interval time (10 min at this moment) in order to know I/O throughput at each used OST. The analysis function generates data in the CSV format and associated heat-map image data are stored in the PNG format.

5   Enhanced MPI-IO Implementation: EARTH on K

MPI-IO is an I/O interface including parallel I/O in the MPI standard [14]. An MPI library for the K computer supports MPI-IO functions for the FEFS using ROMIO [20]. Although two-phase I/O optimization of ROMIO improves collective MPI-IO performance, the implementation on the K computer uses an old implementation of ROMIO which is not optimized for Lustre. Therefore, the original MPI-IO implementation is not suitable for the FEFS to achieve high I/O performance.

The recent ROMIO with the improved two-phase I/O for Lustre has a potential to improve performance on the FEFS. An enhanced implementation named

"EARTH on K" (hereinafter, EARTH) [21,22] has been developed for the K computer by introducing the improved two-phase I/O with some performance optimizations for collective MPI-IO at the FEFS.

Its advanced functions are summarized in the following three key optimization parameters described by `agg`, `rr`, and `req`, respectively:

- `agg`: Striping-aware aggregator layout
- `rr`: Round-robin aggregator layout among compute nodes
- `req`: I/O throttling and associated stepwise data aggregation with a given number of I/O requests per step

The striping-aware aggregator layout mitigates data transfer congestion by suitable layout of processes performing I/O (aggregators) in collective MPI-IO operations using ROMIO. By placing aggregators so that I/O flows of every I/O path towards a target OSS are evenly distributed with paying attention into a striping access pattern against OSTs, we can eliminate data transfer congestion on those I/O paths. Besides, the round-robin aggregator layout can distribute I/O workload evenly among compute nodes, and it also prevent aggregators from I/O congestion on the same compute node if we have multiple aggregators on a subset of compute nodes. The I/O throttling alleviates I/O request contention on OSSes by issuing I/O requests from aggregators on compute nodes in a step-wise manner. Stepwise data aggregation is an optimization associated with the I/O throttling, where data transfer congestion among compute nodes can be mitigated.

Although the above enhancements outperformed the original version in an empirical study using I/O benchmark runs, there were not any examinations to know performance impact of those optimizations because there were no tools to characterize optimization effect in data transfers among I/O nodes and I/O accesses against the LFS at the K computer. By using the proposed framework, we examine their advanced features at the K computer in the following section.

6   Experimental Evaluation

Evaluation for the proposed framework was carried out among the original MPI-IO implementation and EARTH using two I/O benchmarks; IOR [5] and HPIO [2]. In both benchmark runs, we initiated 12,288 processes on 3,072 compute nodes forming $8 \times 12 \times 32$ in a logical 3D layout in order to eliminate I/O interference from other jobs. According to the 3D layout of assigned compute nodes, 192 OSTs were assigned for parallel I/O, and we set 192 in stripe count to use all available OSTs. We set 256 MiB and 64 MiB in stripe size in the IOR run and the HPIO run, respectively.

In the both runs, 1,536 processes worked as aggregators, where aggregator assignment was aligned to ascending order in MPI ranks from zero in the original MPI-IO, while aggregator assignment was defined according to optimization configuration of the EARTH. We have executed the two I/O benchmark runs so that we could observe I/O activities of each run under the trial 10 min monitoring intervals.

In this paper, `original` stands for the original one, while a combination of the three optimization parameters (`agg`, `rr` and `req`) indicates the EARTH case. Concerning the EARTH case, `agg=1` stands for striping-aware aggregator layout and `rr=1` denotes round-robin aggregator layout among compute nodes. A zero value in each case stands for deactivation in the corresponding layout optimization. The last parameter `req` with a number describes the number of I/O requests going to each OST per step in I/O throttling and step-wise data aggregation except that `req=0` denotes deactivation of I/O throttling and stepwise aggregation.

6.1   Benchmark Configuration

We evaluated collective MPI-IO in the two benchmark runs with enabling two-phase I/O implemented in ROMIO. Every run took around 10 min to cover the 10 min intervals of `Tofu` `stats` and `I/O` `rates`.

IOR. The following command was executed in write operations to generate a shared file of 3 TiB (= 256 MiB × 12,288) per iteration:

```
$ ior -i 5 -a MPIIO -c -U hints_info -k -m -vvv -w -t 256m -b 256m \
    -o ${TARGET_DIR}/test-IOR.dat -d 0.1
```

The same command with just changing "-w" by "-r" was executed, followed by write operations in every parameter configuration. "hints_info", is a file describing some hints to set the number of processes per node, and so forth. A target file (`test-IOR.dat`) was generated under a directory `${TARGET_DIR}` with 192 stripe count.

HPIO. We executed the following command for write operations, followed by read operations to generate a shared file of about 2.1 TiB ($\sim$ (5,992 B + 256 B) × 12,288 × 30,729 $-$ 256 B) per iteration in non-contiguous access pattern on a target file with specifying the number of processes per node (`-H cb_config_list=*:4`):

```
$ hpio -n 0010 -r 6 -B -s 5992 -c 30729 -p 256 -m 01 -O 11 -f 0 \
    -S 0 -a 0 -g 2 -H cb_config_list=*:4 -d ${TARGET_DIR} -w 1
```

The target file was generated under a directory `${TARGET_DIR}` with 192 stripe count.

6.2   Benchmark Results

Figure 4 shows mean I/O throughput values with standard deviations by IOR and HPIO benchmarks. The original case (`original`) shows low performance in both read and write operations. EARTH with full optimization in aggregator layout and I/O request throttling and stepwise data aggregation outperformed other cases by setting four requests per step (`agg=1,rr=1,req=4`) in the IOR runs and eight requests per step (`agg=1,rr=1,req=8`) in the HPIO runs. However, performance was degraded by changing the number of requests per step or deactivating aggregator layout optimization. Although we have learned optimization effect through such empirical benchmark runs, it has not been clear about performance impact of the optimization configuration on I/O nodes and the LFS.

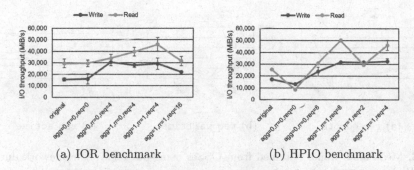

(a) IOR benchmark   (b) HPIO benchmark

Fig. 4. Benchmark results of the original MPI-IO and EARTH with several optimization configurations by using (a) IOR and (b) HPIO benchmarks

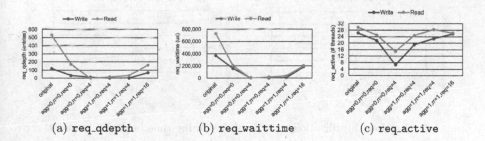

(a) `req_qdepth`   (b) `req_waittime`   (c) `req_active`

Fig. 5. Mean stats values obtained from OSSes using our analysis framework during the IOR benchmark run

6.3   Analysis of OSS Stats Files

Figure 5 shows mean values of `req_qdepth`, `req_waittime`, and `req_active` obtained during I/O operations at the IOR benchmark run. The original case had the largest number of requests in a request queue as shown in Fig. 5(a). Figure 5(b) tells that this case also took the longest times to proceed requests. Besides, Fig. 5(c) shows the highest number of active I/O threads in the original case. Note that the maximum number of threads at each OSS of the LFS was 32 at the K computer. Through the observed results, it has turned out that the original case was not suited for I/O request processing at OSSes.

While the EARTH case with good I/O performance (agg=1,rr=1,req=4) showed quite small number of requests in queue as shown in Fig. 5(a). Figure 5(b) also gives the fact that this case took quite short times to process I/O requests. Besides, Fig. 5(c) tells us relatively high number of threads for those cases.

Figure 6 shows same statistics obtained in the HPIO benchmark run. Similar to the IOR run, the original case was not good compared with the EARTH case with good optimization configuration indicated by "agg=1,rr=1,req=8".

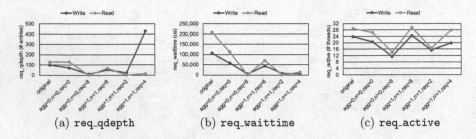

(a) req_qdepth   (b) req_waittime   (c) req_active

Fig. 6. Mean stats values obtained from OSSes using our analysis framework during the HPIO benchmark run

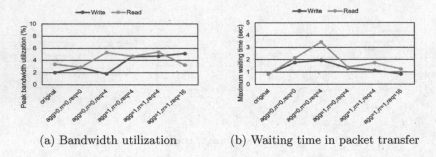

(a) Bandwidth utilization   (b) Waiting time in packet transfer

Fig. 7. Mean values for packet transfers on Tofu interconnects among used I/O nodes during the IOR benchmark run

6.4 Bandwidth Utilization and Waiting Times in Packet Transfers on Tofu Interconnects of I/O Nodes

Figure 7 shows mean values of (a) the peak bandwidth utilization ratios and (b) the maximum waiting times in packet transfers on links of used I/O nodes.

Figure 7(a) indicates that the original case shows the lowest utilization, while the full set of EARTH optimizations such as "agg=1,rr=1,req=4" performed higher bandwidth utilization relative to other cases. By considering effectiveness in packet transfers among I/O nodes via Tofu interconnects, higher utilization is preferable. In this context, the above optimized case was suitable for I/O optimization.

The enhanced implementation without aggregator layout optimization indicated by "agg=0,rr=0,req=4" took the longest times in Fig. 7(b). It is also noted that this case also performed the lowest bandwidth utilization in write operations as shown in Fig. 7(a). It is remarked that the lack of aggregator layout optimization in the EARTH case led to negative impact in packet transfers on Tofu interconnects among I/O nodes.

Figure 8 shows similar bandwidth utilization ratios and waiting times in packet transfers on Tofu links of used I/O nodes at the HPIO benchmark run. The EARTH case with the best configuration (agg=1,rr=1,req=8) also outperformed other cases in Fig. 8(a). This case also showed shorter times in both read and write operations among the EARTH cases in Fig. 8(b).

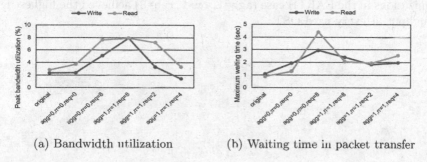

(a) Bandwidth utilization   (h) Waiting time in packet transfer

Fig. 8. Mean values for packet transfers on Tofu interconnects of used I/O nodes at the HPIO benchmark run

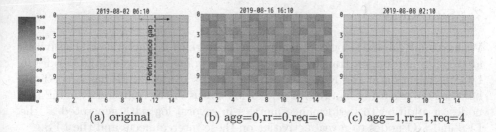

(a) original   (b) agg=0,rr=0,req=0   (c) agg=1,rr=1,req=4

Fig. 9. Write bandwidth heat-maps of used 192 OSTs at the IOR benchmark run

6.5   Load Balancing in I/O Throughput at OSTs

Figure 9 shows write bandwidth heat-maps of used 192 OSTs during the IOR benchmark runs. Each heat-map shows write bandwidth of each OST ranging from 0 to 160 MiB/s, where horizontal and vertical axes represent subjected relative 2D positions of used OSTs from the logical 3D layout of the K computer, ranging from 0 to 15 and from 0 to 11 in horizontal and vertical directions, respectively.

In the original case in Fig. 9(a), we can observe performance gaps among the left and right sides separated by the dotted line. Figure 9(b) also shows performance gaps among OSTs. The both cases are not suitable because total I/O performance was limited by the slowest OST in parallel I/O. While the most optimized case in Fig. 9(c) shows a well-balanced situation in write throughput among OSTs. In the context of parallel I/O characteristics, this case is suitable for the benchmark run.

Write bandwidth heat-maps at the HPIO run are also shown in Fig. 10. The EARTH case with insufficient configuration (agg=0,rr=0,req=8) showed lower performance compared with the original case. Meanwhile, a full set of the three optimizations in the EARTH case (agg=1,rr=1,req=8) achieved the highest I/O throughput at every used OST.

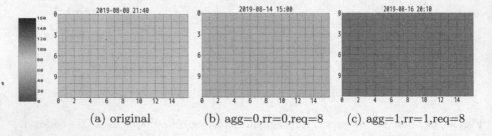

(a) original   (b) agg=0,rr=0,req=8   (c) agg=1,rr=1,req=8

Fig. 10. Write bandwidth heat-maps of used 192 OSTs at the HPIO benchmark run

7   Summary

We have built a holistic log data analysis framework to characterize I/O activities at the LFS and packet transfers through the Tofu interconnects of I/O nodes in I/O optimization at the K computer. The proposed framework has carried out holistic analysis using bandwidth utilization status of the Tofu links among I/O nodes in addition to performance metrics in several log data generated at the LFS and I/O nodes to reveal activities on those interconnects and the LFS.

Two I/O benchmark runs showed distinct differences in I/O activities at the LFS and packet transfers through the Tofu links among I/O nodes between the original MPI-IO implementation and the enhanced MPI-IO implementation named EARTH. Obtained profiling information also gave insights to understand why the EARTH gained I/O performance relative to the original MPI-IO. Besides, the framework also informed us how much the impact in I/O activities at the LFS and bandwidth utilization of the Tofu links of I/O nodes among several optimization configurations of the EARTH. Our future work is building the similar framework in our next HPC system named Fugaku [16] to cover essential information from log data with a fine-grained monitoring interval.

Acknowledgment. This research used computational resources of the K computer provided by the RIKEN Center for Computational Science.

References

1. Ajima, Y., Inoue, T., Hiramoto, S., Takagi, Y., Shimizu, T.: The Tofu interconnect. IEEE Micro **32**(1), 21–31 (2012)
2. Ching, A., Choudhary, A., keng Liao, W., Ward, L., Pundit, N.: Evaluating I/O characteristics and methods for storing structured scientific data. In: Proceedings 20th IEEE International Parallel and Distributed Processing Symposium, p. 49. IEEE Computer Society, April 2006
3. fluentd. https://www.fluentd.org/
4. Ida, K., Ohno, Y., Inoue, S., Minami, K.: Performance profiling and debugging on the k computer. Fujitsu Sci. Tech. J. **48**(3), 331–339 (2012)
5. IOR. https://github.com/hpc/ior
6. Kumar, M., et al.: Understanding and analyzing interconnect errors and network congestion on a large scale HPC system. In: 2018 48th Annual IEEE/IFIP International Conference on Dependable Systems and Networks, DSN 2018, pp. 107–114. IEEE, June 2018
7. Kunkel, J.M., et al.: The SIOX architecture – coupling automatic monitoring and optimization of parallel I/O. In: Kunkel, J.M., Ludwig, T., Meuer, H.W. (eds.) ISC 2014. LNCS, vol. 8488, pp. 245–260. Springer, Cham (2014). https://doi.org/10.1007/978-3-319-07518-1_16
8. Liu, Y., Gunasekaran, R., Ma, X., Vazhkudai, S.S.: Automatic identification of application I/O signatures from noisy server-side traces. In: Proceedings of the 12th USENIX Conference on File and Storage Technologies (FAST 2014), USENIX, pp. 213–228 (2014)
9. Liu, Y., Gunasekaran, R., Ma, X., Vazhkudai, S.S.: Server-side log data analytics for I/O workload characterization and coordination on large shared storage systems. In: Proceedings of the International Conference for High Performance Computing, Networking, Storage and Analysis, SC 2016. ACM (2016)
10. Lockwood, G.K., Wright, N.J., Snyder, S., Carns, P., Brown, G., Harms, K.: TOKIO on ClusterStor: connecting standard tools to enable holistic I/O performance analysis. In: 2018 Cray User Group Meeting (CUG) (2018)
11. Lustre. http://lustre.org/
12. Luu, H., Winslett, M., Gropp, W., Ross, R., Carns, P., Harms, K., Prabhat, M., Byna, S., Yao, Y.: A multiplatform study of I/O behavior on petascale supercomputers. In: Proceedings of the 24th International Symposium on High-Performance Parallel and Distributed Computing, HPDC 2015, pp. 33–44. ACM (2015)
13. Madireddy, S., et al.: Analysis and correlation of application I/O performance and system-wide I/O activity. In: Proceedings of the 2017 International Conference on Networking, Architecture, and Storage (NAS), pp. 1–10. IEEE (2017)
14. MPI Forum. https://www.mpi-forum.org/
15. Patel, T., Byna, S., Lockwood, G.K., Tiwari, D.: Revisiting I/O behavior in large-scale storage systems: The expected and the unexpected. In: Proceedings of the International Conference for High Performance Computing, Networking, Storage and Analysis, SC 2019, pp. 65:1–65:13. ACM (2019)

16. Post-K (Fugaku) Information. https://postk-web.r-ccs.riken.jp/index.html
17. Saini, S., Rappleye, J., Chang, J., Barker, D., Mehrotra, P., Biswas, R.: I/O performance characterization of Lustre and NASA applications on Pleiades. In: 19th International Conference on High Performance Computing (HiPC), pp. 1–10 (2012)
18. Sakai, K., Sumimoto, S., Kurokawa, M.: High-performance and highly reliable file system for the K computer. Fujitsu Sci. Tech. J. **48**(3), 302–309 (2012)
19. Schmuck, F., Haskin, R.: GPFS: a shared-disk file system for large computing clusters. In: Proceedings of the 1st USENIX Conference on File and Storage Technologies, FAST 2002, USENIX Association (2002)
20. Thakur, R., Gropp, W., Lusk, E.: On implementing MPI-IO portably and with high performance. In: Proceedings of the Sixth Workshop on Input/Output in Parallel and Distributed Systems, pp. 23–32 (1999)
21. Tsujita, Y., Hori, A., Ishikawa, Y.: Locality-aware process mapping for high performance collective MPI-IO on FEFS with Tofu interconnect. In: Proceedings of the 21th European MPI Users' Group Meeting, EuroMPI/ASIA 2014, pp. 157:157–157:162. ACM (2014). Challenges in Data-Centric Computing
22. Tsujita, Y., Hori, A., Kameyama, T., Uno, A., Shoji, F., Ishikawa, Y.: Improving collective MPI-IO using topology-aware stepwise data aggregation with I/O throttling. In: Proceedings of HPC Asia 2018: International Conference on High Performance Computing in Asia-Pacific Region, 28–31 January 2018, pp. 12–23. ACM (2018)
23. Uselton, A., Wright, N.: A file system utilization metric for I/O characterization. In: 2013 Cray User Group Meeting (2013)
24. Xie, B., et al.: Characterizing output bottlenecks in a supercomputer. In: Proceedings of 2012 International Conference for High Performance Computing, Networking, Storage and Analysis, SC 2012, pp. 1–11. IEEE (2012)
25. Xu, C., et al.: LIOProf: exposing Lustre file system behavior for I/O middleware. In: 2016 Cray User Group Meeting, May 2016
26. Yang, B., et al.: End-to-end I/O monitoring on a leading supercomputer. In: Proceedings of the 16th USENIX Symposium on Networked Systems Design and Implementation, NSDI 2019, pp. 379–394. USENIX (2019)
27. Zimmer, C., Gupta, S., Larrea, V.G.V.: Finally, a way to measure frontend I/O performance. In: 2016 Cray User Group Meeting (CUG) (2016)

The Importance of Temporal Behavior When Classifying Job IO Patterns Using Machine Learning Techniques

Eugen Betke[1]([☒]) and Julian Kunkel[2]

[1] DKRZ, Hamburg, Germany
betke@dkrz.de
[2] University of Reading, Reading, UK
j.m.kunkel@reading.ac.uk

Abstract. Every day, supercomputers execute 1000s of jobs with different characteristics. Data centers monitor the behavior of jobs to support the users and improve the infrastructure, for instance, by optimizing jobs or by determining guidelines for the next procurement. The classification of jobs into groups that express similar run-time behavior aids this analysis as it reduces the number of representative jobs to look into. It is state of the practice to investigate job similarity by looking into job profiles that summarize the dynamics of job execution into one dimension of statistics and neglect the temporal behavior.

In this work, we utilize machine learning techniques to cluster and classify parallel jobs based on the similarity in their temporal IO behavior to highlight the importance of temporal behavior when comparing jobs. Our contribution is the qualitative and quantitative evaluation of different IO characterizations and similarity measurements that work toward the development of a suitable clustering algorithm.

We explore IO characteristics from monitoring data of one million parallel jobs and cluster them into groups of similar jobs. Therefore, the time series of various IO statistics is converted into features using different similarity metrics that customize the classification. We discuss conventional ML techniques that are applied to job profiles and contrast this with the analysis of time series data where we apply the Levenshtein distance as a distance metrics. While the employed Levenshtein algorithms aren't yet optimal, the results suggest that temporal behavior is key to identify related pattern.

Keywords: IO fingerprinting · Performance analysis · Monitoring

1 Introduction

Scientific large-scale applications of different domains have different needs for IO and, thus, exhibit a variety of access patterns on storage. Even re-running the same simulation may lead to different behavior. We can distinguish between

© Springer Nature Switzerland AG 2020
H. Jagode et al. (Eds.): ISC High Performance 2020 Workshops, LNCS 12321, pp. 191–205, 2020.
https://doi.org/10.1007/978-3-030-59851-8_12

a temporal behavior, i.e., the operations performed over time such as long read phases, bursty IO pattern, and concurrent metadata operations, and spatial access pattern of individual processes of the application as they can be, e.g., sequential or random.

On different supercomputers, the same IO patterns may result in different application runtimes depending on the nature of the access pattern. For example, machines equipped with burst buffers [1,10] may significantly reduce application runtimes by absorbing bursty IO traffic. IO congestion and file system performance degradation can occur when several IO intensive jobs are running on the same machine at the same time.

In our environment at DKRZ, the raw monitoring data of a job is captured in form of a time series of nine metrics per node, each metric sampled at five seconds intervals. When comparing the time series of such metrics between two jobs, the key question is how do we define the similarity between multiple time series. From the user support side, we might be interested in grouping similar suboptimal jobs and aim to provide one recipe to optimize all that exhibit such a behavior. Similarly, we might be interested to optimize the pattern for a single IO phase. We may be interested to ignore computation time and focus on IO phases only. Regardless of the segment of the time series we look at, we naively would consider an IO pattern to be identical if the time series for all metrics of one job is identical to those of another job.

Utilizing time series data of a job for clustering if difficult as it firstly, depends on runtime, the number of nodes, the gathered metrics, and possibly number of file systems; secondly, the temporal IO behavior of parallel jobs depends on the conditions of the cluster it is executed. For various reasons, even re-running the same job may lead to variations in execution time and, thus, observed statistics. Moreover, variants of workflows may lead to slight variations of behavior that might be relevant for a data analyst.

In this article, we discuss and demonstrate the benefit of utilizing time series data in contrast to profiles. First, we briefly discuss related work in Sect. 2. Next, we describe our previous work and the monitoring system used in Sect. 3. Our approach is described in Sect. 4. As jobs are of different length, a similarity metrics must be able to handle time series of different length. Two classes of approaches are investigated: (1) we generate job profiles and apply existing ML techniques to cluster data; (2) we create a string from the time series, and we apply the Levenshtein distance which indicates the number of changes that need to be made between two job strings. The experimental conditions for our evaluation are described in Sect. 5. To evaluate these approach, we perform a qualitative analysis in Sect. 6 discussing the statistics about the generated clusters and a quantitative evaluation in Sect. 7 where we search jobs similar to a given job. Finally, the paper is concluded in Sect. 8.

2   Related Work

There are many tracing and profiling tools that are able to record IO information [6]. Most of them focus on individual jobs, and only a few of them apply machine learning for data analysis, in particular across jobs. As the purpose of applications is computation and, thus, IO is just a byproduct, applications often spend less than 10% time with IO.

The Ellexus tools[1] include the Mistral tool which purpose is to report on and resolve IO performance issues when running complex Linux applications on high performance compute clusters. Darshan [2,3] is an open source IO characterization tool for post-mortem analysis of HPC applications' IO behavior. Its primary objective is to capture concise but useful information with minimal overhead. This is accomplished by eschewing end-to-end tracing in favor of compact statistics such as elapsed time, access sizes, access patterns, and file names for each file opened by an application. Darshan can be used not just to investigate the IO behavior of individual applications but also to capture a broad view of system workloads for use by facility operators and IO researchers.

There are approaches that monitor record storage behavior and aim to identify inefficient applications in a cluster. TOKIO [7] integrates logs from various sources to allow an analysis of data. It allows finding certain inefficient access patterns in the data.

The LASSi tool [9] was developed for detecting victim and aggressor applications. To identify such applications, LASSi calculates metrics from Lustre jobstats and information from the job scheduler. The correlation of these metrics can help to identify applications that cause the file system to slow down. In the LASSi workflow this is a manual step, where a support team is involved in the identification of applications during file system slow down. LASSi's indicates that the main target group are system maintainers. Understanding LASSi reports may be challenging for ordinary HPC users, who do not have knowledge about the underlying storage system.

In [5], the authors utilized probes to detect file system slow-down. A probing tool measures file system response times by periodically sending metadata and read/write requests. An increase of response times correlates to the overloading of the file system. This approach allows the calculation of a slow-down factor identification of the slow-down time period. This approach is able to detect a file system slow-down, but cannot detect the jobs that cause the slow-down.

HiperJOBVIZ [8] is a visual analytic tool for visualizing the resource allocations of data centers for jobs, users, and usage statistics. It provides an overview of the current resource usage and a detailed view of the resource usage via multi-dimensional representation of health metrics. TimeRadar[2] is a part of the tool, which summaries the resource usage via radar charts, creating a kind of comprehensible profile for different user groups.

In contrast to existing approaches, the approach discussed in this paper focuses on the analysis of job data and investigates clustering strategy to group similar jobs.

---

[1] https://www.ellexus.com/products/.
[2] https://idatavisualizationlab.github.io/HPCC/TimeRadar.

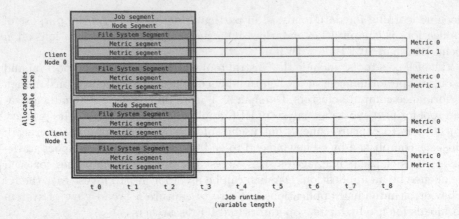

Fig. 1. A generic example of 4-dimensional raw monitoring data (Node × File System × Metric × Time) and different levels of segmentation (colored boxes).

3   Preliminary Work

The German Climate Computing Center (DKRZ) maintains a monitoring system that gathers various statistics from the Mistral HPC system. Mistral has 3,340 compute nodes, 24 login nodes, and two Lustre file systems (lustre01 and lustre02) that provide a capacity of 52 PB.

Raw Monitoring Data. On each node, every five seconds nine IO metrics are gathered on client nodes for each Lustre file system and stored. Five of them (md_read, md_mod, md_file_create, md_file_delete, md_other) capture metadata activities and the remaining four (read_bytes, read_calls, write_bytes, write_calls) capture data access. Figure 1 illustrates a generic example of raw monitoring data. In the example the data is captured on 2 nodes, on 2 file systems, for 2 metrics, and at 9 time points t_i.

Segmentation. We split the time series of each IO metric into equal-sized time intervals (segments) and computes a mean performance for each segment. This stage preserves the performance units (e.g., Op/s, MiB/s) for each IO metric. The generic example in Fig. 1 creates segments out of three successive time points just for illustration purposes. Actually, the real raw monitoring data is converted to 10 min segments, which we found is a good trade-off to represent the temporal behavior of the application while it reduces the size of the time series. Depending on aggregation function, segments can be created of metrics, of file systems, of nodes, or even over all dimensions.

Categorization. Next, to get rid of the units, and to allow calculations between different IO metrics, we introduced a categorization pre-processing step that takes into account the performance of the underlying HPC system and assigns a unitless ordered category to each metric segment. We use a three category system, which contains the LowIO = 0, HighIO = 1 and CriticalIO = 4 categories. The category split points are based on the observed file system usage and the score values assigned to each category represent their weight. We investigated both concepts in our previous work [4]. This node-level data can then be used to compute job-statistics by aggregating across dimensions such as time, file systems, and nodes.

In summary, this data representation has the following key advantages for data analysis. The ordered categories make the calculations between different metrics feasible, which is not possible with raw data. Furthermore, the domains are equally scaled and compatible, because the values are between 0 and 4, and a value has a meaning. Besides, the resulting data representation is much smaller compared to the raw data. This allows us to apply compute-intensive algorithms to large datasets. Finally, irrelevant data is hidden by the LowIO category and doesn't distract from significant parts of jobs.

In our previous work, we computed three high-level Job-IO-metrics per job that aid users to understand job profiles: **Job-IO-Balance** indicates how IO load is distributed between nodes during job runtime. **Job-IO-Utilization** shows the average IO load during IO-phases but ignores computation phases. **Job-IO-Problem-Time** is the fraction of job runtime that is IO-intensive; it is approximated by the fractions of segments that are considered IO intensive.

We will use them in job profiles as well to capture some temporal behavior.

4   Methodology

The goal of this article is to research the impact of the temporal dimension when applying clustering strategies on many jobs. Therefore, we compare job-profiles that neglect the temporal dimension and time series of different length represented as strings.

Generally, machine learning algorithms expect a fixed number of features. Thus, the time series that are retrieved on the node-level needs to be pre-processed. The application of a "specific algorithm" can be understood as a number of successive processing steps on data. Roughly speaking, there are three basic steps that we apply: data pre-processing including coding, similarity computation, and clustering. We call one of such a combination a *clustering stack*. The pre-processing converts the dynamic-sized monitoring data which depends on the number of captured IO metrics, allocated nodes, used file systems, and application runtime into a suitable representation for the clustering algorithm. Then the clustering is applied. Finally, the clustering result needs to be assessed, i.e., how suitable is this strategy for our IO statistics and use cases? In the following, we have dedicated a section to each step discussing potential alternatives.

Data Pre-processing. The 4-dimensional data (Node × File System × Metric × Time) from our monitoring system is too fine-grain for mass analysis. To be able to analyse millions of jobs, we must reduce the dimensionality.

Depending on reduction techniques, the result of the data-preprocessing is either a dataset of feature vectors for general-purpose algorithms, or a set of job codings for specific clustering algorithms.

We decided to distinguish how the different dimensions of a job are reduced and aggregated (if at all); for example, for general-purpose clustering algorithms we may summarize a metric over the node dimension and then compute the mean across time to obtain a profile for each metric and file system. For specific algorithms, that work with time series, we can reduce monitoring data by node, file system, and across metrics, leaving the time dimension untouched. At this point you can see clearly, why it is beneficial to have the same unit for all dimensions, and why we use a category classification which creates a unitless order.

Coding. Segmented data contains a numeric floating-point value for each data, which can be too much information for the analysis. Therefore, we introduce two condensed data representations called binary and hexadecimal coding. Additionally, we introduce zero-aggregation, that is an operation that aggregates continuous zero segments to one zero segment.

Binary coding represents monitoring data as a sequence of numbers, where each number stands for a specific file system usage. Reduction of data by nodes and file system, and aggregation by the sum() function creates a 2d data structure with the metric and the time dimension. In the next reduction step, each conceivable combination of active IO metrics can be mapped to unique number. In our implementation, we do this by a 9-bit number where each bit represents a metric. The approach maps the three categories to two states: LowIO is mapped to 0 (compute intense state), and HighIO and CriticalIO are mapped 1 (IO intense state). On one side, by doing this, we lose information about performance intensity, but on other side, this simplification allows later a more comprehensible comparison of job activities.

Using this kind of coding we can compute a number for each segment, that describes unambiguously the file system usage, e.g., a situation where intensive usage of md_read (Code = 16) and read_bytes (Code = 32) occur at the same time and no other significant loads are registered is coded by the value 48. Coding is reversible, e.g., when having value 48, the computation of active metrics is straightforward.

In the example below, we reduce the 4d data to 1d data (1) by aggregating the node and the file system dimensions, (2) by summing up the score values (3) and mapping each segment in the metric dimension to a number. Additionally, sequences of zero segments can be reduced to just one zero segment to neglect the length of an application's IO phase. For presentation purposes, in the resulting table we leave zero scores. An example encoded job before and after the reduction of zero segments is shown here:

```
jobA (after coding):    [1:5:0:0:0:0:0:0:96:96:96:96:96:96:96], 'length':15
jobA (after reduction): [1:5:0:96:96:96:96:96:96:96], 'length':15
```

Hexadecimal coding preserves monitoring data for each metric and each segment. As the name suggests, the value of a segment is converted into a hexadecimal number. The numbers are obtained in two steps. Firstly, the dimension reduction aggregates the file system and the node dimensions and computes a mean value for each metric and segment, which lies in interval [0,4]. Secondly, the mean values are quantized into 16 levels – 0 = [0,0.25), 1 = [0.5,0.75), ..., f = [3.75, 4]. The following example shows a five segment long hexadecimal coding:

```
jobB: 'length': 6, 'coding':
  'metric_read'    : [0:2:2:2:9],
  'metric_write'   : [0:0:0:0:0],
  ...,
  'metric_md_other': [0:0:0:f:f]
```

Similarity. We use euclidean distance to determine the similarity between two job profiles. For time series, we use Levenshtein distance that is the number of operations (inserts/deletes/changes) required to convert one coding in another.

Clustering. In the last step, similar jobs need to be grouped in clusters. To handle millions of jobs, the algorithm must be performant. We developed two strategies that meet the requirement, one based on widely used general-purpose algorithms, and a specific algorithm.

ClusteringTree Algorithm. As we do not know the number of different classes of jobs are in the dataset, a traditional k-means classification turned out to be not productive in our experiments. Therefore, we explored the usage of agglomerative clustering, however, with its complexity of $\geq O(N^2)$, it wasn't applicable to our dataset. Thus, we simplified the application into this algorithm. This algorithm involves three steps: (1) Agglomerative clustering of a small dataset and labeling data, (2) training of a decision tree model, and (3) clustering with the decision tree of the remaining jobs.

SimplifiedDensity Algorithm. Clusters are formed around centroids. That are job codings that form clusters by attracting similar jobs. All jobs in a cluster fulfill only one condition, the similarity (SIM) to the centroid has to be larger than the user defined value. The algorithm takes a non-assigned job and iterates through existing clusters looking if the similarity to the cluster centroid is larger than the user defined values. The job is assigned to the first cluster, where the condition is fulfilled. If there is no such a cluster, the job forms a new cluster and becomes a centroid of this cluster.

Clustering Stacks. There are various combinations of the different strategies possible. For simplicity, we refer to one clustering stack just as algorithm. During our research, we explored various combinations out of the possible combinations. The paths are visualized Fig. 2 and discussed further in the following section.

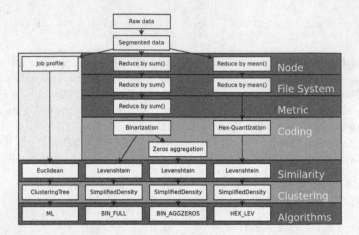

Fig. 2. Algorithms and their actual clustering stacks.

4.1   Algorithms

ML. To apply existing clustering algorithms, first, a job-profile is created in the pre-processing. The 4d time series can be transformed into the required fixed-size input format accepted by the general-purpose ML clustering algorithms. In the preprocessing step, the MinMaxScaler scales the features to values between 0 and 1 using MinMax normalization. Therefore, the highest distance between two points can be at most $\epsilon_{\max} = d^{1/d}$, where d is the dimension of the dataset.

We explored two job profiles: IO-metric and IO-duration. The **IO-metric job profile** utilizes three features, Job-IO-Balance, Job-IO-Utilization, and Job-IO-Problem-Time (as defined in [4]). After the data pre-processing, we obtain a set of 3-dimensional data points with a domain between 0 and 1. The maximum distance between any two jobs ($\epsilon_{\max}$) is 1.44.

The **IO-duration job profile** contains the fraction of runtime, a job spent doing the individual IO categories leading to 27 columns. The columns are named according to the following scheme: metric_category, e.g., bytes_read_0 or md_file_delete_4. The first part is the one of the nine metric names and the second part is the category number (LowIO = 0, HighIO = 1 and CriticalIO = 4). These columns are used for machine learning as input features. There is a constraint for each metric (metric_0 + metric_1 + metric_4 = 1), that makes 9 features redundant, because they can be computed from the other features. So we have to deal with 18 features; $\epsilon_{\max}$ is 1.17.

In experiments, we observed that the agglomerative clustering algorithm that is used in this work can handle around 10,000 jobs in a reasonable amount of time as the complexity is $O(N^2)$. With the following additional classification steps, we are able to cluster 1,000,000 samples:

1. Clustering and labeling 10,000 jobs with agglomerative clustering algorithm.
2. Training of a decision tree model with data from the previous step.
3. Predict labels of 1,000,000 jobs with the trained decision tree model.

BIN_ALL and BIN_AGGZEROS. For these algorithms, we encode the time
series of 9 metrics into one time series that is then assessed using Levenshtein
distance. The similarity between two jobs is determined by the following formula:

$$\text{similarity}\,(\text{job}_A,\text{job}_B) = 1 - \frac{\text{levenshtein}\,(\text{coding}_A,\text{coding}_B)}{\max\,(\text{length}_A,\text{length}h_B)} \tag{1}$$

It computes the number of operations (changes/deletes/inserts) divided by
the length of the longest sequence, and subtracted from the value one. According
to this equation, the similarity between the following two jobs is 73%:

```
jobA: [1:5:0:0:0:0:0:0:0:96:96:96:96:96:96:96], 'length': 15
jobB: [0:0:0:0:0:0:0:0:0:96:96:96:96:96:96:98], 'length': 15
```

As a variation of this approach, we investigated also the case where consecutive zero-sequences are reduced to a single zero segment. This allows us to focus
on IO intensive parts of the job. The example below shows reduced codings from
the previous example. Note, that this operation has no effect on the job length
and similarity computation. The similarity between the following two codings is
53%:

```
jobA: [1:5:0:96:96:96:96:96:96], 'length': 15
jobB: [0:96:96:96:96:96:98], 'length': 15
```

HEX_LEV. This similarity function works on the same principle as the BIN
algorithms, with the difference that instead of a single pre-reduced time series
per job, it computes the similarity between all 9 metrics of two different jobs
first and then compute the mean.

This adaption allows applying Levenshtein-based similarity on hexadecimal
coding as follows:

$$\text{similarity}\,(\text{job}_A,\text{job}_B) = 1 - \frac{\sum_{m\in Metric}\text{levenshtein}\,(\text{coding}_{A,m},\text{coding}_{B,m})}{N\cdot L_B}, \text{with } L_B \geq L_A \tag{2}$$

4.2 Assessment

Lastly, the quality of the obtained clusters must be assessed. Overall, we will
assess their suitability using quantitative metrics such as the number of generated clusters and their sizes and qualitatively by manually exploring clusters of
relevant jobs. We want to emphasize that our goal is to find similar jobs. Unfortunately, it is not feasible to analyse all of them qualitatively with reasonable
effort and there are no tools that can assess the cluster quality automatically.
For the qualitative analysis, we start by looking into a job that is given to user
support, then similar jobs need to be found. In the same cluster, we expect the
sequences to be similar. If not, the clustering algorithm is not effective.

5 Experimental Setup

5.1 Data

This section describes the job data extracted from Mistral, originally we gathered 1 million jobs from a period of 203 days. Mostly jobs are allowed to run up to 8-hours, leading to time series with up to 48 segments. The general procedure for monitoring data shorter than 10 min, that occur inevitable in short jobs and in many last job segments (if job runtime is not divisible by 10 min) is the following: We compute the mean segment performance, extend the runtime to 10 min, and create a 10 min segment with the computed mean performance. From the perspective of this work, analysis of non-IO-intensive jobs (jobs with zero in all segments) is irrelevant. These jobs can be grouped into one class easily. For that reason, we detect zero-jobs early and remove them from the dataset; these are about 40% of jobs.

The number of zero-jobs is different for hexadecimal and absolute mode codings. For BIN algorithms we create 583,000 codings and for HEX algorithms 444,000 codings. The reason is the quantization to HEX coding, which firstly computes mean performance values for all segments, and then quantizes them to 16 levels. Hereby, some segments can be quantized to zeros, if the mean value becomes sufficiently low. Therefore, it may happen that some jobs fall into the zero-job category if all segments are quantized to zeros. It can not happen in BIN coding, because it preserves all the active segments, so that no job may change the category. Interestingly, it affects around 14% of jobs.

5.2 Test Environment

For the performance tests, we allocate a compute node on Mistral supercomputer. It is equipped with 2x Intel® Xeon® CPU E5 2680 v3 @ 2.50 GHz, 64 GB DDR4 RAM. For clustering of job profiles, we use the agglomerative clustering algorithm, decision trees, and the MinMaxScaler from the scikit-learn 0.22.1 library and python 3.8.0. For clustering of binary and hexadecimal codings we a clustering algorithm implemented in Rust and run it on a single core.

5.3 Algorithm Parameters

ML. We explored our discussed job profiles: IO-metric and IO-duration. For both datasets we explore $\epsilon \in [0.03, 0.06, 0.09, 0.1, 0.2, 0.3]$.

BIN/HEX. We conduct experiments with BIN_ALL, BIN_AGGZEROS, and HEX_LEV algorithms, varying the SIM $\in [0.1, 0.3, 0.5, 0.7, 0.9, 0.95, 0.99]$ parameter and capturing clustering progress each time after clustering 10,000 jobs.

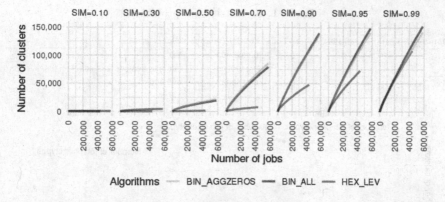

Fig. 3. Clustering progress.

6 Evaluation

ML. The jobs within clusters have indeed a similar job profile, the time series and, therefore, the binary coding differs significantly. For example, a cluster can contain sequences with different IO behavior like in Table 1. Obviously, the approach don't work stable enough. We omit further details.

BIN/HEX. In the introduced algorithms, the user-defined similarity (SIM) defines the closeness a job must fulfill to the cluster centroid to be assigned to the cluster. It is expected that low SIM values produce a few large but noisy clusters and a high SIM value produces a large amount of small but clean clusters. Although an optimal SIM value is dependent on use case and dataset, a parameter exploration may provide important hints to find a good value and achieve optimal cluster qualities.

Figure 3 shows the number of clusters created when clustering an increasing total number of jobs for different SIM values; each point represents the number for an analyzed number of jobs in increments of 10,000 jobs. For all algorithms, we can see that with an increase in SIM value, the number of clusters created increases, and the number of total clusters created slows down the more jobs have been processed as jobs are allocated to existing clusters. For a SIM of 99%, BIN and HEX_LEV can barely group jobs together.

To understand the aggregation behavior better, alternative visualizations are investigated. In Fig. 4, the number of clusters created for a given similarity value is plotted. The red line approximates the overall number of clusters, the green line shows how many contain at least two jobs and the blue line shows how many of them contain at least 10 jobs. On the red line we can observe increasing number of cluster with increasing SIM value, but we can also see on the green line that for the BIN algorithms the number of cluster with two jobs decreases after SIM $\geq$ 0.7. The maximum number of clusters is equivalent to the number of jobs; it is visualized by the gray line. Coding with 100% similarity are of the same job phenotype, i.e., they have exactly the same length and IO behavior.

Table 1. IO-metrics job profiles

Job-IO-Utilization	Job-IO-Problem-Time	Job-IO-Balance	Binary coding
4	1	0.4375000	118
4	1	0.4450206	368:368:368:368:368:368:374:368:368:368
4	1	0.4583333	496:496

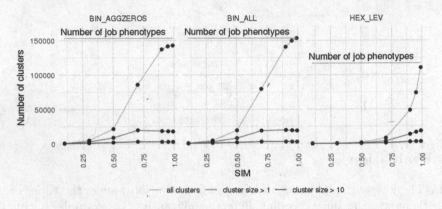

Fig. 4. Similarity value exploration. (Color figure online)

This kind of investigation could help a user to find the right SIM for a particular use case. A user can read off the line generalization capabilities of the algorithm with the particular SIM value. The less clusters are created, the more job phenotype they contain in average. The green line shows the point where the algorithms begin to create job clusters with 1 job only. In some use case, this might be an unwanted behavior.

7   Use Case: Investigating an IO-Intensive Job

The demonstration in this section shows how this approach can be used to identify a cluster of IO-intensive jobs similar to an existing job.

Based on the parameter investigation, we choose the sim value by the following criteria. The BIN algorithms work best for SIM ≥ 0.7, and the HEX algorithm requires a higher SIM value, hence we chose 0.9. A further increase of the SIM value doesn't make significant improvements in our experiments.

Firstly, we determined an IO intensive job that we use to identify similar jobs. The IO intensive metric of the selected job is visualized in Fig. 5. Other metrics contain only zero segments or negligible IO. We can see that this job reads data over the whole runtime. At beginning, only a subset of the nodes is reading most of the data, later more nodes participate in the reading. The amount of transmitted data is not large, but the amount of read calls is exceptionally high and may potentially degrade the file system performance.

The SIM value selection strategy can vary from use case to use case. As criteria, we choose a SIM value that creates a moderate number of clusters

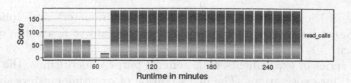

Fig. 5. IO intensive metric of one high IO intensity job running on 46 nodes. Other metrics have negligible IO and are omitted. Score is the sum of all nodes stacked by the node. A color represents the contribution of one of the nodes.

Table 2. Cluster statistics.

	SIM	Cluster size	Number of job types
BIN_ALL	0.7	27	17
BIN_AGGZEROS	0.7	8	8
HEX_LEV	0.9	209	189

Table 3. Job and the cluster centroid. Other jobs in the clusters are similar.

Binary coding	Type
192:192:192:192:192:192:196:192:192:192:192:192:192:192:192:192:192:192:192:192:192:64:64:64:64:64	job
192:192:192:192:192:192:192:192:192:192:454:230:192:192:192:192:192:192:192:192:192:192:192:192:192	centroid

(a) BIN_ALL

Binary coding	Type
192:192:192:192:192:196:192:192:192:192:192:192:192:192:192:192:192:192:192:192:64:64:64:64:64	job
511:238:192:510:192:224:228:192:192:192:192:192:192:192:192:192:192:192:192:192:64:64:64:64:64	centroid

(b) BIN_AGGZEROS

Hexadecimal coding (partially)

read_calls	Type
3:3:8:8:8:5:6:8:8:8:8:8:8:8:8:8:8:8:8:8:8:8:8:8:8	job
8:8:8:8:8:2:6:8:8:8:8:8:8:8:8:8:8:8:8:8:8:8:8:8:8	centroid

(c) HEX_LEV

(around 50% of job phenotypes) and keeps its generalization capabilities (the number of clusters with more than 1 job is considerable). For the BIN algorithms we chose a SIM of 0.7, and the HEX algorithm SIM of 0.9.

In the following, we investigate the cluster that contains this job for the different algorithms. The number of jobs found in the cluster are listed in Table 2. It shows that all algorithms find relatively small clusters. In Table 3, we can see that the jobs are relatively close to the cluster centroid. All other jobs in the clusters appear to be subjectively similar (not shown in the table). Thus, we conclude the approach generally works.

8   Summary

In this article, we applied clustering strategies to job-profile and time series of IO metrics. We conducted a short quantitative analysis to understand generalization capabilities of the algorithms and to select the parameters and conducted a qualitative analysis, i.e., manual inspection of the data to assess the quality of the approach.

After a series of experiments with general purpose algorithms, the outcome didn't meet our expectations. The investigation of resulting clusters shows that they are noisy. One problem might be the devised approach to use a clustering and a classification algorithm. It is likely that the reason is that the temporal behavior is compressed too much into the job-profile neglecting the important information.

On binary coding, the Levenshtein-based algorithms produce better clusters, especially with zero aggregation enabled. But the results are not sufficient for short jobs. Codings like [0:6:0:0] and [0:388:174:0] have the same Levenshtein distance to the centroid [0:388:0:0] but have different IO behavior.

Using the hexadecimal coding instead of binary coding leads to qualitative better results with the price that a higher similarity must be chosen. Presumably one reason is that hexadecimal coding sequences are nine times longer, which provides better conditions for the Levenshtein similarity.

Despite the suboptimal results of the algorithms when inspecting clusters, the final experiment actually shows that all the developed algorithms can actually be applied to identify jobs similar to a given job. The definition of similarity differs between these algorithms and may make them applicable to specific use cases. More research is needed to understand the needs of users and data center staff, and to define the appropriate similarity levels. We believe that the temporal pattern plays a key role in the definition of similarity as our comparison shows. In the future, we intend to refine the algorithms to account for different definitions of similarity.

References

1. Betke, E., Kunkel, J.: Benefit of DDN's IME-FUSE for I/O intensive HPC applications. In: Yokota, R., Weiland, M., Shalf, J., Alam, S. (eds.) High Performance Computing, pp. 131–144. Springer, Cham (2018). https://doi.org/10.1007/978-3-030-02465-9_9
2. Carns, P.: Darshan. In: High Performance Parallel I/O. Computational Science Series, pp. 309–315. Chapman & Hall/CRC (2015)
3. Carns, P., et al.: Understanding and improving computational science storage access through continuous characterization. ACM Trans. Storage (TOS) 7(3), 8 (2011)
4. Eugen Betke, J.K.: Semi-automatic assessment of I/O behavior by inspecting the individual client-node timelines – an explorative study on 10^6 jobs. In: 2014 43rd International Conference on Parallel Processing Workshops. ISC Events (2020)
5. Kunkel, J., Betke, E.: Tracking user-perceived I/O slowdown via probing. In: Weiland, M., Juckeland, G., Alam, S., Jagode, H. (eds.) High Performance Computing: ISC High Performance 2019 International Workshops, Frankfurt/Main, Germany, Revised Selected Papers. LNCS, 20 June 2019, pp. 169–182 Springer, Cham (2019). https://doi.org/10.1007/978-3-030-34356-9_15

6. Kunkel, J., et al.: Tools for analyzing parallel I/O. In: Yokota, R., Weiland, M., Shalf, J., Alam, S. (eds.) High Performance Computing: ISC High Performance 2018 International Workshops, Frankfurt/Main, Germany, 28 June 2018, Revised Selected Papers. LNCS, ISC Team, vol. 11203, pp. 49–70. Springer, Cham (2019). https://doi.org/10.1007/978-3-030-02465-9_4
7. Lockwood, G.K., Wright, N.J., Snyder, S., Carns, P., Brown, G., Harms, K.: TOKIO on ClusterStor: connecting standard tools to enable holistic I/O performance analysis. Technical report, Lawrence Berkeley National Lab. (LBNL), Berkeley, CA, United States (2018)
8. Nguyen, N., Chen, Y., Hass, J., Dang, T.: HiperJobViz: Visualizing Resource Allocations in HPCC via Multivariate Health-Status Data (2019). https://texastechuniversity-my.sharepoint.com/:p:/g/personal/tommy_dang_ttu_edu/EewObo2LMz5Gt1tLBTg1wFYBoMGrvVZ3wLZIRqVGY_50EA?rtime=xSv7VWIt2Eg
9. Sivalingam, K., Richardson, H., Tate, A., Lafferty, M.: LASSi: metric based I/O analytics for HPC. CoRR abs/1906.03884 (2019). http://arxiv.org/abs/1906.03884
10. Wang, T., Oral, S., Wang, Y., Settlemyer, B., Atchley, S., Yu, W.: BurstMem: a high-performance burst buffer system for scientific applications. In: 2014 IEEE International Conference on Big Data (Big Data), pp. 71–79 (2014)

1st Workshop "Machine Learning on HPC Systems" (MLHPCS)

Preface on the 1st Workshop "Machine Learning on HPC Systems" (MLHPCS)

Janis Keuper[1,6], Juan J. Durillo[2], Dennis Hoppe[3], Jenia Jitsev[4]
and Sunna Torge[5]

[1] IMLA, Offenburg University
[2] LRZ, Munich
[3] HLRS, Stuttgart
[4] JSC, Jülich
[5] ZIH, Dresden
[6] Fraunhofer ITWM, Kaiseslautern

1 Workshop Description

Over the last few years, Machine Learning (and in particular Deep Learning) (ML/DL) has become an important research topic in the High Performance Computing (HPC) community. Bringing new users and data intensive applications on HPC systems, ML/DL is increasingly affecting the design and operation of compute infrastructures. On the other hand, the ML/DL community is just getting started to utilize the performance of HPC, leaving many opportunities for better parallelization and scalability. The intent of this workshop is to bring together researchers and practitioners to discuss three key topics in the context of High Performance Computing and Machine Learning/Deep Learning: parallelization and scaling of ML/DL algorithms, ML/DL applications on HPC systems, and HPC systems design and optimization for ML/DL workloads.

1.1 Scope

The aim of the workshop is to provide a platform for technical discussions and the presentation of work in progress, as well as, unsolved problems, which is complementary to the "Machine Learning Day" in the main conference program.

- Unsolved problems in ML/DL on HPC systems
- Scalable ML/DL algorithms
- Parallelization techniques
- Libraries for ML/DL

- Tools + workflows for ML/DL on HPC systems
- Optimized HPC systems design and setup for efficient ML/DL
- ML/DL applications on HPC Systems

1.2 Recorded Talks

Video recordings of all MLHPCS talks are available at: www.mlhpcs.org.

GOPHER, an HPC Framework for Large Scale Graph Exploration and Inference

Marc Josep-Fabregó[1], Xavier Teruel[1(✉)], Victor Gimenez-Abalos[1],
Davide Cirillo[1], Dario Garcia-Gasulla[1], Sergio Alvarez-Napagao[1],
Marta García-Gasulla[1], Eduard Ayguadé[1], and Alfonso Valencia[1,2]

[1] Barcelona Supercomputing Center (BSC), C/ Jordi Girona 29,
08034 Barcelona, Spain
{marc.josep,xavier.teruel,victor.gimenez,davide.cirillo,dario.garcia,
sergio.alvarez,marta.garcia,eduard.ayguade,alfonso.valencia}@bsc.es
[2] ICREA, Pg. Lluís Companys 23, 08010 Barcelona, Spain

Abstract. Biological ontologies, such as the *Human Phenotype Ontology* (HPO) and the *Gene Ontology* (GO), are extensively used in biomedical research to investigate the complex relationship that exists between the phenome and the genome. The interpretation of the encoded information requires methods that efficiently interoperate between multiple ontologies providing molecular details of disease-related features. To this aim, we present *GenOtype PHenotype ExplOrer* (GOPHER), a framework to infer associations between HPO and GO terms harnessing machine learning and large-scale parallelism and scalability in High-Performance Computing. The method enables to map genotypic features to phenotypic features thus providing a valid tool for bridging functional and pathological annotations. GOPHER can improve the interpretation of molecular processes involved in pathological conditions, displaying a vast range of applications in biomedicine.

Keywords: Biological ontologies · Genomics · ML · HPC · Graph exploration

1 Introduction

Understanding the complex processes taking place in a cell or disease requires powerful computational frameworks, able to effectively provide meaningful interpretations of large volumes of high-throughput data and clinical information [6]. In the grand challenge of biomedical data integration and interpretation, biological ontologies are recognized as essential tools [11]. An ontology is a domain-specific knowledge formalization, based on sets of entities and relations [16]. Two of the most popular biological ontologies are the Human Phenotype Ontology (HPO) [12], describing phenome abnormalities, and the Gene Ontology (GO) [20], describing genome activities.

The integration of multiple ontologies, *i.e.*, ontology mapping or alignment, is posing great challenges to Artificial Intelligence (AI) [5]. Despite substantial

© Springer Nature Switzerland AG 2020
H. Jagode et al. (Eds.): ISC High Performance 2020 Workshops, LNCS 12321, pp. 211–222, 2020.
https://doi.org/10.1007/978-3-030-59851-8_13

efforts have been put on the integration of ontology-based biological information [17], computationally tractable approaches exploiting the interconnectivity between multiple large-scale ontological graphs still needs substantial investigation. To this aim, it is crucial to design HPC solutions and novel parallel algorithms that support fine-grained parallelism, while overcoming memory costs.

We develop and evaluate GOPHER, a system for the efficient traversing and exhaustive path enumeration in interconnected biological ontologies, enabled by the large-scale parallelism and scalability of HPC. In addition to efficient graph exploration functionalities, GOPHER harnesses machine learning to infer a precise mapping between given ontologies, allowing knowledge processing and discovery beyond limited cross-references. We applied GOPHER to study associations between disease-related phenotypic features and distinct molecular processes in humans, as well as in other model organisms (e.g., mouse and fruit fly). The approach exploits a very simple and yet very strong principle of biological ontologies: Preferential attachment, also known as *rich get richer*. The huge accuracy obtained in our experiments illustrates the utility of such property.

2   Related Work and Context

Biological ontologies are widely used. For instance, the functional interpretation of sets of genes is commonly achieved through statistical enrichments of ontological annotations, such as GO terms [15]. Given the pervasive application of biological ontologies in the biomedical area, community efforts like the Open Biomedical and Biological Ontologies (OBO) Foundry [18] have been created to disseminate best practices and curated corpora of ontologies.

A pivotal application of biological ontologies is to study the relationships between phenotypic and genotypic characteristics [9,22]. While the genome refers to the full set of genetic material, the phenome is defined as the totality of all traits expressed by an organism [1]. Finding associations between the phenome and genome is of utmost priority in biomedicine as it could lead to the identification of the molecular drivers underlying human diseases.

Although genome-wide association studies (GWAS) have been carried out to dissect phenome-genome associations [19], biological complexity [3] and lack of consensus on pathogenicity and susceptibility [4] entail great limitations. By querying on annotated datasets to infer novel associations, the grand challenge of characterizing phenome-genome relationships would greatly benefit from the fine mapping of ontological terms that tools such as GOPHER are able to generate.

Along the years, *Artificial Intelligence* (AI) approaches have enabled to model the behavior of a given system or agent. Recently, data oriented modeling solutions have been gaining popularity and skill, thanks to the increasing digitalization of data. Nowadays, its increasingly frequent to see how *simple models and a lot of data trump more elaborate models based on less data* [10]. Furthermore, when working with biological data, complex and detailed modeling solutions can be plain unfeasible. For this reason, in this work we chose to produce a very simple modeling solution which is based on the most basic aspects of interaction, empowered by a network structure thoroughly refined by experts along years. This is made possible by the power, scalability and parallelism provided by *High-Performance Computing* (HPC). A series of popular graph processing frameworks already exist (*e.g.*, igraph, networkX), however, since our task is highly specific, we choose to implement an ad-hoc solution which can be thoroughly optimized.

HPC systems allow to process data and run complex computations at a high degree of productivity (in terms of runtime speed, memory usage, or allowed storage). These HPC solutions are commonly based on supercomputers, containing thousands of compute nodes (e.g., processors) working together to complete one single task (i.e., parallel processing).

In order to manage such a complex scenario exist a vast number of tools that ease the use of HPC systems by abstracting the user from the underlying architecture: the *Message Passing Interface (MPI)* [13] is the most used parallel programming model in distributed systems (where memory is not shared, and thus the data must be explicitly sent by messages); the *Open Multi-Processing (OpenMP)* [14] is the standard de facto parallel programming model for shared memory environments (where the communication is done implicitly via the same Memory Address Space); and/or the *OpenMP SuperScalar (OmpSs)* [7], a task-based parallel programming model, considered as a forerunner for OpenMP (its ideas have been transferred into the OpenMP standard on several occasions).

3   GOPHER: Analysis, Design, and Implementation

Our goal is to predict when a pair of ontology terms, henceforth referred to as <genotype, phenotype>, could be directly associated through an intermediate gene. We build a model to represent direct association, and another to represent the lack of direct association. Given both models we can measure the probability with which a new pair belongs to either one of those. To build these models we use examples from the ontologies. Models are designed to strive for simplicity, prioritizing volume over complexity. To that end, we estimate the distribution of distinct paths (of a given maximum length) that connect <genotype, phenotype> pairs for both sets. We hypothesize that the type of path (the ordered sequence of vertex type traversed) may contribute to an accurate modeling.

For simplicity, we assume that the frequency of type of path follows a Gaussian distribution, which has a *mean* and *standard deviation* that can be estimated empirically. We note that this assumption is taken due to the unimodal distribution empirically observed, and we use the pervasive Gaussian to be able to perform inference. Therefore, given a <type of path, number of paths>, we can compute the probability of that number of paths being generated by each of the two corresponding gaussians (one for each of the two sets) using Eq. 1.

$$P(c|\mu,\sigma) = \frac{1}{\sigma\sqrt{2\pi}}e^{-(x-\mu)^2/2\sigma^2} \tag{1}$$

By making the quotient of these two probabilities we obtain the *odds* of each path type. We model the odds of connection of a new pair as the product of each path-specific odds, for a finite number of path types (*i.e.*, all paths up to a maximum length) as seen in Eq. 2.

$$Odds(connected|Counts) = \prod_{pt \in pathtypes} \frac{P(Count(pt)|\mu_{con}(pt), \sigma_{con}(pt))}{P(Count(pt)|\mu_{discon}(pt), \sigma_{discon}(pt))}$$

(2)

3.1   Analysis of Requirements

Modelling the association between <genotype,phenotype> pairs is subject to scientific investigation. It is desirable that both the design and the implementation of the system is highly programmable. Besides programmability, we also pursue a modular design to enable possible extensions of the system components.

GOPHER offers an efficient solution to modelling an embarrasingly parallel problem. Indeed, building the model is achieved by sampling pairs of directly associated (or not) pairs and finding all possible paths of a maximum length taking from one element of the pair to the other. Meanwhile, the total number of possible pairs to sample from is huge, which calls for a parallel approach.

3.2   Design and Implementation

Graph Topology. We create a comprehensive graph based on the relationships between phenotypes, genotypes, and genes. Figure 1 shows an example of this graph's structure. Ontology relations between phenotypes (blue nodes) and genotypes (green nodes) are shown as pointed arrows, and association to genes (red nodes) as dashed lines.

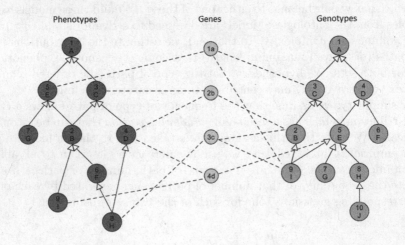

Fig. 1. Example of the graph's structure. (Color figure online)

We define a *type of path* as the sequence of steps between two nodes in the graph, according to the nature of each one. We label phenotypes as 'p', genotypes as 'g' and genes as 'G'. Then, a path of type *ppGg* starts on a phenotype (**p**), connects to another phenotype (**p**) (either its parent or its child), which is associated to a gene (**G**), which in its turn is finally associated to a genotype (**g**). We also define as a "directly associated pair" a pair of phenotype and genotype where there exists at least one path of type *pGg*.

Data Structures. An element is the basic component of the graph, and it can either be a phenotype, a genotype or a gene. In terms of implementation and of element structure, there is no difference between phenotypes, genotypes, and genes. As depicted in Fig. 2a, an element has the following fields:

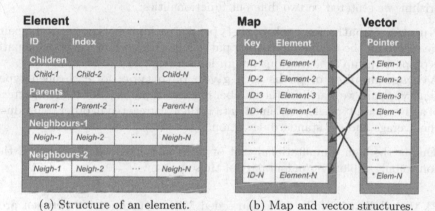

(a) Structure of an element.   (b) Map and vector structures.

Fig. 2. Ontology and pool structures used to represent a GOPHER graph.

- **Id:** The identifier is an integer defined by the input files. Not all sequential integer values need to be defined (i.e., phenotype 4 may exist without the need of the existence of phenotype 3).
- **Index:** The index is an integer defined by the application. The index can take values from zero up to the total number of nodes minus one (no gaps, no duplications within each ontology).
- **Children:** Vector of pointers to all the children of the element. If the element is a leaf or a gene, this vector will be empty.
- **Parents:** Vector of pointers to all the parents of the element. If the element is a root or a gene, this vector will be empty.
- **Neighbours:** According to the element type, these vectors can have two differents uses:
  - If the element is a phenotype or genotype, it will have a single vector containing pointers to its associated genes. It may be empty if the element has no associations.

- If the element is a gene, it will have two vectors, one containing pointers to its phenotypes associations, and another one pointing the its genotypes associations. Vectors may be empty, if the gene has no associations to one of the two ontologies.

Each ontology and the gene pool are defined by two different types of structures (see Fig. 2b). First, the **Map** structure allows to access any element of the graph providing its *Id* as the key value. Second, the **Vector** structure allows to access any element of the graph providing its *Index* as a key value (i.e., which actually matches with its position in the vector)[1].

Algorithms. GOPHER's core algorithm is a recursive exploring function, which searches for all existing paths between a given pair of elements. Using this core algorithm, we centered on two different functionalities:

- **Number of paths for each path type:** for each phenotype-genotype pair, we search for the number of existing paths following each of the possible path type patterns up to a given maximum length (e.g., 5).
- **Average number of paths of a given path type:** for each phenotype-genotype pair, we search for the number of existing paths following the pattern of a given path type. The obtained data is then aggregated in order to produce the average and the standard deviation.

Due to the high computational cost of these functions, we implemented the option to only explore a random part of those pairs.

MPI Parallelization. To avoid unneeded MPI communication between processes, there is no graph data distribution; all processes read the input files an populate a whole graph each. Our first MPI parallelization approach consists of equally distribute one of the two ontologies (e.g., phenotypes) between the processes, and each process explore the pairs starting from its assigned elements.

When finding the number of paths for each path type, no additional communication is needed (see Algorithm 1). Instead, when we want the average number of paths of a certain path's type and its standard deviation, we need to share the results between processes to calculate the average values after all processes have finished its assigned iterations. Algorithm 2 describes this functionality. We can see that there are two communication phases. The first one adds up the obtained number of paths and pairs from all processes, so each process can calculate the global average number of paths per pair. When all processes have the average value, each one calculates its local standard deviation. During the second communication phase, the local standard deviations values are reduced at the first process, which afterward calculates the global standard deviation.

This first approach of distributing phenotypes among MPI processes produces a huge load imbalance between processes. We tracked the origin from this

---

[1] Vectors are parallel-friendly structures that allow to easily split the elements among different compute elements.

Algorithm 1. MPI parallelization without communication

1: $chSize \leftarrow Ontology\,1\,size\,/\,num\,Ranks$
2: $(start, end) \leftarrow (my\,Rank * chSize, my\,Rank * chSize + chSize)$
3: **for** $i \leftarrow start, end$ **do**
4:     **for** $j \leftarrow 0, Ontology\,2\,size$ **do**
5:         **for** $k \leftarrow 0, num\,path\,types$ **do**
6:             Search Paths(Ontology 1(i), Ontology 2(j), path type(k))

Algorithm 2. MPI parallelization with communication

1: $chSize \leftarrow Ontology\,1\,size\,/\,num\,Ranks$
2: $(start, end) \leftarrow (my\,Rank * chSize, my\,Rank * chSize + chSize)$
3: $(nPaths, nPairs) \leftarrow (0, 0)$
4: **for** $i \leftarrow start, end$ **do**
5:     **for** $j \leftarrow 0, Ontology\,2\,size$ **do**
6:         $nPaths \leftarrow nPaths+$ Search Paths(Ontology 1(i), Ontology 2(j), path type)
7:         $nPairs \leftarrow nPairs + 1$
8: MPI_AllReduce (nPaths, nPairs)
9: $(average, st\,dev) \leftarrow (nPaths/nPairs, Calculate\,Local\,St\,Dev)$
10: MPI_Reduce (st dev)
11: **if** $my\,Rank = 0$ **then**
12:     $st\,dev \leftarrow Calculate\,Overall\,St\,Dev$

---

imbalance down to the number of direct connections per element. As can be seen in Fig. 3, there is a correlation between the average number of first-degree connections the elements assigned to a processor have and the time it takes to explore the paths starting from these elements.

To improve the load balance, we change the work distribution policy. As described in Algorithm 3, the new approach distributes the elements from the starting ontology among processes based on the number of the first-degree connections. First, we calculate the total number of connections, and then we distribute the phenotypes between the MPI processes trying to keep this number balanced among processes. In Sect. 4 we will compare these two versions.

Algorithm 3. MPI parallelization with new work distribution

1: $total\,work \leftarrow 0$
2: **for** $i \leftarrow 0, Ontology\,1\,size$ **do**
3:     $total\,work \leftarrow total\,work + connections(i)$
4: $chSize \leftarrow total\,work\,/\,num\,Ranks$
5: $(start, end) \leftarrow (begin(my\,Rank, chSize), end(my\,Rank, chSize))$

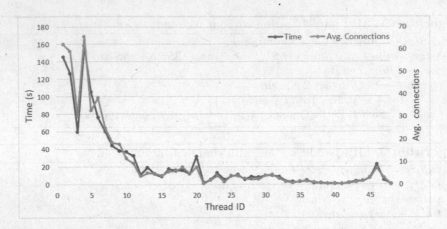

Fig. 3. Correlation between the average number of connections per element and the useful execution time per thread ID.

OpenMP/OmpSs Parallelization. A second level of parallelism based in shared memory has been implemented to palliate even more the imbalance problem previously described. OpenMP and other parallel programming models based on shared memory are inherently easier to load balance, as the threads share memory is easy to redistribute work among them without data exchange.

In our case we use OmpSs, as it offers the same benefits as OpenMP but it simplifies the use of task reductions and, in addition, it has better interoperability with respect to future techniques we also want to analyze in the future (see Sect. 5). Our approach is to create a task per *path exploration* function call.

Algorithm 4. OmpSs parallelization with reduction

1: $(nPaths, nPairs) \leftarrow (0, 0)$
2: **for** $i \leftarrow start, end$ **do**
3:     **for** $j \leftarrow 0, Ontology\, 2\, size$ **do**
4:         # pragma omp task reduction(+, nPaths)
5:         $nPaths \leftarrow nPaths+$ Search Paths(Ontology 1(i), Ontology 2(j), path type)
6:         $nPairs \leftarrow nPairs + 1$
7: # pragma omp taskwait / barrier
8: MPI All Reduce (num paths, num pairs)
9: $(average, st\, dev) \leftarrow (nPaths/nPairs, 0)$
10: # pragma omp parallel for reduction(+, st dev)
11: **for** $i \leftarrow 0, start - end$ **do**
12:     $st\, dev \leftarrow st\, dev + (nPaths(i) - average)^2$
13: MPI Reduce (st dev)

In addition, when we calculate the average number of paths of a certain type, we need to perform a local reduction on the number of found paths. In this case, we also parallelize the computation of the standard deviation. This approach can be seen in Algorithm 4.

4   Experimental Results

We obtained all the results on the *MareNostrum IV* system located at the Barcelona Supercomputing Center. Each node contains two Intel Xeon Platinum 8160, each one with 24 processors running at 2.1 GHz and 33 MB L3 Cache. Memory is organized in two NUMA sockets (i.e., one socket per processor), with a total amount of 192GB per socket (*high-mem* nodes).

For software, we used: *GNU Compilers Collection* (gcc) version 7.2.0; *Mercurium* source-to-source compiler (mcxx) version 2.3.0, *Nanos++* Runtime Library version 0.16a, and the OpenMPI Message Passage Interface version 3.1.1.

4.1   Evaluation of Model Results

As introduced in Sect. 3.2, we estimate the parameters of the gaussians for each path type, so that we can perform inference on unseen pairs by using the odds ratio. To validate we use the *Receiver Operating Characteristic* (ROC) and *Precision-Recall* (PR) curves, which illustrate overall performance. These curves are typically evaluated through the *area-under-the-curve* (AUC). To validate the outcomes of GOPHER, we evaluate under the following conditions:

- **Ontologies:** GO and HPO, only human, version: January 2019.
- **Path size:** all types of paths with size 4 or 5 elements.
- **Pairs nature:** from phenotypes to genotypes.
- **Samples:** 85,750 randomly sampled pairs.
- **Direct edge removal:** yes[2].

We estimate the components of the gaussians required for classification using an equal number of connected and disconnected pairs. To validate the classification results we extract the ROC and PR curves from the odds ratio obtained from Eq. 2, from 85,750 pairs of each type (different from the previous ones). The AUC of both curves is 0.96, significantly close to perfect performance (*i.e.*, 1). This means that, even though we removed relevant information (the edges connecting pairs directly in the graph), our classifier is able to correctly discriminate connected from disconnected pairs with minimal error. Further experimentation on older versions of the ontology is not conducted, as these are known to include a significant amount of noise [21].

4.2   Performance Results

Performance experiments have been executed with the algorithm *Number of paths for each path type* (as described in Sect. 3.2). The decision is based upon the complexity of the function, which clearly shows the imbalance problem between MPI processes. It is also the most relevant function for our studies. For experimenting purposes, we have run this function with the following parameters:

---

[2] Path frequencies for connected pairs are computed without considering the edges that directly connect the phenotype and genotype to the same gene, to avoid biasing the model towards already existing pairs.

- **Ontologies:** GO and HPO, only human, version: January 2019.
- **Path size:** all types of paths up to a size of 5 elements.
- **Pairs nature:** from phenotypes to genotypes.
- **Samples:** 100,000 randomly sampled pairs (constant seed).
- **Direct edge removal:** yes.

The timing results have been collected only from the computation (graph exploration) phase, since it takes most of the execution time in relevant cases. Previous phases, such as graph population and work distribution between processes, have been ignored.

Both versions of the algorithm have been tested and compared. In the initial version (labeled as *baseline* in Fig. 4), we equally distribute elements from the origin ontology just considering the number of elements (see Algorithms 1 and 2). While in the second version, labeled as *balancing* in the same Figure, we try to equally distribute the number of direct connection from the origin ontology (see Algorithm 3) rather than just the number of elements.

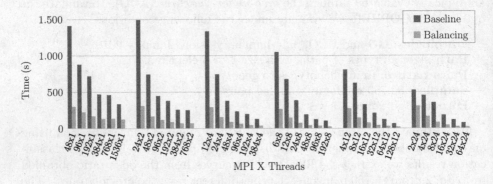

Fig. 4. Overall performance results (including baseline and balancing).

When we execute enabling none of those optimizations, shown as blue bars in Fig. 4, in all the case we achieve our better results when we running a MPI-Threads configuration which uses a high number of threads (and, therefore, a small number of MPI processes). This is because imbalance problems in GOPHER reside mostly in its MPI parallelization, not in OmpSs'.

When we apply the MPI balancing technique, depicted in orange bars in Fig. 4, we achieve an average speedup of 4,24x (comparing *balancing* with *non-balancing* versions) for the cases with 1, 2 and 4 threads for each MPI processes, and of 3,21x for the case with 24 threads per MPI process (mostly due to the lower baseline). When executing within a single node (i.e., first pair of columns in each group: 48 × 1, 24 × 2, etc.) is when it yields a higher impact, showing no significant differences among the different MPI-Threads configurations. As we increase the number of nodes, this version produces better results with higher thread counts, the gap getting wider with each additional node.

5   Conclusions and Future Work

In this paper we introduce the GOPHER framework for large graph exploration and inference, specially designed to run on HPC systems. GOPHER is developed to investigate the relationship between the phenome and genome using machine learning techniques to infer these complex relationships. In particular, it enables to estimate the likelihood that two ontology terms are associated when missing a direct connection through a co-annotated gene.

The work presented is extremely interdisciplinary, starting at understanding the biological questions that we want to answer through *preferential attachment*. We use a machine learning approach to infer associations between HPO and GO terms while working on large graphs. Built on top of an HPC oriented framework, designed to be modular and adaptable to solve a broad range of questions regarding a variety of ontologies.

We show that our approach obtains an AUC score of 0.96 over 1. We have also studied the parallel performance of GOPHER detecting that the main issue is related to the inherent load imbalance produced by the disparity in the number of connections. To address this issue we present an improved load balancing implementation, the evaluation shows that the load balancing implementation can overcome the performance loss due to the different number of connections and that it can scale up to 32 nodes with a relative speed-up of 4.24x.

This work opens a wide range of future work opportunities, we plan to study in detail the performance of GOPHER to find optimization opportunities in different architectures, including the use of a *Dynamic Load Balancing* library [2,8]. We will apply GOPHER to actionable use cases, such as anticancer treatment recommendations, as well as other biological ontologies, such as those of key model organisms (mouse and fruitfly).

Acknowledgements. This work has been developed with the support of the Severo Ochoa Program (SEV-2015-0493); the Spanish Ministry of Science and Innovation (TIN2015-65316-P); and the Joint Study Agreement no. W156463 under the IBM/BSC Deep Learning Center agreement.

References

1. What exactly are genomes: genotypes and phenotypes? And what about phenomes? J. Theor. Biol. **186**(1), 55–63 (1997)
2. Garcia, M., Labarta, J., Corbalan, J.: Hints to improve automatic load balancing with LeWI for hybrid applications. J. Parallel Distrib. Comput. **74**(9), 2781–2794 (2014)
3. Embracing complex associations in common traits: Critical considerations for precision medicine. Trends Genet. **32**(8), 470–484 (2016)
4. Garcia, M., Labarta, J., Corbalan, J.: Evaluating the clinical validity of gene-disease associations: an evidence-based framework developed by the clinical genome resource. Am. J. Hum. Genet. **100**(6), 895–906 (2017)
5. Choi, N., Song, I.Y., Han, H.: A survey on ontology mapping. ACM Sigmod Rec. **35**(3), 34–41 (2006)

6. Cirillo, D., Valencia, A.: Big data analytics for personalized medicine. Curr. Opin. Biotechnol. **58**, 161–167 (2019). https://doi.org/10.1016/j.copbio.2019.03. 004. SBN

7. Duran, A., Ayguadé, E., Badia, R.M., et al.: OmpSs: a proposal for programming heterogeneous multi-core architectures. Parallel Process. Lett. **21**(2), 173–193 (2011)

8. Garcia-Gasulla, M., Josep-Fabrego, M., Eguzkitza, B., Mantovani, F.: Computational fluid and particle dynamics simulations for respiratory system: Runtime optimization on an arm cluster. In: Proceedings of the 47th International Conference on Parallel Processing Companion, p. 11. ACM (2018)

9. Gkoutos, G.V., Schofield, P.N., Hoehndorf, R.: The anatomy of phenotype ontologies: principles, properties and applications. Briefings Bioinform. **19**(5), 1008–1021 (2017)

10. Halevy, A., Norvig, P., Pereira, F.: The unreasonable effectiveness of data. IEEE Intell. Syst. **24**(2), 8–12 (2009)

11. Hoehndorf, R., Schofield, P.N., Gkoutos, G.V.: The role of ontologies in biological and biomedical research: a functional perspective. Briefings Bioinform. **16**(6), 1069–1080 (2015). https://doi.org/10.1093/bib/bbv011

12. Köhler, S., Carmody, L., Vasilevsky, N., et al.: Expansion of the Human Phenotype Ontology (HPO) knowledge base and resources. Nucleic Acids Res. **47**(D1), D1018–D1027 (2018). https://doi.org/10.1093/nar/gky1105

13. Message Passing Interface Forum: MPI: A message-passing interface standard. Version 3.1. University of Tennessee, June 2015

14. OpenMP Architecture Review Board: OpenMP Application Programming Interface, version 5.0 (2018)

15. Rhee, S.Y., Wood, V., Dolinski, K., Draghici, S.: Use and misuse of the gene ontology annotations. Nat. Rev. Genet. **9**, 509–515 (2008)

16. Schulze-Kremer, S.: Ontologies for molecular biology and bioinformatics. In Silico Biol. **2**, 179–93 (2002)

17. Shefchek, K.A., Harris, N.L., Gargano, M., et al.: The Monarch Initiative in 2019: an integrative data and analytic platform connecting phenotypes to genotypes across species. Nucleic Acids Res. **48**(D1), D704–D715 (2019). https://doi.org/10. 1093/nar/gkz997

18. Smith, B., Ashburner, M., Rosse, C., Bard, J., et al.: The obo foundry: coordinated evolution of ontologies to support biomedical data integration. Nat. Biotechnol. **25**, 1251–5 (2007)

19. Tam, V., Patel, N., Turcotte, M., Bossé, Y., Paré, G., Meyre, D.: Benefits and limitations of genome-wide association studies. Nat. Rev. Genet. **20**, 467–484 (2019)

20. The Gene Ontology Consortium: The gene ontology resource: 20 years and still GOing strong. Nucleic Acids Res. **47**(D1), D330–D338 (2018)

21. Tomczak, A., et al.: Interpretation of biological experiments changes with evolution of the gene ontology and its annotations. Sci. Rep. **8**(1), 1–10 (2018)

22. Zhang, W., Zhang, H., Yang, H., et al.: Computational resources associating diseases with genotypes, phenotypes and exposures. Briefings Bioinform. **20**(6), 2098–2115 (2018)

Ensembles of Networks Produced from Neural Architecture Search

Emily J. Herron[1,2], Steven R. Young[1,2(✉)], and Thomas E. Potok[2]

[1] Bredesen Center, University of Tennessee-Knoxville, Knoxville, TN, USA
herronej@ornl.gov
[2] Computational Data Analytics, Oak Ridge National Laboratory,
Oak Ridge, TN, USA
youngsr@ornl.gov

Abstract. Neural architecture search (NAS) is a popular topic at the intersection of deep learning and high performance computing. NAS focuses on optimizing the architecture of neural networks along with their hyperparameters in order to produce networks with superior performance. Much of the focus has been on how to produce a single best network to solve a machine learning problem, but as NAS methods produce many networks that work very well, this affords the opportunity to ensemble these networks to produce an improved result. Additionally, the diversity of network structures produced by NAS drives a natural bias towards diversity of predictions produced by the individual networks. This results in an improved ensemble over simply creating an ensemble that contains duplicates of the best network architecture retrained to have unique weights.

Keywords: Neural architecture search · Ensembles · High performance computing

1 Introduction

There has been much work in recent years in developing methods for automatically designing neural networks for various challenges and datasets. This work in neural architecture search (NAS) largely focuses on finding a single best network. However, throughout this process many networks are created and evaluated.

Notice: This manuscript has been authored in part by UT-Battelle, LLC under Contract No. DE-AC05-00OR22725 with the U.S. Department of Energy. The United States Government retains and the publisher, by accepting the article for publication, acknowledges that the United States Government retains a non-exclusive, paid-up, irrevocable, world-wide license to publish or reproduce the published form of this manuscript, or allow others to do so, for United States Government purposes. The Department of Energy will provide public access to these results of federally sponsored research in accordance with the DOE Public Access Plan (http://energy.gov/downloads/doe-public-access-plan).

© Springer Nature Switzerland AG 2020
H. Jagode et al. (Eds.): ISC High Performance 2020 Workshops, LNCS 12321, pp. 223–234, 2020.
https://doi.org/10.1007/978-3-030-59851-8_14

This provides the opportunity to find not just a single network that performs well, but an ensemble of networks that perform well together on problems of interest.

In this work, we will study the results of ensembling networks produced by one such NAS method. The NAS method used is Multi-node Evolutionary Neural Networks for Deep Learning (MENNDL). It produces a variety of deep learning networks that perform well on the given dataset. However, the single network that gives optimal performance may still be limited in its knowledge of the distribution of the data or be over or under-fitted to the training data. Combining the outputs of multiple deep neural network classifiers has been demonstrated as an effective approach that offers significantly better prediction accuracies than that of individual models [11]. Neural network ensembles do so by combining outputs from a finite number of neural networks with different parameters that have been trained on the same data. In this report, we create and evaluate the performances of ensembles of the best performing networks produced by one or more runs of MENNDL. We consider two approaches to creating ensembles from this NAS approach and apply these approaches to two traditional image dataset benchmarks. The key contribution of this work is a study detailing the effects of ensembling networks from an NAS method including:

1. The effect of using ensembles created from multiple instantiations of the NAS method.
2. The effect of the size of the ensemble on performance.
3. The resulting performance measured as accuracy on the problem and the diversity in the ensemble.

2   Background and Related Work

Deep learning is a branch of machine learning based on the concept of learning features from multiple layers of abstraction [14]. In recent years, deep learning models have advanced the state of the art of tasks in fields like image recognition and generation in computer vision; language translation, text classification; and sentiment analysis in natural language processing; and automatic speech identification and generation in speech recognition [3]. Scientific research applications that involve analysis of large volumes of images produced with specialized instruments in particular also rely on the use of these models.

2.1   Neural Architecture Search

The features of deep learning models are controlled by a set of hyperparameters, which in the case of a deep convolutional neural network (CNN), include the number of hidden layers as well as each layer's number of nodes, activation function, and kernel size. The learning capacity of deep neural networks is dependent upon these hyperparameters, which must be selected appropriately to suit a particular dataset. The process of tailoring a deep neural network architecture to a particular data set can be computationally expensive and time consuming even with the guidance of experts. Furthermore, the features of scientific datasets often differ from that of traditional datasets. Hence, models optimized for traditional datasets may not be well-suited to scientific datasets. Hyperparameters have traditionally been selected either by manual trial and error or grid search. Manual search often requires expert users and involves selecting a set of hyperparameters from a region thought to be best-suited to the data [14]. Grid search, in contrast, finds an optimal solution after evaluating models assembled with each possible combination of hyperparameters. This method is preferred to manual search due to its ease of implementation and tendency to provide a better solution; however, it fails to be efficient in high dimensional feature spaces. If the selection is carried out this way, it can be a time-intensive task owning both to the expansive range of hyperparameters and the evaluation time of each possible network [13,14]. To overcome the drawbacks of these methods, researchers have suggested other approaches, including evolutionary algorithms.

We use an evolutionary optimization approach to NAS in this work known as MENNDL [13]. MENNDL is a GPU-based high performance computing framework that uses an asynchronous steady-state evolutionary algorithm to parallelize the large-scale evaluation of networks on individual nodes, with selection, mutation, and crossover procedures controlled by a master node. This allows for a more efficient search of a high dimensional hyperparameter space than grid search, and improves upon random search by considering previous results [13,14]. Networks produced by evolution-based optimization frameworks like MENNDL have demonstrated increased accuracy and efficiency compared to those suggested by domain experts [12].

2.2 Neural Network Ensembles

Neural network ensembles have been defined as a collection of neural networks that have been trained on the same task before their results are combined to produce a model with better generalization ability than individual networks. They have been applied to a variety of problems including handwritten digit recognition, scientific image analysis, face recognition, and OCR [15]. The idea behind the use of neural network ensembles is that the success of a deep learning model is predicated upon its ability to learn the distribution of a dataset. However, a single model that performs optimally on a training dataset may be over-fit to the training set and perform poorly on unseen data. Ensembles of networks with different parameters and architectures can reduce this risk since different networks may learn varying aspects of the training set before being combined to produce the desired outputs. The networks are typically combined by taking an average or weighted average of the outputs of each model in order to obtain the final result [2].

Constructing ensembles of networks can be a challenging task. Traditionally, ensemble techniques have relied on networks with randomly generated topologies, weights, or topologies that have learned random subsets of the training data. The intuition behind this that the networks will be diverse in the sense that they differ in terms of their errors [7]. It has been shown that the generalization ability of an ensemble is directly dependent upon its average generalization ability (e.g. accuracy) and average diversity of individual networks in the model. Previous work has found that the accuracy of an ensemble model can be improved by constructing and weighting multiple base learners and that the diversity of a model can be enhanced by selecting only learners that are less correlated in terms of training error [2]. Other studies have concluded that the ideal ensemble is one comprised of accurate networks that make errors on different parts of the input space [7]. A range of solutions have aimed to address the problem of assembling neural network ensembles that balance fitness and diversity. One work demonstrated that large ensembles of neural network models can be summarized with a relatively small number of representative models selected via clustering based on distances between model outputs. This method was demonstrated to, in certain cases, yield better prediction accuracies [1]. Elsewhere, a cluster-based selective algorithm was proposed for building a neural network ensemble based on the idea that more effective ensembles are comprised of networks that are both accurate and diverse. Clustering was used to identify subsets of similar networks before selecting the most accurate network from each cluster to form an ensemble. Experiments showed that this approach out-performed traditional ensemble approaches such as Boosting and Bagging [9]. In another study, an ensemble-based model was implemented by using a genetic algorithm to calculate the weights of individual networks to create a population with high overall accuracy. K-means clustering was then used to select an optimal subset of learners to improve the diversity of the model. This approach was compared to other ensemble techniques including the traditional average, weighted average, and kriging models and demonstrated to outperform each [2]. A different study examined the relationship between the generalization abilities of neural network ensembles and correlations between networks based on correctly and incorrectly classified samples selected at random. It was discovered that, in some instances, selecting a subset of networks was superior to ensembles of all of the individual networks. The authors proposed an approach that uses a genetic algorithm to select an optimal set of neural networks given a set of pre-trained networks to serve as an ensemble. They demonstrated that this method worked well compared to a popular ensemble approach and produced ensembles with high generalizing ability with a relatively low computational cost [15]. Another publication introduced a method known as Addemup, which leveraged a diverse population of neural networks generated by a genetic algorithm in creating an ensemble of neural networks. The genetic algorithm used for this purpose was designed to meet an objective function that seeks to maximize the accuracy of the networks while ensuring dissimilarity between members of the population. Ensembles were evaluated during training following an approach that focuses on more difficult examples in order to quickly produce good results. The authors demonstrated that their algorithm yielded significantly better results than uses of the single best network alone, the Bagging ensemble approach, and a similar algorithm with an objective function that only considers validation accuracy [7].

3   Methods

3.1   MENNDL

Multi-node Evolutionary Neural Networks for Deep Learning (MENNDL) is a software framework that implements an evolutionary algorithm for optimizing neural network topology and hyperparameters. More specifically, it can optimize the number of layers, layer type for each layer, and the corresponding layer hyperparameters. MENNDL utilizes an asynchronous approach to evaluate the networks it generates in parallel in order to maximize utilization of available computation resources. Evolutionary algorithms mimic the process of natural selection, treating a population of neural networks as individuals, each with their own 'genes' or set of architectural hyperparameters. The fitnesses of individuals in each generation are evaluated before a selection protocol chooses a subset of individuals in the population who will pass their features on to the next generation of networks, following crossover and mutation. Given proper initialization, parameterization, and a sufficient number of generations, this framework produces high-performing networks by focusing on regions of the parameter space containing individuals selected at each generation, while avoiding searches in the neighborhoods of less-fit individuals [3,10]. Figure 1 illustrates the architectures of the top networks produced by eight separate runs of MENNDL against the CIFAR-10 image dataset. Note that the architectures of the best performing networks produced by each run are diverse, yet each network performs comparably on the validation sets. The specific details of the evolutionary algorithm implemented by MENNDL are provided in [13].

3.2   Ensembles of MENNDL Generated Networks

We created ensembles of the top networks across one or more runs of MENNDL against two different datasets: MNIST and CIFAR-10. For each dataset, MENNDL was run 24 times on 8 nodes for 6 h each. For each of these runs, a 'keep best' flag was used in order to automatically select the individual with the highest fitness at each generation. The validation accuracies and networks from each run were saved. Following these runs, four categories of ensembles were assembled from the networks with the highest validation accuracies. The first three ensembles were of the top 2, 4, and 8 networks and the fourth was of 8 separately trained versions of the top network. The networks were selected from each run as well as from pools of 2, 4, and 8 randomly selected runs for the same dataset. Each of the chosen networks were evaluated on the test set, producing softmax outputs that were averaged to obtain the final predictions. The ensembles were repeated 24 times for each combination of ensemble type and selection pool size. Each MENNDL run and ensemble experiment was carried out on the Summit supercomputer at Oak Ridge National Laboratory. The system has a total of 4608 nodes, each with two IBM POWER9 CPUs and six NVIDIA Volta GPUs [8]. The diversity of each ensemble was measured by averaging the total disagreement between the predicted outputs for each sample, following a method similar to the one described in [6]. Given two arrays of sample predictions for a test set of length m, p_i and p_j, the average disagreement between the two sets of predictions is calculated using the equation

$$d(p_i, p_j) = \frac{1}{m} \sum_{k=1}^{m} \psi(p_{ik}, p_{jk}) \tag{1}$$

where the disagreement between two predictions for a sample at index k is given by

$$\psi(p_{ik}, p_{jk}) = \begin{cases} 0, & p_{ik} = p_{jk} \\ 1, & \text{otherwise} \end{cases} \tag{2}$$

The average disagreements between the predictions of an ensemble of size n are then averaged:

$$\frac{1}{n^2} \sum_{i=1}^{n} \sum_{j=1}^{n} d(p_i, p_j) \tag{3}$$

The result is a value that measures the probability that two networks in the ensemble will disagree with one another given a sample in the test set.

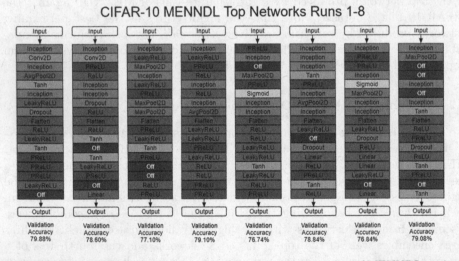

Fig. 1. Top network architectures produced by eight separate runs of MENNDL against the CIFAR-10 training dataset. The validation accuracies are listed for each network.

3.3   Datasets and Experiments

A set of experiments were carried out to compare the accuracies of top individual networks to those of four different ensembles of top performing networks. Three ensembles were created by selecting the top 2, 4, and 8 networks from a pool of runs. A fourth ensemble was constructed by combining the outputs of 8 separately trained versions of the top network architecture. The top networks for each of the 24 MENNDL runs against the dataset were evaluated against ensembles comprised of networks from 1, 2, 4 or 8 randomly selected MENNDL runs. The top networks and ensembles were selected and evaluated 24 times for per configuration.

The CIFAR-10 [4] and MNIST [5] image datasets were used in these experiments. The CIFAR-10 dataset consists of 60,000 32 by 32 multicolor images, each belonging to one of 10 classes. It is divided into a training set of size 50,000 and test set of size 10,000. The MNIST dataset consists of training and test sets of 60,000 and 10,000 28 by 28 grayscale images of handwritten digits ranging from 0 to 9. Upon initializing each run of MENNDL, the CIFAR-10 samples were normalized with the mean and standard deviation transforms (0.4914 0.4822 0.4465) and (0.2023 0.1994 0.2010) and MNIST with (0.1307) and (0.3081). 10% of the samples in each training set were selected at random and held out as a validation set. Individual networks were trained with a batch size of 64 on the remaining training samples. Afterward, the networks were evaluated on the validation set to obtain the fitnesses for selection. The CIFAR-10 and MNIST test sets were used to obtain the accuracies of each ensemble. No data augmentation or transformation beyond the simple normalization given above was used in this work.

4   Results

The means of the total networks, generations, and maximum fitnesses across 24 runs of MENNDL against each dataset are listed in Table 1. We note that the datasets' mean total networks and generations per run were similiar. However, the average maximum fitness was significantly higher with MNIST than with CIFAR-10. The standard deviation of this statistic was also much lower with the MNIST than CIFAR-10.

The mean test set accuracies for each ensemble and pool size configuration are listed in Tables 2 and 3 and plotted in Fig. 2. The ensemble accuracies were generally higher when ensembles were composed of more of the top networks. This trend was consistent in the case of both when going from the top individual network to the ensemble of the top 8 networks. Creating an ensemble of only the top two networks offered accuracy improvements over that of individual networks of as much as $3.0900 \pm 0.3698\%$ on CIFAR-10 and $0.1821 \pm 0.0432\%$ on MNIST. This finding is consistent with our expectations and demonstrates that creating ensembles of the top two or more MENNDL runs is an effective means of improving upon the generalizability of the single best-performing network across one or more runs.

The CIFAR-10 ensembles also tended to achieve higher overall test set accuracies when larger pools of runs were used. However, this trend was not the case with the MNIST ensembles. This is likely because the average best individual network fitnesses of the MENNDL runs against the MNIST dataset had considerably lower standard deviations than that of the runs against the CIFAR-10 dataset. In other words, the top network accuracies from the CIFAR-10 dataset varied more than those from MNIST. Hence, selecting the top overall networks from larger pools of MENNDL runs against this dataset would more likely result in top networks with higher generalization ability than top networks chosen from a smaller pool or single run. Additionally, as the misclassification rate was much smaller for the best MNIST networks, there is little room to add functionally diverse networks to the ensemble while still maintaining high classification rates.

The mean accuracies and diversities of ensembles of the top 8 networks and the top network trained 8 separate times are listed in Tables 4 and 5. These results reveal that ensembles of the top 8 networks yielded diversities that were consistently higher than the ensembles of 8 separately trained versions of the top network. The ensemble diversities' tendency to decrease as larger pools of runs were used was likely an artifact of the larger pools of runs' increased likelihood of having access to top networks with better generalizability, resulting in outputs that were less likely to differ from one another.

Table 1. CIFAR-10 and MNIST mean total networks, generations, and fitness of best network across 24 runs of MENNDL.

Statistic	Dataset	
	CIFAR-10	MNIST
Total networks	607.63 ± 86.35	589.63 ± 73.71
Generations	13.54 ± 1.76	13.08 ± 1.61
Best network fitness	78.47 ± 1.26	99.33 ± 0.10

Table 2. MNIST mean top network and ensemble test set accuracies for run pool sizes of 1, 2, 4, and 8. Note that the ensembles of the top 8 networks from run pool sizes of 2 and 4 achieved the highest mean accuracies out of all configurations.

MENNDL runs	Ensemble method				
	Top network	Top 2 networks	Top 4 networks	Top 8 networks	Top network 8x
1	99.4067 ± 0.1225	99.2471 ± 0.1225	99.4929 ± 0.0658	99.4929 ± 0.0624	99.4092 ± 0.1226
2	99.2554 ± 0.1129	99.4375 ± 0.0697	99.4742 ± 0.0815	$\mathbf{99.5487 \pm 0.0550}$	99.4471 ± 0.0897
4	99.2858 ± 0.0953	99.3954 ± 0.0816	99.5029 ± 0.0443	99.5125 ± 0.0673	99.4629 ± 0.0666
8	99.2629 ± 0.1154	99.4117 ± 0.0860	99.4646 ± 0.0587	99.5229 ± 0.0501	99.4038 ± 0.0933

Table 3. CIFAR-10 mean top network and ensemble test set accuracies for run pool sizes of 1, 2, 4, and 8. Note that the ensemble of the top 8 networks from a run pool size of 8 achieved the highest mean accuracy out of all configurations.

MENNDL runs	Ensemble method				
	Top network	Top 2 networks	Top 4 networks	Top 8 networks	Top network 8x
1	77.9025 ± 1.5848	80.9925 ± 1.2150	82.5629 ± 1.1345	83.0067 ± 0.9954	82.7583 ± 1.5473
2	78.3483 ± 1.1599	80.8808 ± 1.6867	83.0500 ± 0.8213	83.5075 ± 0.7859	83.4538 ± 1.2226
4	79.9271 ± 1.5532	81.6767 ± 1.2697	83.5146 ± 0.8869	$\mathbf{83.9796 \pm 0.6361}$	83.1325 ± 1.0810
8	79.7904 ± 1.3920	81.7825 ± 1.7717	83.6996 ± 0.7334	84.3708 ± 0.6521	84.0350 ± 1.0589

Table 4. MNIST mean diversities and accuracies for ensembles of top 8 and of top network trained 8 separate times selected from run pools of size 1, 2, 4, and 8.

MENNDL runs	Ensemble method			
	Top 8 networks		Top network 8x	
	Diversity	Accuracy	Diversity	Accuracy
1	0.0077 ± 0.0007	99.4929 ± 0.0624	0.0058 ± 0.0016	99.4092 ± 0.1226
2	0.0071 ± 0.0005	99.5487 ± 0.0550	0.0052 ± 0.0013	99.4471 ± 0.0897
4	0.0068 ± 0.0008	99.5125 ± 0.0673	0.0057 ± 0.0014	99.4629 ± 0.0666
8	0.0065 ± 0.0007	99.5229 ± 0.0496	0.0061 ± 0.0009	99.4038 ± 0.0933

Table 5. CIFAR-10 mean diversities and accuracies for ensembles of top 8 and of top network trained 8 separate times selected from run pools of size 1, 2, 4, and 8.

MENNDL runs	Ensemble method			
	Top 8 networks		Top network 8x	
	Diversity	Accuracy	Diversity	Accuracy
1	0.2118 ± 0.0199	83.0067 ± 0.9954	0.1798 ± 0.0200	82.7583 ± 1.5473
2	0.1984 ± 0.0146	83.5075 ± 0.7859	0.1801 ± 0.0148	83.4538 ± 1.2226
4	0.1943 ± 0.0110	83.9796 ± 0.6361	0.1676 ± 0.0135	83.1325 ± 1.0810
8	0.1794 ± 0.0131	84.3708 ± 0.6521	0.1594 ± 0.0118	84.0350 ± 1.0589

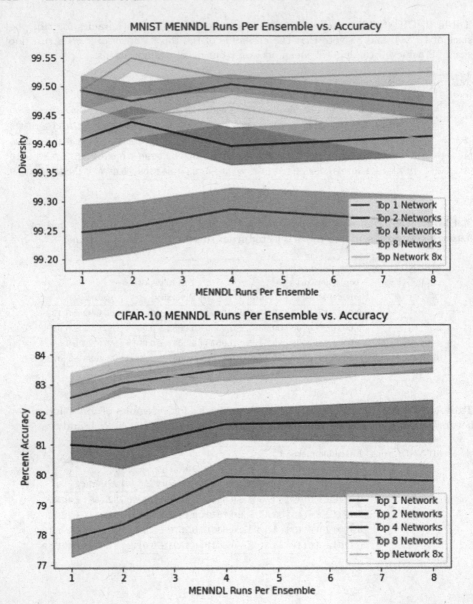

Fig. 2. MNIST and CIFAR-10 MENNDL run pool size vs. mean accuracy for the top network, ensembles of the top 2, 4, and 8 networks, and an ensemble of 8 separately trained versions of the top network.

5   Conclusion and Future Work

We have presented a study demonstrating that creating ensembles of multiple different networks from a NAS method produces a better result than simply using the best network produced by the NAS, even if we use multiple copies of that best network retrained several times. This demonstrates that the increased diversity of network structure in the ensemble produces increased diversity in predictions of the networks leading to improved ensemble performance. These results open the door to several promising directions of future work. As we have demonstrated the diversity of network structures improves performance, we will look to explicitly leverage this by evolving ensembles of networks within a NAS approach instead of simply creating an ensemble as a post-process, thus allowing the NAS to explicitly identify networks that complement each other.

Acknowledgements. This material is based upon work supported by the U.S. Department of Energy, Office of Science, Office of Advanced Scientific Computing Research, Robinson Pino, program manager, under contract number DE-AC05-00OR22725.

This research used resources of the Oak Ridge Leadership Computing Facility, which is a DOE Office of Science User Facility supported under Contract DE-AC05-00OR22725.

References

1. Bakker, B., Heskes, T.: Clustering ensembles of neural network models. Neural Netw. **16**(2), 261–269 (2003)
2. Chatterjee, S., Bandopadhyay, S., Machuca, D.: Ore grade prediction using a genetic algorithm and clustering based ensemble neural network model. Math. Geosci. **42**(3), 309–326 (2010)
3. Coletti, M., Lunga, D., Berres, A., Sanyal, J., Rose, A.: Ramifications of evolving misbehaving convolutional neural network kernel and batch sizes. In: 2018 IEEE/ACM Machine Learning in HPC Environments (MLHPC), pp. 106–113 (2018)
4. Krizhevsky, A., et al.: Learning multiple layers of features from tiny images (2009)
5. LeCun, Y., Cortes, C., Burges, C.: MNIST handwritten digit database. ATT Labs. 2 (2010). http://yann.lecun.com/exdb/mnist
6. Melville, P., Mooney, R.J.: Creating diverse ensemble classifiers (2003)
7. Opitz, D.W., Shavlik, J.W.: Actively searching for an effective neural network ensemble. Connection Sci. **8**(3–4), 337–354 (1996)
8. Patton, R.M., et al.: Exascale deep learning to accelerate cancer research. In: 2019 IEEE International Conference on Big Data (Big Data), pp. 1488–1496 (2019)
9. Qiang, F., Shang-xu, H., Sheng-ying, Z.: Clustering-based selective neural network ensemble. J. Zhejiang Univ.-Sci A **6**(5), 387–392 (2005). https://doi.org/10.1631/jzus.2005.A0387
10. Real, E., et al.: Large-scale evolution of image classifiers (2017)
11. Sharkey, A.J.: Combining Artificial Neural Nets: Ensemble and Modular Multi-Net Systems. Springer, London (2012). https://doi.org/10.1007/978-1-4471-0793-4
12. Young, S.R., et al.: Evolving energy efficient convolutional neural networks. In: 2019 IEEE International Conference on Big Data (Big Data), pp. 4479–4485. IEEE (2019)
13. Young, S.R., et al.: Evolving deep networks using HPC. In: Proceedings of the Machine Learning on HPC Environments, pp. 1–7 (2017)

14. Young, S.R., Rose, D.C., Karnowski, T.P., Lim, S.H., Patton, R.M.: Optimizing deep learning hyper-parameters through an evolutionary algorithm. In: Proceedings of the Workshop on Machine Learning in High-Performance Computing Environments, MLHPC 2015. Association for Computing Machinery, New York (2015). https://doi.org/10.1145/2834892.2834896
15. Zhou, Z.H., Wu, J.X., Jiang, Y., Chen, S.F.: Genetic algorithm based selective neural network ensemble. In: Proceedings of the 17th International Joint Conference on Artificial Intelligence, vol. 2, pp. 797–802 (2001)

SmartPred: Unsupervised Hard Disk Failure Detection

Philipp Rombach[✉] and Janis Keuper

Institute for Machine Learning and Analytics (IMLA), Offenburg University,
Offenburg, Germany
{rombach,keuper}@imla.ai

Abstract. Due to the rapidly increasing storage consumption world-wide, as well as the expectation of continuous availability of information, the complexity of administration in today's data centers is growing permanently. Integrated techniques for monitoring hard disks can increase the reliability of storage systems. However, these techniques often lack intelligent data analysis to perform predictive maintenance. To solve this problem, machine learning algorithms can be used to detect potential failures in advance and prevent them. In this paper, an unsupervised model for predicting hard disk failures based on Isolation Forest is proposed. Consequently, a method is presented that can deal with the highly imbalanced datasets, as the experiment on the Backblaze benchmark dataset demonstrates.

Keywords: Unsupervised learning · Hard disk drives · Anomaly detection

1 Introduction

The prediction of the reliability of hard disk drives was born out of the need to protect stored information on hard disks from data loss. For this purpose, several hard drive manufacturers have developed a technology that monitors and analyzes the current state of a hard drive, also known as Self-Monitoring, Analysis and Reporting Technology (SMART). SMART uses sensors to collect information about the state of magnetic hard disks and Solid State Drives (SSDs). From the collected sensor values, SMART creates an overview of the hard disk's health and can indicate a current failure. However, no intelligence analysis is performed by combining several sensor values. In particular, a predictive analysis of the sensor values would make it possible to detect potential errors or failures in advance. Such predictive maintenance would make it possible to increase the reliability of storage systems by replacing hard disks before they fail.

The recorded performance values of SMART cover 62 attributes. Each attribute has assigned a threshold value based on the experience of the manufacturer. If an attribute exceeds its threshold value, the drive is marked as faulty [15]. Since it is possible to return the drive to the manufacturer for a

© Springer Nature Switzerland AG 2020
H. Jagode et al. (Eds.): ISC High Performance 2020 Workshops, LNCS 12321, pp. 235–246, 2020.
https://doi.org/10.1007/978-3-030-59851-8_15

warranty replacement if the threshold is exceeded, it is reasonable to assume that manufacturers carefully reduce the false alarm rates of their predictions. This assumption is backed by the evaluation in [6], which showed that the current SMART algorithms implemented in the drives have failure detection rates ranging from only 3 to 10%.

Hard disk failures can be divided into two different categories. On the one hand, there are predictable failures that can be detected before a hard disk fails. On the other hand, there are unpredictable failures. In this case, the sudden death of the hard disk occurs [20]. Unpredictable failures occur quickly and suddenly and mean that no prediction can be made at the time of failure. The SMART attributes remain constant during this type of failure and therefore show no variance in the recorded values. These failures cannot be detected using the values logged with SMART. Predictable failures are caused by the worsening of at least one of the SMART attributes overtime before the hard disk fails. By monitoring these SMART attributes, predictive failure analysis is possible, and it can be determined whether the hard disk needs to be replaced. In [11], the percentage of predictable hard disk failures is given as 60%.

There are already several research papers that deal with the failure detection of hard disks [3–5,7,12–14,16,18,19], they evaluate the results using a binary classification and thus predict whether a hard disk will fail. However, differences in the experimental setups make it challenging to compare the performance of the models created. This includes the choice of dataset and the choice of metrics used to evaluate the model.

The objective of this paper is to perform a predictive analysis based on the SMART values and to divide the results into two categories. These categories reflect the failure probability of a hard disk over a specified period. The analysis is carried out using an anomaly detection algorithm since faulty hard disks represent only a tiny minority and can be referred to as anomalies.

In summary, the major contributions in this paper are the following:

- Transfer of anomaly detection techniques to the failure prediction in hard disk drives.
- By choosing the Isolation Forest algorithm, a model is presented to handle the highly imbalanced dataset without preprocessing. Therefore no downsampling or upsampling of the instances is necessary.
- The unsupervised method can be performed on a few samples without the need to generate a training data set. Thus, there is no significant delay between data acquisition and prediction.
- The detected anomalies are divided into two categories based on their failure probability. Depending on the classified category, a replacement process for the hard disk is proposed.

The structure of this work is divided into four basic sections. Section 2 deals with the research work done so far and its results. In Sect. 3, the model created to predict hard disk failures is presented. The results achieved are described and evaluated in Sect. 4. Furthermore, possible limitations of the dataset are discussed. The work is rounded off by Sect. 5 with a conclusion.

2   Related Work

This section provides an overview of research work focusing on predicting disk failure. All studies of investigation take the SMART attributes into account. The metrics used to evaluate the results are Failure Detection Rate (FDR), False Alarm Rate (FAR), and the failure rate of hard disks in the dataset. Recall, or in the context of hard disk failure detection, also called FDR, shows how complete the results are. FDR is a good metric for unbalanced datasets because it only refers to the anomalies. In Eq. 1 the calculation of FDR is shown.

$$FDR = \frac{TP}{TP + FN} \tag{1}$$

False Positive Rate (FPR) is referred to as the FAR value when detecting hard disk failure. FAR is the ratio of correctly detected normal instances to false positive anomalies. In anomaly detection, the goal is to keep the FAR value as low as possible. In Eq. 2 the calculation of FAR is shown.

$$FAR = \frac{FP}{FP + TN} \tag{2}$$

Hamerly and Elkan [3] use two Bayesian approaches, Naive Bayes Expectation Maximization (NBEM), and naive Bayesian classifier, to create semi-supervised models. Their data is provided by Quantum Inc. and includes 1927 good drives and nine failed drives. They achieve failure detection rates of 35% to 40% for NBEM and 55% for the naive Bayes classifier at approximately 1% FAR. Hughes et al. [4] use the Wilcoxon rank-sum test to create predictive models. Since they observed that most of the SMART attributes are distributed more non-parametrically, their model has tested 3780 drives, with a failure rate of 0.9%. They achieve a detection rate of 60% with a false alarm rate of 0.5%. In their later research [7], they used several methods, including rank-sum testing, Support Vector Machine (SVM), and unsupervised clustering. The dataset was substantially smaller, with a population of 369 drives and a failure rate of 51%. SVM achieved the best results with a FDR of 50.6% and a FAR of 0%. 25 SMART attributes were used to create the SVM model. By additionally using the change rates of the SMART attributes, Zhu et al. in [19] were able to improve the SVM model to achieve a FDR of 80% at 0.3% FAR.

Wang et al. [14] proposed a strategy to predict drive anomalies based on Mahalanobis distance. They used the same dataset as in [4,7] and showed that the method with prioritized attributes selected by the Failure Modes, Mechanisms and Effects Analysis (FMMEA) performed better than the method with all attributes. In their subsequent study [13], minimum Redundance Maximum Relevance (mRMR) was used to remove redundant information from the attribute selected by the FMEA. Using these critical parameters, they built a baseline Mahalanobis space. This model could detect 68% of the faulty disks with 0% FAR.

The research work of Zhu et al. in [19] not only included the improvement of the SVM model, they furthermore created a second model with Back Propagation Artificial Neural Network (BP ANN). BP ANN aimed to increase the failure detection rate significantly while keeping the FAR low. The models were created on a real dataset with 23395 drives, and this dataset has a failure rate of 1.9%, which is significantly lower than the dataset used in [4,7]. The collected SMART attributes covered eight weeks and were provided from the Baidu data center. The BP ANN failure detection rate was 95%, and the FAR was reported as reasonably low. In another paper by Zhu et al. [5], the Classification and Regression Trees (CART) algorithm is used to create a model for predicting hard disk failures. Compared to the BP ANN, the advantages of a CART model are improved prediction results and better stability and interpretability. On the Baidu dataset, they achieve a FDR of 95% with a FAR of 0.1%.

The proposed model of Xu et al. [17] used a Recurrent Neural Network (RNN) to predict hard disk failures and to assess the health of hard disks. The SMART attributes divided by their timestamp are used as input data. The results from the model are divided into six levels that reflect the health of a hard disk. The smaller the level, the higher the risk of hard disk failure. Level 6 means that there is no limitation on the hard disk, and it is functioning reliably. If the hard disk is assigned to level 1, it means that the hard disk will fail in less than 72 h. Several RNN-based models were created, focusing on maximizing the FDR and minimizing the FAR. As a result, the predicted results were a FDR of 87% with a very low FAR of 0.004% and a FDR of 97.7% and a FAR of 0.59%.

Shen et al. [12] and Xiao et al. [16] both use the random forest as the underlying technology in their research. They also use datasets provided by Backblaze [1] to train and test their models. In [12], the Random Forest (RF) based model is improved by additional voting. For this purpose, a sliding window is created that always trains samples from a hard disk of 30 days, and if the number of bad samples exceeds a limit, this hard drive is marked as faulty. The model achieves a FDR of 95% with a FAR of 0.4%. In [16], the focus is on training the model to handle streaming data and process it on-the-fly. This is also called Online Random Forest (ORF) [9]. By using ORF, performance is increased, and less memory is used. However, the ORF model takes up to six months to converge to offline random forest models' performance. The FDR on ORF is 98%, with a FAR of 0.7%.

Anomaly detection is performed by Zhang et al. in [18] using Isolation Forest. The dataset is again from Backblaze in the second quarter of 2018 and is trained on several training datasets where the number of failed disks varies from 2% to 10%. The FDR was not specified in the research work, but the accuracy is described with up to 95% and an average FAR of 5%. Also, the better performance in terms of training duration compared to the Random Forest is highlighted.

The presented research papers are sorted chronologically, starting with the oldest research [3] from the year 2001 up to the newest paper [18] from the year 2019. Most of the research has been focused on the development of supervised models, resulting in improved predictive performance over the years as measured by the FDR and FAR values. However, it must be taken into account that the used supervised models provide their results in the form of a binary classification, which cannot reflect the deterioration of a hard disk in reality.

3   The Proposed Method

This section describes the process of creating the Isolation Forest models to predict hard drive failures, intending to predict a failure probability for all hard drives, group the drives based on this probability, and identifying the suspect drives by their serial number. As a first step, exploratory data analysis is performed, and relevant features are selected prior to creating the model and optimize the hyperparameters.

3.1   Dataset

The dataset used to predict disk failure is derived from Backblaze [1]. Backblaze is a cloud storage provider that enables users to store their backups online. The company provides data storage for both private and business purposes. All hard drives used by Backblaze are monitored, and the SMART attributes are logged daily. The collected SMART data is provided in datasets that are publicly available and can be used freely.

Since 2013, Backblaze provides its SMART datasets for each quarter. These are compressed and contain one file for each day, which is stored as structured data. The number of features has been continuously increased since 2013 and reached 129 features in 2019, of which the first five features are reserved for identifying the hard disk.

The *date* feature contains the day on which the values were recorded. The *serial_number* feature is used to identify the disk in the dataset. All hard disks of the same type are combined in the feature *model*. The storage capacity of the hard disk is specified in the feature *capacity_bytes* in bytes. The *failure* feature is an integer in the value range [0, 1] and contains the value 0 if the disk is healthy and the value 1 if this is the last recorded sample of the disk before the failure.

The remaining 124 features are used for the SMART attributes, divided into *smart_x_raw* and *smart_x_normalized*. The features for the raw values contain the real values recorded; these are stored as floating-point numbers. In contrast, for the normalized values, a vendor-specific function has been executed based on the raw values to store them in a specific value range.

To highlight the deterioration of a hard disk, the list of features is extended. For this purpose an additional feature *smart_x_raw_diff* is created for each feature of *smart_x_raw*. These features contain the difference value of a disk to the previous day. The hard disks must be grouped by their serial numbers and sorted by date to calculate the difference value. Afterward, for each feature of *smart_x_raw*, the calculation of the difference value to the previous value is performed. Since no difference can be calculated for the first entry in the dataset, this value is set to 0.

The Backblaze dataset consists of all in all 136568 hard disks with 40737546 samples for the year 2019 and is, therefore, one of the largest SMART datasets publicly available. The failure rate and wear and tear of hard disks vary according to the model and manufacturing process [8,10]. In order to minimize the effects of the different models, this work concentrates on one specific model. This limitation is negligible as the same methodology can be conducted for other hard disk models in the same manner. The number of hard disks and the number of failed disks were used as selection criteria for the model. Thus, the model *ST12000NM0007* from Seagate is taken into account and, for simplification, is referred to as *ST1* in the following. The model *ST1* contains a total of 38256 hard disks, of which 1155 hard disks fail over a period of one year. Over this period, 12721076 samples were recorded.

3.2   Feature Selection

To determine the relevant features for prediction, the correlation coefficient between all SMART Attributes is calculated concerning the feature *failure*. The correlation is a bivariate analysis that measures the strength of the association between two features and the direction of the relationship.

To select the relevant features for the Isolation Forest, features that show a positive correlation with the feature *failure* are filtered. The Table 1 shows all features with a positive correlation.

Table 1. Descriptive statistics of *ST1*

	5_raw	187_raw	197_raw	5_diff	187_diff	197_diff
mean	27.85	1.1	0.14	0.65	0.03	0.01
std	697.15	201.08	15.52	117.97	40.52	9.09
min	0.0	0.0	0.0	−63368.0	−13.0	−280.0
25%	0.0	0.0	0.0	0.0	0.0	0.0
50%	0.0	0.0	0.0	0.0	0.0	0.0
75%	0.0	0.0	0.0	0.0	0.0	0.0
max	65528.0	65535.0	30960.0	57056.0	65535.0	30944.0

The measurements representing the selected raw features are described below:

Reallocated Sectors Count (SMART 5): is the total number of defective sectors that have been detected and reallocated.

Reported Uncorrectable Errors (SMART 187): is the number of errors that could not be recovered with Error Correcting Codes (ECCs).

Current Pending Sector Count (SMART 197): is the number of sectors waiting to be reassigned to the spare area due to uncorrectable errors in reading and writing a sector.

3.3   Preprocessing

To determine whether a hard disk will fail, the values in each feature must have a variance greater than 0 concerning this hard disk. If the disk features have a constant value of 0, they are among the 40% of disks that fail without significant SMART attributes [11] and are therefore considered false negative by the model. This is due to the fact that the values do not differ from healthy disks and, therefore, cannot be detected as anomalies. For this reason, the failed disks without variance are removed from the dataset.

An important step to avoid incorrect predictions is to inspect the dataset for possible inconsistent data and to correct them. This process is also called data cleaning and is divided into four steps:

1. Check the dataset for possible duplicates, if duplicates exist, remove these samples from the dataset
2. Search in the dataset for values without content. This can result from incorrect data collection and processing. If there are missing values in the dataset, delete these samples from the dataset.
3. Check for each disk whether the values are complete. This means that for a working disk, the last sample must match the last day of the dataset, and for a failed disk, the last sample in the *failure* feature must contain a value of 1. If these conditions are not met, all samples from that disk will be removed from the dataset.
4. For each failed hard disk, check if it has a variance greater than 0 in its features. If not, the hard disk will be removed from the dataset.

After data cleaning, the dataset *ST1* contains 37768 disks with 12614746 samples. Thus 1.28% of the data is removed by the cleanup process. With the failing disks, 287 disks fail without the required variance in features, leaving 868 disks marked as failed in the dataset, which is 75.2%.

3.4   Setup

In order to be able to group the failure probabilities for all hard disks, two Isolation Forest models are created, which differ in their parameters. The metrics used to evaluate the Isolation Forest models are also different. For the first Isolation Forest Model *IF_FDR*, the failure detection rate is used as the relevant metric to detect as many faulty disks as possible. In the second Isolation Forest Model *IF_FAR*, the false alarm rate and precision are the metrics used to minimize the number of false positive instances.

The implementation of Isolation Forest in scikit-learn provides several hyperparameters that have a decisive influence on the prediction results. The most essential hyperparameter is the *contamination* value. This value is critical for mapping between anomalies and normal instances, as it defines the relationship between abnormal and normal instances for the dataset.

In Fig. 1 a grid search is performed for the parameter *contamination* and evaluated with the metrics FDR and FAR. To achieve a FDR of 100%, the value

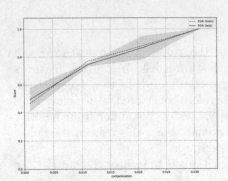
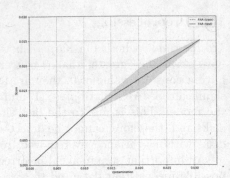

Fig. 1. GridSearch CV for contamination FDR

Fig. 2. GridSearch CV for contamination FAR

for *contamination* must be 0.031, which is 3.1% of the complete dataset. However, the FAR value must also be considered, which is 3%. Since the FAR value is calculated from the ratio between the true negative and false positive instances, the number of false positive instances is too high. A detailed representation of the FAR value is illustrated in Fig. 2. To achieve a tradeoff between FDR and FAR, the value for *contamination* is defined as 0.01 for the model *IF_FDR*.

For the model *IF_FAR*, the main focus is on the false alarm rate and precision, so that the model only predicts hard disk failures if they have a high probability of failure. For the model *IF_FAR* the value 0.0002 is set as suitable for *contamination*.

Once the parameters for the models are set, the models can be created, and the prediction for the dataset can be made. This process is described below:

1. The cleaned-up dataset *ST1* is loaded, it contains the date of the sample and the serial number as indices, as well as the six selected features. In addition, the dataset *STF* with the feature *failure* is loaded for later evaluation of the prediction.
2. The period for which the predictions are to be made is specified.
   (a) The dataset *ST1* is reduced to the samples of one day.
   (b) The Isolation Forest model is created with the parameters, and the prediction for the samples is performed.
   (c) The anomaly score is attached to a list together with the serial number and date.
3. Steps a), b), and c) are repeated for each day in the specified period.
4. The anomaly score and the *contamination* parameter are used to classify each sample in the list as an anomaly or normal instance.
5. The predicted values are compared with the true values from *STF*. If the failure date of a disk is within one week after prediction, it is considered true positive.
6. Based on the analysis of the data, the confusion matrix is built, and the values for FDR, FAR, and precision are calculated.

The different values of *contamination* and the calculated value of precision in both models can be used to define the failure probability of the hard disk. The failure probability is stored in a structured text file together with the prediction date and the serial number.

4 Experimental Results

In this section, the results of the model are presented and evaluated with different metrics. Furthermore, a comparison with other common models is carried out. Finally, gained insights and possible limitations of the dataset are discussed.

Figure 3 shows the results for the Isolation Forest model *IF_FDR*. In this model, the focus is on detecting the largest possible number of faulty disks with the lowest possible FAR. The FDR is 84.54%, with a FAR of 0.0073%. Also, the precision is 44.21%, reflecting the probability of failure of the hard drive over seven days.

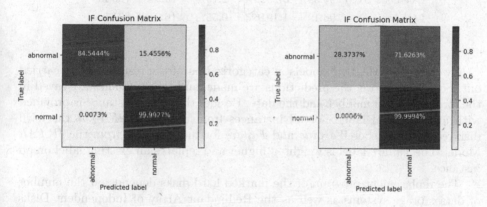

Fig. 3. FDR confusion matrix   **Fig. 4.** Precision confusion matrix

In contrast to the *IF_FDR* model, the *IF_FAR* model was developed with the focus on keeping the number of false positive instances as low as possible. The results are shown in Fig. 4. All instances detected as faulty have a probability of failure of 77.85%, which reflects the precision. Due to the high value of the failure probability, the FAR is also significantly lower, with a value of 0.0006%. The FDR is 28.37% and thus far below the value of the *IF_FDR* model.

4.1 Comparative Analysis

Table 2 shows a comparison between different anomaly detection algorithms. On the dataset *ST1*, the predictions were additionally performed for the algorithms One-class SVM and Local Outlier Factor (LOF). One-class SVM and LOF were

244 P. Rombach and J. Keuper

selected because they are among the most widely used algorithms in anomaly detection and provide good results for imbalanced datasets [2]. The FDR is higher for both algorithms than for the Isolation Forest, but the FAR is also markedly higher, which harms precision. Additionally, the computation time, calculated on the prediction of one day, is a multiple of the Isolation Forest. Precision is an essential factor for the evaluation of the results, as the probability of failure in the replacement process serves as the underlying principle. Therefore, the Isolation Forest, out of these three algorithms investigated, is best suited for prediction.

Table 2. Comparison of Isolation Forest, One-class SVM and LOF

	FDR	FAR	Precision	Computation time
IF_FDR	84.54%	0.0073%	44.21%	1.10 s ± 10 ms
IF_FAR	28.37%	0.0006%	77.85%	1.10 s ± 10 ms
One-class SVM	95.39%	0.2925%	2.19%	15.9 s ± 780 ms
LOF	96.19%	1.1916%	0.55%	16.0 s ± 671 ms

By combining the two models, a categorization of the results can be carried out. For this purpose, the predictions are made, and the anomalies are saved in the form of a serial number and the date. Besides that, each instance is provided with an additional label. For all instances from the model *IF_FDR* the hard disk receives the label *Warning* and *Failure* for the instances from the *IF_FAR* Model. The *Failure* label is weighted higher and replaces an existing label on an instance.

The replacement program of the marked hard disks depends on the number of data storage systems as well as the Redundant Array of Independent Disks (RAID) technology used, since the reliability of a RAID array changes depending on the RAID level.

The goal is to distribute the hard disks with the label *Warning* over several RAID arrays in such a way that in each array, a maximum of one marked hard disk operates. This means that there are no additional costs for the provision of a new hard disk, and the reliability of the array is not endangered. If it is not possible to replace the marked hard disks in the array, they must be replaced with a new hard disk. The marked hard disks from model *IF_FAR* with the label *Failure* are to be regarded as critical due to their high failure probability and should, therefore, be replaced with a new hard disk.

4.2 Limitations

It was discovered that the features *smart_5_raw* and *smart_187_raw* are in a value range of $[0, 65535]$, which is exactly 2 bytes in size. Thus it can be concluded that a buffer overflow occurs with these two features, and then the values are reset to 0. A buffer overflow can lead to a degradation of the prediction, but was taken into account in the created models and compensated by the additional features $smart\_5\_raw\_diff$ and, $smart\_187\_raw\_diff$.

The logging interval of one day is not optimal because there are disks whose values deteriorate significantly within one day and fail the same day. Hourly logging would make it easier to identify these disks, but it would also increase the dataset's storage requirements considerably. For 10% of the disks detected as faulty, only one sample indicates the possible failure. Hourly logging could increase the number of samples that indicate a failure.

5   Conclusion

In this work, it has been shown that the prediction of faulty disks by techniques of anomaly detection achieves good results, particularly for models that were created based on the Isolation Forest. The decision for the algorithm was based on the highly imbalanced dataset, the comprehensible behavior, and low linear time complexity of the models. Many machine learning methods cannot handle imbalanced datasets without preprocessing as they tend to overestimate the majority class. The Isolation Forest does not require preprocessing for an imbalanced dataset, so there is no need to downsample or upsample the instances. Furthermore, the training phase is omitted with the unsupervised approach, which significantly reduces the time between data acquisition and prediction.

Two models were created with a different focus. The model IF_FDR concentrates on a high failure detection rate and a low false alarm rate. This model achieved a FDR of 84.54% with a FAR of 0.0073%. Furthermore, the failure probability of the predicted failing disks is 44.21%. The second model IF_FAR focused on providing a prediction to find the faulty disks that were very likely to fail within the next seven days. A failure probability of 77.85% was achieved for the hard disks marked as faulty. The model IF_FAR determines which hard disks require urgent action by infrastructure administration.

Several aspects can improve the accuracy of the models. For applications in data centers, it would make sense to include the location of the hard disks and the corresponding array in the dataset, so that the decision whether a hard disk should be replaced does not have to be performed manually, and can be calculated by the model. It was also shown that the prediction is limited to the SMART attributes alone since 25% to 40% of all hard disks fail without any variance in the data. To improve the prediction, a combination of system log files and SMART attributes could be used to perform a hard disk assessment in the future.

References

1. Backblaze: Hard drive stats (2013–2019). https://www.backblaze.com/b2/hard-drive-test-data.html. Accessed 16 Apr 2020

2. Goldstein, M.B.: Anomaly Detection in Large Datasets. Verlag Dr. Hut, Munich (2014)
3. Hamerly, G., Elkan, C., et al.: Bayesian approaches to failure prediction for disk drives. In: ICML, vol. 1, pp. 202–209 (2001)
4. Hughes, G.F., Murray, J.F., Kreutz-Delgado, K., Elkan, C.: Improved disk-drive failure warnings. IEEE Trans. Reliab. **51**(3), 350–357 (2002)
5. Li, J., et al.: Hard drive failure prediction using classification and regression trees. In: 2014 44th Annual IEEE/IFIP International Conference on Dependable Systems and Networks, pp. 383–394. IEEE (2014)
6. Murray, J.F., Hughes, G.F., Kreutz-Delgado, K.: Hard drive failure prediction using non-parametric statistical methods. In: Proceedings of ICANN/ICONIP (2003)
7. Murray, J.F., Hughes, G.F., Kreutz-Delgado, K.: Machine learning methods for predicting failures in hard drives: a multiple-instance application. J. Mach. Learn. Res. **6**(May), 783–816 (2005)
8. Pinheiro, E., Weber, W.D., Barroso, L.A.: Failure trends in a large disk drive population. In: 5th USENIX Conference on File and Storage Technologies (FAST 2007), San Jose, CA. USENIX Association, February 2007
9. Saffari, A., Leistner, C., Santner, J., Godec, M., Bischof, H.: On-line random forests. In: 2009 IEEE 12th International Conference on Computer Vision Workshops, ICCV Workshops, pp. 1393–1400. IEEE (2009)
10. Schroeder, B., Gibson, G.A.: Understanding disk failure rates: what does an MTTF of 1,000,000 hours mean to you? ACM Trans. Storage (TOS) **3**(3), 8-es (2007)
11. Seagate: Get S.M.A.R.T. for reliability. Technical report, Seagate Technology Paper (1999)
12. Shen, J., Wan, J., Lim, S.J., Yu, L.: Random-forest-based failure prediction for hard disk drives. Int. J. Distrib. Sensor Netw. **14**(11) (2018)
13. Wang, Y., Ma, E.W., Chow, T.W., Tsui, K.L.: A two-step parametric method for failure prediction in hard disk drives. IEEE Trans. Industr. Inf. **10**(1), 419–430 (2013)
14. Wang, Y., Miao, Q., Ma, E.W., Tsui, K.L., Pecht, M.G.: Online anomaly detection for hard disk drives based on Mahalanobis distance. IEEE Trans. Reliab. **62**(1), 136–145 (2013)
15. Wang, Y., Miao, Q., Pecht, M.: Health monitoring of hard disk drive based on Mahalanobis distance. In: 2011 Prognostics and System Health Management Conference, pp. 1–8. IEEE (2011)
16. Xiao, J., Xiong, Z., Wu, S., Yi, Y., Jin, H., Hu, K.: Disk failure prediction in data centers via online learning. In: Proceedings of the 47th International Conference on Parallel Processing, pp. 1–10 (2018)
17. Xu, C., Wang, G., Liu, X., Guo, D., Liu, T.Y.: Health status assessment and failure prediction for hard drives with recurrent neural networks. IEEE Trans. Comput. **65**(11), 3502–3508 (2016)
18. Zhang, T., Wang, E., Zhang, D.: Predicting failures in hard drivers based on isolation forest algorithm using sliding window. J. Phys. Conf. Ser. **1187**(4) (2019)
19. Zhu, B., Wang, G., Liu, X., Hu, D., Lin, S., Ma, J.: Proactive drive failure prediction for large scale storage systems. In: 2013 IEEE 29th Symposium on Mass Storage Systems and Technologies (MSST), pp. 1–5. IEEE (2013)
20. Züfle, M., Krupitzer, C., Erhard, F., Grohmann, J., Kounev, S.: To fail or not to fail: predicting hard disk drive failure time windows. In: Hermanns, H. (ed.) MMB 2020. LNCS, vol. 12040, pp. 19–36. Springer, Cham (2020). https://doi.org/10.1007/978-3-030-43024-5_2

1st International Workshop on Monitoring and Data Analytics (MODA20)

1st International Workshop on Monitoring and Data Analytics (MODA20)

Florina Ciorba[1], Nicolas Lachiche[2], Aurélien Cavelan[1], Daniele Tafani[3],
and Utz-Uwe Haus[4]

[1] University of Basel, Switzerland
[2] University of Strasbourg, France
[3] Leibniz Supercomputing Centre, Germany
[4] Cray/HPE EMEA Research Lab, Switzerland

1 Introduction

The Exascale computing race poses significant challenges for the collection and analysis of the vast amount of data that current Petascale, and future (pre-)Exascale HPC systems will produce, in terms of increasing complexity of the machines, intrusiveness and scalability of the adopted monitoring solution, and effective inference and interpretability driven by the acquired data.

The main scope of the 1st ISC-HPC International Workshop on Monitoring and Operational Data Analytics (MODA20) is to provide insights into the current state and trends in monitoring and operational data analytics of HPC systems and data centres, identify potential gaps, and offer an outlook into the future of MODA at increasingly large scales together with possible solutions for the upcoming Exascale systems.

MODA is becoming common practice at HPC sites and data centres around the world. However, each site adopts a different, insular approach, rarely adopted in production environments and mostly limited to the visualisation of the system and building infrastructure metrics for system health check purposes. This creates a gap between the collection of operational data and its meaningful and effective analysis and exploitation, which prevents the closing of the feedback loop between the monitored HPC system, its operation, and its end users. Under these premises, the goals of the MODA20 workshop are:

1. Gather and share knowledge and establish a common ground within the international community with respect to best practices in monitoring and operational data analytics.
2. Discuss future strategies and alternatives for MODA, potentially improving existing solutions and envisioning a common baseline approach in HPC sites and data centres.
3. Establish a debate on the usefulness and applicability of Artificial Intelligence and Machine Learning techniques to the collected operational data for optimising the operation of production systems through novel systems research methods (e.g., for practices such as predictive and prescriptive maintenance, runtime optimisation, optimal resource allocation and scheduling).

The workshop offered a forum for invited presentations, technical contributions, and discussions on:

- State-of-the-practice methods, tools, techniques in monitoring at various HPC sites.
- Solutions for monitoring and analysis of operational data that work very well on large- to extreme-scale systems with a large number of users.
- Solutions that have proven limitations in terms of efficiency of operational data collection in real-time or in terms of the quality of the collected data.
- Opportunities and challenges of using machine learning methods for efficient monitoring and analysis of operational data.
- Integration of monitoring and analysis practices into production system software (energy and resource management) and runtime systems (scheduling and resource allocation).
- Discuss explicit gaps between operational data collection, processing, effective analysis, highly useful exploitation, and propose new approaches to closing these gaps for the benefit of improving HPC and data centres planning, operations, and research.
- Other monitoring and operational data analysis challenges and approaches (data storage, visualisation, integration into system software, adoption).

2   Workshop Organisation

The workshop organising and program committees consist of academics, researchers at leading HPC sites and in industry. The workshop is unique to the European HPC arena being the first to address the topic of monitoring and operational data analytics for improving HPC operations and research.

Organising Committee

Florina Ciorba	University of Basel, Switzerland
Nicolas Lachiche	University of Strasbourg, France
Aurélien Cavelan	University of Basel, Switzerland
Daniele Tafani	Leibniz Supercomputing Centre, Germany
Utz Uwe Haus	Cray/HPE EMEA Research Lab, Switzerland

Program Committee

Andrea Bartolini	University of Bologna, Italy
Valeria Bartsch	Fraunhofer ITWM Kaiserslautern, Germany
Norm Bourassa	NERSC LBNL, USA
Jim Brandt	Sandia National Labs, USA
Rubén Cabezón	sciCORE, University of Basel, Switzerland
Carlo Cavazzoni	CINECA, Italy

Daniele Cesarini	CINECA, Italy
Todd Gamblin	LLNL, USA
Victor Holanda	CSCS, Switzerland
Thomas Ilsche	Technische Universität Dresden, Germany
Jacques-Charles Lafoucriere	CEA, France
Erwin Laure	KTH, Sweden
Filippo Mantovani	BSC, Spain
Diana Moise	Cray/HPE, Switzerland
Ariel Oleksia	Poznan Supercomputing Center, Poland
Melissa Romanus	NERSC LBNL, USA
Karthee Sivalingam	Cray/HPE, UK
Heiko Schuldt	University of Basel, Switzerland
Martin Schulz	TU Munich/Leibniz Supercomputing Centre, Garching, Germany
Keiji Yamamoto	RIKEN, Japan

The reviewing of the submitted papers was balanced among the program committee members and ensured a high quality of the reviews. Based on the submissions and their reviews, three papers were accepted and presented at MODA20:

- Application IO analysis with Lustre Monitoring using LASSi for ARCHER, by Karthee Sivalingam and Harvey Richardson
- Characterising HPC Performance Variation with Monitoring and Unsupervised Learning, by Gence Ozer, Alessio Netti, Daniele Tafani, and Martin Schulz
- AI-Driven Holistic Approach to Energy Efficient HPC, by Robert Tracey, Lan Hoang, Felix Subelet, and Vadim Elisseev

MODA20 was initially envisioned as a full-day workshop with a balanced mix between technical paper presentations, keynote and invited talks. As part of the ISC 2020 Digital program, MODA20 was held digitally online, as a live half-day workshop, with a keynote address, three paper presentations, and one debate panel. The full live program is available on the MODA20 website[1].

MODA20 gathered experts that described the current solutions and best practices for monitoring systems at HPC sites and data centres, as well as their strategies for analysing and interpreting the collected operational data.

The workshop debuted with the live keynote address by Prof. Martin Schulz (TUM and LRZ, Germany) entitled Challenges and Opportunities in Actively Monitoring and Managing Power and Energy on HPC Systems followed by an lively questions and answers (Q&A) session.

The workshop continued with three live paper presentations, that initiated an interactive real time exchange of questions and answers via the chat functionality. A strikingly positive aspect of this setup was that the answers to these questions in certain came from other members of the audience and not always from the authors or

---

[1] https://moda20.sciencesconf.org/resource/page/id/4.

presenters. This demonstrates the active engagement and interest of the attendees in the topics addressed by MODA20.

The last part of the workshop was a panel discussion on Monitoring and Operational Data Analysis: past, present, and future which very early turned in to a free-form discussion with the entire audience.

2.1 Keynote Address

Prof. Martin Schulz (TUM and LRZ, Germany) gave a keynote address on the Challenges and Opportunities in Actively Monitoring and Managing Power and Energy on HPC Systems.

In his keynote, he highlighted that monitoring is very important for the efficient management of power and energy given the increase in energy costs. He emphasised the need for an active feedback loop regarding energy and power management during system design, during infrastructure setup, and especially during system operation. He described the approach taken by LRZ towards energy efficiency, which is holistic and addresses all levels of the ecosystem: from infrastructure to applications. Highlights from this keynote include the data centre data base or DCDB (an open-source tool developed at LRZ for high-frequency, high-resolution HPC monitoring) and the Wintermute analytics framework. Martin Schulz also highlighted the challenges that lie ahead for monitoring: variable data granularity, frequency and usage, in-situ analytics, and application integration and incentives thereof.

2.2 Research Papers

The first paper, Application IO analysis with Lustre Monitoring using LASSi for ARCHER, presented by Karthee Sivalingam and co-authored by Harvey Richardson, described how a combination of the LASSi tool (developed by Cray) and the SAFE software (developed by EPCC) is used to collect and analyse Lustre I/O performance data for all jobs running on the UK national supercomputing service (ARCHER), to provide reports on I/O usage for users in the standard reporting framework, while also enabling analysis of parallel I/O use on ARCHER to quantify the potential impact of different applications on file system performance using metrics derived from the LASSi data. They highlighted that the performance data from LASSi reveals how the same application can stress different components of the file system depending on how it is run, and how the LASSi risk metrics permit identification of cases that could potentially cause issues for global I/O performance.

The second paper, entitled Characterising HPC Performance Variation with Monitoring and Unsupervised Learning, was presented by Gence Ozer, and co-authored by Alessio Netti, Daniele Tafani, and Martin Schulz. Gence Ozer first pointed out the many challenges of big systems, the different available metrics, and the need for automated analyses of this big data. Data were collected on their CooLMUC-3, using their own Data Centre Data Base (DCDB) framework. They propose an approach to detect variation based on the distance to normal cases learned by clustering. They experimented at three levels of a HPC system: core, compute node, and infrastructure. Gence Ozer presented the analysis of long term thermal trends of compute nodes.

A second example concerns the cooling consistency of the racks. Future work is to do more, and more quantitative, experiments on bigger systems.

Robert Tracey presented the work he conducted with his collaborators (Lan Hoang, Felix Subelet and Vadim Elisseev) on the design and implementation of an AI-Driven Holistic Approach to Energy Efficient HPC. In his presentation Robert claimed that, in order to cope with the ever-increasing energy demanded by HPC and data centres (and its associated costs), it is necessary to have in place a holistic monitoring solution which allows to comprehensively collect data at different system levels. Such framework should be hardware-agnostic, with interchangeable software components, and should facilitate the integration of AI techniques to dynamically control applications and workflows. Robert's proposed monitoring solution has been implemented following these design principles. His framework collects metrics from different data sources, i.e. at hardware, software and building infrastructure level. The monitored data is then stored in an OpenTSDB database instance and conveniently visualised via Grafana dashboards. As expected, the proposed framework introduces very low overhead in terms of CPU, memory, network and disk usage.

The collected data allowed Robert and his collaborators to efficiently analyse and, in some instances, successfully predict the behaviour of their monitored HPC testbed: in his experiments, workloads could be sorted into different groups, potentially influencing future node assignment; also, thanks to the collected historical data, the power draw of single racks could be predicted. Robert's future research efforts will mainly focus on collecting more in-band data, investigating security features and implementing mechanisms to efficiently control cooling infrastructure.

2.3   Panel Discussion

To conclude the workshop, and to partially compensate for the missing in-person coffee breaks, a panel discussion with open discussion was held. Panelists were invited to represent both the work discussed in the presentations (Martin Schulz, Karthee Sivalingam, Robert Tracey), as well as expert experience from among the reviewers (Daniele Cesarini, Jim Brandt, Valeria Bartsch). The discussion was moderated by Utz-Uwe Haus.

Asked what they see as the most critical aspect of MODA today, or in the near future, the panel members' answers exhibited a surprising overlap, despite very different angles of experience: The adaptivity of future systems poses significant new challenges to MODA, and performance tuning will needs to be driven by data collected by more sophisticated monitoring tools (M. Schulz). This poses new data management challenges, both due to data accumulation, but also in order to support run-time analysis and feedback (J. Brandt), in particular since the holistic view on all data available is the only way to get meaningful insight into big systems (R. Tracey). Even if the monitoring, data collection, analysis and correlation issue is solved, presenting feedback to application developers and sysadmins is a separate, challenging, but essential problem (K. Sivalingam), in particular with respect to non-traditional HPC users in machine learning and data science, which are often not accustomed or aware of the monitoring possibilities (V. Bartsch).

What was planned to be a 30 minute discussion with questions and comments from the audience continued for more than 1 hour, driven by experience reports by audience members. <u>Time to insight</u>, a criterion often employed in semi-qualitative benchmarking of scientific codes was cited as a critical measure of success for deployment of MODA approaches: Dashboards with drill-down interfaces for operators, alert indicators based on both categorial and artificial-intelligence data analytics, and tools as approachable as profilers in in IDE, to enable application developers and users to understand system behaviour.

While mostly centred around technical aspects of MODA, security and privacy concerns were discussed as a critical topic that needs to be addressed with more generality: System monitoring data typically contains data that is considered sensitive for the operator, but also include personally identifiable information as well as business secrets or intellectual property of users. This makes even the exchange of monitoring data for research purposes nontrivial. Open source and platform agnostic monitoring tools were seen as an avenue to offer a path towards open data interfaces that make it possible to exchange analytics and visualisation components across sites, avoiding the need to exchange the raw data.

3   Conclusion

We believe that MODA20, despite the unexpected format change to a virtual workshop, provides a crystallisation point for future growth of the topic, and paves the way to a recurring series of events. Presentations and discussions showed that the scope of topics is even wider than we thought, and that some aspects seem to warrant significantly more attention. In this direction we want to specifically mention

- visualisation aspects, in particular reusable methods instead of one-off designs for it,
- user experience design and the cost of such these solutions that are essential to wide adoption of MODA,
- the wider HPC and scientific programming usage of monitoring data, i.e., beyond the system operations view point,
- application of Operations Research methods in HPC MODA,
- the challenge of monitoring the behaviour of scripting language and container-based applications, which appear much more opaque than traditional HPC applications due to missing monitoring APIs,
- data privacy and security issues, as they relate to the raw data collection, handling, storage and use of the conclusions.

The latter topic has many facets, as MODA may provide a front line defence against security breaches and system abuse like the recent cryptocurrency mining events at supercomputing centres[2] or the data breach at many European HPC centers earlier this year[3] in the spring of this year. At the same time, MODA itself can be abused for information disclosure or privacy breaks.

We hope that many of these aspects will figure prominently in submissions to the next edition of this workshop.

---

[2] https://csirt.egi.eu/academic-data-centers-abused-for-crypto-currency-mining/.

[3] https://www.hpcwire.com/2020/05/18/hacking-streak-forces-european-supercomputers-offline-in-midst-of-covid-19-research-effort/.

Application IO Analysis with Lustre Monitoring Using LASSi for ARCHER

Karthee Sivalingam$^{(\boxtimes)}$ and Harvey Richardson

HPE EMEA Research Lab, Broad Quay House, Prince Street, Bristol, UK
{karthee.sivalingam,harvey.richardson}@hpe.com

Abstract. Supercomputers today have to support a complex workload with new Big Data and AI workloads adding to the more traditional HPC ones. It is important that we understand these workloads which constitute a mix of applications from different domains with different IO requirements. In some cases these applications place significant stress on the filesystem and may impact other applications making use of the shared resource. Today, ARCHER, the UK National Supercomputing service supports a diverse range of applications such as Climate Modelling, Bio-molecular Simulation, Material Science and Computational Fluid Dynamics. We will describe LASSi, a framework developed by the ARCHER Centre of Excellence to analyse application slowdown and IO usage on the shared (Lustre) filesystem.

LASSi combines application job information from the scheduler with Lustre IO monitoring statistics to construct the IO profile of applications interacting with the filesystem. We show how the metric-based, application-centric approach taken by LASSi was used both to understand application contention and reveal interesting aspects of the IO on ARCHER. In this paper we concentrate on new analysis of years of data collected from the ARCHER system. We study the general IO usage and trends in different ARCHER projects. We highlight how different application groups interact with the filesystem by building a metric based IO profile. This IO analysis of projects and applications enables project managers, HPC administrators, Application developers and Scientist to not only understand IO requirements but also plan for future. This information can be further used for reengineering applications, resource allocation planning and filesystem sizing for future systems.

Keywords: IO · LUSTRE · Monitoring · ARCHER · LASSi

1 Introduction

Supercomputers need to meet the demands of complex large workloads consisting of many application types at the same time as providing an environment to support highly-scalable applications. High performance networks, storage systems

Supported by EPRSC.

and workload schedulers all play a part in delivering consistent high performance to applications. However there will still be circumstances where a workload/application can place stress on the system to the extent that users experience variations in runtime (perceived as a *slowdown*) which can result in the loss of jobs (running past walltime limits) and an increased cost to users. In such an environment it is crucial to have tools to analyse application behaviour. This is a complex problem, for example expected run time depends on application parameters, available hardware characteristics and any contention for resources. In this paper, we analyse the broad I/O patterns for a set of applications and introduce a framework that we have used both for triage of issues in the filesystem and for analysis of IO workload.

2   ARCHER

ARCHER is the UK national supercomputer and has been supporting multiple scientific communities such as Ocean science, Plasma Science, Bio-molecular simulation and Material science since 2014. It is a Cray XC30 [7] supercomputer comprising of 4920 nodes, high-speed Aries network and a High-performance Lustre storage system [3]. It has three Lustre file systems based on Cray Sonexion 1600 technology. Two file systems have 12 Object Storage Servers (OSS) and one file system has 14 OSS. There is one Metadata Server (MDS) and one backup MDS per file system. Each MDS is a Cray Sonexion 1600 MDS controller module. Each client accesses the three file systems via 18 Lustre router nodes internal to the ARCHER system.

3   LASSi

ARCHER typically has thousands of jobs running at the same time and most jobs access the Lustre filesystem for file I/O. From time to time there are reports of application slowdown with users reporting issues with interactive access to the filesystem. Sometimes this would be due to rogue application making great demands on the filesystem compared to the norm. In order to analyse slowdown causes, LASSi [16] was developed by Cray Center of Excellence for ARCHER. This was further developed to provide better understanding of the complex workloads and the applications using a shared resource. Even though network and storage are shared in ARCHER, LASSi focuses only on storage. LASSi uses the Lustre statistics aggregated by a site-developed tool (LAPCAT) at 3 min intervals along with job metadata from the scheduler. LASSi combines the Lustre statistics and job metadata to build an application IO profile over time. Job IO profiles can be analysed to study the interaction of jobs with the filesystem and with each other due to shared filesystem usage. The results of the analysis has been used to triage issues and support further analysis.

LASSi moves beyond existing tools like *UMAMI, MELT, ldiskfs, LMT, LLView* and *NERSC's FSU* [16] (mainly provide raw filesystem or application statistics) by also focusing on applications that exhibit unusual I/O behaviour

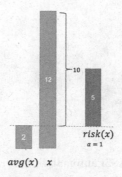

Fig. 1. Example of risk calculation

resulting in filesystem slowdown. LASSi is non-invasive (to the filesystem and application) and does not require user involvement.

3.1 Metric Based Approach

In this section, we give a brief overview of LASSi's metric based approach as described in detail in [16]. LASSi uses the following Lustre statistics for analysis which can be categorised as *OSS* and *MDS* based on the server (Object Storage Server or MetaData Server) as shown below.

- **OSS:** *read_kb, read_ops, write_kb, write_ops, other*
- **MDS:** *open, close, mknod, link, unlink, mkdir, rmdir, ren, getattr, setattr, getxattr, setxattr, statfs, sync, sdr, cdr*

In analysing the statistics, we use the following metrics: *risk* and *ops* for an application run. The *risk* metric denotes the quantity whereas the *ops* metric denotes the quality of IO. The *risk* metric is calculated by accumulating the risk of individual operations. For every *OSS* or *MDS* operation x on a file system *fs*, the risk metric is calculated as follows:

$$risk_{fs}(x) = \frac{x - \alpha \cdot \text{avg}_{fs}(x)}{\alpha \cdot \text{avg}_{fs}(x)} \qquad (1)$$

where α is an arbitrary scaling factor. Figure 1 illustrates the risk calculation for any quantity. Individual *risk* calculations are aggregated to give an overall risk attributed to *OSS* or *MDS*. Any negative risk is ignored when aggregating.

$$\begin{aligned} risk_{oss} = \ &risk_{read\_kb} + risk_{read\_ops} + \\ &risk_{write\_kb} + risk_{write\_ops} + risk_{other} \end{aligned} \qquad (2)$$

$$\begin{aligned} risk_{mds} = \ &risk_{open} + risk_{close} + risk_{getattr} + risk_{setattr} \\ &+ risk_{mkdir} + risk_{rmdir} + risk_{mknod} + risk_{link} \\ &+ risk_{unlink} + risk_{ren} + risk_{getxattr} + risk_{setxattr} \\ &+ risk_{statfs} + risk_{sync} + risk_{cdr} + risk_{sdr} \end{aligned} \qquad (3)$$

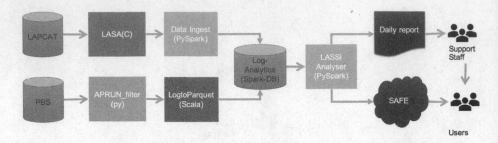

Fig. 2. LASSi automated daily workflow

On Lustre, 1 MB (and larger) aligned accesses are optimal and much more efficient than small accesses, our *ops metric* is used to quantify the *quality* of IO and is defined as follows:

$$read\_kb\_ops = \frac{read\_ops \cdot 1024}{read\_kb} \qquad (4)$$

$$write\_kb\_ops = \frac{write\_ops \cdot 1024}{write\_kb} \qquad (5)$$

where $read\_kb\_ops$ denotes the read quality and $write\_kb\_ops$ denotes the write quality. The *risk* and *ops* metrics are designed so that higher value indicate higher risk of slowdown and bad quality respectively.

3.2   Automated Workflow and Architecture

Figure 2 shows the LASSi workflow. Lustre statistics (collected in the LAPCAT mysql database) and application data (from PBS) are exported (using custom tools, *LASA* and *APRUN_filter*) and ingested to LASSi (using *Data Ingest* and *LogtoParquet* scripts). LASSi uses Spark [19] for data analytics and matplotlib for generating reports. Daily risk plots are generated and are made available to helpdesk staff. Aggregated data for each application run is exported to SAFE[1], a portal for ARCHER users. Users can view high-level application IO usage and generate reports. Custom risk plots and raw Lustre operation data plots can also be generated manually.

4   ARCHER Analysis

In this section, we build on top of the preliminary analysis of LASSi data, presented at CUG [17]. For this ARCHER analysis, we use Lustre statistics collected from April 2017 to November 2019. Whereas our previous analysis focused only on slowdown with analysis of applications causing slowdown, this analysis focuses on analysis at three levels

---

[1] https://www.archer.ac.uk/documentation/safe-guide.

– ARCHER Projects comprising of multiple application
– Application type based on the executable name
– Application run profiling

ARCHER users are grouped in projects and sub projects based on their consortia and science areas[2]. These projects are a good representation of the science area in general. The Project information is extracted from SAFE and is then ingested to LASSi to map application runs to Projects. For Application level analysis, we group application runs based on the executable used in the run command. The run command used for application launch is available from the PBS logs.

4.1   Projects IO Usage

In order to analyse application IO from different projects we made use of a mapping of jobs to projects from SAFE. Table 1 lists the different project names, project types and the total reads and writes to filesystem. For simplicity we will use the project type names to refer to the project. Only the top 10(based on read/write quantity) projects are listed. With a total of 59 PB reads and 192 PB writes, ARCHER applications in general write 3 bytes for every byte of data read. This trend is reversed for *Mesoscale Engineering* and *Astrophysics and Cosmology* where the application read more data than they write. *Computational Fluid Dynamics* and *Ocean Science* have lesser write proportion. Projects like *Climate Science, Material Chemistry, Atomistic simulation, Geophysics and Seismology, Plasma Physics* and *Combustion* follow the general trend and write more than 6 bytes of data for every byte read.

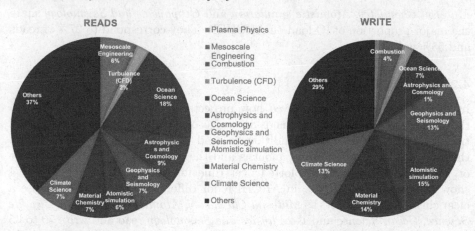

Fig. 3. Proportion of total read and writes in ARCHER for different projects

Figure 3 shows the proportion of total read and writes in ARCHER for different projects. The large proportion of application in *others* (37%) illustrates the huge variety of applications using the ARCHER system. *Climate Science,*

---

[2] https://www.archer.ac.uk/community/consortia.

Table 1. Total read and writes (in petabytes) of projects in ARCHER.

Project name	Project area	Read (PB)	Write (PB)
Plasma Physics Consortium	Plasma Physics	0.05	1.47
UK Consortium on Mesoscopic Engineering Sciences	Mesoscale Engineering	3.57	1.48
UKCTRF Consortium	Combustion	0.28	7.01
UK Turbulence Consortium	Computational Fluid Dynamics	1.40	4.00
Global Ocean Modelling Consortium	Ocean Science	10.35	14.56
UK Atomic, Molecular and Optical Physics R-matrix Consortium (UKAMOR)	Astrophysics and Cosmology	5.08	1.69
Computational Mineral Physics Consortium	Geophysics and Seismology	4.32	25.76
UK Car-Parrinello	Atomistic Simulation	3.38	29.17
Materials Chemistry HPC Consortium	Material Chemistry	4.12	26.01
NCAS (National Centre for Atmospheric Science)	Climate Science	4.08	24.09
Others	Multiple	21.94	55.32

Material Chemistry, *Atomistic simulation* and *Geophysics and Seismology* share the major proportion of IO load on ARCHER. They correspond to 27% of reads and 55% writes.

4.2   Projects IO Trends

In the previous section we showed how projects do IO in general. We expand this further with analysis of trends in usage over time. We also investigated trends in metadata usage in addition to read/write usage. For this analysis, the data was accumulated over months and the cumulative sum of read/write or metadata operations are plotted over time for different projects. Figure 4 show the Read/Write trends in ARCHER for different projects. We can see a clear clustering of projects as *Material Chemistry, Atomistic simulation, Climate Science, Ocean Science* and *GeoPhysics and Seismology* read and write 20 to 35 PB of data (highlighted in yellow), 5 other projects had less than 5 PB.

GeoPhysics and Seismology shows a sharp increase in the start of 2019, but their usage slowed down after that. *Atomistic simulation* usage is not comparable to other projects in 2017-18 but this has increased exponentially in 2019. The *Combustion* project has shown a increase in usage compared to previous years.

Figure 5 shows the trends in metadata usage in ARCHER for different projects. Two projects, *Material Science* and *Ocean Science* show bigger usage

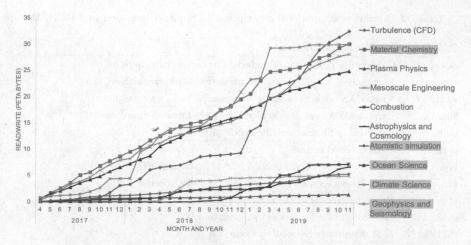

Fig. 4. Trends in Read/Write in ARCHER for different projects. Reads and Writes are cumulatively added over time.

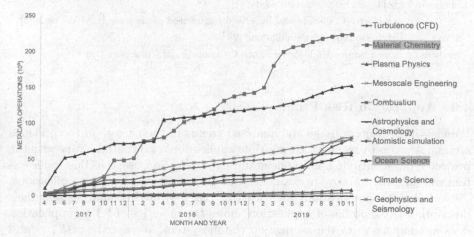

Fig. 5. Trends in metadata usage in ARCHER for different projects. Metadata operations are cumulatively added over time.

compared to other projects, with *Material science* showing considerable increases in the recent years. Projects like *Combustion, Turbulence, Atomistic Simulation, Climate Science* and *GeoPhysics and Seismology* uses around 50 billion operations. We also see a considerable increase in the metadata usage of *Atomistic Simulation* and *Climate Science*. These trends and usage reports can be used by Project managers and the HPC manager to better plan for projects in the future. For example, Project usage can be used to allocate projects across filesystem to enable isolation. IO trends are more important for predicting usage and planning allocation in future for expansion or new hardware.

Table 2. Application code and description of applications used in ARCHER

Code name	Application description
castep	Calculating properties of materials from first principles [6]
solver	Flow Solver, https://www.ukturbulence.co.uk/flow-solvers.html
vasp	Vienna Ab initio Simulation Package, https://www.vasp.at
lammps	Large-scale Atomic/Molecular Massively Parallel Simulator [15]
boffin	Large Eddy Simulation(LES) code [4]
python	Python based codes
Foam	Open Source Computational Fluid Dynamics (CFD) Toolbox [9]
xios	XML-IO-Server - I/O management in climate codes [14]
atmos	Numerical model of the atmosphere [5]
axisem3d	Simulation of Seismic wave propagation [13]
HYDRA	A Multi-physics Simulation Code [12]
incompact	A high-order finite-difference flow solvers [11]
senga	Direct Numerical Simulation (DNS) of turbulent combustion [10]
mitgcmuv	MIT general circulation model [1]
elk	all-electron full-potential linearised augmented-plane wave (LAPW) code [8]
aims	ab initio molecular simulations [2]
nwchem	Open Source High-Performance Computational Chemistry [18]

4.3   Application Risk Profile

We identified projects usage and analysed trends in their usage in the previous section. A project users may use multiple applications and this may vary with the project type. Identifying and understanding application usage of Lustre filesystem will not only improve performance but also avoid slowdown in applications. Table 2 lists the applications used for this risk and quality analysis and their description. Risk profile of application shows the quantity of IO an application does in comparison to the average on the filesystem. We use the $risk\_oss$ and $risk\_mds$ to build the application profile for this scatter plot. For an application, $risk\_oss$ and $risk\_mds$ values for all corresponding application runs are identified using their run command and then we use only the 95th percentile to characterise more risky runs.

Figure 6 shows the risk profile of different Applications with the size of the circle denoting the number of application runs. In Fig. 6, most applications are clustered closer to the axis. This shows application either using the OSS or MDS but not both heavily. $axisem3d$, $senga$ and $solver$ application have a higher $risk\_oss$ compared to $risk\_mds$, but the number of runs is relatively low. $HYDRA$, $xios$, $mitgcmuv$, $incompact$, $Foam$ and $python$ application have a higher $risk\_mds$ compared to $risk\_oss$ with $xios$ having a considerably higher number of runs. Applications $atmos$, $vasp$ and elk have more runs but have lower risks. In the case of elk, it is run as task farms where hundreds of similar runs are started

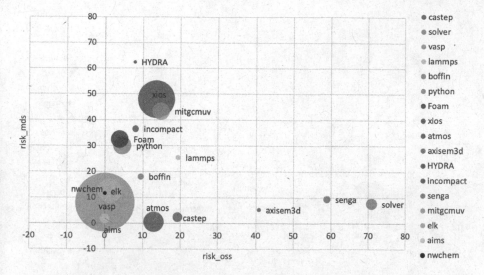

Fig. 6. Profile of different Application risk with the size of the circle denoting the number of application runs

at the same. Even with lower risk, the risk of such application gets multiplied based on the number of simultaneous runs.

4.4 Application Quality Profile

We build the quality profile of application using the ops metrics: $read\_kb\_ops$ for read quality and $write\_kb\_ops$ for write quality. Figure 7 shows the quality profile of applications. The application used are described in table 2 and we use the 95th percentile as described in the previous section. We see many application clustered near the read quality axis, this shows that the application have a poor read quality in general compared to write quality. Writes are usually buffered and this is one of the reasons for better write quality. There are three outliers that is not shown in the Fig. 7, *senga* and *HYDRA* showing poorer read quality (800–1000) compared to others and *boffin* showing the poorest write quality (6000). Application *boffin* breaks the trend in quality of IO of ARCHER applications as its write quality is poorer than its read quality.

In Fig. 7, the size of the circle relates to the number of application runs of this type. *castep*, *mitgcmuv*, *aims*, *incompact* and *incompact3d* show poorer read quality compared to write quality. *Foam*, *solver* and *lammps* show poor quality of read and writes. Application like *atmos*, *elk* and *xios* show good quality of read and write as they are clustered near the origin.

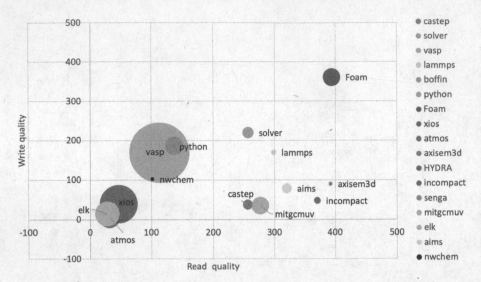

Fig. 7. Profile of different Application quality with the size of the circle denoting the number of application runs. This is same as Fig. 7 but with reduced axis scale

4.5 Application Run IO Tracing

Having identified applications that cause stress on the filesystem the next step is to engage with users to gain better understanding of the application. The IO timelines we can generate are quite course (3 min) although on other more recent platforms this can be reduced. The second problem is that the application profile does not identify individual operations that contribute to the summed statistics. Our approach is to obtain a system level trace of (potentially) all processes in the application using the *strace* command. We post-process the output using a tool we developed to obtain a detailed profile showing how applications interact with the filesystem through system calls. We can graph rates of operations (open/close/write), data rates, metadata rates, timelines etc. and attribute operations to individual files. Using this tool we have been able to identify applications that open and close the same files repeatedly (hundreds of times per second), where many processes write to the same file and where many small I/O operations mixed with large ones lead to serious performance degradation. The final step is to make changes to applications.

5   Future Work

The ARCHER service will be replaced with a new service (ARCHER2) in 2020. Moving forward, we are interested in extending the framework in a number of areas. We would like to make the framework more holistic so that we include information from the high-speed network and possibly power consumption information. Another area we would like to investigate is the use of ML approaches to classify applications from their 'telemetry'—be that IO or Network. This may allow us to not only identify applications but also any unusual behaviour from their norms. We plan to integrate LASSi into the data collection framework provided by *Cray View for ClusterStor*[3] so that sites with this software can take advantage of the alternative view that LASSi can provide.

6   Conclusions

Understanding application requirements for shared resources such as filesystem and network in a super computer is important for sustained performance and avoiding contention. We presented the LASSi framework which collects Lustre statistics and application job metadata and analyses them via derived metric like *risk* and *ops* that represent quantity and quality of application IO respectively. Based on 32 months of data, we presented analysis of ARCHER project's IO usage showing how this changed over time. We characterised different application types based on the *risk* and *quality* metrics. We observed clear patterns in application usage and highlighted outliers that have unusual requirements. This framework is enhanced with a tracing based IO profiler to study finer details. Such analysis at project and application level will help project managers, application developers and scientists understand their IO requirements This can enable better planning for reengineering applications, resource allocation and filesystem sizing for future systems. As we approach the Exascale, application IO requirements are evolving. Storage environments will change to support them. It will always prove valuable to understand how application interact with the memory/storage system to gain new insights on future performance challenges.

Acknowledgement. This work used the ARCHER UK National Supercomputing Service. We would like to acknowledge EPSRC, EPCC, Cray-HPE, the ARCHER helpdesk and user community for their support.

References

1. Adcroft, A., et al.: MITgcm user manual. Massachusetts Institute of Technology (2008)
2. Blum, V., et al.: Ab initio molecular simulations with numeric atom-centered orbitals. Comput. Phys. Commun. **180**(11), 2175–2196 (2009)
3. Braam, P.J., et al.: The Lustre storage architecture. White Paper, Cluster File Systems Inc., October 23 (2003)
4. Brauner, T., Jones, W., Marquis, A.: LES of the Cambridge stratified swirl burner using a sub-grid pdf approach. Flow Turbul. Combust. **96**(4), 965–985 (2016). https://doi.org/10.1007/s10494-016-9719-4
5. Brown, A., Milton, S., Cullen, M., Golding, B., Mitchell, J., Shelly, A.: Unified modeling and prediction of weather and climate: a 25-year journey. Bull. Am. Meteorol. Soc. **93**(12), 1865–1877 (2012). https://doi.org/10.1175/BAMS-D-12-00018.1

---

[3] https://www.cray.com/products/storage/clusterstor/view.

6. Clark, S.J., et al.: First principles methods using castep. Zeitschrift für Kristallographie-Cryst. Mater. **220**(5/6), 567–570 (2005)
7. Cray: Cray XC series supercomputers. https://www.cray.com/products/computing/xc-series (2018)
8. Dewhurst, K., et al.: The elk fp-lapw code. ELK. http://elk.sourceforge.net (2016)
9. Jasak, H., Jemcov, A., Tukovic, Z., et al.: OpenFOAM: a C++ library for complex physics simulations. In: International Workshop on Coupled Methods in Numerical Dynamics, vol. 1000, pp. 1–20. IUC Dubrovnik Croatia (2007)
10. Jenkins, K.W., Cant, R.S.: Direct numerical simulation of turbulent flame kernels. In: Knight, D., Sakell, L. (eds.) Recent Advances in DNS and LES. Fluid Mechanics and its Applications, vol. 54, pp. 191–202. Springer, Dordrecht (1999). https://doi.org/10.1007/978-94-011-4513-8_17
11. Laizet, S., Li, N.: Incompact3d: a powerful tool to tackle turbulence problems with up to o (105) computational cores. Int. J. Numer. Methods Fluids **67**(11), 1735–1757 (2011)
12. Langer, Steven H., Karlin, Ian, Marinak, Michael M.: Performance characteristics of HYDRA – a multi-physics simulation code from LLNL. In: Daydé, Michel, Marques, Osni, Nakajima, Kengo (eds.) VECPAR 2014. LNCS, vol. 8969, pp. 173–181. Springer, Cham (2015). https://doi.org/10.1007/978-3-319-17353-5_15
13. Leng, K., Nissen-Meyer, T., Van Driel, M., Hosseini, K., Al-Attar, D.: AxiSEM3D: broad-band seismic wavefields in 3-D global earth models with undulating discontinuities. Geophys. J. Int. **217**(3), 2125–2146 (2019)
14. Meurdesoif, Y.: Xios: an efficient and highly configurable parallel output library for climate modeling. In: The Second Workshop on Coupling Technologies for Earth System Models (2013)
15. Plimpton, S.: Fast parallel algorithms for short-range molecular dynamics. Technical report, Sandia National Labs., Albuquerque, NM (United States) (1993)
16. Sivalingam, K., Richardson, H., Tate, A., Lafferty, M.: LASSi: metric based I/O analytics for HPC. In: SCS Spring Simulation Multi-Conference (SpringSim 2019), Tucson, AZ, USA (2019)
17. Turner, A., Sloan-Murphy, D., Sivalingam, K., Richardson, H., Kunkel, J.M.: Analysis of parallel I/O use on the UK national supercomputing service, ARCHER using cray LASSi and EPCC SAFE. CoRR abs/1906.03891 (2019). http://arxiv.org/abs/1906.03891
18. Valiev, M., et al.: NWChem: a comprehensive and scalable open-source solution for large scale molecular simulations. Comput. Phys. Commun. **181**(9), 1477–1489 (2010)
19. Zaharia, M., et al.: Apache spark: a unified engine for big data processing. Commun. ACM **59**(11), 56–65 (2016). https://doi.org/10.1145/2934664

AI-Driven Holistic Approach to Energy Efficient HPC

Robert Tracey[1,2](✉), Lan Hoang[1](✉), Felix Subelet[1,3](✉),
and Vadim Elisseev[1,2](✉)

[1] IBM Research, STFC Daresbury Laboratory, Sci-Tech Daresbury,
Cheshire WA4 4AD, UK
{Robert.Tracey,Lan.Hoang,Vadim.V.Elisseev}@ibm.com
[2] Wrexham Glyndwr University, Mold Road, Wrexham LL11 2AW, UK
[3] The University of Liverpool, Liverpool L69 3BX, UK
Felix.Soubelet@liverpool.ac.uk

Abstract. Rapid growth of the world-wide Information Technology (IT) infrastructure fueled by demands of the global Digital Economy and associated demands for electrical power creates significant impact on the environment. Over the past decade power usage effectiveness (PUE) was the major focus for improving energy efficiency of Data Centres in particular. While PUE did result in significant energy efficiency improvements, it is not sufficient by itself. Huge energy efficiency gains are expected from optimizing hardware utilization, cooling and software stacks. We present an AI-Driven Holistic Approach to energy and power management in data centres, which can be described as Energy Aware Scheduling (EAS). EAS uses AI-driven workloads aware software-hardware co-design to optimize energy efficiency of a data centre.

Keywords: AI · Energy efficiency · Holistic · Energy aware
scheduling · Co-design

1 Introduction

Rapid growth of the world-wide Information Technology (IT) infrastructure fueled by demands of the global Digital Economy and associated demands for electrical power creates significant impact on the environment. At present data centres consume 3% of the worlds power usage, which is more than most countries [3] and have a significant impact on carbon footprint. Thus, current Data Centres and systems, including High Performance Computers (HPC) must be built considering *energy efficiency* as one of the foremost design goals [10].

There is a substantial amount of research and development focused on Energy Efficiency as a core metric [10,34], with some sites reporting up to 40% reduction in cooling costs [4,20,27]. However, most approaches only consider parts of the IT system and therefore improve energy efficiency of a component. There is a strong need for a holistic approach that joins up all the components and augments information available across the system [5].

© Springer Nature Switzerland AG 2020
H. Jagode et al. (Eds.): ISC High Performance 2020 Workshops, LNCS 12321, pp. 267–279, 2020.
https://doi.org/10.1007/978-3-030-59851-8_17

In this paper we present our ongoing work on Holistic Approach to energy and power management, which can be described as Energy Aware Scheduling (EAS). We are looking at energy efficiency across both hardware and software stacks of the IT infrastructure: i) data centres, servers, network, cooling, IoT and Edge devices in one dimension, ii) software stack from firmware through to the OS, applications and workload managers. EAS uses Machine Learning(ML) and Artificial Intelligence (AI) methods for modelling of performance and power consumption and software hardware co-design for implementing various energy/power aware scheduling policies at different levels of the infrastructure.

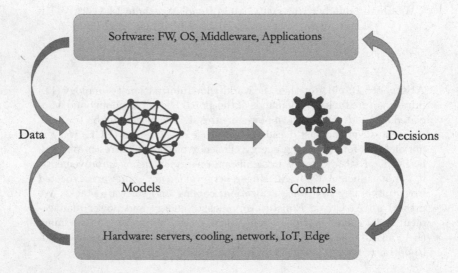

Fig. 1. EAS Concept: data, continuously collected across hardware and software stacks is fed to the AI-based models for performance and power consumption predictions, which are used by scheduling components to send control decisions back to hardware and software stacks.

Figure 1 introduces main components of the Holistic EAS: data collected from a broad range of hardware devices and software components is fed into an AI component, which produces optimal decisions to meet required criteria, which are then sent back to hardware and software system components ti implement. Current work is a continuation from of our previous efforts on EAS [1,2],but it has more ambitious goals of building a fully automated, AI-driven system for optimizing energy efficiency of data centres.

The rest of the paper is structured as follows: Sect. 2 presents our Data Collection Framework. Section 3 describes our choice of ML and AI methods for analysing the data. Section 4 presents preliminary results of our research. Finally, we conclude with Sect. 5.

2 Data Collection Framework

2.1 Architecture

The architecture used for data collection is displayed in Fig.2. Each component is housed in a Docker [21] container, which provides numerous benefits. Firstly, each software component can be easily upgraded independently from the other components in the system. This allows a rolling upgrade model, which allows us to take advantage of newer features in components that require it without altering other components. Secondly, it allows us to swap out easily databases or graphing components if required. Finally it allows us the possibility of being able to easily move this system to a different set of nodes if required as Docker is multi architecture, we have also built our components to be the same so that when moving to different nodes they do not have to be IBM POWER™ servers.

The inputs to the system come from three areas: software level, hardware level and data centre. This has been a crucial factor from the initial design of this system to facilitate and bridge all three of these areas into a single interface.

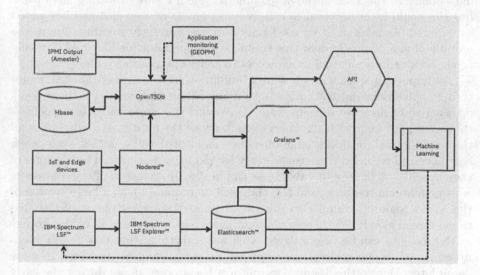

Fig. 2. Intelligent data collection framework architecture

2.2 Monitoring Tools

An important factor that went into the choice of monitoring tools was to ensure that they have as small as possible impact on the cluster as we can. We are aware that monitoring tools will always have some impact but one of our main design goals was to keep this to a minimum. One factor that we were keen to avoid very early on is to avoid having clients running on the nodes or having multiple relay nodes. In order to achieve this we have moved all of the major components onto a single node and also chose tools that required little to no interaction with the other nodes.

The first tool used is Amester, this gathers data from the Baseboard Management Controller (BMC) port on IBM POWER^{TM} systems and handles data from the hardware level. As the BMC port connects to the BMC which is a specialized service processor used to monitor the physical state of the running system. This means that all results gathered from other nodes are classed as out-of-band results, as they will have zero impact on the running of the system and it's resources. This zero impact is very important and useful as it allows us to gather a more accurate reading of the data based on user workloads without outside interference. This was chosen based on previous work done on the DiG [12] where similar tools were used to generate data with successful results.

The second tool selected to look at the software layer and workloads being submitted was IBM Spectrum LSF Explorer. We chose this as we were already using IBM Spectrum LSF as our workload manager and this integrates well with it. Also as LSF is already running and gathering this data it requires no extra overhead on the nodes than is already happening. This currently collects 700+ data points, as this is an initial development system we are capturing all of these but this could be customized to collect fewer points or new custom ones added as required. As mentioned we used LSF as it was currently running, due to the module design of this system this could be swapped out for Slurm [32] or any other workload manager allowing access to other open source tools.

An important consideration whilst building this system was that the monitoring applications did not consume to many resources. Even with them being on a separate node we did not want to overuse this node with these tools as that would not help with the energy efficiency of the cluster as a whole. As all the applications are docker containers we monitored using docker stats, each container and recorded there usage every second for one minute. The averages of these results can be seen in Table 1. As can be clearly seen each of the containers is using minimal resources and together still do not add up to a large section of the node's resources. Similar to this the amount of storage to be used also had to monitored closely. As there is no point in a system that uses all of the storage so that no jobs can be run or saved. this was something that was closely monitored as we altered some of the sampling rates, this will be discussed in more detail later. Due to this keeping watch over the storage usage during the early phases was a priority. In Table 2 you can see the databases do use a significant amount of storage but it is manageable as the metrics can be altered to record fewer metrics and also after the initial first year we can remove data every three months.

This system could easily scale for exascale size as all of the tools were picked so that they could handle large quantities of data at any given time. This allows us to upgrade our current system without worrying or port this to a much larger exascale system.

Table 1. Resource usage by the Data Collection Framework component averaged from 60 samples over one minute period.

Application	CPU (% of a core)	Memory usage	Memory	Net I/O
Nodered	1.57%	147.615 MiB	0.013%	4.32 MB
Grafana	0.11%	26.59 MiB	0%	1.05 GB
LSF Explorer	12.35%	3.26 GiB	0.32%	581.38 MB
OpenTSDB	2.5%	3.84 GiB	0.38%	825.75 MB

Table 2. Disk space usage by the Data Collection Framework components over a four month period.

Application	Disk usage
Nodered	37 MB
Grafana	24 MB
LSF Explorer	221 GB
OpenTSDB	25 GB

2.3   Metrics

When deciding what data to collect for the system we were faced with a difficult challenge as there is a high number of metrics to choose from. We have decided to choose metrics that would:

a) be useful to our analysis of the system both for general monitoring and ML,
b) be present on as many of our systems as possible.

From the hardware metrics we decided to focus on ones such as fan power, CPU power and GPU power as they fit both of our criteria. We set the tools to record the results every 250 ms as this is how fast the servers read from the sensors. This would allow for sufficient resolution to see power fluctuations, even if they were for just a short period of time.

For collecting information about workloads, we used IBM Spectrum LSF Explorer [26], which collects over 700 metrics. During this early analysis stage of the project this has been left to collect all metrics so that we can identify the most useful ones for monitoring and feeding into our ML systems.

At present all data is being kept for the first year to allow for the detailed analyses and training of our models. Once we are confident in quality of our results, we will look into reducing amount of historical data to the minimum required.

Going forward we plan to use tools like PAPI [29] and nvprof [29] for collecting performance and power consumption metrics from applications and GEOPM [8] and Variorium [11] for controlling hardware knobs and dials during applications run time. Based on the work done at the LRZ [13] we feel that this would expand this level of detail that we would be able to see from our system without adding too much jitter.

Table 3 shows the average sample rate used in each of the three main areas of data collection. Sampling at different rates creates a challenge of misalignment among data points from different metrics. We used linear interpolation in order to smooth over any gaps that appeared in the data.

Table 3. Average sampling rates per data collection area

Sensor set	Average sample rate (secs)
LSF	10
Amester	0.25
IoT	5

2.4   Databases

As part of our system we have utilized two separate databases, due to the containerized architecture of this system a variety of databases could be used instead and it would not be difficult to add more or substitute out some of the databases we have used. This is due to the isolation that being in containers creates and also due to Grafana supporting many different data sources.

For collecting data from LSF, Elasticsearch [22] was used as it comes packaged with LSF Explorer and is therefore optimized to work with the high frequency data sent from this tool. This is especially required as we have altered the sampling rate in LSF in order to capture more granular data. The Table 4 shows the original values that are set in the LSF data collector and the values they were changed to. These were altered in order to capture a more granular view of the running jobs and to also capture more detail on smaller jobs. This has had no effect to the running of the system or the jobs running on the nodes. The only issue that has to be monitored is this can create large quantities of data, so the area storing the elastic search database has to be large enough to accommodate all of the data that will be generated.

The second database chosen was OpenTSDB [30] which is built on top of HBase [18]. This was used as it has great support with Grafana, it allows custom metrics which we would need as we developed and added new custom sensors from sources not typically used, such as directly from IPMI. Also it has been known to out perform rival databases such as KairosDB by quite a significant margin [6].

2.5   Visualisation and API

An important part of any system that capture data is how that data is used and is made accessible to other users. With this in mind we have used different methods in order to extract this data.

Table 4. Original and new values for LSF Explorer Sampling

Metric	Original value (secs)	New value (secs)
hostgrouploader	3600	60
hostmetricsloader	600	10
lsfbhostsloader	600	10
lsfeventsloader	300	10
lsfjobstatusloader	600	10

The first was to use the open source tool Grafana [25] to generate graphs and dashboards to visualise the initial data that was being generated. This gave us two benefits, firstly we were able to easily identify the data being generated as we added new components and sensors and adapt them as required and secondly it has allowed us to create live rotating dashboards that we have running on screens in the office so that we have a live picture of the state of the cluster and the in use resources.

The second method we added to access the data was via API, it was decided very early on in the design of this system that this would be a vital component as with so many data sources being used a critical element would be the ability for the data to be accessed by a single point of entry. We started developing the API as a Python library as the libraries we use in ML are all Python based such as Keras [28], PyTorch [31] and Tensorflow [33]

3   Machine Learning Analysis

This section presents the Machine Learning components of the framework to analyse and predict energy consumption of the system.

3.1   Clustering

We use clustering analysis to classify events according to their power consumption, fan speed and CPU/GPU utilisation. The clustering technique is based on k-mean classification [16] and provides a breakdown of events that show a different levels of load on the HPC cluster.

3.2   Predictive Management

For this paper, we propose to use Long Short Term Memory(LSTM) network [7], a type of Recurrent Neural Network [14] which is highly suitable for time series data. The LSTM network consists of multiple block units. Each block unit has a cell, an input gate, a forget gate and an output gate. These gates allow including the influence of the previous time step data for more accurate time series prediction. The network is trained based on the fan power and CPU Utilisation of the cluster in three previous time steps. Output from the Network provide ongoing predictions for the cluster.

4   Preliminary Results

4.1   Experimental Setup

We are conducting our research on a cluster of IBM POWER8/9™servers
(2 CPUs per node, 10/12 cores per CPU, Nominal frequency 3.6–4.2 GHz,
512/1024 GB RAM, 4 NVIDIA Tesla P100/V100 GPUs per node, 16 GB/GPU,
NVIDIA NVLink) with IBM Spectrum Scale™ storage subsystem, 100 Gb/s
EDR Infiniband and 10 GigE networks and RHEL 7.x operating system. This
cluster is used as a research system in our lab, which we use to develop and test
our new projects for IBM clients and IBM internal use. In order to get a good
baseline of workloads we encourage the researchers on site to also submit jobs
to it as well so that we can collect real world information.

At a room level we are using ESP8266 [24] micro controllers with DHT22
[17] sensors to gather temperature and humidity data. Within the room we are
also making use of existing monitoring infrastructure which consists of room and
rack level IoT devices, Trendpoint Enkapsis [23] Power Management Devices and
CSIM Babel Buster [19] edge devices. These gather data from different parts
of the data centre environment including, power usage at the breaker, room
temperature and current information about the main room cooling systems.
The benefit of using edge devices such as the Babel Buster is that it is able
to communicate on multiple protocols to various IoT devices in the room. It
is then able to process this data and present key metrics via Simple Network
Management Protocol (SNMP) [35] to our Data Collection Framework.

4.2   Generated Graphs

In Fig. 3 we can see the temperature of the water going into and out of the
data centre cooling systems over a period of time. This allows us to see if any
problems arise in the cooling systems and also allows us to see if our cluster is
negatively impacting the cooling. We will use such data in our clustering and
prediction analyses.

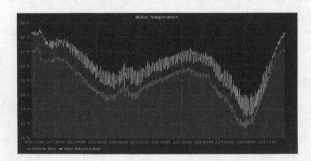

Fig. 3. Generated stats showing water temperature used for the cooling systems in the
data centre

4.3   Clustering and Prediction Analysis

In this section, we inspect a time series over 3 months of CPU Utilisation, Fan Power and Rack Power see Fig. 4. The CPU Utilisation time series have a high frequency of sampling, with 765,986 data points from mid November 2019 to mid February 2020. Meanwhile, the Fan Power time series and Rack Power time series have 647 and 663 data points respectively. As a result, we performed linear interpolation to upsample the Fan Power and Rack Power time series. The time series of total CPU Utilisation and Fan Power show similar spikes at the same time in the overall rack power. This suggests that CPU Utilisation and Fan Power are the main factors dominating the energy consumption of the rack.

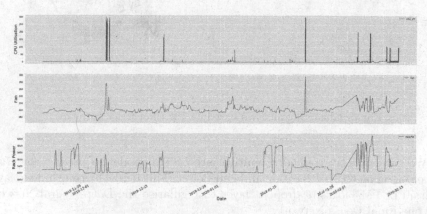

Fig. 4. Graph showing the time series of Rack Power, Fan Power and CPU Utilization.

The correlation matrix of the timeseries further demonstrates positive correlations across the timeseries, in particular between RackPW and Fan Power, and between Fan Power and CPU_UT, shown in Table 5. Further clustering analysis using the k-means methods show that the data points of Rack Power, Fan Power and CPU utilisation can fall into 3 to 6 groups. Figure 5 shows the analysis using the elbow method ([9]) to determine the number of clustering group (in this case k = 3) and the corresponding 3D plotting of the data points. The 3D graph indicates that the clustering boundary demonstrates the different levels of Rack Power, which is influenced by both CPU Utilisation and Fan Power, which

Table 5. Correlation matrix of the timeseries for CPU_UT, Fan Power and Rack Power

	CPU_UT	FanPW	RackPW
CPU_UT	1.00	0.37	0.15
FanPW	0.37	1.00	0.40
RackPW	0.15	0.40	1.00

increases or decreases in response to the HPC cluster's temperature and workloads. These graphs allow us to pinpoint groups of workloads in Fig. 5 Group 2
can be classified as a ML series of jobs, these have high power consumption, but
low CPU utilization, which means that GPU's are being heavily used, this is a
common theme for ML jobs.

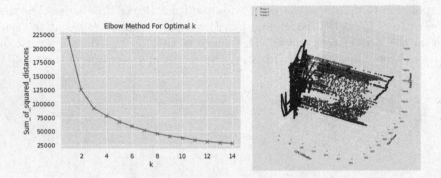

Fig. 5. Clustering analysis based on the time series variables

We subsequently trained a multivariate LSTM model to predict the Rack
Power based on CPU Utilisation and Fan Power. This model has one hidden layer
with 50 LSTM blocks, a dropout layer to regularise the Deep Neural Network
and one Final Dense Network.

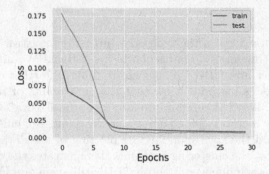

Fig. 6. Loss curve of the Machine Learning model across epochs

The model was trained in 30 epochs, each using a batch of 5,000 data points
(out of the total 432,000 points for training and 300,113 points for testing). The
loss curve of the model in Figure 6 shows that learning has converged after 30
epochs and the final model performs well in prediction mode, with an $R^2 = 99.7$
when used on the test data set (Fig. 7).

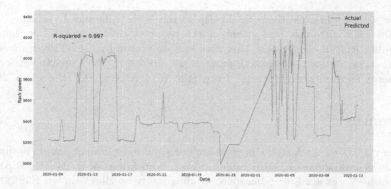

Fig. 7. Machine Learning prediction of Rack Power based on CPU Utilisation and Fan Power

Overall the LSTM prediction model shows that Rack Power can be predicted with high precision based on corresponding CPU Utilisation and Fan Power of the current and previous timesteps. While the number of parameters used in this analysis is limited, the framework and methodology are transferable and scalable to include more variables and parameters. This AI-driven holistic approach contributes building an architecture towards an intelligence control system that utilise these correlation for predictive control. As a direction for future research, we plan to apply a technique called Deep Reinforcement Learning [15].

5   Conclusions and Future Work

We have presented our on-going work on AI driven Holistic Approach to Energy Efficient Computing. We have outlined our vision of using ML and AI in combination with software-hardware co-design for analysing and optimizing energy efficiency throughout different parts of software and hardware stacks. We have described details of the Data Collection Framework and ways to access the data via GUI and APIs. We have also presented preliminary results from AI based analysis of the data to support our vision.

Going forward we plan to evolve our system by extending the number and types of IoT devices in use to get a better map of the Data Centre and its environment. This will include extending the use of Edge devices to help with the processing of streaming data to reduce data processing load of the main cluster. We also plan to integrate in-band data collection from applications into our Data Collection framework. Feeding results of our models into a scheduler, e.g. LSF and cooling system controlling software are also on our list. Note that while we are using certain proprietary software in our tests, our architecture is very open and can be utilized in different environments. In terms of Machine Learning algorithm, directions for future research include further implementation of AI-driven control techniques that combines Predictive Analytics and Deep Reinforcement Learning.

Acknowledgements. Authors would like to thank S. Hills and J. Whittle, UKRI-STFC for help with the deployment of the test-bed cluster and K. Jordan, IBM Research for fruitful discussions. This work was supported by the STFC Hartree Centres Innovation Return on Research programme, funded by the Department for Business, energy and Industrial Strategy. Copyright. (c) UKRI-STFC, IBM Corp. 2020

References

1. Puzovic, M., et al.: A study on cross-architectural modelling of power consumption using neural networks. Supercomput. Front. Innovations **5**(4), 24–41 (2018)
2. Elisseev, V., et al.: Energy aware scheduling study on BlueWonder, E2SC@SC18
3. Andrae, A.S.G., Edler, T.: On global electricity usage of communication technology: trends to 2030. Challenges **6**, 117–157 (2015)
4. Bartolini, A., et al.: The D.A.V.I.D.E. big-data-powered fine-grain power and performance monitoring support. In: Proceedings of the 15th ACM International Conference on Computing Frontiers, pp. 303–308. CF 2018, Association for Computing Machinery, New York, NY, USA (2018). https://doi.org/10.1145/3203217.3205863
5. Bashroush, R.: A comprehensive reasoning framework for hardware refresh in data centers. IEEE Trans. Sustain. Comput. **3**(4), 209–220 (2018)
6. Greenberg, H.N., DeBardeleben, N.: Tivan: a scalable data collection and analytics cluster. In: SC (2018)
7. Hochreiter, S., Schmidhuber, J.: LSTM can solve hard long time lag problems. In: Advances in Neural Information Processing Systems, pp. 473–479 (1997)
8. Kunkel, Julian M., Yokota, Rio., Balaji, Pavan, Keyes, David (eds.): ISC 2017. LNCS, vol. 10266. Springer, Cham (2017). https://doi.org/10.1007/978-3-319-58667-0
9. Kodinariya, T.M., Makwana, P.R.: Review on determining number of cluster in k-means clustering. Int. J. **1**(6), 90–95 (2013)
10. Brochard, L., et al.: Energy-Efficient Computing and Data Centers. Wiley, Hoboken (2019). https://doi.org/10.1002/9781119422037.fmatter
11. Labasan, S. et al.: Variorum: extensible framework for hardware monitoring and contol. In: E2SC at SC (2017)
12. Libri, A., Bartolini, A., Benini, L.: Dwarf in a giant: enabling scalable, high-resolution HPC energy monitoring for real-time profiling and analytics. CoRR abs/1806.02698 (2018). http://arxiv.org/abs/1806.02698
13. Ozer, G., et al.: Towards a predictive energy model for HPC runtime systems using supervised learning, August 2019
14. Sherstinsky, A.: Fundamentals of recurrent neural network (RNN) and long short-term memory (LSTM) network. arXiv preprint arXiv:1808.03314 (2018)
15. Sutton, R.S., Barto, A.G., et al.: Introduction to Reinforcement Learning, vol. 135. MIT Press, Cambridge (1998)
16. Teknomo, K.: K-means clustering tutorial. Medicine **100**(4), 3 (2006)
17. ADAFRUIT: Dht22. https://learn.adafruit.com/dht
18. APACHE: Hbase. https://hbase.apache.org/
19. CONTROL SOLUTIONS MINNESOTA: Modbus to SNMP Gateway (2020). https://www.csimn.com/CSI_pages/BBPRO-V210.html
20. DEEPMIND: DeepMind AI Reduces Google Data Centre Cooling Bill by 40% (2016). https://deepmind.com/blog/article/deepmind-ai-reduces-google-data-centre-cooling-bill-40

21. DOCKER: Docker. https://docker.com/
22. ELASTICSEARCH: Elasticsearch: The Official Distributed Search Analytics Engine (2020). https://www.elastic.co/elasticsearch/
23. ENKAPSIS: Enkapsis - Trendpoint (2020). https://trendpoint.com/branch-circuit-monitoring/enkapsis/
24. ESPRESSIF: Esp8266.   https://www.espressif.com/en/products/socs/esp8266/overview
25. GRAFANA: Grafana: The open observability platform — Grafana Labs (2020). https://www.grafana.com/
26. IBM: IBM Spectrum Scale LSF Explorer (2020). https://www.ibm.com/support/knowledgecenter/en/SS6MQM_10.1.0/getting_started/about.html
27. KATHY KINCADE: Less is more: Lbnl breaks new ground in data center optimization. https://www.nersc.gov/news-publications/nersc-news/nersc-center-news/2020/less-is-more-lbnl-breaks-new-ground-in-data-center-optimization/
28. KERAS: Keras. https://keras.io/
29. NVIDIA: Profiler. https://docs.nvidia.com/cuda/profiler-users-guide/index.html
30. OPENTSDB: Opentsdb. http://opentsdb.net/
31. PYTORCH: PyTorch. https://pytorch.org/
32. SCHEDMD: Slurm. https://slurm.schedmd.com/
33. TENSORFLOW: Tensorflow. https://www.tensorflow.org/
34. THE HPC POWERSTACK: The HPC PowerStack (2019). https://powerstack.caps.in.tum.de/index.html
35. Snmp. https://en.wikipedia.org/wiki/Simple_Network_Management_Protocol

Characterizing HPC Performance Variation with Monitoring and Unsupervised Learning

Gence Ozer[1(✉)], Alessio Netti[1,2], Daniele Tafani[2], and Martin Schulz[1]

[1] Technische Universität München, Boltzmannstr. 3, 85748 Garching, Germany
gence.ozer@tum.de, schulzm@in.tum.de
[2] Leibniz-Rechenzentrum, Boltzmannstr. 1, 85748 Garching, Germany
{alessio.netti,daniele.tafani}@lrz.de

Abstract. As HPC systems grow larger and more complex, characterizing the relationships between their different components and gaining insight on their behavior becomes difficult. In turn, this puts a burden on both system administrators and developers who aim at improving the efficiency and reliability of systems, algorithms and applications. Automated approaches capable of extracting a system's behavior, as well as identifying anomalies and outliers, are necessary more than ever.

In this work we discuss our exploratory study of Bayesian Gaussian mixture models, an unsupervised machine learning technique, to characterize the performance of an HPC system's components, as well as to identify anomalies, based on sensor data. We propose an algorithmic framework for this purpose, implement it within the DCDB monitoring and operational data analytics system, and present several case studies carried out using data from a production HPC system.

Keywords: HPC systems · Monitoring · Operational data analytics · Clustering · Anomaly detection

1 Introduction

As the demand for more capable *High-Performance Computing* (HPC) systems increases, supercomputing centers keep adding hardware and software resources to build significantly more complex and heterogeneous platforms: on top of their extreme power consumption [19], these systems also introduce new major challenges regarding hardware reliability [6] and performance variability [13], which in turn hinder the optimization of system operations. To address these issues, monitoring frameworks can be used to capture fine-grained sensor data (e.g., power or temperature) from all components in a production HPC system, allowing users and administrators alike to understand and characterize the system's behavior, as well as identify potential anomalies: processes of this kind are referred to as *Operational Data Analytics* (ODA) [4]. This knowledge subsequently can support tuning strategies to improve energy efficiency and system reliability, among other aspects.

© Springer Nature Switzerland AG 2020
H. Jagode et al. (Eds.): ISC High Performance 2020 Workshops, LNCS 12321, pp. 280–292, 2020.
https://doi.org/10.1007/978-3-030-59851-8_18

The majority of HPC centers still relies on the domain knowledge and expertise of system administrators, who manually analyze key monitoring metrics and log streams, to steer operations and thus enact ODA [5]. As systems become more complex, however, manual tuning becomes impractical and correlations between metrics become both more critical and at the same time difficult to spot: this can be addressed by partially automating the ODA processes, using data mining algorithms to construct a global overview of the performance of a system and to find outliers, allowing system administrators to focus on root cause analysis and mitigation actions. In the context of this paper, we focus on *performance variation* and *anomaly* detection: the first is a systematic approach to characterize the performance of an HPC system and extract behavioral patterns both in time and across system components. The latter can be seen as an extreme case of performance variation, where the behavior of a set of components severely deviates from the others due to abnormal events, such as faults or failures [11].

Related Work. Many approaches to performance variation and anomaly detection have been proposed, relying on either text log streams or monitoring sensors as sources of data. These approaches can be classified according to the techniques they employ, starting from supervised machine learning: Tuncer et al. proposed an approach to detect performance anomalies based on monitoring data, which is processed and fed to classifiers [18]. Similarly, Baseman et al. proposed a framework using density estimation and random forest classification to detect anomalies [2]. Wang et al. combined instead independent component analysis with Bayesian classifiers to spot anomalies in virtual machines [20].

In contrast, others employ unsupervised machine learning techniques: Dani et al. performed classification using the K-means algorithm to find abnormal log streams [8]. Similarly, Münz et al. applied K-means to network traffic data in order to detect anomalous activity [14]. Zhang et al. targeted the domain of cloud computing and applied DBSCAN clustering to fine-grained, thread-level resource usage metrics to detect performance anomalies [21]. Finally, Borghesi et al. developed a semi-supervised approach based on auto-encoders, which leverages the reconstruction error to detect anomalous states [3].

Less common is the use of traditional statistical analysis techniques: Gabel et al. developed a fault detection model for cloud services using statistical tests such as the Tukey test or the sign test [10]. Cohen et al. used tree-augmented Bayesian networks to achieve anomaly detection based on performance data [7]. Guan et al. [12], instead, used a most relevant principal components method to characterize faults based on the correlations between monitoring sensors. Among commercial solutions, *Datadog* utilizes median absolute deviation algorithms to identify anomalous states in the servers.[1] However, while there is an abundance of anomaly detection techniques, there is to our knowledge a lack of techniques combining the former with a systematic performance characterization of an HPC system's components. Moreover, the feasibility of current approaches in an online context and their associated details are not clear, yet.

---

[1] https://docs.datadoghq.com/monitors/monitor_types/outlier/.

Contributions. In this work we explore and evaluate the effectiveness of unsupervised machine learning for characterizing performance variation in HPC systems. In particular, we present an experimental approach using *Bayesian Gaussian mixture models* applied to HPC monitoring data, which allows us to extract statistical descriptions of the behavior of components at any level in an HPC system via Gaussian distributions. Based on this, we also propose an anomaly detection method that employs the *Mahalanobis distance*. We conduct an exploratory analysis on available monitoring data from the *CooLMUC-3* cluster operated by the *Leibniz Supercomputing Centre* (LRZ), and present the insights on early experiences with our approach. Monitoring is performed via the *Data Center Data Base* (DCDB) framework [15], and the online implementation of our approach is realized with its *Wintermute* ODA extension [16].

Organization. The paper is structured as follows. In Sect. 2 we present our exploratory analysis of the CooLMUC-3 monitoring data. In Sect. 3 we then describe our approach to performance variation characterization, and in Sect. 4 we present several case studies. Section 5 concludes the paper.

2 HPC Environment and Monitoring Data

First, we introduce the CooLMUC-3 system on which we conduct our exploratory analysis and the associated monitoring metrics. In particular, we highlight the relationships between metrics as well as variation across components.

2.1 HPC Environment

We employ the CooLMUC-3 HPC system hosted at LRZ:[2] it is composed of 148 compute nodes, each equipped with an Intel Xeon Phi 7210 CPU with 64 physical cores each having 4 threads. Each node has 96 GB of RAM, 16 GB of high-bandwidth memory (HBM) and a dual-rail Intel OmniPath network interface. In addition, CooLMUC-3 uses warm water cooling for all of its components: this includes, for example, the network switches and allows all racks to be completely isolated from the environment, reducing heat dispersion to ambient air. We leverage the *Data Center Data Base* (DCDB) framework developed at LRZ [15] to perform monitoring on CooLMUC-3. DCDB operates continuously on this system, collecting fine-granularity production sensor data from both compute nodes and the system's infrastructure. The data is collected by plugin-based daemons called *Pushers* and is sent via the MQTT protocol to *Collect Agents*, which act as data brokers. The data is finally stored in an *Apache Cassandra* database, from which it can be queried.

Monitoring data is collected from a variety of sources: in compute nodes, we collect CPU performance counters (e.g., number of instructions) via a *Perfevents* plugin, paired with additional CPU activity information from the *stat* interface,

---

[2] https://doku.lrz.de/display/PUBLIC/CoolMUC-3.

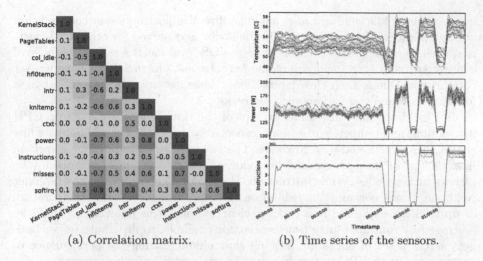

(a) Correlation matrix.   (b) Time series of the sensors.

Fig. 1. The correlation matrix associated to the sensors monitored in the CooLMUC-3 system, and an excerpt of the time series for the compute node power, CPU instructions and temperature sensors.

as well as memory usage information from *meminfo* and *vmstat* with a *ProcFS* plugin. Moreover, we collect network-related metrics and additional sensors (e.g., power consumption or temperature) via a *SysFS* plugin. We also collect out-of-band data for rack-level power consumption via a *REST* plugin, as well as a series of metrics related to the warm water cooling system (e.g., inlet water temperature) with an *SNMP* plugin. All sensors follow a numerical time series format and are sampled every 10 s.

2.2 Analysis of Monitoring Data

In order to characterize the DCDB metrics and their behavior under a uniform workload, we execute a series of proxy applications from the Coral-2 suite[3] on a set of 32 CooLMUC-3 nodes, with DCDB activated. Specifically, we use *LAMMPS*, *Kripke* and *Nekbone*, which were configured to use one MPI rank per node and 64 threads, as many as the physical CPU cores per node. In our experience on this system, this type of configuration leads to good performance and makes full use of available resources such as the HBM memory. As the applications have diverse performance profiles, we expect our analysis to be general, with minimal resulting bias. The results are shown in Fig. 1: for space reasons, we do not present the analysis in its full extent, but focus on the aspects that are most relevant in the context of this work.

Figure 1a shows the correlation matrix for a subset of DCDB metrics that exhibit interesting behaviors. Strong correlation patterns can be observed in this subset, with most metrics related to computational intensity such as CPU

---

[3] https://asc.llnl.gov/coral-2-benchmarks.

instructions or idle time (col_idle) having a direct impact on power consumption and temperature (knltemp). A similar behavior is observed for other CPU metrics, such as cache misses (misses), whereas OS-level metrics such as number of context switches (ctxt) and size of the kernel stack (Kernelstack) have weaker correlations. Due to their clear interactions, these metrics provide a robust base for statistical analysis and anomaly detection.

In Fig. 1b we show instead an excerpt of the time series for the power, CPU instructions and temperature sensors respectively, for each of the 32 nodes, while running LAMMPS and then Nekbone. The two runs are separated by a vertical line: on top of the applications' behavior, we observe a large variance in the metrics across nodes. While instructions show only light variance, mostly under Nekbone, power consumption exhibits a spread of up to 30W, and temperature of up to 3°. If expressed in a concise, clear manner, this information could be leveraged by runtime tuning frameworks, for example, to distribute power budgets across a set of nodes [9], proving that characterizing the performance of components in an HPC system in a systematic way is indeed necessary.

3   The Variation Detection Framework

Based on our experience described in Sect. 2, we propose an approach for capturing HPC performance variation in a generic fashion. Our variation detection framework is based on unsupervised machine learning applied to monitoring sensor data and, as shown in Fig. 2, comprises three steps: data preparation, clustering and outlier detection. The framework is designed to operate in online and offline scenarios, and can be easily integrated in any monitoring system.

Data Preparation. First, the sensor data collected by the underlying monitoring system must be prepared for the clustering stage. We fill in missing values in the time series of each sensor by means of linear interpolation, and we transform all monotonic sensors that come in the form of accumulators (e.g., instructions or energy) into their first-order derivative, by applying the delta operation to consecutive readings. This way, we are able to count the number of occurrences of a certain event in each time range rather than the total number of events since boot time. Finally, the data is smoothed over specified aggregation windows, depending on the desired type and granularity of the analysis, supplying the input that will be used for the clustering process.

Clustering with Lookback. After the data transformation operations are complete, clustering can be performed in N dimensions in order to characterize performance variation. The selected subset of sensors out of the full dataset determines the number of dimensions in the clustering space as well as the scope of the analysis: an analysis focused on CPU performance variation will use metrics such as the per-CPU instructions or cache misses, whereas an energy efficiency-oriented analysis will consider metrics such as the compute node-level power consumption. Each HPC component involved in the analysis (e.g., CPU cores,

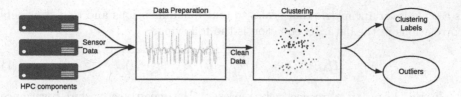

Fig. 2. Overview of the proposed variation detection framework.

compute nodes or racks) will represent a point in the clustering space whose coordinates are identified by the values of its selected metrics. In general, however, due to the limitations of most clustering algorithms, we expect our approach to be effective only when using a low number N (i.e., less than 10) of dimensions.

We use *Gaussian Mixture Models* (GMM) as a clustering approach: they try to explain the data by fitting multiple Gaussian distributions over it, typically using the *Expectation-Maximization* (EM) algorithm. Once the parameters of the individual distributions have been identified, each individual point in the data can be assigned to one of them, thus creating a series of clusters. This method generalizes well to different datasets, provides good results with minimal parameter tuning and produces compact statistical descriptions of the data clusters. Among existing GMM algorithms, we use *Bayesian Gaussian Mixture Models* (BGMM) [17]: compared to ordinary GMM algorithms, these are able to identify the optimal number of Gaussian distributions to use in the fitting process autonomously, further reducing model tuning and proving useful in online, continuous scenarios, where HPC systems exhibit highly diverse states. The maximum number of Gaussian distributions that are potentially generated by the BGMM algorithm can be specified as a parameter. We also experimented with algorithms such as DBSCAN, but we were not able to produce good results without tuning of parameters on a per-dataset basis.

We apply BGMM clustering to the points in the clustering space using a configurable *lookback* approach, considering not only the points corresponding to the most recent aggregation window for each HPC component, but also those corresponding to past ones. This approach has several benefits: it allows us to compare the characteristics of components over time, making in turn the clustering process more stable due to the increased number of points. Upon completion, the BGMM algorithm provides the mean vector and covariance matrix of each Gaussian distribution and assigns each point to one of them.

Outlier Detection. Since the BGMM algorithm does not label outliers automatically, we introduce a two-step outlier detection approach. First, due to the BGMM optimization process, small clusters grouping multiple outlier points can potentially be formed. As such, we label as outliers all points belonging to clusters that have a number of points lower than a configurable threshold. Second, some points might be assigned to certain clusters even though the associated probabilities are extremely low. To identify these points, we calculate their distance from the respective distributions using the *Mahalanobis distance*, which is a scale-invariant metric that scales to multiple dimensions and that considers correlations in the data. Its equation is the following:

$$D_M(x) \quad = \quad \sqrt{(x-\mu)^T S^{-1}(x-\mu)} \tag{1}$$

In Eq. 1, μ and S respectively represent the mean vector and covariance matrix of the Gaussian distribution to which the point x is assigned by the BGMM algorithm. If the resulting distance is higher than a configurable threshold, the point is classified as an outlier. Since the Mahalanobis distance is proportional to the number of standard deviations that separate a point from a distribution's mean, this threshold is generic and does not need to be tuned ad-hoc for each experiment, but only in extreme scenarios.

Implementation. We implemented our approach for both offline and online operation: the first offline implementation was made in Python, using the popular *scikit-learn* library. This implementation is suitable for experiments focusing on large historical datasets and requiring extensive data manipulation. Conversely, the second implementation is tailored for lightweight online operation in production HPC systems. This was carried out using the DCDB monitoring framework for HPC systems [15] and its Wintermute extension for online operational data analytics [16]. The resulting plugin is written in C++ and is based on the *OpenCV* GMM implementation: due to the lack of implementations in C++, we use a simple GMM model in the plugin in place of the more sophisticated BGMM one, relying on our offline implementation for hints on the ideal number of clusters to use in a certain scenario.

4   Case Studies

Here we present several case studies carried out using cluster-wide CoolMUC-3 data from Summer 2019: we target different aspects of the HPC system, starting from application phases at the CPU core level, up to power consumption and temperature at the compute node level and finally up to the rack level, analyzing the cooling system's efficiency. This way we evaluate the effectiveness of our framework with different granularities and data sources. For convenience, the experiments were carried out offline using archived data, but can be reproduced online using the DCDB Wintermute framework.

4.1   CPU Core-Level Analysis

We start with a short-term analysis of application behavior at the CPU core level. To this end, we execute the Kripke and LAMMPS proxy applications on 4 compute nodes of CoolMUC-3 and analyze the 1-min averages of the CPU instructions and cache misses (*misses*) metrics. Specifically, each point in the 2-D clustering space is a CPU core from a single node we selected out of the 4 available. We use the lookback feature to consider all data in the past 5 min and highlight the applications' behavior over time.

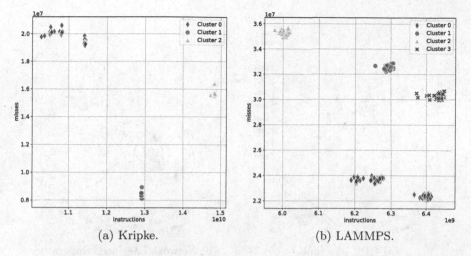

(a) Kripke.   (b) LAMMPS.

Fig. 3. Results of clustering applied at the CPU core level to perform application phase detection in Kripke (a) and LAMMPS (b). Each point is a CPU core in a CooLMUC-3 compute node with its 1-min averages of the instructions and cache misses metrics.

The results are shown in the scatter plots in Fig. 3 for the Kripke and LAMMPS proxy applications respectively. In the scatter plots we show the outlier points as not belonging to any distribution, since this information is not reliable due to the very low probabilities involved. In Fig. 3a, Kripke exhibits a clear separation between its different phases on both axes, which are captured by 3 distinct Gaussian distributions. No outliers were identified, as variance across CPU cores appears to be limited. This is especially true for Clusters 1 and 2, which likely correspond to the compute-intensive phases of Kripke due to their higher instructions count. Cluster 0, on the other hand, may be associated with the application's initialization phase, due to its low instructions and high cache misses counts, and shows higher variance across CPU cores.

The behavior associated to LAMMPS, in Fig. 3b, is similar to what we observed with Kripke: Cluster 2 captures the initialization phase of the application, on the top left corner, while the other 3 clusters capture more compute-intensive phases. Interestingly, it can be observed that, while the point clouds associated to Clusters 1 and 3 were separated into two low-variance Gaussian distributions, Cluster 0 captures several distinct point clouds, resulting in a single distribution with higher variance. We attribute this behavior to the optimization process behind the EM algorithm. In general, it can be noted that LAMMPS exhibits both higher cache misses and lower instructions counts than Kripke, indicating stronger memory activity for this specific configuration. Since we only aim to characterize performance patterns, our approach's effectiveness at distinguishing the applications themselves is not clear: for this purpose, supervised learning models relying on a wide pool of metrics have been shown to be effective [1].

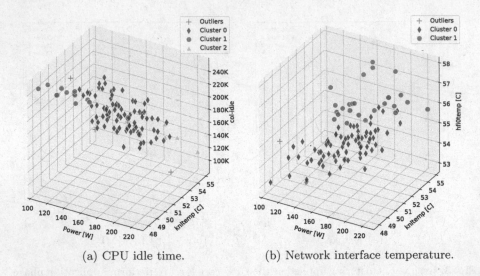

(a) CPU idle time.   (b) Network interface temperature.

Fig. 4. Results of clustering applied at the compute node level. Each point represents a compute node in CooLMUC-3 with its 2-week average power consumption, temperature and CPU idle time (a) or network interface temperature (b).

4.2 Compute Node-Level Analysis

Here we perform a long-term compute node-level analysis, using data between September 2nd and 15th from CooLMUC-3. In particular, for each of its 148 compute nodes we use the 2-week averages of their power consumption, temperature (*knltemp*) and CPU idle time (*col_idle*), and the resulting points are clustered in a 3-D space with a maximum of 4 Gaussian distributions. The last of the three metrics is replaced by the network interface temperature (*hfi0temp*) in a second experiment. Although we have no knowledge of the running jobs in this time frame we expect the 2-week averages, given the maximum allowed job execution time of 48 h, to mitigate the bias of single applications and extract real node performance. We do not use lookback.

Results are shown in the scatter plots in Fig. 4a, which uses the CPU idle time as third metric, and Fig. 4b, which uses the network interface temperature. In both cases, a strong linear correlation can be observed among the metrics: as expected, a compute node with low CPU idle time consumes more power and has higher temperatures, due to the workload and communication of HPC applications. Despite the 2-week aggregation, a large spread in node behavior can still be observed: in Fig. 4a, compute nodes in Cluster 0 have higher CPU idle times with lower power and temperature values. Conversely, nodes in Cluster 2 exhibit heavier load, with up to 200W of average power consumption; this behavior is likely the symptom of a job scheduling policy that does not account for inter-node workload balance. Furthermore, a few nodes were classified as outliers: one of them shows a peculiar behavior, consuming 20% more power than other nodes with similar CPU idle time. We are currently monitoring this anomaly, in order

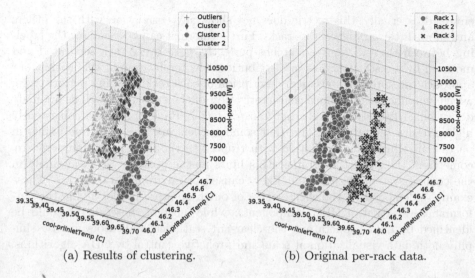

(a) Results of clustering.   (b) Original per-rack data.

Fig. 5. Results of clustering applied at the rack level. Each point represents a rack in CooLMUC-3 with its hourly averages of the cooling system's warm water inlet temperature, return temperature and heat removed, at different points in time.

to identify its root cause. The same considerations apply for Fig. 4b: in this case, nodes belonging to Cluster 1 show higher network interface temperatures, which are likely caused by cooling inefficiency or manufacturing variability. A single node is classified as an outlier, with a higher network interface temperature than other nodes under similar load.

4.3   Rack-Level Analysis

For this last case study, we analyze several infrastructure metrics related to the 3 racks composing CooLMUC-3. Each rack contains roughly 50 nodes, as well as sensors for its section of the warm water cooling system. We consider two weeks of data, from June 28th to July 11th, for three sensors: the water's inlet temperature in the racks (*cool-priInletTemp*), its return temperature (*cool-priReturnTemp*) and finally the amount of heat removed from the racks (*cool-power*) quantified in Watts. We compute hourly averages for each metric, obtaining the 3-D points on which clustering is performed, with a maximum of 4 Gaussian distributions. Finally, we use the lookback feature to extend the number of points, so as to cover the entire 2 week range of available data.

The results are shown in the scatter plots in Fig. 5a, with the points labeled according to their Gaussian distributions, and in Fig. 5b according to the rack they belong to. Unlike in Sect. 4.2, only the return temperature and the heat removed metrics appear to be strongly correlated: this is expected, as the greater is the temperature difference between the inlet and return water, the greater is the amount of heat removed from the system. As the inlet temperature is enforced externally, this metric does not show any correlation with the others and shows little variance across racks. Furthermore, it can be seen how the labeling between the two figures matches perfectly, with every rack separated and modeled by a distinct Gaussian distribution: the implication of this is that our approach can supply a statistical description of each rack's cooling performance, which simplifies performance characterization of the system, as well as anomaly detection. It can also be seen that Cluster 1 (i.e., Rack 2) shows a consistently higher return temperature, and that some outliers are present: three points in particular, which show deviation with respect to the inlet water temperature, come from the same time frame. This hints at the presence of an anomaly in the cooling system at that time, likely caused by environmental factors. These examples demonstrate the effectiveness of our framework in identifying the performance variation of HPC components: while most of these effects could be identified by human operators, the clear-cut statistical indicators we use simplify both data visualization at scale and proactive control by ODA algorithms.

5   Conclusions

In this paper we have presented a framework to characterize performance variation in the components of HPC systems: we employ Bayesian Gaussian mixture models applied to sensor monitoring data, so as to extract the behavioral groups associated to the components and their statistical description. Based on this, we proposed an anomaly identification mechanism that uses the Mahalanobis distance of the single clustering points to the fitted Gaussian distributions and also provided the online implementation of our approach in the DCDB Wintermute framework. We then presented the early findings of an exploratory analysis using our approach on production monitoring data from the CooLMUC-3 HPC system at LRZ, discussing several case studies carried out at different granularity levels effectively: our approach can capture different behaviors both in time and across different components, as well as flag suspicious behaviors as anomalies.

As future work, we plan to validate our approach in a quantitative way, identifying use cases with clear accuracy metrics. Moreover, we plan to further test our approach in combination with dimensionality reduction techniques, in order to enrich the information encoded within the clustering space, as well as devise techniques to identify relevant metrics for clustering automatically.

References

1. Ates, E., et al.: Taxonomist: application detection through rich monitoring data. In: Aldinucci, M., Padovani, L., Torquati, M. (eds.) Euro-Par 2018. LNCS, vol. 11014, pp. 92–105. Springer, Cham (2018). https://doi.org/10.1007/978-3-319-96983-1_7
2. Baseman, E., Blanchard, S., DeBardeleben, N., Bonnie, A., et al.: Interpretable anomaly detection for monitoring of high performance computing systems. In: Proceedings of the ACM SIGKDD 2016 Workshops (2016)
3. Borghesi, A., Libri, A., Benini, L., Bartolini, A.: Online anomaly detection in HPC systems. In: Proceedings of AICAS 2019, pp. 229–233. IEEE (2019)

4. Bourassa, N., Johnson, W., Broughton, J., Carter, D.M., et al.: Operational data analytics: optimizing the national energy research scientific computing center cooling systems. In: Proceedings of the ICPP 2019 Workshops, pp. 5:1–5:7. ACM (2019)
5. Bourassa, N., Ott, M.: EEHPCWG operational data analytics survey (2019). https://eehpcwg.llnl.gov/assets/sc19_11_425_525_operational_data_analytics_ott_bourassa.pdf
6. Cappello, F., Geist, A., Gropp, W., Kale, S., et al.: Toward exascale resilience: 2014 update. Supercomput. Front. Innovations 1(1), 5–28 (2014)
7. Cohen, I., Chase, J.S., Goldszmidt, M., Kelly, T., Symons, J.: Correlating instrumentation data to system states: a building block for automated diagnosis and control. In: OSDI, vol. 4, p. 16 (2004)
8. Dani, M.C., Doreau, H., Alt, S.: K-means application for anomaly detection and log classification in HPC. In: Benferhat, S., Tabia, K., Ali, M. (eds.) IEA/AIE 2017. LNCS (LNAI), vol. 10351, pp. 201–210. Springer, Cham (2017). https://doi.org/10.1007/978-3-319-60045-1_23
9. Eastep, J., et al.: Global extensible open power manager: a vehicle for HPC community collaboration on co-designed energy management solutions. In: Kunkel, J.M., Yokota, R., Balaji, P., Keyes, D. (eds.) ISC 2017. LNCS, vol. 10266, pp. 394–412. Springer, Cham (2017). https://doi.org/10.1007/978-3-319-58667-0_21
10. Gabel, M., Gilad-Bachrach, R., Bjorner, N., Schuster, A.: Latent fault detection in cloud services. Microsoft Research, Technical report MSR-TR-2011-83 (2011)
11. Gainaru, A., Cappello, F.: Errors and faults. In: Herault, T., Robert, Y. (eds.) Fault-Tolerance Techniques for High-Performance Computing. CCN, pp. 89–144. Springer, Cham (2015). https://doi.org/10.1007/978-3-319-20943-2_2
12. Guan, Q., Fu, S.: Adaptive anomaly identification by exploring metric subspace in cloud computing infrastructures. In: Proceedings of SRDS 2013, pp. 205–214. IEEE (2013)
13. Inadomi, Y., Patki, T., Inoue, K., Aoyagi, M., et al.: Analyzing and mitigating the impact of manufacturing variability in power-constrained supercomputing. In: Proceedings of SC 2015, pp. 1–12. IEEE (2015)
14. Münz, G., Li, S., Carle, G.: Traffic anomaly detection using k-means clustering. In: Proceedings of the GI/ITG Workshop MMBnet, pp. 13–14 (2007)
15. Netti, A., Mueller, M., Auweter, A., Guillen, C., et al.: From facility to application sensor data: modular, continuous and holistic monitoring with DCDB. In: Proceedings of SC 2019. ACM (2019)
16. Netti, A., Mueller, M., Guillen, C., Ott, M., et al.: DCDB Wintermute: enabling online and holistic operational data analytics on HPC systems. In: Proceedings of HPDC 2020. ACM (2020)
17. Roberts, S.J., Husmeier, D., Rezek, I., Penny, W.: Bayesian approaches to Gaussian mixture modeling. IEEE Trans. Pattern Anal. Mach. Intell. 20(11), 1133–1142 (1998)
18. Tuncer, O., Ates, E., Zhang, Y., Turk, A., et al.: Online diagnosis of performance variation in HPC systems using machine learning. IEEE Trans. Parallel Distrib. Syst. 30, 883–896 (2018)
19. Villa, O., Johnson, D.R., Oconnor, M., Bolotin, E., et al.: Scaling the power wall: a path to exascale. In: Proceedings of SC 2014, pp. 830–841. IEEE (2014)

20. Wang, G., Yang, J., Li, R.: An anomaly detection framework based on ICA and Bayesian classification for IaaS platforms. KSII Trans. Internet Inf. Syst. (TIIS) **10**(8), 3865–3883 (2016)
21. Zhang, X., Meng, F., Chen, P., Xu, J.: TaskInsight: a fine-grained performance anomaly detection and problem locating system. In: Proceedings of CLOUD 2016, pp. 917–920. IEEE (2016)

15th Workshop on Virtualization in High-Performance Cloud Computing (VHPC'20)

Preface to the 15th Workshop on Virtualization in High-Performance Cloud Computing (VHPC'20)

Michael Alexander and Anastassios Nanos

Introduction

Containers and virtualization technologies constitute key enabling factors for flexible resource management in modern data centers, and particularly in cloud environments. Cloud providers need to manage complex infrastructures in a seamless fashion to support the highly dynamic and heterogeneous workloads and hosted applications customers deploy. Similarly, HPC environments have been increasingly adopting techniques that enable flexible management of vast computing and networking resources, close to marginal provisioning cost, which is unprecedented in the history of scientific and commercial computing. Most recently, Function as a Service (Faas) and Serverless computing, utilizing lightweight VMs-containers widens the spectrum of applications that can be deployed in a cloud environment, especially in an HPC context. Here, HPC-provided services become accessible to distributed workloads outside of large cluster environments.

Various virtualization-containerization technologies contribute to the overall picture in different ways: machine virtualization, with its capability to enable consolidation of multiple underutilized servers with heterogeneous software and operating systems (OSes), and its capability to live-migrate a fully operating virtual machine (VM) with a very short downtime, enables novel and dynamic ways to manage physical servers; OS-level virtualization (i.e., containerization), with its capability to isolate multiple userspace environments and to allow for their coexistence within the same OS kernel, promises to provide many of the advantages of machine virtualization with high levels of responsiveness and performance; lastly, unikernels provide for many virtualization benefits with a minimized OS/library surface. I/O Virtualization in turn allows physical network interfaces to take traffic from multiple VMs or containers; network virtualization, with its capability to create logical network overlays that are independent of the underlying physical topology is furthermore enabling virtualization of HPC infrastructures.

The VHPC program committee invited talks, research papers and demos related to virtualization across the entire software stack with a special focus on the intersection of HPC, containers-virtualization and the cloud. The main areas of focus were design/architecture, low-level systems software, management, performance management, modeling and configuration/tooling.

Program

The workshop ran for approximately 10 hours, starting from 4pm CEST, ending at 2am CEST (the next day). There were 8 research papers presented, two lightning talks, three invited talks and two keynote presentations. The main focus of the workshop was the evolution of virtualization and container technologies in relation to packaging, deploying, and executing HPC applications in public infrastructure. Highlighted talks from the program include Daniel Walsh's talk from RedHat on Podman, Krzysztof Rzadca's talk on Autopilot from Google, as well as the unikernel paper from Stefan Lankes (RWTH Aachen) about RustyHermit. The second part of the workshop covered hardware acceleration (talks by Seetharami Seelam from IBM Watson, orchestration issues for agriculture use-cases from Yiannis Georgiou (RYAX) and an interesting survey about performance variability for containerized applications on GRNET's supercomputer by Dimitris Dellis (GRNET).

The workshop was held as a fully virtual event via Zoom, peaking at 80 attendees, sustaining more than 40 participants during most of the workshop's running time. At the panel discussion, 25 people were online, and of those, 20 engaged in a fruitful panel debate about where containers, orchestrators and low-level systems virtualization stacks are going.

Five papers were submitted, and after a double-blind review process, four papers were accepted. The workshop was held virtually with live presentations on June 24, 2020.

Organization

Chairs

Michael Alexander	BOKU, Vienna, Austria
Anastassios Nanos	Nubis, Greece

Program Committee

Stergios Anastasiadis	University of Ioannina, Greece
Paolo Bonzini	Red Hat, Italy
Jakob Blomer	CERN, Europe
Eduardo César	Universidad Autonoma de Barcelona, Spain
Taylor Childers	Argonne National Laboratory, USA
Stephen Crago	USC ISI, USA
Tommaso Cucinotta	St. Anna School of Advanced Studies, Italy
François Diakhaté	CEA DAM Ile de France, France
Kyle Hale	Northwestern University, USA
Brian Kocoloski	Washington University, USA

Simon Kuenzer	NEC Laboratories Europe, Germany
John Lange	University of Pittsburgh, USA
Giuseppe Lettieri	University of Pisa, Italy
Klaus Ma	Huawei Technologies, China
Alberto Madonna	Swiss National Supercomputing Center, Switzerland
Nikos Parlavantzas	IRISA, France
Anup Patel	Western Digital, USA
Kevin Pedretti	Sandia National Laboratories, USA
Amer Qouneh	Western New England University, USA
Carlos Reaño	Queen's University Belfast, UK
Adrian Reber	Red Hat, Germany
Riccardo Rocha	CERN, Europe
Borja Sotomayor	University of Chicago, USA
Jonathan Sparks	Cray, USA
Kurt Tutschku	Blekinge Institute of Technology, Sweden
John Walters	USC ISI, USA
Yasuhiro Watashiba	Osaka University, Japan
Chao-Tung Yang	Tunghai University, Taiwan

The chairs would like to thank the ISC-HPC and Workshop organizers and the members of the program committee, along with the speakers and attendees, whose interaction contributed to a stimulating environment. VHPC is planning to continue the successful co-location with ISC-HPC in 2021.

Service Function Chaining Based
on Segment Routing Using P4
and SR-IOV (P4-SFC)

Andreas Stockmayer, Stephan Hinselmann, Marco Häberle[✉],
and Michael Menth

Chair of Communication Networks, University of Tuebingen, Tuebingen, Germany
{andreas.stockmayer,marco.haeberle,menth}@uni-tuebingen.de,
stephan.hinselmann@student.uni-tuebingen.de

Abstract. In this paper we describe P4-SFC to support service function chaining (SFC) based on a single P4-capable switch and off-the-shelf components. It utilizes MPLS-based segment routing for traffic forwarding in the network and SR-IOV for efficient packet handling on hosts. We describe the P4-SFC architecture and demonstrate its feasibility by a prototype using the Tofino Edgecore Wedge 100BF-32X as P4 switch. Performance test show that L2 throughput for VNFs on a host is significantly larger when connected via SR-IOV with the host's network interface card instead of over a software switch.

1   Introduction

Packet processing at the network ingress or egress typically requires network functions (NFs) such as firewalls, IDS/IPS, NAT, and others. In the past, these functions have been provided as hardware appliances. To reduce costs, many of them are today implemented as applications running on standard server hardware as so-called virtual NFs (VNFs). Complex services may be composed of multiple VNFs. This is called service function chaining (SFC). As the VNFs of a SFC are generally located on different hosts, SFC requires forwarding support in the network. That means, a packet which is classified for a specific SFC must be forwarded along a path that visits all VNFs of the respective SFC in a predefined order.

The IETF has proposed various approaches for this problem. One approach requires per-SFC state in the network, the other requires the ability of a node – we call it the SFC ingress node – to encode a source route in the packet header. Segment routing based on MPLS is one preferred option for source route encoding. It requires the SFC ingress node to push a stack of MPLS labels, but intermediate SFC forwarders just need to pop individual labels. While the latter

This work was supported by the bwNET2020+ project which is funded by the Ministry of Science, Research and the Arts Baden-Württemberg (MWK). The authors alone are responsible for the content of this paper.

H. Jagode et al. (Eds.): ISC High Performance 2020 Workshops, LNCS 12321, pp. 297–309, 2020.
https://doi.org/10.1007/978-3-030-59851-8_19

is simple, pushing a large header stack is hardly supported by today's affordable hardware.

In recent years, programmable data planes have been developed with the goal to facilitate new headers and forwarding behavior on software and hardware switches. P4 is a widespread programming language to specify switch behavior. It utilizes match-and-action tables for packet forwarding which are populated by a controller. We leverage this technology in this work and refer to [4] for further background.

The contribution of this paper is a simple architecture (P4-SFC) using MPLS-based segment routing for SFC forwarding, a P4-programmable switch as SFC ingress node, and communication with VNFs using SR-IOV hardware virtualization on hosts. To demonstrate the feasibility of P4-SFC, a prototype of P4-SFC is implemented using the Tofino Edgecore Wedge 100BF-32X as hardware platform. It forwards packets at a speed of 100 Gb/s and pushes large header stacks in line speed. Apart from the P4 switch, the prototype consists only of commodity hardware and comprises an SFC orchestrator that allows customers to submit their own VNF implementations that do not need to be SFC-aware.

The paper is structured as follows. In Sect. 2, we give an overview of segment routing, SFC-supporting protocols, and summarize SFC-related activities. Section 3 presents P4-SFC including the P4 pipeline of the SFC ingress node and an P4-SFC orchestrator. Section 4 reports on a prototype implementation of P4-SFC and experiments for validation purposes. Section 5 discusses some performance issues and compares the L2 throughput of VNFs with and without SR-IOV. Section 6 summarizes the work and gives conclusions.

2   Related Work

In this section, we first explain segment routing, then we give an overview of existing protocol stacks for SFC, and summarize selected SFC-related activities.

2.1   Segment Routing

With label switching, an MPLS label identifies a connection. The ingress label switching router (LSR) pushes a label onto a packet, intermediate LSRs switch the label according to their forwarding tables, and the egress LSR pops the label. Segment routing (SR) is a new approach for source routing and may leverage MPLS forwarding. Here, a label identifies a segment, which may be a link, a path, a node, etc. The ingress LSR pushes a label stack onto a packet. LSRs forward the packet according to the topmost label and possibly pop it. Thus, with SR, the network can remain unaware of individual connections as only ingress LSRs need to know them to push the right label stack. However, most MPLS nodes can push only few labels. In this work, we utilize SR and program a P4-capable switch for pushing large label stacks.

2.2   Protocol Stacks for SFC

The IETF has identified SFC as a problem for traditional networks due to their topological dependencies [16]. Traditional networks have a rather static configuration but SFC requires a highly dynamical network limiting high availability and scaleability.

A major result of te IETF's SFC working group is the network service header (NSH) [17]. It consists of three parts: a base header providing information about the header structure and the payload protocol, a service path header containing the path identification and location within a service path, and a context header for metadata.

Another document proposes an MPLS-based forwarding plane for SFC [9]. It suggests tuples consisting of an "SFC context label" and an "SF label" similar to the NSH. The context label identifies the SFC by the contained service path identifier (SPI), and the SF label identifies the next service function to be actioned. In case of label switching, the context label is maintained and used by LSRs to switch consecutive SF labels for VNFs. In case of segment routing, tuples of context/SF labels are stacked by the ingress LSR and are consecutively popped with completed VNF operations. A similar approach is described in another working group draft [7].

These protocols are partly competing and not fully compatible. In all proposed protocol suites, all devices involved in an SFC, e.g., forwarding nodes and NFs, need to be SFC-aware, i.e., they need to respect protocol specifics. P4-SFC allows customers to use VNFs that are not SFC-aware. Furthermore, it leaves the network unaware of SFCs, utilizes only common MPLS labels, and requires forwarding nodes to pop only single labels, i.e., no special hardware features are needed. Only the SFC ingress node pushes a label stack.

2.3   Selected SFC-Related Activities

The ETSI has published a set of documents describing an architecture for networking operations and orchestration (MANO) of NFVs [8]. It provides an overview with focus on interoperability, but it does not offer an NFV/SFC networking stack.

The Open Platform for NFV (OPNFV) [2] has been started by the Linux Foundation in 2014. It is a cooperative project among 20 companies with the goal to develop an NFV infrastructure (NFVI) software stack to build and test NFV functionality. Its long-term goal is to provide a standard platform for NFVI.

Most commercial cloud operators, e.g., Amazon [3] or Microsoft [15], offer configurable, complex services to their customers based on NFV/SFC. Examples of such NFs are firewalls, gateways, and load balancers. These services are comfortable for customers but are limited to functions provided by the cloud operators. P4-SFC allows customers to upload their own VNF binaries.

NFVnice [14] is a user-space scheduler on a host that decides whether a packet is delivered to its desired VNF. It also monitors all VNFs in the system. If VNFs in a later stage of an SFC are overloaded, NFVnice drops packets already at an early stage of the SFC to reduce wasted work.

P4NFV [10] and P4SC [6] propose to implement NFs based on P4-capable hardware because general purpose hardware is too slow for fast packet processing. Their contribution is an architecture for the management of VNFs on P4 switches. The work is applicable to P4-based hardware and software switches.

3   Architecture of P4-SFC

In this section we explain the implementation of the P4-based SFC ingress node and how VNFs are efficiently integrated on hosts so that they remain SFC-unaware and transparent for routing.

3.1   Implementation of the SFC Ingress Node

We briefly describe the requirements of the SFC ingress node and explain a P4 pipeline for implementation of this functionality in P4.

Requirements. In P4-SFC, the SFC ingress node classifies traffic and adds appropriate MPLS label stacks to packets that require processing by a specific SFC. The classifier identifies flows for a specific SFC. We utilize flow descriptors consisting of source and destination IP addresses, port numbers, and IP protocol number for that purpose. Wildcards are supported. That label stack encodes both the forwarding in the network and the identification of the VNFs. Therefore, the label stack can be large. To keep things simple, we support up to $n = 10$ labels in our small testbed (see Sect. 4). However when using jumbo frames, large numbers of labels are possible.

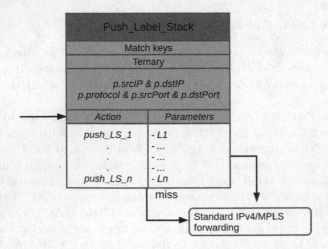

Fig. 1. Match-and-action table "push_Label_Stack" to push label stacks of different size.

P4 Pipeline. We describe the supported header stacks, the ingress and egress control flow, and the `pushLabelStack` control block in more detail.

Supported Header Stacks. Incoming packets are parsed so that their header values can be accessed within the P4 pipeline. To that end, we define up to n MPLS labels, an IP header, and a TCP/UDP header.

Ingress and Egress Control Flow. The ingress control flow consists of a `Push_Label_Stack` control block and an `IP_MPLS_Forward` control block. The `push_Label_Stack` control block adds an appropriate label stack to the packet, i.e., it serves as classifier. The `IP_MPLS_Forward` control block performs simple IP/MPLS forwarding. The egress flow just sends the packet and does not implement any special control blocks.

Implementation of the `Push_Label_Stack` *Control Block.* The implementation challenge is that an arbitrary number of up to n labels need to be pushed. Header sizes are fixed. An intuitive approach is pushing a single label per pipeline execution and recirculating the packet for another pipeline execution until the desired label stack is fully pushed. The drawback of this approach is that pushing n labels requires n-fold packet processing capacity, which reduces the throughput of the SFC ingress node.

Our solution uses the match-and-action table (MAT) push_Label_Stack whose structure is given in Fig. 1. The MAT utilizes the fields of the source and destination addresses and port numbers as well as the IP protocol number as match keys. A ternary match is used so that wildcards are supported. We provide actions `push_LS_i` to push a stack of i labels onto the packet. This action has i parameters but the table has n label entries (L1, ..., Ln). In case of a match, the corresponding action is executed with the appropriate number of arguments. Afterwards, the `IP_MPLS_Forward` control block is carried out. For the implementation of the `IP_MPLS_Forward` control block we reuse available demo code.

3.2   Transparent and Efficient VNF Integration on Hosts

We now specify how packets are forwarded from a switch to a VNF on a host and back. This is challenging since the VNF should remain unaware of the label stack, and the packet forwarding from the host's network interface card (NIC) to the VM hosting the VNF should be efficient. The following steps are illustrated by Fig. 2.

We assume that up to N VNFs are supported by a host, either within a container or a separate VM. Each potential VNF constitutes a logical network segment while the corresponding physical network segment is the switch over which the VNF is reachable. The forwarding table of the switch is configured such that an incoming packet with a topmost label pointing at a specific VNF is equipped with a VLAN tag pointing at the VNF and forwarded to the respective host.

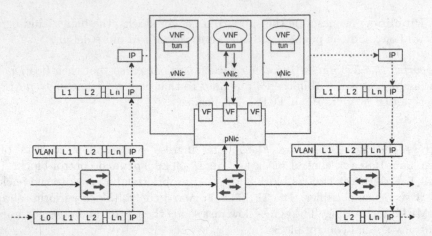

Fig. 2. P4-SFC utilizes label stacks in packets for segment routing in the network, but passes only IP packets to VNFs. Therefore, VNF remain unaware of the SFC.

The NIC of the host is statically configured to map packets with VLAN tags to virtual PCI devices that serve as virtual NICs (vNICs) for VMs or containers. These features are enabled by virtual machine device queue (VMDq) and single root I/O virtualization (SR-IOV). These technologies are supported by most contemporary NICs and CPUs. With VMDq, a NIC can have multiple internal queues and with SR-IOV, a so-called Physical Function (PF) can be virtualized into Virtual Functions (VFs). A VF can be passed-through as PCI device to a VM or container. We utilize SR-IOV to pass through a queue of the NIC as a VF to a VM/container in order to serve as a vNIC. The NIC used in our prototype provides up to 128 VFs so that up to $N = 128$ VNFs can be supported on a host. More powerful NICs providing even more VFs also exist.

Within a VM/container, the forwarding table of the MPLS Router Module in the Linux kernel is utilized to deliver the IP packet to the VNF without the label stack, to store the label stack, to push the label stack again when the packet is returned from the VNF, and to send the packet to the appropriate egress interface. Then, the packet is returned from the host to the switch in the corresponding VLAN. The switch removes the VLAN tag and the label for the next segment.

3.3 P4-SFC Orchestrator

The P4-SFC orchestrator is written in Python and leverages the libvirt and LXD framework for VM/container management. It interacts with administrators for management purposes and with customers for the specification of SFCs. It places VNFs on hosts and computes paths for SFCs, it launches and terminates SFCs, it adds new hosts and migrates VNFs among hosts.

Administrator/Customer Interaction and SFC Specification. The orchestrator offers a CLI interface for maintenance, e.g., for adding a new host to the system or moving VNFs.

Customers provide a configuration file in json format with a description of their SFCs. The specification of an SFC includes a flow descriptor, a list of VNFs, their executable binaries, their resource requirements (CPU, RAM, I/O), and information whether they are to be deployed as VMs or containers. Customers may request permanent storage for a VNF, e.g., for logging purposes, so that it has permission to write to shared network storage. The VNF binaries provided by customers are also saved to shared network storage. VNF applications are required to receive and send packets via /dev/net/tun, but they can remain unaware of SFCs.

VNF Placement and Path Calculation. The orchestrator determines hosts to run VNFs such that resource requirements communicated by the customers are met. Storage is not part of these requirements since shared network storage is used. If resources are not sufficient, VNFs may be migrated or new hosts may be added. While there is an extensive body of literature on VNF placement, our prototype uses only simple algorithms for this task.

The orchestrator knows the network topology. Either the network topology is static like in our prototype or it can be dynamically discovered with protocols like LLDP [11]. Based on this information, the orchestrator computes paths from the SFC ingress node to desired destinations including the VNFs specified by SFCs. The path calculation is performed whenever a forwarding entry for the SFC ingress node needs to be modified.

Launch and Termination of SFCs. The orchestrator holds a disk image as template for VMs/containers supporting VNFs. P4-SFC requires an appropriate configuration of the forwarding table of the MPLS Router Module which is initially applied to the template. The template is copied to every host so that VMs/containers can be cloned from it. Resources required by a VNF are provided by the customer's SFC description and are enforced by the orchestrator using appropriate configuration files for the VM/container. A libvirt xml definition specifies the hardware resources assigned to a VM. Similarly, an LXD configuration file uses cgroup statements to limit the kernel space resources available to the container.

If an SFC is to be launched, the orchestrator determines for each VNF a host with sufficient resources and finds a free VF on the NIC of that host. This VF determines the label for the VNF. The orchestrator defines a VM/container with suitable parameters, i.e., the VM/container template, sufficient resources, the VF, and a pointer to the VNF binary. It then starts the VM/container and the appropriate VNF binary from the shared network storage. Finally, the SFC ingress node is configured. To that end, a path is computed for the SFC and an entry is added to the MAT push_Label_Stack (see Fig. 1) containing the flow descriptor and the label stack for the SFC. The flow descriptor is needed for packet classification.

If an SFC is to be stopped, the VMs/containers with its VNFs are terminated and the corresponding entry is removed from the MAT push_Label_Stack.

Adding a New Host. To add a new host to P4-SFC, the orchestrator needs ssh access and permissions for VM/container management on the new host. It initially scans for available resources on the new host and adds them to its pool of available capacities. It then copies the VM/container templates to the host and configures the virtualization frameworks.

To make the new host and its potential VNFs reachable in the network, the forwarding table of the switch to which the host is attached is equipped with forwarding entries for the labels of all potential VNFs on the new host. If a host is removed, the corresponding labels are removed from the switch.

VNF Migration. VNFs may need to be migrated to another host, e.g., for maintenance purposes. The orchestrator supports this process by first cloning and starting the VNF on the new host, changing the respective entry of its SFC in the MAT push_Label_Stack, and terminating the VNF on the old host.

4   P4-SFC Prototype

We first give an overview of the testbed and describe functional tests. Finally, we report on the virtualization platform of the hosts.

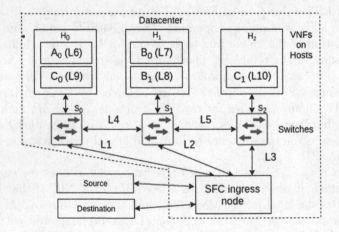

Fig. 3. Testbed for functional tests of P4-SFC.

4.1   Testbed

Figure 3 illustrates the testbed setup. A small datacenter which consists of an
SFC ingress node, three forwarding nodes, and three servers hosting VNFs.
Traffic is forwarded using segment routing using the bidirectional labels associated with the links. The MPLS forwarding nodes are standard Linux PCs with
software switches using the mpls_router kernel module and iproute2. The SFC
ingress node is a Tofino Edgecore Wedge 100BF-32X with the implementation
as reported in Sect. 3.1. In addition, an orchestrator as outlined in Sect. 3.3, but
omitted in the figure, controls the testbed.

4.2   Functional Tests

We conduct the following experiments. An external source sends traffic via the
datacenter to a destination. Within the datacenter, traffic is treated by an SFC.
We experiment with three different SFCs that consist of the SFCs A, B, and
C. We run tcpdump on source, destination, and the hosts to observe whether
a packets are sent, received, or delivered to a specific VNF. We describe three
experiments in which traffic was received by the destination.

SFC A contains only the single VNF A_0 and the label stack is $(L1, L6)$.
The successful experiment demonstrates that the implemented segment routing
works.

SFC B contains two VNFs B_0 and B_1 on the same host and the label stack
is $(L2, L7, L8)$. The successful experiment shows that multiple VNFs can be
reached on the same host. To that end, the traffic is forwarded from B_0 via S_2
to B_1.

SFC C contains two VNFs C_0 and C_1 on different hosts with the label stack
$L1, L9, L4, L5, L10$. The successful experiment shows the correct operation of
alternating VNF delivery and network forwarding.

4.3   Host Virtualization Platform

We use servers with a Xeon Gold 6134 processor, 8 cores, and 128 GB RAM as
hosts. Linux kernel 5.3.10 serves as operating system. We leverage the Intel VT-
x feature to enable hardware-accelerated virtualization. We use Linux Kernel-
based Virtual Machine (KVM) [13] as a hypervisor. VMs are created based
on QEMU and are managed using the libvirt [18] framework. This approach
enables almost native performance for VMs [12]. Containers are supported with
the LXD [5] framework using cgroups [1] to isolate containers from each other
and manage resource allocation.

In contrast to VMs, containers are lightweight so that many of them can be
accommodated on a single host. However, isolation among them is not perfect.
In addition, there is some risk that malicious VNFs exploit security breaches
and compromise the host. This tradeoff influences the choice whether VMs or
containers should be used for VNFs. Thus, trusted VNFs can be deployed as

containers so that they can benefit from a smaller resource footprint and a faster starting time compared to VMs.

We presented only one specific instantiation of P4-SFC. KVM-based virtualization on host could by easily substituted by e.g. XEN [20] without modification of the orchestrator. Segment routing could be implemented with IPv6 instead of MPLS but this requires changes to the SFC ingress node and the orchestrator.

5   Performance Evaluation

We first compare the forwarding efficiency VNF interconnection with SR-IOV and a virtual switch on the host and then we discuss additional performance aspects.

5.1   Performance Comparison

We compare the throughput for a VNF integrated with SR-IOV as presented in Sect. 3.2 with the one of a VNF connected via the Open vSwitch (OVS) software switch [19]. We utilize the same host platform as in Sect. 4.1 and two Mellanox ConnectX-5 NICs with 100 Gb/s. We set up 2 VMs with 8 cores each and utilize both iperf2 and iperf3 for TCP throughput test for 10 s. Iperf2 supports multiple threads, but iperf3 is the newer version. To test SR-IOV-based integration, each of the two VMs uses one VF on different NICs. To test OVS-based integration, both VMs are connected only via the OVS and not via a real NIC, which is an optimistic approximation for OVS-based VNF communication.

Table 1. L2 throughput for VNFs with different integration.

L2 packet size	Forwarding technology	iperf3 1 flow	iperf2 1 flow	iperf2 8 flows
1500	OVS	3.11 Gb/s	3.3 Gb/s	3.24 Gb/s
bytes	SR-IOV	32.3 Gb/s	36.3 Gb/s	93.4 Gb/s
104	OVS	54.3 Mb/s	2.24 Mb/s	4.24 Mb/s
bytes	SR-IOV	2.24 Gb/s	2.17 Gb/s	7.64 Gb/s

Table 1 shows the results. With iperf3, multithreading is not supported so that we used it only for experiments with a single flow. For large packets and OVS, around 3 Gb/s L2 throughput are achieved, both with iperf2 and iperf3, with 1 and 8 flows. Thus, 3.3 Gb/s seems to be the upper limit of OVS. With SR-IOV, we obtain a L2 throughput of 32.3 Gb/, 36.3 Gb/s, and 93.4 Gb/s in different experiments. Thus, the L2 throughput is up to 28 times larger than with OVS. For small packets, the L2 throughput is significantly reduced for both OVS and P4-SFC. In addition, we observe TX errors on the OVS NICs. With iperf2 and a single flow we even witness interface resets. Therefore, the throughput is extremely low in those cases. These problems were not observed with SR-IOV.

5.2   Additional Performance Aspects

We discuss additional performance aspects.

Ingress Node Forwarding Speed. Tofino performs P4 code in line speed so that its full capacity 100 Gb/s can be used for packet classification and encapsulation with label stacks.

Encapsulation Overhead. The segment routing approach used in P4-SFC imposes multiple labels per packet. Each MPLS label is only 4 bytes large. Thus, the header overhead for a stack of 10 labels amounts only to 40 bytes which is the size of a single IPv6 header, which has hardly any impact on forwarding performance.

Ingress Node Scalability. The SFC ingress node needs to support a large number of SFCs, therefore, the size of the entries in the MAT push_Label_Stack (see Fig. 1) is critical. Each entry consists of ingress and egress IPv4 addresses (2 × 4 bytes), ingress and egress ports (2 × 2 bytes), IPv4 protocol number (1 bytes) for SFC classifier and 10 MLPS labels (10 × 4 bytes) for segment routing. This amounts to 53 bytes per table entry, which allows for a number of SFCs in an order of magnitude of 100 K.

Traffic Engineering. Segment routing has potential for traffic engineering so that a smart orchestrator could optimize network performance.

6   Conclusion

In this work, we proposed P4-SFC as an architecture for SFC. It has a P4-based SFC ingress node which can push large header stacks needed for segment routing. It uses SR-IOV-based host virtualization to achieve high VNF throughput. It uses plain MPLS forwarding and allows VNFs to be SFC-unaware and allows customers to upload own binaries as VNFs. P4-SFC has been demonstrated as a prototype. The SFC ingress node has been implemented on the Tofino Edgecore Wedge 100BF-32X. The orchestrator controls both the SFC ingress node and hosts. Experiments showed that the chosen approach for host virtualization is more powerful than using software switches.

References

1. Linux control groups. http://man7.org/linux/man-pages/man7/cgroups.7.html. Accessed 14 July 2020
2. Open Platform for NFV (OPNFV). https://www.opnfv.org/. Accessed 14 July 2020
3. Amazon: Amazon Web Services. https://aws.amazon.com. Accessed 14 July 2020

4. Bosshart, P., et al.: P4: programming protocol-independent packet processors. ACM SIGCOMM Comput. Commun. Rev. **44**(3), 87–95 (2014)
5. Canonical: Linux Containers. https://linuxcontainers.org/lxd/introduction/. Accessed 14 July 2020
6. Chen, X., Zhang, D., Wang, X., Zhu, K., Zhou, H.: P4SC: towards high-performance service function chain implementation on the P4-capable device. In: IFIP/IEEE Symposium on Integrated Network and Service Management (IM) (2019)
7. Clad, F., et al.: Service Programming with Segment Routing, November 2019. http://www.ietf.org/internet-drafts/draft-ietf-spring-sr-service-programming-01.txt
8. ETSI OSM Team: ETSI Open Source Mano. https://www.etsi.org/technologies/nfv/open-source-mano. Accessed 14 July 2020
9. Farrel, A., Bryant, S., Drake, J.: RFC8595: An MPLS-Based Forwarding Plane for Service Function Chaining, June 2019. https://tools.ietf.org/html/rfc8595
10. He, M., Basta, A., Blenk, A., Deric, N., Kellerer, W.: P4NFV: an NFV architecture with flexible data plane reconfiguration. In: International Conference on Network and Services Management (CNSM) (2018)
11. IEEE: 802.1AB-2016 - IEEE Standard for Local and metropolitan area networks - Station and Media Access Control Connectivity Discovery (2016)
12. Intel: Enabling Intel Virtualization Technology Features and Benefits. https://www.intel.com/content/dam/www/public/us/en/documents/white-papers/virtualization-enabling-intel-virtualization-technology-features-and-benefits-paper.pdf. Accessed 14 July 2020
13. Kivity, A., Kamay, Y., Laor, D., Lublin, U., Liguori, A.: KVM: the Linux virtual machine monitor. In: Ottawa Linux Symposium (2007)
14. Kulkarni, S.G., et al.: NFVnice: dynamic backpressure and scheduling for NFV service chains. In: ACM SIGCOMM, pp. 71–84 (2017)
15. Microsoft: Microsoft Azure. https://azure.microsoft.com. Accessed 14 July 2020
16. Quinn, P., Nadeau, T.: RFC7498: Problem Statement for Service Function Chaining, April 2015. http://www.rfc-editor.org/rfc/rfc7498.txt
17. Quinn, Ed.,P., Elzur, Ed.,U., Pignataro, Ed.,C.: RFC8300: Network Service Header (NSH), January 2018. https://tools.ietf.org/html/rfc8300
18. Hat, R.: libvirt: The Virtualization API. http://libvirt.org. Accessed 14 July 2020
19. The Linux Foundation: Open vSwitch. https://www.openvswitch.org/. Accessed 14 July 2020
20. The Linux Foundation: Xen Project. http://xenproject.org/. Accessed 14 July 2020

Seamlessly Managing HPC Workloads
Through Kubernetes

Sergio López-Huguet[1]([✉]), J. Damià Segrelles[1], Marek Kasztelnik[2],
Marian Bubak[2], and Ignacio Blanquer[1]

[1] Instituto de Instrumentación para Imagen Molecular (I3M),
Centro mixto CSIC - Universitat Politècnica de València,
Camino de Vera s/n, 46022 Valencia, Spain
serlohu@upv.es, {dquilis,iblanque}@dsic.upv.es
[2] ACC Cyfronet, Sano Centre for Computational Medicine,
AGH University of Science and Technology,
Nawojki 11, 30-950 Kraków, Poland
ymkaszte@cyfronet.pl, bubak@agh.edu.pl

Abstract. This paper describes an approach to integrate the jobs management of High Performance Computing (HPC) infrastructures in cloud architectures by managing HPC workloads seamlessly from the cloud job scheduler. The paper presents *hpc-connector*, an open source tool that is designed for managing the full life cycle of jobs in the HPC infrastructure from the cloud job scheduler interacting with the workload manager of the HPC system. The key point is that, thanks to running *hpc-connector* in the cloud infrastructure, it is possible to reflect in the cloud infrastructure, the execution of a job running in the HPC infrastructure managed by *hpc-connector*. If the user cancels the cloud-job, as *hpc-connector* catches Operating System (OS) signals (for example, SIGINT), it will cancel the job in the HPC infrastructure too. Furthermore, it can retrieve logs if requested. Therefore, by using *hpc-connector*, the cloud job scheduler can manage the jobs in the HPC infrastructure without requiring any special privilege, as it does not need changes on the Job scheduler. Finally, we perform an experiment training a neural network for automated segmentation of Neuroblastoma tumours in the Prometheus supercomputer using *hpc-connector* as a batch job from a Kubernetes infrastructure.

The work presented in this article has been partially funded by the regional government of the Comunitat Valenciana (Spain), co-funded by the European Union ERDF funds (European Regional Development Fund) of the Comunitat Valenciana 2014–2020, with reference IDIFEDER/2018/032 (High-Performance Algorithms for the Modeling, Simulation and early Detection of diseases in Personalized Medicine). The work is also co-funded by PRIMAGE (PRedictive In-silico Multiscale Analytics to support cancer personalised diaGnosis and prognosis, empowered by imaging biomarkers) a Horizon 2020 RIA project funded under the topic SC1-DTH-07-2018 by the European Commission, with grant agreement no: 826494.

H. Jagode et al. (Eds.): ISC High Performance 2020 Workshops, LNCS 12321, pp. 310–320, 2020.
https://doi.org/10.1007/978-3-030-59851-8_20

Keywords: Integrating cloud and HPC · Kubernetes · Docker and Singularity containers

1   Introduction

Most scientific workloads combine requirements that could be efficiently addressed using a combination of *High-Throughput Computing* (HTC) and *High-Performance Computing* (HPC) workloads [7,8,20]. Focusing on Medical Imaging, HPC is extensively used for artificial intelligence model building and simulation. HTC is widely used in image post-processing and applying trained models to new datasets. HTC workloads can be efficiently tackled on cloud computing infrastructures, which fit to massive, coarsely coupled and embarrassingly parallel jobs. HPC workloads typically require infrastructures composed of a large number of highly-coupled computing nodes. HPC infrastructures are typically provided by singular data centers through specific interfaces.

Cloud computing platforms provide access to a large variety of computing resources on demand and without needing on-premise resources. Therefore, cloud services assist on reducing the cost contention and the ecological impact thanks to the self-adaptive mechanisms that dynamically adjust the cloud infrastructure depending on different aspects. Furthermore, it is possible to build hybrid cloud platforms depending on the institution necessities. Cloud infrastructures are much more flexible than HPC systems. Contrary to Cloud infrastructures, which can be adapted to the applications requirements, in HPC systems applications must be adapted to the execution environment. One important aspect for final users relies on the job management.

On the other hand, an *HPC* cluster delivers a huge amount of specialized and already configured computation resources to the researchers. Clusters can run free and commercial set of toolboxes which are already prepared to be used efficiently in distributed environments. As a result, running an application in this scenario can be easier than in a pure cloud model for the researcher (who wants to perform calculations and does not want to focus on the hardware and software installation and fine tuning).

The institutions can take benefit of employing a hybrid processing platform composed of HPC and cloud infrastructures. The architecture platform can be complex because there are a lot of aspects to consider: authentication, authorization, data storage, software requirements, special hardware, etc. Furthermore, the majority of the institutions that use HPC infrastructures, use infrastructures that are provided by third parties. Therefore, they must adapt their other processing infrastructures (for example, a public or private cloud platform) to use the different HPC infrastructures. This work presents *hpc-connector*[1], an open source tool that allows to seamlessly integrate the cloud architecture with the access to the HPC cluster, without administrator privileges.

---

[1] https://gitlab.com/primageproject/hpc-connector.

2   Scenario and Related Work

2.1   Architecture

Cloud application architectures typically comprise front-end services and back-end nodes. Front-end services provide external access and manage back-end resources through a job scheduler API or a graphical interface. In some cases, front-end nodes use resource manager tools in order to scale in or out the resources, depending on usage metrics to provide an agreed Quality of Service. The back-end nodes are a set of heterogeneous resources that run the jobs sent by the users through the job scheduler.

There are examples of cloud platforms in the literature that use the previous architecture scheme. In [14], the authors present an architecture to process Internet of Things (IoT) data collected from smart agriculture. In our previous works, we presented a cloud architecture for data analysis [19] and for processing medical imaging [18].

However, there are no examples of hybrid cloud and HPC infrastructures that could provide a seamless interface for both types of workloads. The PRIMAGE project [21] is an ongoing research project that uses artificial intelligence techniques for the processing of medical imaging in paediatric cancer. In this project, the platform architecture combines an HPC infrastructure (the Prometheus supercomputer [10]) and an on-premise cloud platform. The tool presented in this work was designed to solve the problem of combining the execution of some applications in several infrastructures with no administrator privileges.

Job schedulers (or workload managers) manage the remote execution of the applications on the available resources. The most popular job schedulers designed for containers technologies are Docker Swarm, Kubernetes[2], some frameworks of Apache Mesos[3] and Nomad[4]. Regarding workload managers in the HPC environment, there are a lot that are widely used: SLURM [22], Torque[5] or HTCondor[6]. It should be pointed out that *hpc-connector* was designed to integrate any cloud architecture (provided with any job scheduler) with an HPC infrastructure (also provided with any workload manager). In this work, we will use Kubernetes as the cloud job scheduler, and SLURM for the HPC infrastructure.

Application portability and delivery are key issues not only in cloud computing environments but also in HPC. Containers probably are now the most popular technology for application delivery, thanks to the reproducibility, traceability, provenance, isolation, and portability. Docker[7] has reached the maximum popularity as container technology on cloud infrastructures, thanks to its rich ecosystem of tools and great versatility. However, Docker containers run under the root user space and do not provide easily multi-tenancy (it is necessary to

---

[2] https://kubernetes.io.

[3] http://mesos.apache.org/.

[4] https://www.nomadproject.io/.

[5] https://adaptivecomputing.com/cherry-services/torque-resource-manager/.

[6] https://research.cs.wisc.edu/htcondor/.

[7] https://www.docker.com/.

create previously the users during the container building stage). Singularity containers [17] are widely used in the HPC environments because they run under user space, support multi-tenancy and provide mechanisms to use Message Passing Interface (MPI). There are other container technologies and runtimes, such as Podman[8], Charliecloud[9], Shifter[10], etc., but we will use Docker and Singularity as container technologies for cloud and HPC infrastructures, respectively. It should be noted that the common used HPC workload managers (such as SLURM) can run unprivileged containers without requiring changes or installing a plugin (as containers are processes that are executed in the user space).

2.2 Objectives and Requirements

The goal of this work is to provide a tool that permits the combination of a job scheduler that runs applications embedded in Docker containers (for example, Kubernetes) on the cloud environment, with the HPC workload managers that run applications bare metal or in unprivileged containers. Considering the scenario described in the previous section, the identified requirements and assumptions needed to fulfill are:

(R1) Users must use the same method to submit or cancel jobs to the HPC workload manager, as the job scheduler on the cloud environment does.
(R2) The job scheduler used on the cloud environment must manage the full life cycle of a job in the HPC infrastructure. For example, the job scheduler should be able to submit, cancel, get execution state, get the logs, etc.
(R3) The data required to run the job must be accessible in the HPC infrastructure. There are several options: users upload it in advance, the job downloads it before starting, or there is a shared storage between the HPC infrastructure and any other environments that could use the data.
(R4) Any user authorised to access the cloud and the HPC resources must be able to execute jobs without requiring special privileges in neither the HPC nor the cloud infrastructures.
(R5) The solution should be extensible to deal with different job schedulers and workload managers.

2.3 State of the Art

The combination of the potential of High Performance Computing for simulation and Big Data and cloud computing for massive data processing has become a driving forces for complex disciplines such as Brain science [9]. The relevance of High Performance and Cloud Computing for addressing challenges related to medical imaging has boosted with the take off of the application of Artificial Intelligence [4,5]. A revision study [11] highlights 83 articles applying some kind

---

[8] https://podman.io/.
[9] https://hpc.github.io/charliecloud/.
[10] https://www.nersc.gov/research-and-development/user-defined-images/.

of HPC techniques in Medical Imaging [2], many of them also suitable of being addressed using cloud computing.

Although there are authors that propose hardware specific configurations based on FPGAs and GPUs [12,16], current tendencies propose the use of cloud computing platforms, especially public offerings [13] with special examples on solutions provided directly by main industry players in cloud [1]. However, in most of the cases, the use of clouds is limited to the storage and access of medical imaging data with low processing capabilities [2,15]. Recently, solutions proposing the combination of container-based platform with computing accelerators have arisen [3].

3   The Proposed Solution: *HPC-Connector*

Institutions that manage HPC and cloud environments can integrate job schedulers by developing the appropriate plug-ins and extending the current job types to make them compatible between both environments. Large HPC consortia and institutions may follow this approach. However, in most cases users face a situation in which they can acquire both types of resources from different providers.

Another approach is to adapt the job scheduler on the cloud platform to be able to communicate with the workload manager, as cloud infrastructures are widely accessible and much more flexible than an HPC infrastructure for a regular user. This option could be complex and cumbersome, as it would require continuous work as new updates to the job scheduler arise. If the job scheduler is released under open-source licenses, the institution must extend it with the desired functionality following the rules from the project developers. It should be pointed out that, if the institution wants to use more than one HPC infrastructure with different configurations (for example, in one case you only can interact using a REST API but, in the other case, you can only interact using ssh commands), the software extension could be even more complex.

Adapting the job scheduler to the workload managers could be complex and, besides, it forces to keep using the adapted job scheduler in the future for making the adaption effort profitable. For this reason, we propose a solution by creating an external tool (*hpc-connector*) that manages the jobs in the HPC infrastructure from the cloud infrastructure, as any other job without special privileges.

The key point of the proposed solution is the following: once a user submits a job to the job scheduler that wants to be executed in the HPC infrastructure (fulfilling R1), a special job is executed in the cloud infrastructure. The special mirror job is a an instance of *hpc-connector*, which will manage the job in the HPC infrastructure (R2). Thus, the mirror job updates the job scheduler as the execution of the HPC job progresses in the HPC infrastructure. As *hpc-connector* does not need any special privilege (like mounting a directory or accessing special kernel directives), the special mirror job can run in the user space (fulfilling R4). After submitting the job, *hpc-connector* will monitor it (R2) until the end or its cancellation by the HPC workload manager. Once the job ends, *hpc-connector* can retrieve, if the HPC infrastructure allows it, the job output (R2). Furthermore, *hpc-connector* is able to catch the SIGINT signal that the job scheduler

can send to the job before killing it. Therefore, if an appropriate cloud job configuration is performed (the cloud job receives a SIGINT signal and it has a grace
period before killing it after the signal is received) and the job still running,
hpc-connector will cancel the job in the HPC infrastructure (R2).

The tool presented is designed to be running in any environment (even in
a local machine) because it is implemented in Python, so it can be running
embedded in a any type of container or bare metal. Regarding the support of
HPC infrastructures, as each HPC backend has its own methods for managing
the jobs and the data, it is necessary to implement some specific functionality
for each backend in *hpc-connector* to interect with the job submission, information retrieval about the job execution, canceling, or deleting jobs. Furthermore,
if the institution wants to retrieve the logs, it is required to implement how to
operate with files (like upload, download, or remove) and operations with directories (list, create, or delete). The tool uses the super-class `Backend` so, for each
new HPC infrastructure, a new subclass from the `Backend` class must be created with the name of the HPC infrastructure. For example, let's consider two
different HPC infrastructures: *cluster1* and *cluster2*. The infrastructure *cluster1*
uses SLURM as workload manager with a REST API. On the other hand, *clus-
ter2* also uses SLURM but only provides a REST API to manage the files, so
the users must interact with SLURM via ssh. Thus, *cluster2* implementation is
different from *cluster1* because, although both use SLURM, the job operations
must be performed using ssh for *cluster2*. Therefore, `cluster1` and `cluster2`
sub classes from `Backend` class must be implemented. Thus, *hpc-connector* fulfils R5 because it is designed to be running in any environment and it can be
extended for new HPC infrastructures.

4   Use Case: Segmentation of Neuroblastoma Tumours

To validate the usefulness of the *hpc-connector*, we performed a test case. The
scenario uses a private cloud platform and the Prometheus HPC infrastructure.
The cluster deployed on the private cloud infrastructure is composed of 3 virtual
nodes with 4 vCPUs, 32 GB of memory RAM, 80 GB of Solid State Disk and 1
NVIDIA Tesla V100 each. The job scheduler used is Kubernetes (version v1.15.9)
and the container technology is Docker (version 18.06.2-ce).

The HPC infrastructure is the Prometheus supercomputer [10], which is
located in the 289th position of the TOP500 list (June 2020). Prometheus cluster
provides REST API to interact with SLURM (version 19.05.5) called Rimrock
(Robust Remote Process Controller)[11] and PLGData service[12] to interact with
the file system.

The selected use case is a training of a neural network using Tensorflow for
performing an automated segmentation of neuroblastoma tumours. Neuroblastoma is the most frequent solid cancer of the early childhood [6]. This use case
belongs to the PRIMAGE project [21].

---

[11] https://submit.plgrid.pl/.
[12] https://data.plgrid.pl/?locale=en.

First, we define two ConfigMap objects, which store non-confidential data in key-value pairs). The Fig. 1 shows the definition (in YAML[13] format) of the ConfigMap that contains the information required by *hpc-connector* to use the backend Prometheus. This ConfigMap will be used for all jobs that want to connect with Prometheus. If we were using another HPC infrastructure, the configuration value would maybe contain other dictionary keys.

```
apiVersion: v1
kind: ConfigMap
metadata:
  name: hpc-prometheus
  namespace: serlohu-at-upv-dot-es
data:
  name: Prometheus
  configuration: |
    {
      "ENDPOINT": "https://submit.plgrid.pl",
      "PROXY": "XXXXXX"
    }
```

Fig. 1. ConfigMap definition to specify the Prometheus configuration required by *hpc-connector*.

Once the ConfigMap for accessing properly to the HPC infrastructure is defined, the users must define the job configuration. As we are using Rimrock service from Prometheus cluster, the required parameters are at least, the host and the SLURM script in plain text. In this script, we specify the amount of resources, the special hardware (GPUs), and the batch queue (plgrid-gpu). Then, we implement the tasks: show the hostname, load modules and run the Singularity image (available at the directory **$SCRATCH/singularity/neuroblastoma.sandbox**).

```
apiVersion: v1
kind: ConfigMap
metadata:
  name: hpc-job-gibi230-segmentation
  namespace: serlohu-at-upv-dot-es
data:
  job: |
    {
      "host": "prometheus.cyfronet.pl",
      "script": "#!/bin/bash \n#SBATCH -J gibi230 \n#SBATCH -N 1 \n#SBATCH --ntasks-per-node=24
      \n#SBATCH --time=72:00:00 \n#SBATCH --mem=40gb \n#SBATCH -A primage1gpu \n#SBATCH -p plgrid-gpu
      \n#SBATCH --gres=gpu \n#SBATCH --output=\"gibi230_segmentation.out\" \n#SBATCH
      --error=\"gibi230_segmentation.err\" \ncd $SLURM_SUBMIT_DIR \nsrun /bin/hostname \nmodule load
      plgrid/tools/singularity \nsingularity run --bind $SCRATCH/gibi230_segmentation/Input:/training
      --bind $SCRATCH/gibi230_segmentation/Output:/output --bind $SCRATCH/gibi230_segmentation/
      user_application/:/user_application $SCRATCH/singularity/neuroblastoma.sandbox python /
      user_application/batch.py /training /output"
    }
  monitoring_period: "1800"
```

Fig. 2. Job definition to specify the job configuration required by *hpc-connector* to launch the job using, in this HPC backend, Rimrock.

---

[13] https://yaml.org/.

Figure 2 shows the ConfigMap definition for the job configuration. This new ConfigMap is specific for each job in Prometheus cluster.

Figure 3 shows the Kubernetes batch job definition. As it is described in Sect. 3, the job executed in the cloud infrastructure consists of running *hpc-connector* to managing the job in Prometheus cluster. It should be noted that his job is configured with a termination grace period and, if the users cancel this Kubernetes job, it has 30 s to execute the command `kill -SIGINT 1`. If this occurs, *hpc-connector* will catch the signal and immediately cancel the job in the HPC infrastructure. Once the job is submitted to Kubernetes, it is possible to check (in real time) the progress of the execution consulting the logs of *hpc-connector*. Figure 4 is a screenshot of the Kubernetes dashboard showing the logs of the created job.

```
apiVersion: batch/v1
kind: Job
metadata:
  name: hpc-job-gibi230-segmentation
  namespace: serlohu-at-upv-dot-es
spec:
  template:
    spec:
      restartPolicy: "Never"
      terminationGracePeriodSeconds: 30
      containers:
      - name: hpc-job-gibi230-segmentation
        image: registry.gitlab.com/primageproject/hpc-connector:0.0.1
        imagePullPolicy: Always
        lifecycle:
          preStop:
            exec:
              command. ["kill","-SIGINT","1"] # send SIGINT to hpc-connector in order to cancell the job
        args: [ "--backend", "$(BACKEND_NAME)", "--backend-conf", "$(BACKEND_CONF)", "simulate",
        "--job-config", "$(JOB_CONF)", "--monitoring-period", "$(MONITORING_PERIOD)", "--print-logs"]
        env:
          - name: BACKEND_NAME
            valueFrom:
              configMapKeyRef:
                name: hpc-prometheus
                key: name
          - name: BACKEND_CONF
            valueFrom:
              configMapKeyRef:
                name: hpc-prometheus
                key: configuration
          - name: JOB_CONF
            valueFrom:
              configMapKeyRef:
                name: hpc-job-gibi230-segmentation
                key: job
          - name: MONITORING_PERIOD
            valueFrom:
              configMapKeyRef:
                name: hpc-job-gibi230-segmentation
                key: monitoring_period
```

Fig. 3. *hpc-connector* job definition.

Fig. 4. Consulting the logs of *hpc-connector* using the Kubernetes dashboard.

5   Conclusions

This paper has presented *hpc-connector*, which is an open source tool for seamlessly integrating HPC workloads in cloud infrastructures without requiring administrator privileges or changes on the workload manager, providing the users with the same user interface even across different HPC infrastructures. The tool implemented fulfils the requirements identified in Sect. 2.2: running in the user space, and agnosticism of the workload manager (it is implemented as a Python tool easy extendable to other HPC infrastructures) to manage the jobs in an HPC infrastructure.

The experiment performed in Sect. 4 demonstrated that this approach can address a wider range of complex problems in a convenient way. In this experiment, we successfully trained a neural network using GPUs in an HPC supercomputer (Prometheus) using *hpc-connector* from a Kubernetes job hosted in a private cloud infrastructure.

Future work includes improving the functionality of *hpc-connector*: upload the data (from a repository or from a directory in the Docker container) before submitting the job (if necessary) or consider retrieving the results and storing them in an external repository or in the Docker container itself (for example, if the container has mounted a shared filesystem). Another possible enhancement could be the ability to refresh the HPC credentials when they expire.

References

1. Azure for health. https://azure.microsoft.com/en-us/industries/healthcare/#security. Accessed 07 May 2020
2. Cloud access to mammograms enables earlier breast cancer detection. https://www.itnonline.com/content/cloud-access-mammograms-enables-earlier-breast-cancer-detection. Accessed 07 May 2020

3. Getting to the heart of the HPC and AI the edge in healthcare. https://www.nextplatform.com/2018/03/28/getting-to-the-heart-of-hpc-and-ai-at-the-edge-in-healthcare/. Accessed 07 May 2020

4. High Performance Computing and deep learning in medicine: Enhancing physicians, helping patients. https://ec.europa.eu/digital-single-market/en/news/high-performance-computing-and-deep-learning-medicine-enhancing-physicians-helping-patients. Accessed 07 May 2020

5. Medical Imaging Gets an AI Boost. https://www.hpcwire.com/2019/12/03/medical-imaging-gets-an-ai-boost/. Accessed 07 May 2020

6. Bhatnagar, S.: An audit of malignant solid tumors in infants and neonates. J. Neonatal Surg. **1**, 5 (2012)

7. Cabellos, L., Campos, I., Fernández-Del-Castillo, E., Owsiak, M., Palak, B., Płóciennik, M.: Scientific workflow orchestration interoperating HTC and HPC resources. Comput. Phys. Commun. (2011). https://doi.org/10.1016/j.cpc.2010.12.020

8. Callaghan, S., Maechling, P., Small, P., Milner, K., Juve, G., et al.: Metrics for heterogeneous scientific workflows: a case study of an earthquake science application. Int. J. High Perform. Comput. Appl. (2011). https://doi.org/10.1177/1094342011414743

9. Chen, S., He, Z., Han, X., He, X., et al.: How big data and high-performance computing drive brain science (2019). https://doi.org/10.1016/j.gpb.2019.09.003

10. Cyfronet Krakow, P.: Prometheus supercomputer. www.cyfronet.krakow.pl/computers/15226,artykul,prometheus.html. Accessed 07 May 2020

11. Gulo, C.A.S.J., Sementille, A.C., Tavares, J.M.R.S.: Techniques of medical image processing and analysis accelerated by high-performance computing: a systematic literature review. J. Real-Time Image Process. **16**(6), 1891–1908 (2017). https://doi.org/10.1007/s11554-017-0734-z

12. Hussain, T., Haider, A., Shafique, M., Taleb Ahmed, A.: A high-performance system architecture for medical imaging (2019). https://doi.org/10.5772/intechopen.83581

13. Ivanova, D., Borovska, P., Zahov, S.: Development of PaaS using AWS and Terraform for medical imaging analytics. In: AIP Conference Proceedings (2018). https://doi.org/10.1063/1.5082133

14. Jamalian, S., Rajaei, H.: Data-intensive HPC tasks scheduling with SDN to enable HPC-as-a-service. In: Proceedings - 2015 IEEE 8th International Conference on Cloud Computing, CLOUD 2015, pp. 596–603. Institute of Electrical and Electronics Engineers Inc., August 2015. https://doi.org/10.1109/CLOUD.2015.85

15. Kao, H.Y., et al.: Cloud-based service information system for evaluating quality of life after breast cancer surgery. PLoS ONE (2015). https://doi.org/10.1371/journal.pone.0139252

16. Kovacs, L., Kovacs, R., Hajdu, A.: High performance computing in medical image analysis HuSSaR, June 2018. http://arxiv.org/abs/1806.06171

17. Kurtzer, G.M., Sochat, V., Bauer, M.W.: Singularity: scientific containers for mobility of compute. PLOS ONE **12**(5), 1–20 (2017). https://doi.org/10.1371/journal.pone.0177459

18. López-Huguet, S., García-Castro, F., Alberich-Bayarri, A., Blanquer, I.: A cloud architecture for the execution of medical imaging biomarkers. In: Rodrigues, J., et al. (eds.) ICCS 2019. LNCS, vol. 11538, pp. 130–144. Springer, Cham (2019). https://doi.org/10.1007/978-3-030-22744-9_10

19. López-Huguet, S., et al.: A self-managed Mesos cluster for data analytics with QoS guarantees. Future Gener. Comput. Syst., 449–461. https://doi.org/10.1016/j.future.2019.02.047
20. Manuali, C., et al.: Efficient workload distribution bridging HTC and HPC in scientific computing. In: Murgante, B., et al. (eds.) ICCSA 2012. LNCS, vol. 7333, pp. 345–357. Springer, Heidelberg (2012). https://doi.org/10.1007/978-3-642-31125-3_27
21. Martí-Bonmatí, L., et al.: PRIMAGE project: predictive *in silico* multiscale analytics to support childhood cancer personalised evaluation empowered by imaging biomarkers. Eur. Radiol. Exp. 4(1), 1–11 (2020). https://doi.org/10.1186/s41747-020-00150-9
22. Yoo, A.B., Jette, M.A., Grondona, M.: SLURM: simple linux utility for resource management. In: Feitelson, D., Rudolph, L., Schwiegelshohn, U. (eds.) JSSPP 2003. LNCS, vol. 2862, pp. 44–60. Springer, Heidelberg (2003). https://doi.org/10.1007/10968987_3

Interference-Aware Orchestration in Kubernetes

Achilleas Tzenetopoulos[1]($\boxtimes$), Dimosthenis Masouros[1], Sotirios Xydis[1,2], and Dimitrios Soudris[1]

[1] National Technical University of Athens, Athens, Greece
{atzenetopoulos,demo.masouros,sxydis,dsoudris}@microlab.ntua.gr
[2] Harokopeio University of Athens, Athens, Greece

Abstract. Nowadays, there is an increasing number of workloads, i.e. data serving, analytics, AI, HPC workloads, etc., executed on the Cloud. Although multi-tenancy has gained a lot of attention to optimize resource efficiency, current state-of-the-art resource orchestrators rely on typical metrics, such as CPU or memory utilization, for placing incoming workloads on the available pool of resources, thus, neglecting the interference effects from workload co-location. In this paper, we design an interference-aware cloud orchestrator, based on micro-architectural event monitoring. We integrate our solution with Kubernetes, one of the most widely used and commercially adopted cloud orchestration frameworks nowadays, and we show that we achieve higher performance, up to 32% compared to its default scheduler, for a variety of cloud representative workloads.

Keywords: Cloud-computing · High performance computing · Resource management · Scheduling · Kubernetes · Interference-aware

1 Introduction

The continuous increase in the amount of workloads uploaded and executed on the cloud, has forced data-center (DC) operators and cloud providers, to embrace workload co-location and multi-tenancy as first class system design concern regarding resource efficiency [3]. Workloads placed on the same physical machines continuously contest for shared resources, such as cache, memory occupancy, memory/network bandwidth, and others, causing interference to each other, which, in turn, induces huge negative impact on their performance. Multi-sharing and multi-diversity of resources can cause serious degradation on the performance of running applications, thus the need for interference-aware scheduling of incoming workloads on a cluster is indispensable. This situation becomes even more consecutive, as cloud providers currently provide users with elasticity and resizability of their computing capacity, leading to a dynamic provisioning of resources.

This work is partially funded by the EU Horizon 2020 research and innovation program, under project EVOLVE, grant agreement No 825061.

H. Jagode et al. (Eds.): ISC High Performance 2020 Workshops, LNCS 12321, pp. 321–330, 2020.
https://doi.org/10.1007/978-3-030-59851-8_21

Several research works have administered the problem of resource allocation. Quasar [8], and other works [9,12] were able to determine the right amount of resources to meet QoS constraints. Meanwhile, under-utilized servers contribute to expenses and limit the scaling of the data-center [4], while HPC environments suffer from under-utilization as well [18]. Even the mature Google cluster manager Borg [20], achieves 25–35% and 40% CPU and memory utilization respectively, while reserved resources are 75% and 60% at the same time.

Recently, HPC and Cloud worlds are getting more and more close [1]. The latest advancements and performance improvements of container-based virtualization [10] have driven many HPC applications to be containerized, enabling increased productivity through prompt and seamless updates and rollbacks to previous versions. Indeed, the current trend for the scheduling of arriving workloads on a pool of available resources even in HPC environments [23] is through container orchestrators, such as Kubernetes [6] which provide a common environment for the whole infrastructure, be it on-premises or in the cloud.

Even though container orchestrators provide major benefits, such as ease of use and deployment, abstraction of resources, scaling and others, they are focusing mostly on availability rather than performance optimization, relying on coarse metrics, e.g., CPU or memory utilization, thus neglecting interference effects, overlooking the specifications of the underlying infrastructure and the nature of the imposed stress on the shared resources.

Contention on the low-level shared resources of a system, i.e. low-level caches and bus bandwidth, can lead to unpredictable performance variability [13,24] and degradation, which highly reduces the QoS of applications [16]. Opensourced services like Prometheus [2], and the Elasticsearch, fluentd and Kibana (EFK) stack [22] provide well-organized systems for metrics logging, aggregation and querying. However, the metrics acquired are usually too coarse, not able to reveal the real system state. As a result the resource under contention cannot be identified and the root cause of application degradation remains unmanageable.

In this work, we propose an interference-aware custom scheduler for Kubernetes, able to efficiently place applications on a cluster of available machines. Using a universal approach for every kind of workload behavior and duration our framework aims to maximize resource utilization and minimize application execution delays provoked by interference phenomena. Compared to prior works, we use low-level metrics, which describe micro-architectural events, capable of providing useful information in terms of the resource under contention, namely the origin of system's inability to serve workloads' needs efficiently. Our scheduler outperforms the default one of Kubernetes, improving the performance of the scheduled workloads, up to 32%, by efficiently equilibrating the usage of the aforementioned resources between the different components on the machine.

2   Experimental Setup and Motivational Analysis

In this section, we describe the Kubernetes scheduling process and discuss some of its shortcomings. Motivated by Kubernetes inefficient workload placement, we exploit the insights provided by hardware counters placed in our system.

2.1   System Hardware and Experimental Workloads

System Architecture: We consider a dual-socketed multi-processor system (24 logical cores/socket, 128 GB Memory), referred to as H1, on top of which, we have deployed 5 virtual machines (VMs) with various configurations, serving as the nodes of our cluster. The combination of VMs with containers is currently the common way of deploying cloud clusters at scale, since it establishes the perfect catalyst for reliability and robustness [15].

Each VM's cores range from 4 up to 16 and RAM size from 8192(MB) up to 65536(MB). The virtual cores of each VM have been mapped onto the physical cores of the servers using the CPU pinning options of the `libvirt` library to enable the monitoring of VM-specific metrics. On top of the VMs, we have deployed Kubernetes [6] as our container orchestrator. We used a single-master node cluster with the VM serving as master being deployed in a separate physical machine, not affecting the testing results. All the referenced workloads running on the cluster have been containerized, utilizing the Docker platform. Finally, in order to record low-level performance counters, we utilize the Performance Counter Monitoring (PCM) API [21] that provides micro-architectural events from core up to system level. The PCM tool runs natively on the physical machines, since it requires access to Model-Specific Registers (MSRs) of the system and the corresponding metrics are communicated through a Network File System (NFS) to the Kubernetes orchestrator.

Experimental Workloads: Cloud data-center server machines accommodate a wide range of workloads, which are basically either batch/best-effort (BE) applications, or user-interactive/latency-critical (LC) applications. The former type of workloads require the highest possible throughput, whereas the latter demand to meet their QoS constraints. In order to cover both BE and LC workloads, we consider workloads from three popular scientific benchmarking libraries, i.e. scikit-learn [19] and SPEC 2006 [14] (as BE) and cloudsuite [11] (as LC) suites as referred in Table 1.

2.2   Kubernetes Scheduler

Kubernetes Scheduler, henceforth referenced as kube-scheduler is a core component of Kubernetes. It is responsible for selecting the most viable node for the placement of any incoming application. Briefly, the process is comprised of two different stages.

Table 1. Summary of workloads used as cloud applications.

Benchmark	Setup	Type
Scikit-Learn	Lasso, Linear Regression, Linear Discriminant Analysis, Ada Boost Classifier, Random Forest Regressor, Random Forest Classifier	best-effort
SPEC 2006	astar, leslie, cactus, sphinx	batch
Cloudsuite	data-serving, in-memory analytics, web-serving	latency-critical

First, the scheduler determines the set of feasible placements, which is the set of nodes that meet a set of given constraints. Those constraints, called predicates, are related to affinity and node availability. Secondly, after the filtering, with only the feasible nodes remaining, kube-scheduler using a set of pre-defined rating functions, determines the viability of each node. Those priority functions favor nodes using criteria like `image locality`, `affinity` and `resource usage`.

Container orchestrators provide also the additional utility of explicitly setting resource requirements and limits by the developer for each application deployed. However, resource allocations imposed by users often exaggerate the average resources required by applications, which, in turn, leads to low-utilization in data-centers as it was also mentioned in Sect. 1. Although kube-scheduler usually favors the node with the least requested per capacity ratio of resources (RAM, CPUs), this results in suboptimal pod placement, even in simple deployment scenarios. To show the effects of this suboptimality, we assigned kube-scheduler the task to schedule a `scikit-lasso` pod on a small cluster of two VMs v_1 (4 vcpus, 8 GB RAM) and v_2 (8 vcpus, 16 GB of RAM), in which there were already deployed some resource-stressing micro-benchmarks from the iBench suite [7], specifically $3 \times$`cpu-iBench` in v_1 and $6 \times$`L3-iBench` in v_2. After multiple tests, the scheduler consistently favored v_2. However, by placing the aforementioned application in v_1, we achieved an average speedup of 1.46x.

2.3   Quantifying Interference Level

While offline solutions based on intermittent bench-marking, e.g., [7], offer a great perspective of the performance of co-scheduled applications, by stressing and considering individual low-level resources, to identify the real bottleneck of the system, we need to inspect and examine the low-level performance counters as a whole [17]. In order to quantify socket-level interference, we extract the amount of Last Level Cache (LLC) misses, the C0-state percentage, reads and writes from and to the memory respectively and the Instructions Per Cycle (IPC). Henceforth by performance we refer to the fraction $\frac{1}{latency}$ and by relative performance the fraction of performance when executed isolated divided by the actual performance $\frac{latency}{isolated\_latency}$.

In order to evaluate the impact of each kind of resource stress on the performance of applications, we tentatively co-schedule workloads described in Table 1 with iBench. Figure 1 depicts the relative performance (y-axis) of all our target workloads when co-scheduled with different numbers (x-axis) of specific resource-stressing, iBench micro-benchmarks. The solid line in each plot shows the estimate of the central tendency of the relative performance while the surrounding area illustrates the confidence interval for that estimate. This plot reveals that, as the resource interference moves higher in the memory hierarchy, the impact on the performance increases exponentially. Specifically, we notice that stressing the LLC has the greatest effect on the performance of our workloads.

This can be explained due to the fact that LLC misses require data to be fetched from the off-chip memory. Memory reads and writes are the requests for data on behalf of LLC misses, as well as DRAM traffic due to prefetching,

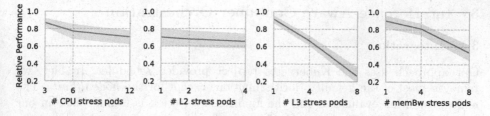

Fig. 1. Impact of stress on different resources on the performance of applications.

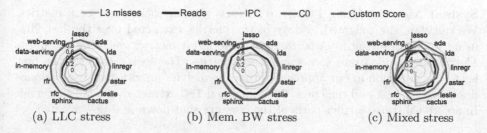

(a) LLC stress   (b) Mem. BW stress   (c) Mixed stress

Fig. 2. Correlation between applications performance degradation and system metrics.

providing a low level performance counter able to depict the number of memory accesses. However, during high volume of interference, different processes are competing for memory access [5], and as the available bandwidth is not able to support all requests at the same time, neither memory reads and writes number nor L3 cache misses are any longer valuable indicators of the contention beyond this point. In this case, we conscript IPC, another low level hardware metric as an indicator of further slowdown caused by delays in process execution due to memory bus competition.

Interference-Aware Node Scoring: Proper scheduling requires a score that reflects the interference on the system. In the previous paragraph, we discussed the preeminence of memory traffic and IPC as contention bottlenecks. We utilize the custom metric

$$S = \frac{Reads + Writes}{IPC} \qquad (1)$$

as a valid system condition depictor, where $Reads/Writes$ are DRAM memory read/write traffic on a socket in GB. To show its effectiveness, we compare different metrics accuracy on reflecting system's condition utilizing the Pearson's correlation between the performance of each application and the metric's average value prior to application's scheduling. Figure 2 shows the correlation between the application's relative performance under different levels of stress. Our custom metric seems to be highly correlated with application's performance in most scenarios. Furthermore, while C0-state seems to be a great system performance indicator, it fails in the last one. As Fig. 2c shows, when different pods (cpu,L3,memBw) are deployed, C0 is not a reliable system state indicator anymore.

3   Interference-Aware Container Orchestration

3.1   Integration

Our approach uses the Kubernetes project provided scheduler. In fact, we removed most of the default priority functions except for the *node affinity*. The nodes' condition evaluation and the final node selection is taking place in our external framework. The customized kube-scheduler is used in order to use the high variety of constraints, predicates and utilities it offers.

System Metrics: Using PCM, we extract system, socket and core metrics. We calculate the weighted average of the metrics extracted over the last 20 s, using weights ranging from 50 to 1 with the latest metrics weighing the most. Metrics are divided into socket and core metrics. The socket consists the first level of abstraction in our approach. From the metrics provided we use the ones described in Eq. 1 and the cores' `C6-state` and `IPC` extracted in a 0.4 s interval. In a core-C6 state, further parts of the core are shut down and power gated.

3.2   System Model

We target conventional data center environments, where applications are arriving on the cluster and an orchestrator is responsible for scheduling them on the available pool of VMs lying on top of the server systems, as shown in Fig. 3.

Target HW Model: Each server is uniquely identified by an identifier $i \in \mathbb{N}^{\leq n}$, where n is the total number of servers available on the cluster. We denote the jth, $j \in \mathbb{N}^{\leq m_i}$ socket of server i as s_j^i, where m_i is the total number of sockets in server i. Every socket $s_j^i \forall i, j$ is characterized by its attributes $\langle C6, IPC, Reads, Writes \rangle$ and is consisted of o_j number of cores. Furthermore, a node (VM) in the cluster consisted of vcpus pinned in socket j is denoted as $n_l^{j,i}$. Every node is characterized by the total number of cores $p_l \leq o_j$ and their average C6-state percentage $\langle C6 \rangle$. In addition, each core of socket s_j^i and node's $n_l^{j,i}$ is denoted as $c_k^{j,i,l}$, $k \in \mathbb{N}^{\leq i}$.

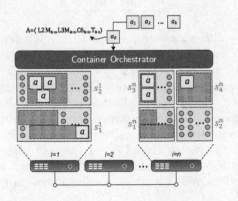

Fig. 3. Target system architecture

Application Model: We consider that each workload arriving on the cluster is characterized by a tuple $\mathcal{A} = \langle Writes_{iso}, Reads_{iso}, C0_{iso} \rangle$, where $Writes_{iso}$, $Reads_{iso}$, $C0_{iso}$ refer to the mean values of the respective low-level performance counters (as described in Sect. 2). As $Writes_{iso}$ and $Reads_{iso}$ refer to socket metrics, $C0_{iso}$ is related to core level metrics and is the average value of the socket's cores belonging to the examined cluster. Those metrics can be easily monitored during the first execution of the application, thus there is no extended profiling and offline analysis required.

3.3 Algorithm

The Algorithm is consisted of 2 levels. In the first level, we consider as a bin every different socket in the system and afterwards, in the second level, we select the most viable node of the ones belonging to the selected socket. As we have pinned underlying system's sockets and their respecting cores in separate VMs, we are able to have insight and take advantage of the real system metrics. This information allows our custom scheduler to greedily schedule applications in a manner that minimizes interference and maximizes the utilization of the server's resources.

First Level: Cores in a socket share their L3 cache. In this stage we are trying to address both interference effects and core availability. Using best-fit heuristic algorithm, with respect to the PCM metrics extracted, we construct a scoring function using Eq. 1. For every batch of incoming applications, our custom scheduler uses socket extracted metrics in order to initialize each socket object with the corresponding metrics. In addition, using the $s_j^i \langle C6 \rangle \forall j$ we add the additional factor c in the Eq. 1 as shown in Algorithm 1. More specifically, we verify core availability for each node associated with the examined socket. If there is not a single core available (**space** <1), we include $s_j^i \langle c6 \rangle$, otherwise we do not. Afterwards, for every application in the current batch, the most viable socket is selected. Algorithm 1 is executed for every socket belonging to the cluster. After the most viable socket selection, we update its measured metrics with the scheduled application stress surcharge and proceed to the next stage.

Second Level: After selecting the most appropriate socket according to our priority function, the L3 cache and memory bandwidth are not prioritizing factors anymore as their are shared between the cores within the socket. The next level of abstraction in our system, are the nodes (VMs). Owing to node heterogeneity, in terms of virtual cores and memory capacity in this stage of our approach we need to choose the most appropriate of the nodes whose cores are pinned to the selected socket. We use the number of cores of each node in combination with the average c6-state of those cores and select the predominant node to schedule the current application. Next we update again the node's c6-state using application's average value. While, our contribution is based on the **node affinity** functionality, Kubernetes will handle cases of resources starvation in an availability-centric way.

Algorithm 1. Calculate Score for server i and socket j

Require: $s_j^i \langle c6 \rangle \geq 0$

1: $space \leftarrow 0$
2: **for** $\forall n_l^{i,j}$ **do**
3:    **if** $n_l^{i,j} \langle c6 \rangle * p_l > 1$ **then**
4:       $space \leftarrow space + 1$
5:    **end if**
6: **end for**
   {Search for c6-state core availability}
7: **if** $space \geq 1$ **then**
8:    $c \leftarrow o_j$
9: **else**
10:    $c \leftarrow o_j * s_j^i \langle c6 \rangle$
11: **end if**
12: **return** $(s_j^i \langle reads \rangle + s_j^i \langle writes \rangle) / s_j^i \langle ipc \rangle * c$

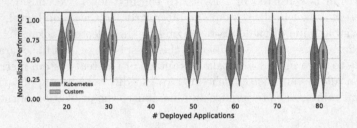

Fig. 4. Applications relative performance in different workload density.

4 Evaluation

Experimental Setup: The cluster is consisted of four worker nodes as described in Sect. 2. For every test-case, we log the application completion time and the socket metrics captured during the makespan of the batch.

Scheduling Under Realistic Workloads: To evaluate our proposed solution, we examine a scenario where various workloads arrive to our system on random intervals, ranging from 10 to 50 s, using the benchmarks described in Table 1. Figure 4 illustrates the results of scheduling workloads varying from 20 to 80 applications in our Kubernetes cluster. As we can see, our custom scheduler outperforms the default kube-scheduler in all the cases, providing an average of 20% and a maximum of 32% improvement over the median performance. In cases of huge amount of workloads (>70), the target system becomes saturated, hurting the overall performance in both cases. However, even in such over-stressed scenarios, we see that our proposed approach achieves higher performance over the naive one, with an average of 25%.

Available Resources Usage: In order to depict the more fair workload balancing, we placed in one of the two sockets L3 stress using iBench. Afterwards, similar to the previous test, we deployed 4–6 random batches of the workloads referenced in Table 1. In Fig. 5, we present some hardware system metrics extracted. More specifically, each figure describes the absolute difference in resource usage between the two sockets during the execution of our workloads. In Fig. 5a, the

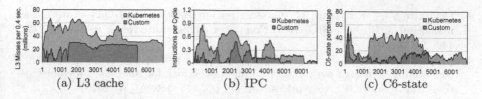

Fig. 5. Resources Usage imbalance between the sockets; x-axis denotes the timestep(400 ms)

imbalance between each socket's cache misses in Kubernetes scheduler is significantly greater than our proposed one. Consequently, one of the two sockets was over-utilized, degrading running applications' performance due to contention, while the other one had that specific resource available and unused. On the other side, our proposed scheduler is aware of the L3 cache interference and distributes applications in a more evenhanded way, trying to share the load between the separate components of the system. Similarly in Fig. 5b and 5c is displayed the more balanced resource usage during the execution of the workload our proposed approach scheduled. C6-state percentage and the IPC seem also to come up against a more equitable sharing in our custom approach.

5 Conclusion

In this paper, we address the problem of interference in multi-tenant cloud infrastructures. We designed an integrated with Kubernetes interference-aware custom scheduler, deployed on the top of a virtualized environment. We experimentally evaluated the pod placement of our proposed scheduler using different scenarios and compared it with the default Kubernetes scheduler. Our results showed that our custom approach can improve the overall performance of the deployed workloads, while, at the same time, achieves a more balanced resource utilization.

References

1. Evolve H2020 official website. https://www.evolve-h2020.eu/
2. Authors, P.: Prometheus-monitoring system & time series database (2017)
3. Barroso, L.A., Hölzle, U.: The case for energy-proportional computing (2007)
4. Barroso, L.A., Hölzle, U.: The datacenter as a computer: an introduction to the design of warehouse-scale machines. Synth. Lect. Comput. Architect. **4**(1), 1–108 (2009)
5. Blagodurov, S., Zhuravlev, S., Fedorova, A.: Contention-aware scheduling on multicore systems. ACM Trans. Comput. Syst. (TOCS) **28**(4), 8 (2010)
6. Burns, B., Grant, B., Oppenheimer, D., Brewer, E., Wilkes, J.: Borg, Omega, and Kubernetes (2016)
7. Delimitrou, C., Kozyrakis, C.: ibench: quantifying interference for datacenter applications. In: 2013 IEEE International Symposium on Workload Characterization (IISWC), pp. 23–33. IEEE (2013)

8. Delimitrou, C., Kozyrakis, C.: Quasar: resource-efficient and QoS-aware cluster management. In: ACM SIGARCH Computer Architecture News, vol. 42, pp. 127–144. ACM (2014)
9. Ebrahimi, E., Lee, C.J., Mutlu, O., Patt, Y.N.: Fairness via source throttling: a configurable and high-performance fairness substrate for multi-core memory systems. In: ACM SIGPLAN Notices, vol. 45, pp. 335–346. ACM (2010)
10. Felter, W., Ferreira, A., Rajamony, R., Rubio, J.: An updated performance comparison of virtual machines and Linux containers. In: 2015 IEEE International Symposium on Performance Analysis of Systems and Software (ISPASS), pp. 171–172. IEEE (2015)
11. Ferdman, M., et al.: Clearing the clouds: a study of emerging scale-out workloads on modern hardware. In: Proceedings of the Seventeenth International Conference on Architectural Support for Programming Languages and Operating Systems (2012)
12. Ferdman, M., Kaynak, C., Falsafi, B.: Proactive instruction fetch. In: Proceedings of the 44th Annual IEEE/ACM International Symposium on Microarchitecture, pp. 152–162. ACM (2011)
13. Guo, J., et al.: Who limits the resource efficiency of my datacenter: an analysis of alibaba datacenter traces. In: Proceedings of the International Symposium on Quality of Service, p. 39. ACM (2019)
14. Henning, J.L.: Spec CPU2006 benchmark descriptions. ACM SIGARCH Comput. Architect. News 34(4), 1–17 (2006)
15. V. Inc.: Containers on virtual machines or bare metal? Deploying and Securely Managing Containerized Applications at Scale, White Paper, December 2018
16. Lo, D., Cheng, L., Govindaraju, R., Ranganathan, P., Kozyrakis, C.: Heracles: improving resource efficiency at scale. In: ACM SIGARCH Computer Architecture News, vol. 43, pp. 450–462. ACM (2015)
17. Masouros, D., Xydis, S., Soudris, D.: Rusty: runtime system predictability leveraging LSTM neural networks. IEEE Comput. Archit. Lett. 18(2), 103–106 (2019)
18. Panwar, G., et al.: Quantifying memory underutilization in HPC systems and using it to improve performance via architecture support. In: Proceedings of the 52nd Annual IEEE/ACM International Symposium on Microarchitecture, pp. 821–835 (2019)
19. Pedregosa, F., et al.: Scikit-learn: machine learning in python. J. Mach. Learn. Res. 12(Oct), 2825–2830 (2011)
20. Reiss, C., Tumanov, A., Ganger, G.R., Katz, R.H., Kozuch, M.A.: Heterogeneity and dynamicity of clouds at scale: Google trace analysis. In: Proceedings of the Third ACM Symposium on Cloud Computing, p. 7. ACM (2012)
21. Willhalm, T., Dementiev, R., Fay, P.: Intel performance counter monitor-a better way to measure CPU utilization (2012). Dosegljivo https://software.intel.com/en-us/articles/intelperformance-counter-monitor-a-better-way-to-measure-cpu-utilization. [Dostopano: September 2014]
22. Yang, K.: Aggregated containerized logging solution with fluentd, elastic search and kibana. Int. J. Comput. Appl. 150(3) (2016)
23. Yenier, D.G., Wolfgang Gentzsch, U.: Kubernetes and HPC applications in hybrid-cloud environments – part II, March 2020. https://www.hpcwire.com/2020/03/19/kubernetes-and-hpc-applications-in-hybrid-cloud-environments-part-ii/
24. Zhuravlev, S., Blagodurov, S., Fedorova, A.: Addressing shared resource contention in multicore processors via scheduling. In: ACM SIGPLAN Notices, vol. 45, pp. 129–142. ACM (2010)

RustyHermit: A Scalable, Rust-Based Virtual Execution Environment

Stefan Lankes[1]([✉]), Jonathan Klimt[1], Jens Breitbart[2], and Simon Pickartz[3]

[1] Institute for Automation of Complex Power Systems, RWTH Aachen University,
Aachen, Germany
{slankes,jonathan.klimt}@eonerc.rwth-aachen.de

[2] Bosch Chassis Systems Control, Robert Bosch GmbH, Gerlingen, Germany
jens.breitbart@de.bosch.com

[3] ParTec Cluster Competence Center GmbH, Munich, Germany
pickartz@par-tec.com

Abstract. System-level development has been dominated by programming languages such as C/C++ for decades. These languages are inherently unsafe, error-prone, and a major reason for vulnerabilities. High-level programming languages with a secure memory model and strong type system are able to improve the quality of the system software. This paper explores the programming language Rust for development of a scalable, virtual execution environment and presents the integration of a Rust-based IP stack into RUSTYHERMIT. RustyHermit is part of the standard Rust toolchain and common Rust applications are able to build on top of RUSTYHERMIT.

1 Introduction

The C programming language is still dominating system-level software development as it was designed for this exact case and is known to provide high performance. However, C is also known to be error-prone and difficult to use in large scale projects as even senior developers can hardly avoid an incorrect usage of C. Dangling pointers and missing boundary checks are other typical reasons for issues within kernel code. This is not a new observation. As described in by Cutler et al. [3], the Pilot kernel [29] and the Lisp machine [8] are early examples of the usage of a high-level language (Mesa and Lisp, respectively) for Operating System (OS) development. However, the approach has not gained acceptance and is hardly used because memory safety of high-level languages often induces runtime overhead (e.g., due to garbage collection).

Furthermore, the OS requirements changed fundamentally over the last years. The basic infrastructure within OSs was established in the seventies when hardware was expensive and resource sharing was the focus. The virtualization of hardware resources has been established for a simplified resource sharing, e.g., sharing a processor in round-robin manner. However, in the era of cloud computing, complete machines are virtualized supporting server consolidations. Virtualization is implemented as another software abstraction layer in an already

© Springer Nature Switzerland AG 2020
H. Jagode et al. (Eds.): ISC High Performance 2020 Workshops, LNCS 12321, pp. 331–342, 2020.
https://doi.org/10.1007/978-3-030-59851-8_22

highly layered software stack. Typical modern OSs still include support for old physical protocols (e.g., floppy disks), irrelevant optimizations (e.g., disk elevator algorithms on SSDs) and backward-compatible interfaces (e.g., POSIX). Anil Madhavapeddy et al. discuss these issues in [20,21] and present unikernels, i.e., specialized library OSs, as a solution. Unikernels are built by compiling high-level languages directly into specialized single-address-space machine images. In doing so, unused code is removed by static code analysis and system calls are replaced by common function calls promising a faster resource handling. Unikernels are able to run directly on a hypervisor or bare metal on the hardware. They provide a smaller footprint compared to traditional OS kernels and have more prospect to optimize the applications, e.g., the application and the kernel can be optimized by means of Link-time Optimization (LTO).

Current Unikernels relinquish backward compatibility, often rely on uncommon programming interfaces, and barely support multi-processor systems. In [16], we present a rewrite of HERMITCORE [14] in Rust called RUSTYHERMIT and demonstrate that the performance of the Rust implementation is on a par with the original C implementation. RUSTYHERMIT is integrated into the standard runtime of Rust and its compiler infrastructure. It is trivial to port pure Rust application to RUSTYHERMIT, as it just requires a configuration change. Only applications, which bypass the Rust runtime and call directly a C library, have to port also the C library to the new system. Furthermore, existing C/C++ and Fortran applications can be linked with RUSTYHERMIT and generate a bootable image. In this paper, we focus on the integration of a Rust-based IP stack enabling the building and deployment of secure and efficient cloud applications.

The rest of this paper is structured as follows: We start with a discussion of the related work in the area of unikernels and the usage of high-level programming languages for kernel development. In Sect. 3, we give a short introduction to Rust, followed by the Sect. 4 on kernel development using Rust and the integration of the IP stack. In the Sect. 5 we compare the performance of our kernel with Linux. Finally, Sect. 6 summarizes the paper and give a short outlook.

2   Related Work

High-level programming languages provide type-safety and memory-safety as well as convenient abstractions of concurrent programming reducing the susceptibility to errors. However, kernel developers are often skeptical to use new languages because they expect them to introduce additional overhead compared to C [37] and require a redevelopment of kernel components. Yet, many research projects use high-level programming languages to benefit from new features such as a safe memory handling. New system programming languages, e.g., D [4], Nim [27], Go [7], and Rust [35], have emerged in the last decade. For nearly every language there exists an OS project.

In Rust, the compiler is able to determine when memory has to be freed avoiding the need for according runtime checks. This results in far less runtime overhead compared to other high-level programming languages, but introduces unique memory handling at the language level. Levy et al. [17,18] show that Rust is attractive for kernel development because it promises memory-safety while providing good performance. In addition, Balasubramanian et al. [1] show that Rust offers software fault isolation (SFI) with lower overhead and Narayanan et al. in [24] steps to realize a Rust-based verified firmware. Currently, Microsoft [22] is also analyzing Rust as a system programming language. Projects such as Redox [31], Tock [36] or teaching kernels such as our eduOS-rs [6] show that Rust is usable for OS development, but all these Rust kernels were not designed for cloud environments.

Both HERMITCORE and RUSTYHERMIT belong to the class of unikernels or library OSs. *MirageOS* [20], *IncludeOS* [2], *rumprun kernels* [9], and *OSv* [10] are typical representatives. The fundamental drawback of unikernels is the porting effort that is required to adapt existing applications to the underlying minimalistic OS. This often requires both expert work and a considerable amount of time. One objective of the Unikraft [38] project is to build unikernels targeted at specific applications, without requiring the time-consuming, expert work. Unikraft is written in C, uses newlib [30] as the C library, and LwIP [5] as the network stack.

Like Unikraft, HERMITCORE relies on *LwIP* as it is easy to combine to a kernel and the list of requirements is small. However, *LwIP* was mainly designed for embedded systems and it is a challenge to get the same performance as provided by common operating systems (e.g., Linux). For instance, Kuenzer et al. [12] can improve the performance by using a low-level API (instead of a socket interface) and to integrate checksum offloading. Further improvements can be achieved by supporting the Data Plane Development Kit (DPDK) [28]. However, this is not available for all devices.

The compatibility of unikernels to common OSs (e.g., Linux) is currently still limited. HermiTux [26] has similar objectives and realizes compatibility to Linux by rewriting system calls and using a modified C library. However, the compatibility of HermiTux is limited as not all Linux system calls have been re-implemented. RUSTYHERMIT is also not compatible to common OSs, but it offers the possibility to write portable Rust applications. Changes to the source code are not required to run the application on Linux or other OSs.

3   Introduction to Rust

Rust is a new programming language originally designed by Graydon Hoare as a replacement for C/C++. Its goal is to provide the same level of performance, but to allow for more comprehensive safety checks at compile time and by default enabled runtime checks when the compile time checks are not sufficient (e.g., array access with indices not known at compile time). We discuss only the features relevant to understand this paper, a detailed overview on Rust can be found in [11].

Rust relies on *ownership* to provide safe memory handling without runtime overhead. Each resource (e.g., memory) in Rust has a variable that is called its

owner. There is exactly one owner at a time and whenever this owner goes out
of scope, the resource will be dropped and the memory freed. Ownership can
be forwarded to another variable invalidating the original owner, or the owner
can borrow the resource to another variable. Read only access can be provided
to multiple variables at a time via immutable borrows, as long as no mutable
borrow is happening at the same time. In general, these rules prevent data races,
the dangling pointer problem, and pointer aliasing for mutable access. For most
tasks it is possible to develop code that these rules are satisfied at compile time,
however it is also possible to use `std::cell::RefCell` to bypass compile time
checks, but enforce runtime checks.

Similarly to these checks, Rust provides compile time checks as well ensuring
the correct execution of concurrent or parallel code. Data that is shared between
threads must implement the so-called `sync` trait (the rust term for an interface)
or must be wrapped into a mutex providing this trait. This rule prevents data
races, as long as the synchronization mechanism (e.g., the mutex) is implemented
correctly. Furthermore, the Rust compiler checks the lifetime of values shared by
threads and will not compile code in which a value is not guaranteed to outlive
the threads borrowing a value.

All checks named before can be circumvented by using the `unsafe` keyword.
Unsafe Rust code provides the same level of control as C, e.g., it provides *raw
pointers* enabling direct, unchecked memory accesses and even supports the
usage of inline assembly. Code in unsafe regions should be reviewed more carefully than code that is checked by the compiler and as a result it is typically
frown upon by the Rust community. Currently, it is not possible to write a kernel without unsafe code. For instance, inline assembly is important to restore
the context of the FPU. However, the RUSTYHERMIT only requires 1170 lines
of unsafe code corresponding to only 1.71% of total code size.

The Rust standard library is divided into an OS-independent and an OS-
dependent part. The library known as *core* library is the major part of the OS-
independent library and already implements basic error/panic handling, string
operations, and atomic operations. Furthermore, Rust offers the possibility to
redefine the global memory allocator. This allocator is used by all other Rust
codes unless explicitly circumvented. In contrast, the part known as *std* con-
denses the OS-dependent libraries and extends them with various data structures, console output, and thread handling. It is easily possible to create a project
that does not use *std* by adding `#![no_std]` to the main file.

4   A Unikernel Written in Rust

RUSTYHERMIT is a rewrite of our 64 bit unikernel HERMITCORE [14,15] which
was written in C. RUSTYHERMIT is completely written in Rust, supports the
Intel 64 Architecture and comes with support for SSE4, AVX2, and AVX512.
It has multi-core and single-core multiprocessing support by the means of multithreading and multiprocessing. The Kernel supports the execution of more
threads than available cores. This is an important feature for dealing with concurrent applications or to integrate performance monitoring tools. Currently, the

scheduler does not support load balancing as explicit thread placement is favored over automatic strategies. Scheduling overhead is reduced to a minimum by the employment of a dynamic timer, i.e., the kernel does not interrupt computation threads which run exclusively on certain cores and do not use any timer. To improve the security behavior, RUSTYHERMIT provides a stack guard and is completely position-independent. Consequently, the loader is able to randomize the memory layout.

4.1   Integration of RustyHermit into libstd

One major goal of RUSTYHERMIT was a complete integration into the Rust toolchain to simplify the application development. Any common Rust application should be buildable with RUSTYHERMIT. To achieve this goal, the kernel provides the required interfaces to the Standard Library (*libstd*) whilst being based only on the *core* library. The operating system abstraction layer of the Rust toolchain is relative small, so only around 26 files within a total of ~3000 lines of code are required to integrate RUSTYHERMIT into the standard library of Rust.

Most operating systems are written in C and use a common C library as interface to the kernel. These functions are typically provided by a helper crate[1] in Rust realizing an interface to the C functions. For instance, the C interface for Rust is published in the crate *libc*[2], however C functions are by definition unsafe.

In case of RUSTYHERMIT, the complete kernel is written in Rust and theoretically, it could be directly integrated into the Rust standard library. However, the kernel uses a set of external crates to detect processor features, programming of the interrupt controller, or log messages. As the Rust community wants to reduce the dependencies of the basic runtime libraries to external crates, we cannot integrate RUSTYHERMIT into *libstd* directly. Instead, we create two helper crates *hermit-abi*[3] and *hermit-sys*[4]. The former describes only the interface to the library operating system for linkage and is included in *libstd*s dependencies, just like the *libc* crate does for the Linux interface of the Standard Library. The latter is a helper crate, with the main purpose of building the kernel as static library from source and linking it to the application.

Separating the kernel and *libstd* into separate compilation units also allows the use of different compiler settings for each of them. Hereby, we are able to compile the kernel without FPU and AVX/SSE support and to enable it for the rest of the application. This is necessary because AVX and SSE is not longer limited to floating-point operations and the compiler would use these instructions to optimize the kernel code. The usage of AVX and SSE within the kernel would trigger interrupts to save the FPU context.

---

[1] Crate is a tree of modules that produces a library or executables. Much like a package in other programming languages.
[2] https://crates.io/crates/libc.
[3] https://crates.io/crates/hermit-abi.
[4] https://crates.io/crates/hermit-sys.

Listing 1.1. Extension of Cargo.toml to integrate RUSTYHERMIT

```
[target.'cfg(target_os = "hermit")'.dependencies]
hermit-sys = "0.1.*"
```

A Rust based RUSTYHERMIT application can be build by adding the *hermit-sys* crate to the application dependencies as shown in Listing 1.1 and declare it as an `external crate` in the applications source. Rust's package manager Cargo [34] will then download the kernel's sources, compile it, and link it to the application.

4.2   Network Support

The library operating system only provides basic features such as interrupt handling, device drivers, memory management, and scheduling. One possible solution to integrate network support, is the use of real hardware drivers. The hypervisor emulates these devices by trapping every request to the device and emulating the behavior of the real hardware (*trap and emulate*). This approach comes with an important overhead.

Another solution is to use *para-virtualization* where the hypervisor provides a simpler and faster interface for the I/O devices to the guest, who is aware of running on a hypervisor. Today, *virtio* is the standard abstraction layer [25] for these para-virtualized I/O devices on KVM-accelerated hypervisors. The driver is split into two parts: the frontend and the backend. The former is provided by the guest kernel while the backend is provided by the host. This abstraction layer can be used for para-virtualization of any I/O device. In case of a network interface, there exist at least two buffers. One buffer is handling all incoming packets, while the second buffer is handling all outgoing packets. The original version of virtio [32] was developed by Rusty Russell for the support of his own virtualization solution. RUSTYHERMIT provides a frontend driver in the kernel that is used to access the file system with *virtio-fs* [39] and network support.

As shown in Fig. 1, RUSTYHERMIT uses *smoltcp* [19] as a dual IPv4/IPv6 stack and is provided by *hermit-sys* to the Rust runtime. *smoltcp* is an event-driven TCP/IP stack written in Rust and designed for bare-metal, real-time systems. In principle, *hermit-sys* creates a thread, which handles all incoming packets including ARP and ICMP packets with the help of *smoltcp*. The IP stack is added to *hermit-sys* and not to the kernel, so it can use the default memory allocator of the Rust runtime and to enable hardware dependent optimizations (e.g., AVX support) as explained before Sect. 4.1. We implemented a direct interface between *smoltcp* and Rust's standard library to forward TCP streams to all common Rust applications. All outgoing messages are directly passed through the IP stack to the virtio interface. Incoming messages triggers an interrupt, where the interrupt handler wakes the IP thread of *hermit-sys*. Acknowledgments and retransmission of lost messages are directly handled by this thread. If the incoming message is intended for a specific thread, which is

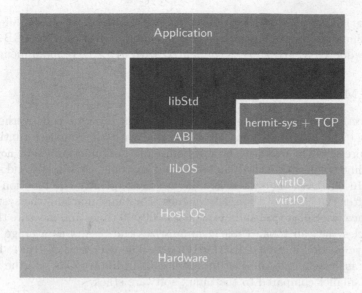

Fig. 1. Architecture overview of RustyHermit.

blocked on a socket, the IP thread wakes the thread and afterwards the thread consumes the data.

This approach works well for communication pattern in which the delay between requesting data and receiving data is high enough to hide the overhead of both the interrupts and the context switches between the threads. To get peak performance for communication pattern with a short delay, the driver switch to a polling mode. In this case, interrupts from the virtio device will be disabled. The complete communication is then realized by the application threads, which are waiting for incoming messages. If the IP stack is not used for 20 ms, the driver switch back to the non-polling mode.

We implemented this behavior with *Futures* [33], which are Rust way of expressing asynchronous computation. This interface provides a polling method to check if the data is available. The usage of this standard mechanism offers the possibilities to easily check several futures asynchronously.

5   Evaluation

All benchmarks were performed on a NUMA system possessing two sockets each with 12 physical cores, exposing 24 cores in total. The CPUs are Intel Skylake CPUs (Xeon Gold 6128) clocked at 3.4 GHz, equipped with 256 GiB DDR4 RAM and 19.25 MiB L3 cache. We used a 4.18.0 Linux kernel with CentOS 8. All benchmarks are compiled with optimization level 3 and LTO.

As said before, unikernels are designed to run within a hypervisor. For the evaluation, qemu-kvm 2.12.0 is used and accelerated by KVM. All benchmarks run within virtual machines with the same setup. The network interface and the storage is integrated by virtio to reduce the overhead. The only difference is that for Linux guests the virtual machine is configured to provide 4 GB of main memory, while RUSTYHERMIT is configured with 512 MByte main memory.

5.1   OS Micro-benchmarks

In this section we present benchmarks regarding system call overhead and scheduling. The getpid system call is the one with the smallest runtime and closely represents the overhead of a system call. The function yield_now of the Rust runtime triggers the scheduler to check if another task is ready and switches to them. In our case, the system is idle and consequently the function returns directly after the check of the ready queues. For benchmarking the system call performance, we call getpid and yield_now 1 000 000 times and measure the number of cycles the call took. Table 1 summarizes the results as average number of CPU cycles for Linux and RUSTYHERMIT. The overhead of RUSTYHERMIT is smaller as system calls are just function calls in library OSs and the runtime system is smaller compared to the Linux software stack.

Table 1. Comparison of basic system services by Linux and RUSTYHERMIT.

System activity	Linux	RustyHermit
Time to boot	≤15 s	≤1.0 s
Reserved memory	748 MByte	58 MByte
Boot image size	1.8 GByte	1.55 MByte
yield_now()	1439 cycles	68 cycles
getpid()	1147 cycles	43 cycles

Table 1 also shows memory consumption of a minimal CentOS 8 configuration, where only a secure shell server is running and compares it with the memory consumption of the smallest possible RUSTYHERMIT application. To determine these numbers, the memory consumption of the hypervisor on the host system is evaluated. The numbers show the physically allocated memory. The reserved memory in the logical address space is clearly larger because the virtual machines are configured to use up to 4 GByte memory for the Linux guest and 500 MByte for RUSTYHERMIT as guest. Both virtual machines are not fully utilized. The low memory consumption and the small image size for RUSTYHERMIT promise a better resource utilization in data centers.

To evaluate the boot time, the time between the start of the virtual machine and the first response of a ICMP-based ping request is measure. To avoid side effects from the storage device, the boot image is stored in *tmpfs*. The last step before entering the main function of the Rust application in RUSTYHERMIT is the initialization of the network stack. Therefore, the results show the minimal time to start the unikernel application within a hypervisor. While it is possible

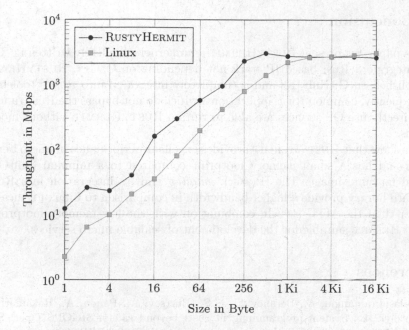

Fig. 2. Comparsion of the network throughput between RustyHermit and Linux

to start applications in Linux before the network services have started, this is a rather unlikely scenario and it is more likely that other services are started between the network service start and the application start. As expected for a unikernel, RustyHermit is clearly faster in comparison to Linux which is beneficial for services requiring low latencies.

5.2   Network Performance

To determine the network performance, a benchmark is used transferring data with Rust's standard TCP stream interface. Both the server and the client are running on the same node. The sender is running in all test scenarios within a VM, while the receiver is running natively on the host system. In case of the senders, the checksums of the IP packets are built within the guest machine. All interfaces use an MTU of 1500 Bytes and the Nagle algorithm [23] is disabled.

Figure 2 compares the performance between RustyHermit and Linux. Up to a message size of the MTU, RustyHermit provides a clearly higher bandwidth in comparsion to Linux. For messages with the size of 512 bytes, RustyHermit is twice as fast. Linux is more efficient at splitting messages larger than the MTU size and as a result Linux currently provides higher performance for large messages. This is something that needs to be worked on in *smoltcp* and is not directly part of RustyHermit.

6 Conclusion

In this paper, we present RUSTYHERMIT a unikernel completely written in Rust. We integrate a Rust-based IP stack not depending on C/C++. RUSTYHERMIT is published on GitHub [13] and is completely integrated into Rust's toolchain. Consequently, common Rust applications, which do not bypass the Rust runtime and directly use OS services are able to run on RUSTYHERMIT without modifications.

We show that RUSTYHERMIT provides excellent performance in micro benchmarks and has a small memory footprint compared to a minimal CentOS 8 virtual machine image. The IP stack *smoltcp* and its integration into Rust's standard library provide a higher bandwidth in comparison to Linux for message smaller than the MTU size. In combination with the low memory footprint is RUSTYHERMIT suitable for the development of scalable micro services.

References

1. Balasubramanian, A., Baranowski, M.S., Burtsev, A., Panda, A., Rakamari, Z., Ryzhyk, L.: System programming in rust: beyond safety. SIGOPS Oper. Syst. Rev. **51**(1), 94–99 (2017). https://doi.org/10.1145/3139645.3139660
2. Bratterud, A., Walla, A., Haugerud, H., Engelstad, P.E., Begnum, K.: IncludeOS: a resource efficient unikernel for cloud services. In: Proceedings of the 2015 IEEE 7th International Conference on Cloud Computing Technology and Science (Cloud-Com) (2015)
3. Cutler, C., Kaashoek, M.F., Morris, R.T.: The benefits and costs of writing a POSIX kernel in a high-level language. In: 13th USENIX Symposium on Operating Systems Design and Implementation (OSDI), pp. 1–19, September 2018
4. D Language Foundation: The D Programming Language. https://dlang.org/. Accessed 4 Mar 2019
5. Dunkels, A.: Design and Implementation of the LwIP TCP/IP Stack. Swedish Institute of Computer Science (2001)
6. eduOS-rs: A teaching operating system written in rust. https://rwth-os.github.io/eduOS-rs/. Accessed 13 Feb 2019
7. Google: The Go Programming Language. https://golang.org. Accessed 4 Mar 2019
8. Greenblatt, R.D., Knight, T.F., Holloway, J.T., Moon, D.A.: A LISP machine. ACM SIGIR Forum **15**(2), 137–138 (1980)
9. Kantee, A.: Flexible operating system internals - the design and implementation of the anykernel and rump kernels. Ph.D. thesis, Department of Computer Science and Engineering, Aalto University, Aalto, Finland (2012)
10. Kivity, A., et al.: OSv - Optimizing the operating system for virtual machines. In: USENIX Annual Technical Conference (2014)
11. Klabnik, S., Nichols, C.: The Rust Programming Language (Manga Guide). No Starch Press, San Francisco (2018)
12. Kuenzer, S., et al.: Unikernels everywhere: the case for elastic CDNs. In: Proceedings of the 13th ACM SIGPLAN/SIGOPS International Conference on Virtual Execution Environments, VEE 2017, pp. 15–29. Association for Computing Machinery, New York (2017). https://doi.org/10.1145/3050748.3050757

13. Lankes, S., Breitbart, J., Pickartz, S.: Rustyhermit - a rust-based, lightweight unikernel. https://github.com/hermitcore/libhermit-rs. Accessed 3 Oct 2019
14. Lankes, S., Pickartz, S., Breitbart, J.: HermitCore: a unikernel for extreme scale computing. In: Proceedings of the 6th International Workshop on Runtime and Operating Systems for Supercomputers, ROSS 2016, pp. 4:1–4:8. ACM, New York (2016)
15. Lankes, S., Pickartz, S., Breitbart, J.: A low noise unikernel for extrem-scale systems. In: Knoop, J., Karl, W., Schulz, M., Inoue, K., Pionteck, T. (eds.) ARCS 2017. LNCS, vol. 10172, pp. 73–84. Springer, Cham (2017). https://doi.org/10.1007/978-3-319-54999-6_6
16. Lankes, S., Breitbart, J., Pickartz, S.: Exploring rust for unikernel development. In: Proceedings of the 10th Workshop on Programming Languages and Operating Systems, PLOS 2019, pp. 8–15. Association for Computing Machinery, New York (2019). https://doi.org/10.1145/3365137.3365395
17. Levy, A., et al.: Ownership is theft: experiences building an embedded OS in Rust. ACM, New York, October 2015
18. Levy, A., Campbell, B., Ghena, B., Pannuto, P., Dutta, P., Levis, P.: The case for writing a kernel in rust. Proceedings of the 8th Asia-Pacific Workshop on Systems (APSys 2017), pp. 1–7 (2017)
19. M-Labs: uhyve - a minimal hypervisor for rustyhermit. https://github.com/m-labs/smoltcp. Accessed 1 Aug 2019
20. Madhavapeddy, A., et al.: Unikernels: library operating systems for the cloud. In: Proceedings of the Eighteenth International Conference on Architectural Support for Programming Languages and Operating Systems, ASPLOS 2013, pp. 461–472. ACM, New York (2013). https://doi.org/10.1145/2451116.2451167
21. Madhavapeddy, A., Scott, D.J.: Unikernels: rise of the virtual library operating system. ACM Queue 11(11), 30 (2013)
22. Microsoft Security Response Center: Why rust for safe systems programming. https://msrc-blog.microsoft.com/2019/07/22/why-rust-for-safe-systems-programming/. Accessed 1 Aug 2019
23. Nagle, J.: Congestion Control in IP/TCP Internetworks. https://tools.ietf.org/html/rfc896. Accessed 10 July 2020
24. Narayanan, V., Baranowski, M.S., Ryzhyk, L., Rakamarić, Z., Burtsev, A.: Redleaf: towards an operating system for safe and verified firmware, pp. 37–44 (2019). https://doi.org/10.1145/3317550.3321449. http://doi.acm.org/10.1145/3317550.3321449
25. OASIS Virtual I/O Device (VIRTIO) TC: Virtual I/O Device (VIRTIO) Version 1.1 (2018). https://docs.oasis-open.org/virtio/virtio/v1.1/csprd01/virtio-v1.1-csprd01.html
26. Olivier, P., Chiba, D., Lankes, S., Min, C., Ravindran, B.: A binary-compatible unikernel. In: Proceedings of the 15th ACM SIGPLAN/SIGOPS International Conference on Virtual Execution Environments, VEE 2019, pp. 59–73. Association for Computing Machinery, New York (2019). https://doi.org/10.1145/3313808.3313817
27. Picheta, D.: Nim in action. http://nim-lang.org/. Accessed 4 Mar 2019
28. DPDK Project: Data Plane Development Kit. https://www.dpdk.org. Accessed 10 July 2020
29. Redell, D.D., et al.: Pilot - an operating system for a personal computer. Commun. ACM 23(2), 81–92 (1980)
30. RedHat: Newlib - a c library for embedded systems. https://sourceware.org/newlib/. Accessed 13 Feb 2019

31. Redox: A unix-like operating system written in rust. https://www.redox-os.org. Accessed 13 Feb 2019
32. Russell, R.: Virtio: towards a de-facto standard for virtual i/o devices. SIGOPS Oper. Syst. Rev. **42**(5), 95–103 (2008). https://doi.org/10.1145/1400097.1400108
33. Rust Project Developers: Future - a Representation of asynchronous computation. https://doc.rust-lang.org/std/future/trait.Future.html. Accessed 10 July 2020
34. Rust Project Developers: Cargo - a rust package manager. https://doc.rust-lang.org/cargo/. Accessed 4 Mar 2019
35. Rust Project Developers: The Rust Programming Language. https://www.rust-lang.org. Accessed 4 Mar 2019
36. Tock: A secure embedded operating system for cortex-m based microcontrollers. https://www.tockos.org. Accessed 4 Mar 2019
37. Torvalds, L.: (2004). http://harmful.cat-v.org/software/c++/linus
38. Unikraft: An easy way of crafting unikernels. http://unikraft.neclab.eu. Accessed 4 Mar 2019
39. Virtio-fs Project Developers: virtio-fs. https://virtio-fs.gitlab.io. Accessed 14 July 2020

Rootless Containers with Podman for HPC

Holger Gantikow[1,2]([✉]) [iD], Steffen Walter[1] [iD], and Christoph Reich[2] [iD]

[1] science+computing AG, Atos, Tübingen, Germany
gantikow@gmail.com, steffen.walter@atos.net
[2] Institute for Cloud Computing and IT Security, Furtwangen University,
Furtwangen, Germany
{holger.gantikow,christoph.reich}@hs-furtwangen.de

Abstract. Containers have become popular in HPC environments to improve the mobility of applications and the delivery of user-supplied code. In this paper we evaluate Podman, an enterprise container engine that supports rootless containers, in combination with runc and crun as container runtimes using a real-world workload with LS-DYNA, and the industry-standard benchmarks sysbench and STREAM. The results suggest that Podman with crun only introduces a similar low overhead as HPC-focused container technologies.

Keywords: Virtualization · Container · Podman · Singularity · runc · crun · Rootless containers · LS-DYNA · Benchmark · Performance analysis

1 Introduction

Over the last half decade, containers have become a valuable asset when it comes to running services and applications. Especially in enterprise environments, where containers have turned into an integral part of the development, deployment and operation of modern microservice architectures, they are well received. They also prove to be particularly suitable for HPC environments, where they improve the mobility of applications and the delivery of user-supplied code. HPC centers are increasingly confronted with these requirements, since users there are not only demanding software for traditional MPI-based simulations but also increasingly novel software stacks and workflows to support workloads from the data science domain. In addition, modern sites call for solutions that open up ways for simplified use of resources distributed across multiple locations and for obtaining supplementary resources from the cloud [18] at a progressive rate. Containers are a suitable component to support the demands for flexibility in a in many ways converging future of compute. They decouple applications and their dependencies from the underlying operating system and encapsulate them in an easily redistributable unit. Due to special requirements of HPC environments in the form of HPC-specific hardware and related libraries [2]

H. Jagode et al. (Eds.): ISC High Performance 2020 Workshops, LNCS 12321, pp. 343–354, 2020.
https://doi.org/10.1007/978-3-030-59851-8_23

this abstraction is not yet fully realized. Despite these limitations and other open issues [17], the achieved state still represents a serious advancement compared to a few years ago.

At the beginning of the containerization trend started by Docker, there was, as already before with LXC, only one runtime available, which could not be integrated easily into HPC environments due to inherent differences in concepts. As a result, a number of HPC-focused container runtimes have been developed over the last few years, most notably *Singularity* [10], but also *Shifter* [8], *Charliecloud* [12] and most recently *Sarus* [1]. They made the concept of containers usable in HPC environments, differentiated by diverging functional extent and implementation. However, due to their HPC focus, these runtimes were not widely accepted beyond HPC environments and only Singularity has achieved a notable degree of adoption in the enterprise HPC market. Even though the interoperability of the individual runtimes has well increased due to the *Open Container Initiative (OCI)* specifications, especially enterprise users show an interest in a common solution, which is suitable for a variety of containerized workloads, including HPC, and that consequently also allows a converging of resources.

The *Podman* [4] container engine fills this gap to a certain extent, as it distinguishes itself by features such as the ability to strongly isolate workloads that are particularly relevant in enterprise container environments, as well as an implementation and process model that is much closer to HPC environments. To the best of our knowledge, the potential of Podman in HPC has not been evaluated beyond basic functional testing [13] yet, a gap we are trying to address with our research. The same applies to performance differences between the OCI compatible runtimes *runc* and *crun*, both supported by the Podman engine for spawning and running containers, insights we consider of use for other container engines that rely on *runc*.

The focus of this paper is to investigate the suitability of Podman in the context of HPC and to identify current limitations. We concentrate on the performance of the container engine, with both *runc* and *crun* as runtime, compared to the native bare metal performance and the HPC-focused Singularity runtime used in enterprise HPC. We are especially interested in the overhead introduced when processing a real-world workload using the *Finite Element Analysis (FEA)* application *LS-DYNA*. This application from the field of *Computer Aided Engineering (CAE)* is widely used in the automotive industry for crash test simulation. This investigation is complemented by a series of industry-standard benchmarks.

The rest of the paper is organized as follows: Sect. 2 introduces related work on container runtimes targeted at HPC environments with focus on performance overhead. Section 3 covers the basic concepts of Podman in the context of HPC. Section 4 presents the results of our evaluation of the Podman engine with the FEA application LS-DYNA using MPI + Infiniband for communication, as well as CPU and memory performance, using the *sysbench* and *STREAM* benchmarks and gives configuration details related to the environment used for the

experimental evaluation. Limitations we came across are discussed in Sect. 5.
The paper concludes in Sect. 6.

2   Related Work

As Docker was not able to make its mark in HPC centers due to technical
challenges, several container platforms were created to address the needs of the
HPC community, each characterized by a specific focus and means to implement
the privilege escalation required to start containers.

Singularity [10] is characterized by its easy integration into existing HPC
workflows, uses a flat single file image format for performance reasons and offers
compatibility with legacy OS installations via a setuid starter. *Shifter* [8] reuses
some components of the Docker workflow and combines the basic concept of
containers with a *chroot* environment. *Charliecloud* [12] is characterized by a very
compact code base and the use of user namespaces to spawn containers. *Sarus*
[1], the latest HPC-specific runtime, is built around OCI specifications, uses the
runtime specification reference implementation *runc* and extends features for
HPC use cases by the use of OCI hooks.

The extent of overhead introduced by container virtualization has been investigated many times over the last years. The study carried out by Felter et al.
[6] represents the central paper when it comes to Docker containers, as it evaluated a variety of typical services, such as MySQL, in conjunction with standard
benchmarks. It concluded that "Docker equals or exceeds KVM performance in
every case we tested". This core statement is true throughout various application
domains: Di Tommaso et al. [5], who investigated the execution speed of genomic
pipelines, shared this conclusion of "negligible impact on the execution performance". Zhang et al. [19] summarized a "much better scalability than virtual
machines" with a Spark-based Big Data workload.

These studies have in common that they usually do not consider HPC-
optimized runtimes. HPC-specific studies are rather sparse and often only examine partial aspects, such as only comparing a single runtime against native performance as in Wang et al. [16] and Younge et al. [18] - or only non-distributed
workloads as in Kovács [9]. The most thorough and recent work is by Torrez et al.
[15], where the three HPC-focused runtimes Charliecloud, Shifter, Singularity are
compared using a number of standard benchmarks, with the conclusion that "the
flexibility gained by using containers does not come at the cost of performance".
Sadly the work lacks the inclusion of the Sarus engine and an evaluation of a
real-world workload.

3   Podman

Although Docker helped containers achieve their current popularity, it met with
disfavor not only in the HPC community, but also in Enterprise Linux distributions. This led to the development of the Podman engine, which integrates
more naturally into a Linux system. In order to avoid potential security risks

caused by the client-server architecture implemented by Docker, Podman uses a classic fork-exec model, which also improves audit capabilities, as, by lacking user switches, the audit subsystem has the possibility to document which user performed container-related operations. The development of Podman is mainly driven by Red Hat, which leads to the integration of corresponding packages in *Red Hat Enterprise Linux (RHEL)* and its derivatives, a detail that is interesting for HPC environments that often rely on RHEL-based distributions.

Coming from the enterprise breed of container runtimes, Podman follows the "as much isolation as possible" paradigm rather than the "as much isolation as necessary" preferred by HPC container runtimes. As expected, the full range of safeguards for workload isolation is therefore supported. In addition to namespaces and cgroups these include seccomp filters, Linux Security Modules (SELinux, AppArmor) and capabilities. These mechanisms, which we presented in more detail in an earlier work in the context of Docker [7], are not necessarily all implemented by HPC-focused runtimes and may be less relevant to traditional HPC workloads. We expect that with the advent of a wider variety of applications, converged resources and the need for additional isolation from bare metal operations and concurrent workloads, these will become more important. How we addressed these mechanisms for MPI workloads is documented in Sect. 4.1.

The most prominent feature of Podman is support for *rootless containers*, which allows the execution of containers without privilege escalation mechanisms, such as root daemon or setuid binary. Podman, like Charliecloud, uses the user namespace functionality for this. Processes inside a new user namespace have different privileges and user IDs than those outside and require corresponding configuration of $/etc/sub\{g,u\}id$. Limitations of rootless containers are discussed in Sect. 5.

The Podman engine uses the runtime *runc*, also used by Docker and Sarus, which is written, as Podman, in Go. It also supports the state-of-the-art runtime *crun*, which is implemented in C and described by the developers as "fast and low-memory footprint". Crun is currently used as the default runtime in Fedora, as it already migrated to the resource limiting feature *cgroups V2*, only supported by crun as of now.

As the name Pod Man(ager) implies, Podman supports the concept of *Pods*, which is used to group a set of containers that collectively implement a complex application. These containers are not completely isolated from each other, but share several namespaces, which simplifies communication. This could be used to provide a group of compute containers with a data sidecar container that only serves the specific input data belonging to a job. In addition, since Kubernetes is based on pods by default, this feature provides increased flexibility in a converged environment to either launch suitable workloads in Kubernetes or to use Kubernetes workloads with Podman.

To build container images Podman relies Buildah and offers the possibility to create OCI compatible images from a Dockerfile without root privileges or background services, which is a notable improvement over Docker-based build processes. It also features functionality to create an image from scratch by using the local package manager to install software as a measure to reduce image bloat over the regular way of running the package manager inside the container itself. It also supports multistage builds, that allow exclusion of build time only tools, as compilers and package managers that are obsolete at run time, from the final build. This can result in smaller image sizes.

A feature that seems more appropriate for HPC environments than for enterprise workloads with stateless containers is the built-in support for *Checkpoint/Restore in Userspace (CRIU)*. It is used to checkpoint containers and restore them at a later time and also to migrate containers to another system, helping with scheduled downtimes and emergency patches. Unfortunately, CRIU cannot be used in combination with rootless containers and when using MPI and Infiniband-based workloads as of now.

Support for OCI Hooks represent a feature we have not yet had the opportunity to gain experience with. OCI Hooks are a mechanism which is used by Sarus to extend the runtime functionality, for example to enable synchronization with the Slurm Scheduler [1]. However, we are aware of an *extended Berkeley Packet Filter (eBPF)*-based hook from the Podman developers, which is used for automated creation of seccomp filters.

4   Evaluation

To investigate the suitability of Podman for HPC workloads we conducted a series of experimental evaluations, comparing rootless Podman to native execution and Singularity as HPC-focused reference runtime. As container runtime for Podman we used both *runc* and *crun* to investigate potential benefits from utilizing the newer implementation written in C (crun) over runtimes in Go (runc, Singularity). This resulted in four distinct runtime environments: *Native, Singularity, Podman-runc* and *Podman-crun*.

Our test environment is part of an automotive industry environment used for crash test simulations, aero dynamics and other CAE workloads. It consists of one cell with 8 nodes and is part of a cluster with several hundred servers using FDR Infiniband and Gigabit Ethernet as interconnect. The nodes are equipped

Table 1. Evaluation cluster details

(a) Hardware Environment		(b) Software Environment	
Component	Details	Component	Version
Server	8x NEC HPC 1816Rf-2	Operating System	CentOS Linux 8.1.1911
Processor	2x Intel Xeon E5-2680 v3 (Hyper Threading enabled)	Kernel	4.18.0-147.3.1.el8_1.x86_64
Memory	128 GB DDR4 (2134 MHz)	Singularity	3.5.2
Interconnect	FDR Mellanox Infiniband HCA MT27500 (ConnectX-3)	Podman	1.6.4
		crun	0.13
		Platform MPI	9.1.4.3r
Local Storage	Intel SSDSC2BB80	LS-DYNA	mpp_r9_3_dm_134916

with SSD-based local storage and use CentOS Linux 8.1 with permissive *SELinux* and a local evaluation user. To ensure meaningful and comparable results all tests were executed on the same systems without configuration changes during the evaluation period. Details related to the evaluation environment are documented in Table 1.

As real-world workload we use two versions of a LS-DYNA crash simulation, the core application the cluster is used with on a daily basis.

To achieve a more detailed view of the overhead induced by containers, we also perform a series of industry-standard benchmarks. To measure *CPU performance* we utilize *sysbench* that calculates the prime numbers between 1 and 40 million using one thread per CPU core. For *memory performance* we rely on STREAM [11]. Benchmark versions, configurations and execution calls are documented in Table 2.

4.1 LS-DYNA

LS-DYNA is used to simulate the impact of automotive crashes, explosions and sheet metal stamping. We use the *car2car* model, a widely used workload originally published by the *National Crash Analysis Center (NCAC)* to measure the performance of LS-DYNA. The model includes 2.4 million single elements and

Table 2. Benchmark Configuration

Component	Version	Compile Flags, Call, Configuration
STREAM	5.10	*gcc -m64 -O3 -mcmodel=medium -ffreestanding -fopenmp -DSTREAM_ARRAY_SIZE=3000000000 -DSTREAM=double stream.c -o stream*
sysbench CPU	1.0.17	*sysbench cpu –threads=24 –cpu-max-prime=40000000 run*
LS-DYNA car2car short	V03c	*memory=600m memory2=60m endtime=0.02*
LS-DYNA car2car long	V03c	*memory=600m memory2=60m [default endtime=0.12]*

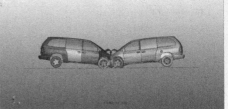

(a) Zoom In Perspective   (b) Side View Perspective

Fig. 1. NCAC car2car Model at time = 95 ms

simulates a frontal crash of two minivans (see Fig. 1) each at the speed of 35 mph and covers the first 120 ms of the crash. For quicker turnaround times we created an additional model that only covers the first 20 ms. We refer to these workloads in the course of this paper as *short run* (20 ms) and *long run* (120 ms) configuration.

We used LS-DYNA on 8 nodes with 24 processes each, as it does not scale very well horizontally and the selected configuration has proven to be efficient. The rest of the configuration is characterized as follows: All processes on one host share a working directory, that is located on a local SSD. The inter-process communication on each host is accomplished via shared memory and the inter-node communication is implemented by remote memory access via FDR Infiniband. We use a hybrid model using compatible MPI implementations on the host and in the container. This is the most common way to execute MPI containers. For this setup *mpirun* is called on the host to start the containers and afterwards connects to the MPI within the containers. This approach reduces the portability of the container image by the need for compatible MPI implementations [2], but is easier to implement. Furthermore, in our test case we are restricted to the MPI implementation required by LS-DYNA anyway. Upon using *mpirun* to start a containerized run, one container is being created for each process. The different jobs were directly started with *mpirun*, omitting batch system integration, but still maintaining an identical LS-DYNA invocation throughout the tests. We extended the shell environment with information regarding the LS-DYNA licence server, *Platform MPI* library path and MPI meta variables, and passed the updated environment into the container that starts the application. To obtain meaningful results, each LS-DYNA run was carried out six times with each configuration in every runtime environment.

Starting the containerized workload with Singularity was straightforward and required no additional parameters or adjustments: *mpirun mpp i=Caravan-V03c-2400k-main-shell16-120ms.k memory=600 memory2=60.*

Since Podman is not developed specifically for HPC workloads, we had to make some adjustments to the container execution call: interprocess communication and shared memory access require *pid* and *ipc* namespace sharing among the containers. The *net* namespace must also be shared between the containers

Table 3. LS-DYNA: Arithmetic mean + overhead

	Native	Singularity	Podman-runc	Podman-crun
Short Run	1097,67 s	1116,17 s	1154,83 s	1120,17 s
Long Run	6393,33 s	6521,17 s	6712,00 s	6521,83 s
Std Dev Short	2,42 (0,22%)	5,12 (0,46%)	4,54 (0,39%)	2,71 (0,24%)
Std Dev Long	12,64 (0,20%)	18,45 (0,28%)	9,78 (0,15%)	12,98 (0,20%)
Overhead Short	–	2,09%	5,63%	2,45%
Overhead Long	–	1,61%	4,58%	1,62%
Mean Overhead	–	1,85%	5,10%	2,04%

350   H. Gantikow et al.

and the host, so that MPI on the host can manage internode communication. These adjustments are achieved by appending the command line parameters – *net=host –pid=host –ipc=host*. Furthermore we used *–env=host* to pass the host environment into the container and *–volume* to bind mount a shared working directory and pass the Infiniband device into the containers.

The analysis of the results[1] (see Fig. 2 and Table 3) from the different runs show: **a)** All container runtimes introduce a certain amount of overhead compared to native execution of the simulation (1,85% - 5,10% for the arithmetic mean of short and long run). **b)** This overhead might be negligible for many workloads over the benefits of containers, as 2/3 runtimes only add 2,04% or less overhead. **c)** Although Singularity causes the least overhead, the differences of Podman in combination with crun as runtime are minor, especially for long runs of LS-DYNA (1,61% vs 1,62%). **d)** Compared to Singularity and crun the performance of runc is noticeably lower.

Discussions with Podman developers indicate that the slight difference of Podman with *crun* compared to Singularity might be related to Podman isolation mechanisms activated by default, such as a seccomp profile or more extensive use of namespaces.

4.2   Benchmarks

To ensure comparability with other evaluations and to get specifics on where the overhead described in Sect. 4.1 comes from, we performed some additional industry-standard benchmarks on a single node. We used sysbench and STREAM to measure CPU and memory performance. *Sysbench* is a multi-threaded benchmark tool that supports different tests to measure performance. The evaluation scope of this paper covers the CPU test. *STREAM* performs simple vector operations and measures the available memory bandwidth. It needs to

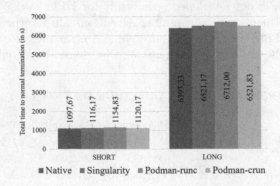

Fig. 2. LS-DYNA: Elapsed time to normal termination for car2car model

---

[1] Values used in Fig. 2 and Table 3 are based on *"elapsed time"* as returned by LS-DYNA and do not include startup and teardown periods, which are further discussed Sect. 5.

be compiled to use a data set that is significantly larger than the CPU caches. To reflect CPU cache size and the amount of memory available in our test systems we modified the preprocessor definition $STREAM\_ARRAY\_SIZE$ to increase the elements per array to 3 billion. When using large data sets, the resulting values are naturally dominated by the bandwidth between the CPU and the memory rather than the handling of cache misses [11]. Details concerning benchmark versions, configurations and execution calls are documented in Table 2.

Figure 3a shows the results of the sysbench CPU benchmark that were sampled over 25 runs with each runtime environment. The variation of the execution times reported by the benchmark reported is ≈300 ms, not counting rare outliers. Therefore, the results only differ by 0,4%, which does not lead to any direct conclusions, except that the results of all container-based runtime environments are virtually identical and there seems to be no added overhead by containerization.

Figure 3b illustrates the arithmetic mean of the performance data collected during five runs of the STREAM benchmark for STREAM's four memory-bound vector kernels in each runtime environment. Again, the measurements are within a very small window, the results differ by less than 1% and containerization does not seem to impose additional overhead in most cases. For this reason the y-axis of the graph starts at a higher value than 0 to illustrate the differences in more detail.

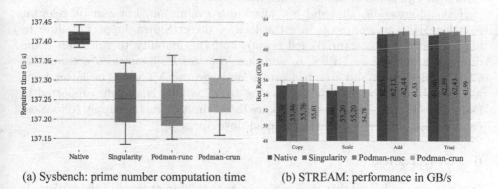

(a) Sysbench: prime number computation time   (b) STREAM: performance in GB/s

Fig. 3. Sysbench + STREAM results

The *Copy* part of STREAM, which only copies the elements of one vector into another ($C[i] = A[i]|i = 1 \dots n$ [11]), shows similarities to the results of the LS-DYNA benchmark. It can be concluded that the overhead of containerized LS-DYNA is at least partially due to memory intensive operations.

5   Limitations

During our evaluation we were affected by limitations of *rootless* Podman: Some Podman commands fail when no subordinate user IDs (subuid) and subordinate group IDs (subgid) are not configured, even though we did not make use of the feature since sub{u,g}ids cannot be used with MPI jobs, since shared memory access and shared file access is not supported.

When using network based authentication systems like LDAP, sub{u,g}ids cannot be configured easily, because the files /etc/sub{u,g}id are not utilized. According to Podman Developers the addition of new directives in the nss-witch.conf to support the *subuid* and *subgid* databases is work in progress. In rare cases when trying to start new containers for a job run, it failed with an error indicating that there already exists a container storage for the requested name, even though none by that name is known to Podman at the time.

We observed that startup and teardown costs of Podman containers are considerably greater than that of Singularity containers. We measured the following deltas when comparing the total *real* wall clock from the start of *mpirun* until successful termination and the *"elapsed time"* as reported by LS-DYNA: native: ≈ 3 s, Singularity: ≈ 5 s, Podman: ≈ 25 s. We are currently working with the developers to clarify the cause, but the most probable reason is due to the layered filesystem that needs to be set up and torn down again in combination with a ≈ 2 GB LS-DYNA image. Further investigations have shown that the measured delta is independent of the number of servers and thus the number of containers (one per physical core). Application runs with 8, 4 and 2 hosts (192, 96 and 48 containers) all resulted in a constant delta of ≈ 25 s.

Other limitations that did not affect our evaluation, but can be relevant to other HPC environments, are the lack of direct Slurm support, failure to bind to ports < 1024 (privileged ports), and the inability to run from home directories on NFS or GPFS. In addition, rootless Podman does not support CRIU's checkpoint and restore features and cgroups V1 yet. The latter issue will be solved in the long run by moving to V2, which is already supported in Fedora 31 for crun [14]. A comprehensive list of limitations that apply to rootless containers is maintained by the Podman developers [3].

6   Conclusion

Our evaluation showed that Podman, despite the different focus of the project, is essentially suitable for use in HPC. In terms of real-world workload performance, Podman performs on a similar level as Singularity, at least in conjunction with crun as runtime. Our results with industry-standard benchmarks are consistent with other studies on other runtimes, namely that containers generate only a small performance overhead, if at all. However, it is still higher with real-world workloads than with benchmarks. At the moment there are still some limitations in Podman, including issues that should be fixed in future versions, but which cause more problems in a production environment than in our evaluation environment. From an administrator's point of view, these include restrictions on the use of directory services such as LDAP, shortcoming of rootless containers in combination with distributed file systems and, from the user's point of view, a more complex integration with MPI workloads than Singularity. Nevertheless, Podman offers a number of advantageous features. These include the ability to create images with user privileges only, support for pods and stronger isolation. This makes it an interesting option for newer workloads and converged environments and bridges the gap between single-node container engines and Kubernetes. In future work we want to examine Podman specific features and explore the possibilities of OCI Hooks, especially for integration with workload managers.

References

1. Benedicic, L., Cruz, F.A., Madonna, A., Mariotti, K.: Sarus: highly scalable docker containers for HPC systems. In: Weiland, M., Juckeland, G., Alam, S., Jagode, H. (eds.) ISC High Performance 2019. LNCS, vol. 11887, pp. 46–60. Springer, Cham (2019). https://doi.org/10.1007/978-3-030-34356-9_5
2. Canon, R.S., Younge, A.: A case for portability and reproducibility of HPC containers, pp. 49–54. IEEE (2019). https://doi.org/10.1109/CANOPIE-HPC49598.2019.00012
3. Containers Organization: libpod: Shortcomings of Rootless Podman. https://github.com/containers/libpod/blob/master/rootless.md
4. Containers Organization: Podman—podman.io. https://podman.io/
5. Di Tommaso, P., Palumbo, E., Chatzou, M., Prieto, P., Heuer, M.L., Notredame, C.: The impact of Docker containers on the performance of genomic pipelines. PeerJ **3**, e1273 (2015). https://doi.org/10.7717/peerj.1273
6. Felter, W., Ferreira, A., Rajamony, R., Rubio, J.: An updated performance comparison of virtual machines and Linux containers. In: 2015 IEEE International Symposium on Performance Analysis of Systems and Software (ISPASS), pp. 171–172, March 2015. https://doi.org/10.1109/ISPASS.2015.7095802
7. Gantikow, H., Reich, C., Knahl, M., Clarke, N.: Providing security in container-based HPC runtime environments. In: Taufer, M., Mohr, B., Kunkel, J.M. (eds.) ISC High Performance 2016. LNCS, vol. 9945, pp. 685–695. Springer, Cham (2016). https://doi.org/10.1007/978-3-319-46079-6_48
8. Jacobsen, D.M., Canon, R.S.: Contain This, Unleashing Docker for HPC. Cray User Group 2015, p. 14 (2015). https://www.nersc.gov/assets/Uploads/cug2015udi.pdf
9. Kovács, Á.: Comparison of different Linux containers. In: 2017 40th International Conference on Telecommunications and Signal Processing (TSP), pp. 47–51. IEEE (2017). https://doi.org/10.1109/TSP.2017.8075934
10. Kurtzer, G.M., Sochat, V., Bauer, M.W.: Singularity: scientific containers for mobility of compute. PLOS ONE **12**(5), 1–20 (2017). https://doi.org/10.1371/journal.pone.0177459
11. McCalpin, J.D.: Memory bandwidth and machine balance in current high performance computers. IEEE Computer Society Technical Committee on Computer Architecture (TCCA) Newsletter (May), 19–25 (1995)
12. Priedhorsky, R., Randles, T.: Charliecloud: unprivileged containers for user-defined software stacks in HPC. In: Proceedings of the International Conference for High Performance Computing, Networking, Storage and Analysis, SC 2017, Association for Computing Machinery, New York (2017). https://doi.org/10.1145/3126908.3126925
13. Reber, A.: Podman in HPC environments. https://podman.io/blogs/2019/09/26/podman-in-hpc.html

14. Suda, A.: The current adoption status of cgroup v2 in containers. https://medium.com/nttlabs/cgroup-v2-596d035be4d7
15. Torrez, A., Randles, T., Priedhorsky, R.: HPC container runtimes have minimal or no performance impact, pp. 37–42. IEEE (2019). https://doi.org/10.1109/CANOPIE-HPC49598.2019.00010
16. Wang, Y., Evans, R.T., Huang, L.: Performant container support for HPC applications. In: ACM International Conference Proceeding Series (2019). https://doi.org/10.1145/3332186.3332226
17. Watada, J., Roy, A., Kadikar, R., Pham, H., Xu, B.: Emerging trends, techniques and open issues of containerization: a review. IEEE Access **7**, 152443–152472 (2019). https://doi.org/10.1109/ACCESS.2019.2945930
18. Younge, A.J., Pedretti, K., Grant, R.E., Brightwell, R.: A tale of two·systems: using containers to deploy HPC applications on supercomputers and clouds. In: Proceedings of the International Conference on Cloud Computing Technology and Science, CloudCom (2017). https://doi.org/10.1109/CloudCom.2017.40
19. Zhang, Q., Liu, L., Pu, C., Dou, Q., Wu, L., Zhou, W.: A comparative study of containers and virtual machines in big data environment. In: IEEE International Conference on Cloud Computing, CLOUD, vol. 2018-July, pp. 178–185 (2018). https://doi.org/10.1109/CLOUD.2018.00030

Bioinformatics Application with Kubeflow for Batch Processing in Clouds

David Yu Yuan(✉) ⑩ and Tony Wildish ⑩

Technology and Science Integration, European Bioinformatics Institute,
European Molecular Biology Laboratory, Hinxton, UK
davidyuan@ebi.ac.uk
https://www.ebi.ac.uk/

Abstract. Bioinformatics pipelines make extensive use of HPC batch processing. The rapid growth of data volumes and computational complexity, especially for modern applications such as machine learning algorithms, imposes significant challenges to local HPC facilities. Many attempts have been made to burst HPC batch processing into clouds with virtual machines. They all suffer from some common issues, for example: very high overhead, slow to scale up and slow to scale down, and nearly impossible to be cloud-agnostic.

We have successfully deployed and run several pipelines on Kubernetes in OpenStack, Google Cloud Platform and Amazon Web Services. In particular, we use Kubeflow on top of Kubernetes for more sophisticated job scheduling, workflow management, and first class support for machine learning. We choose Kubeflow/Kubernetes to avoid the overhead of provisioning of virtual machines, to achieve rapid scaling with containers, and to be truly cloud-agnostic in all cloud environments.

Kubeflow on Kubernetes also creates some new challenges in deployment, data access, performance monitoring, etc. We will discuss the details of these challenges and provide our solutions. We will demonstrate how our solutions work across all three very different clouds for both classical pipelines and new ones for machine learning.

Keywords: Kubernetes · Kubeflow · Workflow · Container orchestration · Deployment · Clouds · Data management · Monitoring · OpenStack · Google Cloud Platform · Amazon Web Services

1 Introduction

Bioinformatics pipelines make extensive use of HPC batch processing farms. The data size is growing exponentially in Terabyte to Petabyte range. The computational complexity is also growing rapidly with job duration reaching weeks to months. HPC facilities can no longer satisfy these rapidly growing requirements. With the modern applications of machine learning algorithms, GPUs become

© The Author(s) 2020
H. Jagode et al. (Eds.): ISC High Performance 2020 Workshops, LNCS 12321, pp. 355–367, 2020.
https://doi.org/10.1007/978-3-030-59851-8_24

critical for batch processing, but long wait times for GPU batch queues are common. With rapidly changing GPU models, high unit price and long procurement cycles, it is impossible to run some pipelines simply due to the lack of specific GPU models on premises.

HPC-in-the-cloud solutions provide VM-based workflow management. Open source tools like Cluster-in-the-Cloud are more portable, but also need lots of maintenance. In general, batch clusters are complex to configure for general users, and don't take good advantage of cloud-native capability. We tried implementations on different clouds: Google Cloud Platform, Microsoft Azure and Oracle Cloud. The solutions are very cloud-specific, and thus unportable.

Container and its orchestration engine Kubernetes is the obvious choice to overcome issues with VM-based batch solutions in clouds. The basic Kubernetes job framework is insufficient for Bioinformatics pipelines. It is more of a framework for frameworks. Kubeflow [1] is a comprehensive and cloud-agnostic workflow engine on Kubernetes. It is designed for machine learning workflows but generic enough to run any workflow on Kubernetes in a simple, portable and scalable fashion.

In this article, we are to deploy Kubernetes and Kubeflow to run two pipelines: one for classic pipeline and the other for machine learning, targeting three clouds: a private cloud based on OpenStack (OSK), and two public clouds of Google Cloud Platform (GCP) and Amazon Web Services (AWS). Although Kubernetes has become the de facto standard on almost all major clouds, there are also some new challenges in data access, performance monitoring, and GPU etc. We will discuss the details of these challenges and our solutions. We will demonstrate how our solutions work across all three very different clouds for both classical pipelines and new ones for machine learning.

2   Method

Docker and Kubernetes have become the de facto standard for container and container orchestration. All major cloud providers and operating systems provide first class support for them. In our previous investigation, we have confirmed that Bioinformatics pipelines can be migrated from HPC into public clouds with ease. In addition, the resulting Kubernetes clusters are almost identical in Google, Amazon and Microsoft [2]. Together, Docker and Kubernetes become universal platforms for Infrastructure-as-a-Service (IaaS) for Bioinformatics pipelines and other workloads.

Kubernetes has a job framework built into its APIs [3]. However, it is in its infancy and incapable to support complex pipelines for Bioinformatics. Google, together with many other major cloud vendors, have just started a new workflow engine, Kubeflow, on Kubernetes to make ML simple, portable and scalable. Kubeflow shows promise as a platform to manage the workflows of Bioinformatics pipelines with efficiency, scalability and portability. In this section, we will focus on the challenges, temporary and long term, and our solutions to address them.

2.1   Deployment

We have Kubernetes clusters for HPC on three clouds: OSK, GCP and AWS. We run Rancher Kubernetes Engine (RKE) [4] on OSK. Public clouds have their Kubernetes engines built in: GKE on GCP and EKS on AWS. Kubernetes provides a good solution for computing. It is relatively weak on integration with storage and network.

We then deployed Kubeflow for batch processing. There are two categories of deployment for Kubeflow:

1. Cloud-agnostic: the deployment scripts are maintained by the open source community or third party, for example the first two scripts in the table [5]. They require the Kubernetes cluster created first.
2. Cloud-specific: the deployment scripts are maintained by cloud providers such as GCP, AWS, IBM and OpenShift. Microsoft is using the community maintained script at present.

We have been using both cloud-agnostic and cloud-specific scripts. The cloud-agnostic script is completely portable. We are able to deploy Kubeflow on Open-Stack, GCP and AWS without modification. This would reduce our operational cost in production and the implementation of the hybrid cloud strategy. The cloud-specific script provides tight integration with the underlying cloud infrastructure. The benefit to end users is minimal at this point. Therefore, we have chosen the cloud-agnostic script (kfctl_istio_dex.v1.0.0.yaml) [6] for all of our three clouds. It provides a consistent mechanism for authentication and authorization [7] as shown in Fig. 1.

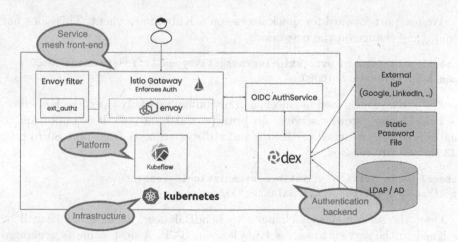

Fig. 1. Multi-user, auth-enabled Kubeflow was modified from Kubeflow documentation (https://www.kubeflow.org/docs/started/k8s/kfctl-istio-dex/) under CC BY 4.0 license.

Storage. Cloud providers only support a very small subset of Volume Plugins, with few overlaps. They all support ReadWriteOnce mode. About 60% of them support ReadOnlyMany. Only 30% of them support the ReadWriteMany model [8]. Bioinformatics pipelines almost always assume local access to POSIX-like file systems for both read and write, so we use an NFS persistent volume as a workaround to make our pipelines cloud-agnostic.

NFS has many limitations in security, performance, scalability and, to a certain extent, data integrity. We only use it to pass a small amount of intermediate data between tasks in the same pipeline. For temporary files within a task, we use the default Storage Classes to create Persistent Volumes. The Volume Plugins for the default Storage Classes always support ReadWriteOnce. The Persistent Volume Claims (PVCs) always use the default Storage Classes if omitted. This makes the PVC manifest syntactically identical in all the clouds to create temporary storage for reading and writing within a task. We mount emptyDir in a pod for caching. If cache is small, we set emptyDir.medium field to "Memory" for fast access as the tmpfs mounted is a RAM-backed filesystem.

Networking. The integration between the internal and external networks of a Kubernetes cluster is another difficulty for users. We use three options to integrate the internal networks created by Kubeflow with the outside world: port-forward, load balancer and Ingress.

Kubeflow creates Istio ingress gateway service with NodePort by default, for example:

```
NAME              TYPE        CLUSTER-IP      EXTERNAL-IP   PORT(S)                                            AGE
istio-ingressgateway NodePort  10.43.184.114   <none>        15020:30024/TCP,80:31380/TCP,443:31390/TCP,31400:31400/TCP,
15029:30610/TCP,15030:30412/TCP,15031:32070/TCP,15032:32526/TCP,15443:30403/TCP   12d
```

We use port-forward for quick access on a Kubernetes client. This does not require any change on the networking.

```
kubectl port-forward svc/istio-ingressgateway -n istio-system 8080:80 &
open http://localhost:8080
```

For public clouds, load balancers can be configured easily to expose Kubeflow. As Istio ingress gateway services on both ports 80 and 443, it is important to enable SSL with a signed certificate and redirect requests from port 80 to port 443 for security reasons.

```
kubectl patch service -n istio-system istio-ingressgateway \
-p '{"spec": {"type": "LoadBalancer"}}'
```

Once the service type is changed to LoadBalancer, an external IP will be assigned to the service to access Kubeflow on GCP. A host name is generated on AWS as well.

```
NAME              TYPE          CLUSTER-IP    EXTERNAL-IP     PORT(S)                                            AGE
istio-ingressgateway LoadBalancer 10.32.7.82   35.190.144.146   15020:31092/TCP,80:31380/TCP,443:31390/TCP,31400:31400/TCP,
15029:31624/TCP,15030:31175/TCP,15031:30963/TCP,15032:30674/TCP,15443:30189/TCP   6d11h
```

There is no load balancer configured for RKE in our private OSK cloud at present. We assign a floating IP to the Kubernetes cluster. We then configure the ingress control to access Kubeflow via the floating IP.

2.2 Data Access

The pipelines usually have very little control over the storage for input and output. Most of Bioinformatics pipelines assume local access to POSIX-like file systems for simplicity. Kubeflow and its orchestrator Kubernetes naturally assume that pipelines use cloud-native storage as the data sources. Persistent Volumes need to be mounted as temporary storage for input and output.

We use commands (e.g., curl, wget, scp etc.) or any special clients, such as Globus or Aspera to download or upload files in the pipelines. This approach has its obvious drawbacks. This biggest issue is scalability. Data files have to be moved in batch mode and then processed. They often require large amounts of storage from Terabytes to Petabytes. As we have discussed before, the only Persistent Volume for multiple clouds is NFS. Accessing input and output data becomes moving many files into and out of NFS server for seemingly local access is very inefficient. It is impractical to move Terabytes to Petabytes of data to persistent volumes before computing.

POSIX-like File System for Bioinformatics Applications. We use Onedata [9] to fill the functionality gap. Onedata presents a globally federated POSIX VFS built out of local storage in Ceph, S3, NFS, Lustre, and other storage backends. There are several limitations:

1. Onedata does not support Kubernetes. There is no storage provisioner for Onedata.
2. There is only n-1 version compatibility between its client and server. Short release cycle essentially eliminates backward compatibility in practice.
3. Both client and server require root privilege.

The only viable option to bypass all the limitations above is to create Docker images with both OneClient and a Bioinformatics application. There are two options to create such merged Docker images:

1. Starting with *onedata/oneclient* : $<version\_tag>$ as the base image, install a Bioinformatics application. Sometimes, it is necessary to use the multi-staged build.
2. Building an image on a Docker server supporting conda, install OneClient with exactly the version as OneProvider.

To merge Samtools, we simply installed it into a given OneClient image which is fairly standard. To merge the latest version of Freebayes with OneClient, we use a two-staged build. The binaries of bamleftalign and freebayes are built from the source in a Python image first. They are then copied into OneClient image. A Dockerfile is available in the repository [10].

The second option of installing OneClient can be tricky. OneClient requires specific versions of libraries. Its installer does not do a good job to ensure that the prerequisite is met correctly.

The utility oneclient is called to mount a POSIX VFS in the container. The Bioinformatics tools will access remote files as if from a local file system as input for just-in-time data ingestion and as output for transparent write-through.

S3-Like Cloud Storage. S3 has firmly established its dominance as a popular cloud storage. We first tried Tensorflow API to download and upload files in S3 buckets as we were using Tensorflow/Keras in our machine learning pipeline, but switched to AWS CLI for S3 based on the Python library Boto 3 for better performance, scalability and resource consumption.

Neither AWS CLI nor Boto 3 provides official Docker images. We have created a custom image. A default Persistent Volume is used as a cache for input and output. We do not accumulate the files on the temporary storage. We download them only when they are needed, and upload them as soon as they are generated. In the pipelines, we use Kubeflow sidecar or a separate component for file transfer in parallel.

As shown in a sidecar snippet in [11], we extend the custom AWS CLI image with some simple shell scripts (`image='davidyuyuan/aws:1000g'`). We then use Kubeflow sidecar API to call our scripts for cloud storage. Both the sidecar and separate components are useful depending on whether we want to transfer files just for a single operation or shared by multiple parallel operations. They enable the classic pipelines to access cloud storage a little easier.

2.3   Monitoring

Logging and telemetry are weak in clouds, including major public clouds. Most of the existing solutions are designed for virtual machines instead of containers (Docker), still less for container orchestration (e.g., Kubernetes) and much less for workloads (e.g., Kubeflow and pipelines on it). Our attempt to establish a cloud-agnostic solution or HPC batch processing via container orchestration adds one more challenge.

We have identified a single tool for both logging and telemetry for both VMs and Kubernetes including Kubeflow and Bioinformatics pipelines on all three clouds. Elasticsearch [12] has been known to the Open Source community for a long time. It is undeniably complex to create a traditional deployment of Elasticsearch with high availability, performance and scalability. We are using the SaaS solution and also investigating the feasibility to run Elasticsearch on Kubernetes [13]. Our goal is to let Kubernetes handle high availability, performance and scalability for a simple deployment. The details of the investigation is beyond the scope of this article. We will focus on how we make use of the SaaS solution for the pipelines on Kubeflow.

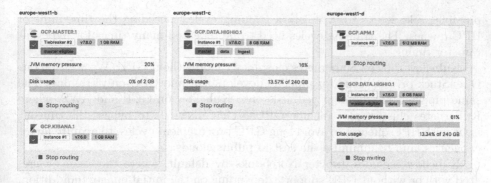

Fig. 2. Deployment architecture of an Elasticsearch instance.

At minimum, Elasticsearch consists of Kibana, Elasticsearch, Logstash or Beats. As shown in Fig. 2, our SaaS instance contains the components on the server side: Elasticsearch and Kibana. We use Beats (Filebeat and Metricbeat) on the client side for logging and telemetry. Beats is simple to use with lower overhead compared with Logstash. DaemonSet is used to run containers (e.g., `docker.elastic.co/beats/metricbeat:7.6.0`) in Kubernetes clusters, instead of classic OS-specific installation packages for VMs.

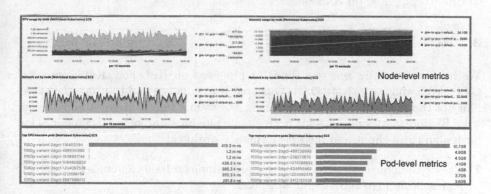

Fig. 3. Monitoring multiple Kubernetes clusters with Elasticsearch.

This allows us to monitor clusters in different clouds in a single pane of glass, for example public GCP and private OSK in Fig. 3. Together with Filebeat container (`docker.elastic.co/beats/filebeat:7.6.0`), we are able to monitor both logging and telemetry of Kubernetes including Kubeflow and Bioinformatics pipelines in all three clouds.

2.4 Using GPUs with Kubeflow

Machine Learning (ML) has wide applications in Bioinformatics, for example, genomic sequence assembly, literature analysis and image processing. Some ML pipelines take weeks to complete a training cycle, exceeding the time-limit of HPC queues. The training cycles need to be repeated many times for hyperparameter tuning.

Kubeflow runs on Kubernetes clusters with or without GPU. We position our OpenStack private cloud for pipeline development and CPU-only training. The same pipelines can be deployed as-is onto Kubeflow on GCP and AWS, where Kubernetes clusters may include GPUs. This allows us to bypass the timeout issue with HPC queues, to avoid long GPU procurement cycles, to acquire larger capacities, and to minimise the cost in public clouds.

Kubeflow includes Jupyter Notebooks by default, where they can be created with or without GPU support, depending on the initial image. In addition, Kubeflow pipeline DSL provides very handy APIs to consume GPU or TPU in a Python package:

```
kfp.dsl.ContainerOp.apply(gcp.use_tpu())
kfp.dsl.ContainerOp.set_gpu_limit()
```

GCP and AWS provide different GPU models. They both support GPU in passthrough mode for bare metal performance. However, GCP provides separate node pools for CPUs and GPUs as well as multiple GPU pools for different GPU models in the same Kubernetes cluster. This allows us to create an ideal platform to run ML pipelines on Kubeflow.

3   Result

We have successfully run two types of pipelines on Kubeflow/Kubernetes on GCP, AWS and our private OSK. Our goal is to enhance and to prove the capability of the platform for Bioinformatics. We want to make it suitable for large scale Bioinformatics research for both classic pipelines and new ML pipelines for both high throughput and high performance workloads.

1. Classic Bioinformatics pipelines - variant calling on 1000 Genomes Project [14] representing high throughput workload
2. Machine Learning pipelines - image classification on cardiomyocytes from Image Data Repository [15] representing high performance workload

3.1   Classic Bioinformatics Pipelines

We have created a brand new pipeline, consisting of two classical tools for genomics: Samtools and Freebayes. Freebayes are to be run in parallel, one set of pods per chromosome. The output VCFs from Freebayes are cached on a shared disk, and then uploaded to an S3 bucket as soon as they arrive at the staging area (Fig. 4).

The data sources and the methods to access them are completely unchanged when we run the pipeline on GCP, AWS or the private OSK clouds:

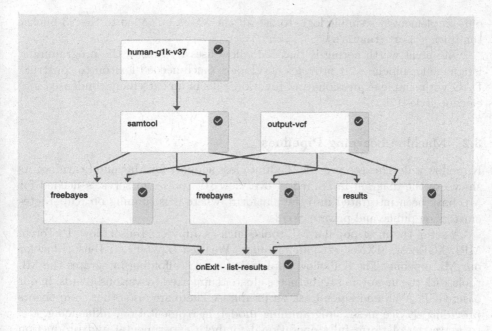

Fig. 4. Example of a simplified classic bioinformatic workflow.

1. Human reference genome is downloaded from an FTP server at EBI [16]. It then gets preprocessed by Samtools to generate fasta files and their indices.
2. Queries or a list of file names of the 1046 genomes is stored in an S3 bucket. It gets downloaded by a sidecar as discussed above. Freebayes is to loop through the list for each genome for each region in batches in parallel.
3. The actual alignments of the 1046 genomes are accessed with Onedata for just-in-time data ingestion from a storage volume at EBI. We have discussed details on how to integrate Onedata with Kubernetes above.

A complete run of 1046 genomes on all 26 regions takes several weeks. We usually scale down to three fastest regions ('GL000207.1', 'MT', 'Y') for a 40-hour-run (Fig. 5). The exit handler gets invoked by Kubeflow where we have

```
C02XD1G9JGH7:.kube davidyuan$ kubectl get po -n kubeflow | grep 1000g
1000g-variant-2qrbq-1034027386          0/1     Completed   0       40h
1000g-variant-2qrbq-1063933343          0/1     Completed   0       40h
1000g-variant-2qrbq-1634016030          0/2     Completed   0       40h
1000g-variant-2qrbq-2080743279          0/2     Completed   0       4m13s
1000g-variant-2qrbq-3651124281          0/2     Completed   0       40h
1000g-variant-2qrbq-3744735513          0/2     Completed   0       40h
1000g-variant-2qrbq-3954814010          0/2     Completed   0       40h
1000g-variant-2qrbq-535586066           0/3     Completed   0       40h
C02XD1G9JGH7:.kube davidyuan$
```

Fig. 5. Pods for the pipeline scale up and down efficiently as needed.

only implemented a simple logic to list all the VCFs uploaded to the S3 bucket (`onExit - list-results`).

One point worth noting is that Kubeflow uses Python as the programming language for pipelines. It provides developers much needed lexicon to construct DAG with simple expressions and function calls in an extremely condensed and elegant style [17].

3.2   Machine Learning Pipelines

Kubeflow is designed to provide the first class support for Machine Learning. As shown in the diagram in Kubeflow overview [1], tools and services needed for ML have been integrated into the platform, where it is running on Kubernetes clusters on public and private clouds.

A set of the most popular ML tools, such as Jupyter, TensorFlow, PyTorch, MPI, XGBoost, MXNet, etc., are included. We used Jupyter and TensorFlow for our ML pipeline. The Kubeflow applications and scaffolding integrates the ML tools with the underlying Kubernetes cluster supported by various clouds, in our case: GCP, AWS and OpenStack on premises. There are also other components providing service mesh, programming model, instrumentation, influencing, etc. to make the platform fully operational for both experimental and production phases.

We have created a notebook for image classification. The images are whole slides of cardiomyocytes published in 2018 [18]. The public data is stored in the IDR hosted by EBI. We have decided to use our Kubeflow on GCP with GPU support to speed up the model training for high performance. A notebook server is created with an Docker image with Tensorflow 2.1.0 and GPU support accordingly.

We use the latest OMERO 5.6.0 JSON API [19] to download the images. There is a limit on the IDR server of maximum downloads of 1000 images, which gives us 1978 images to work with, comparable to the original datasets of 2277 usable images. This is on the smaller side for CNN training and validation. The image quality and annotation are good so it gives us satisfying results (Fig. 6).

The training and validation with GPU are surprisingly fast with 4s for each epoch on the original images and 8 s for augmented images. With the per second billing on both GCP and AWS together with dynamic resource allocation on Kubeflow, the cost to run ML pipelines with GPUs is very low. This fully cloud-native and cloud-agnostic approach provides advantages not only over HPC on premises but also over HPC-in-the-cloud, where GPUs still have to be reserved for the lifecycle of the job, whether they are used well or not.

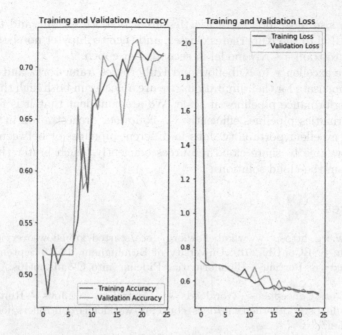

Fig. 6. Training and validation of a CNN model with cardiomyocytes images on Kubeflow

4   Conclusion

We have successfully run pipelines on Kubernetes in OpenStack, Google Cloud Platform and Amazon Web Services, in particular, on Kubeflow with more sophisticated job scheduling, workflow management, and first class support to machine learning. We choose Kubeflow/Kubernetes to avoid the overhead of provisioning of virtual machines, to achieve rapid scaling with containers, and to be truly cloud-agnostic in all three cloud environments.

We have chosen two very typical pipelines in Bioinformatics: one for genomic sequence analysis and the other for image classification; one for classic tools and the other for modern machine learning; one for high throughput and the other for high performance; one for classic pipeline and the other for Jupyter notebook. With the successful deployment of these two pipelines, we can conclude confidently that Kubeflow can satisfy complex requirements by Bioinformatics.

Kubeflow and Kubernetes have also introduced interesting challenges. We have systematically analysed and addressed various aspects in deployment, storage and networking. We have identified and implemented methods to access data for input and output in CLI and Python APIs. We have successfully proposed and implemented a creative solution to combine the strength of Onedata and Docker for the just-in-time data ingestion as well as transparent write-through. For S3 storage, we have created a custom AWS CLI image and run the container as either a sidecar or a separate operation for parallel operations to transfer objects. We also have integrated Elasticsearch for both logging and telemetry. By adding GPU to the Kubernetes cluster, and then to Jupyter notebook server, we are able to train a CNN model in seconds per epoch.

With the excellence in Kubeflow and Kubernetes frameworks and our solutions to compensate for their limitations, we are able to run both high throughput and high performance pipelines at scale. We are confident that it is feasible to run Bioinformatics pipelines efficiently via container orchestration in all major clouds with excellent portability. Jobs in different pipelines or between different runs are now able to share cloud resources efficiently, much better than traditional HPC-in-the-cloud solutions.

References

1. Kubeflow.org. https://www.kubeflow.org/docs/started/kubeflow-overview/
2. Yuan, D.: RSEConUK 2019, University of Birmingham, 17–19 September 2019, Case Study of Porting a Bioinformatics Pipeline into Clouds. https://sched.co/QSRc
3. Kubernetes, Concepts → Workloads → Controllers → Jobs - Run to Completion. https://kubernetes.io/docs/concepts/workloads/controllers/jobs-run-to-completion/
4. Overview of RKE. https://rancher.com/docs/rke/latest/en/
5. Installing Kubeflow. https://www.kubeflow.org/docs/started/getting-started/
6. Cloud-agnostic Kubeflow deployment. https://raw.githubusercontent.com/kubeflow/manifests/v1.0-branch/kfdef/kfctl_istio_dex.v1.0.0.yaml
7. Authentication with Istio + Dex. https://journal.arrikto.com/kubeflow-authentication-with-istio-dex-5eafdfac4782
8. Storage volume. https://kubernetes.io/docs/concepts/storage/persistent-volumes/#access-modes
9. Onedata. https://onedata.org/#/home
10. Two-staged build. https://gitlab.ebi.ac.uk/TSI/kubeflow/blob/master/pipelines/1000g/freebayes/Dockerfile
11. Function samtools_op. https://gitlab.ebi.ac.uk/TSI/kubeflow/-/blob/1.0.1/pipelines/1000g/1000g.py
12. Elasticsearch. https://www.elastic.co/elasticsearch
13. Elastic Cloud on Kubernetes. https://www.elastic.co/downloads/elastic-cloud-kubernetes
14. Data - 1000 Genomes Project. https://www.internationalgenome.org/data/
15. IDR: Image Data Repository. https://idr.openmicroscopy.org/webclient/?show=project-402
16. Human Reference Genome, v37. ftp://ftp.1000genomes.ebi.ac.uk/vol1/ftp/technical/reference/human_g1k_v37.fasta.gz
17. Kubeflow pipeline APIs. https://kubeflow-pipelines.readthedocs.io/en/stable/index.html
18. Nirschl, J.J., et al.: A deep-learning classifier identifies patients with clinical heart failure using whole-slide images of H&E tissue. https://www.ncbi.nlm.nih.gov/pmc/articles/PMC5882098/
19. OMERO 5.6.0 JSON API. https://docs.openmicroscopy.org/omero/5.6.0/developers/json-api.html

Converging HPC, Big Data and Cloud Technologies for Precision Agriculture Data Analytics on Supercomputers

Yiannis Georgiou[1]([✉]), Naweiluo Zhou[2], Li Zhong[2], Dennis Hoppe[2],
Marcin Pospieszny[3], Nikela Papadopoulou[4], Kostis Nikas[4],
Orestis Lagkas Nikolos[4], Pavlos Kranas[5], Sophia Karagiorgou[6],
Eric Pascolo[7], Michael Mercier[1], and Pedro Velho[1]

[1] Ryax Technologies, Saint-Fons, France
{yiannis.georgiou,michael.mercier,pedro.velho}@ryax.tech
[2] HLRS, Stuttgart, Germany
{naweiluo.zhou,li.zhong,dennis.hoppe}@hlrs.de
[3] PSNC, Poznań, Poland
marcin.pospieszny@man.poznan.pl
[4] ICCS, Athens, Greece
{papadopoulou,nikas,nikolos}@cslab.ece.ntua.gr
[5] Leanxscale, Madrid, Spain
kranas@leanxscale.com
[6] Ubitech, Athens, Greece
karagiorgou@ubitech.eu
[7] CINECA, Casalecchio di Reno, Italy
eric.pascolo@cineca.it

Abstract. The convergence of HPC and Big Data along with the influence of Cloud are playing an important role in the democratization of HPC. The increasing needs of Data Analytics in computational power has added new fields of interest for the HPC facilities but also new problematics such as interoperability with Cloud and ease of use. Besides the typical HPC applications, these infrastructures are now asked to handle more complex workflows combining Machine Learning, Big Data and HPC. This brings challenges on the resource management, scheduling and environment deployment layers. Hence, enhancements are needed to allow multiple frameworks to be deployed under common system management while providing the right abstraction to facilitate adoption.

This paper presents the architecture adopted for the parallel and distributed execution management software stack of Cybele EU funded project which is put in place on production HPC centers to execute hybrid data analytics workflows in the context of precision agriculture and livestock farming applications. The design is based on: Kubernetes as a higher level orchestrator of Big Data components, hybrid workflows and a common interface to submit HPC or Big Data jobs; Slurm or Torque for HPC resource management; and Singularity containerization platform for the dynamic deployment of the different Data Analytics frameworks on HPC. The paper showcases precision agriculture

H. Jagode et al. (Eds.): ISC High Performance 2020 Workshops, LNCS 12321, pp. 368–379, 2020.
https://doi.org/10.1007/978-3-030-59851-8_25

workflows being executed upon the architecture and provides some initial performance evaluation results and insights for the whole prototype design.

1   Introduction

High Performance Computing has been traditionally used for scientific computing to solve complex problems which require extreme amounts of computation. HPC is designed with performance as principal focus, leveraging on supercomputers along with parallel and distributed processing techniques. The rise of Big Data came with an increasing adoption of data analytics and Artificial Intelligence in modern applications that make use of data-driven models and analysis engines to facilitate the extraction of valuable insights. Big Data Analytics utilize Cloud data-centers which provide elastic environments based on commodity hardware and adapted software; while instead of performance they focus on flexibility and programming simplicity. Containerization, based on Docker, has greatly improved the productivity and simplicity of Cloud technologies; and together with the advanced orchestration, introduced through systems such as Kubernetes, enabled the adoption of Big Data software by a large community.

Today, Big Data Analytics are becoming more compute-intensive, mainly due to AI and in particular Deep Learning, while needing extremely-fast knowledge extraction for rapid and accurate decisions. The convergence of HPC and Big Data, especially regarding systems software, resource management and programming, is an important concern which appears as top research objective in the Strategic Research Agenda (SRA4) of HPC in Europe as published by ETP4HPC [1].

Big Data analytics are applied extensively, under the digitalization efforts, in various industries such as pharmaceutics, construction, automotive but also agriculture and farming. Supercomputers and HPC can be of great benefit to Big Data Applications since large datasets can be processed in timely manner. But the steep learning curve of HPC systems software and parallel programming techniques along with the rigid environment deployment and resource management remain an important obstacle towards the usage of HPC for Big Data analytics. In addition, the usage of classic Cloud and Big Data tools for containerization and orchestration cannot be applied directly on the HPC systems because of security and performance drawbacks. Hence workflows mixing HPC and Big Data executions cannot be yet combined intelligently using off-the-shelf software.

CYBELE [2] is an EU funded project which aims to provide solutions to the above issues. It brings a prototype architecture combining HPC and Big Data hardware and software tools to enable the deployment of data analytics workflows, in the context of precision agriculture and livestock farming. CYBELE proposes a suite of Cloud-level tools combined with Big Data and HPC systems software and adapted techniques to bring the right abstractions to data scientists with non-HPC systems expertise to optimally leverage HPC platforms.

CYBELE disposes four production HPC platforms across Europe upon which a complete set of demonstrators[1] will be rolled-out, covering 9 topics in total: from protein-content prediction in organic soya yields, to climate smart predictive models, to autonomous robotic systems, to crop yield forecasting, down to sustainable livestock production, aquaculture and open sea fishing.

This paper focuses on the systems software layer and in particular on the basic building blocks of the parallel and distributed execution management tools used in CYBELE. However, the described tools and techniques can be used in any case where Big Data Analytics need to be executed on HPC platforms. We consider an architecture featuring one Big Data partition composed of VMs managed by Kubernetes, using a mix of Docker and Singularity runtimes for containerization, along with one HPC partition, as the typical HPC production system, composed of baremetal machines managed by Slurm or Torque, using only Singularity containerization. The contributions of this paper are the following:

– Meta-scheduling and resource abstraction techniques enabling first the execution of Big Data Analytics as batch jobs on Slurm or Torque managed HPC partitions, through a Kubernetes micro-service submission based on singularity containers and wlm-operator software adapted for multi-user support; and second the possibility to deploy Big Data Analytics and Cloud-level tools such as workflow managers and databases on the VMs of the Big Data partitions, using the typical Kubernetes API. The deployed Cloud-level tools will provide the needed abstractions to non-HPC experts for the Data Analytics execution on the underlying HPC-Big Data hybrid system.
– An Environment deployment tool for the creation of customizable environments based on singularity containerization and a specialized repository with pre-built images featuring Big Data and AI frameworks (such as Pytorch, Tensorflow and Horovod) for specific HPC resources (such as GPUs and Infiniband).

The reminder of the paper goes as follows: Sect. 2 provides the related work, Sect. 3 describes the Meta-scheduling and resource abstraction techniques, Sect. 4 presents the Environment Deployment tool, Sect. 5 the validation using precision agriculture data analytics and finally Sect. 6 the Conclusions and Future Works.

2   Related Work

2.1   Resource Management and Orchestration

Older state-of-the-art HPC resource managers such as Slurm [12] and Torque do not provide integrated support for environment provisioning and hence no orchestration [4] is feasible. However, newer resource managers such as Mesos[2]

---

[1] https://www.cybele-project.eu/demonstrators.
[2] https://github.com/apache/mesos.

and Kubernetes[3] enable the deployment of containers and allow the applications' lifecycle management. Another widely used orchestrator with limited capabilities but simplicity in usage is Docker Swarm[4]. Kubernetes [5] is the de-facto standard for Cloud and Big Data orchestration, it has a rapidly growing community and ecosystem with plenty of platforms being developed upon it. Kubernetes simplifies the deployment and management of containerized applications. It is based on a highly modular architecture which abstracts the underlying infrastructure and allows internal customizations such as deployment of different software defined networking or storage solutions. It supports various Big Data frameworks such as Hadoop MapReduce, Spark and Kafka and has a powerful set of tools to express the application lifecycle considering parameterized redeployment in case of failures, auto-scaling, state management, etc. Furthermore, it provides advanced scheduling capabilities and the possibility to express different schedulers per job.

2.2   Containerization in HPC

Containers have recently started to be applied on HPC clusters. HPC applications are hardware specific, and their applications are often specifically optimized for the nodes. Considering that performance is the focus for HPC applications, it poses the key question for massive usage of containerized applications on HPC cluster [6–8]. Nevertheless, the flexibility of containerization principles and the productivity advantages makes them very interesting for HPC. Singularity[5] [13] is a technology that bears all the benefits of Bring-Your-Own-Environment, composability and portability, also matching the security requirements in HPC environments. While Docker [11] is the popular approach for containerization in cloud environments, it poses security implications when it comes to HPC centers: Docker allows root user operation, which can lead to privilege escalation. In addition, Docker containers rely on Docker daemon, which requires root access. Rootless mode for the Docker daemon is still experimental. On the other hand, Singularity is a container technology that has been designed for use on HPC systems [14]. Singularity containers do not rely on a daemon for execution and are executed as child processes. Moreover, the user within a Singularity container is the same user as the user of the host system who executes the container, with the same privileges, thus preventing privilege escalation. Regarding the transparent use of resources, Singularity also provides native support for MPI and GPUs. Udocker[6] is another basic user tool (written in Python) to execute simple Docker containers in user space without requiring root privileges.

---

[3] https://github.com/kubernetes/kubernetes.
[4] https://github.com/docker/classicswarm.
[5] https://github.com/sylabs/singularity.
[6] https://github.com/indigo-dc/udocker.

3   Orchestration and Resources Abstraction in HPC

For the execution of Data Analytics on supercomputers we propose a combination of Big Data, HPC and Cloud tools. The meta-scheduling and orchestration tasks are based upon Kubernetes. The first role of Kubernetes, in that context, is to allow the deployment of either Big Data (ML, DL, etc.) or HPC (MPI-based) workloads upon Big Data or HPC platforms through the same command line interface (kubectl) or API (Kubernetes API) making use of a common representation using YAML language. The deployment on the Big Data platforms can be done directly through this API. The deployment on the HPC platforms pass through the integration of a specific existing open-source software named wlm-operator[7] which has been adopted and extended to fit our needs. The software wlm-operator, allows the submission of a job on the dedicated HPC resource manager (Slurm or Torque) by using the Singularity containerization. Kubernetes will also perform resource management and containers orchestration on the Big Data platforms of the supercomputing centers, enabling typical widely used cloud-native software, to be introduced to supercomputers. This is the case of the various Cloud services for which, as we can see on Fig. 1, the resource abstraction is provided through the help of Kubernetes.

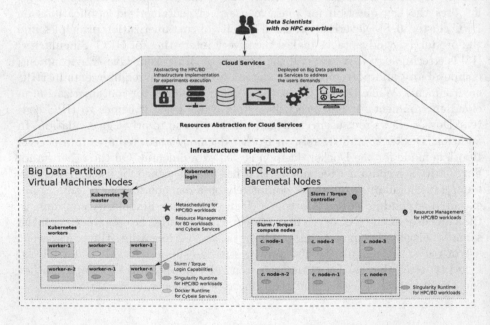

Fig. 1. Architecture for Big Data Analytics on hybrid HPC-Big Data platforms

---

[7] https://sylabs.io/guides/cri/1.0/user-guide/k8s.html.

3.1   Kubernetes and Container Runtimes

Kubernetes controls the deployment lifecycle of containerized applications while managing distributed systems resiliently. Another important part is the resources abstraction through the containerization platform used. As the matter of fact, Kubernetes introduced pods, which specify the resources utilized by a group of application containers. At run time, a pod's containers are instances of container images, packaged and distributed through container image registries. The usage of a containerization platform on Kubernetes goes through the support of specialized Container Runtime Interface (CRI) which has to comply on the Open Container Interface (OCI) standards. Kubernetes uses by default Docker and its specialized CRI, which is the traditional choice and supported out-of-the box by most cloud-Native software. Docker runtime will be used on Big Data partitions to deploy Cloud services which will then be used to abstract the complexity of deploying experiments on hybrid HPC/BD platforms. For the actual execution of the Big Data Analytics which can take place either on the Big Data or the HPC partition, we adopt Singularity platform. The maintainers of Singularity have proposed Singularity CRI[8] to allow the usage of Singularity for the pods runtime within Kubernetes and the particular mechanism wlm-operator[9] which can enable the direct connection between Kubernetes pods and execution on HPC partition through Singularity containers.

In the installation and configuration phase of each worker we need to distinguish the nodes that will use Singularity or Docker as runtime. To perform a rightly matched scheduling we need to define specific label per node to show which runtime is used and then on the application submission (yaml of the pod) we need to provide the right node-selector to determine the need in terms of runtime and divert the pod to be scheduled on the right node. As shown in Fig. 1 the workers with Docker runtime will be used to deploy the Cloud services while those with Singularity will allow the deployment of BD/HPC workloads.

3.2   Integration of Kubernetes and Slurm/Torque with Multi-user Support

At least one of the Kubernetes workers that will be deployed with Singularity runtime will also need to have Slurm or Torque login nodes capabilities, which will enable the connection with the HPC cluster. This means that from that worker node we should have the capability to run Slurm or Torque commands and in particular job submissions. Based on that we have installed and deployed the wlm-operator software which will open a communication protocol with the Slurm or Torque Resource Manager to submit and monitor containerized HPC jobs through Kubernetes API. The wlm-operator integrates with Slurm by default but in the context of our project and to respect the needs of a particular testbed we have extended it to also support Torque. Furthermore

---

[8] https://github.com/sylabs/singularity-cri.
[9] https://github.com/sylabs/wlm-operator.

we have enhanced the mechanism of wlm-operator with multi-user support. The prerequisites of wlm-operator software are to have Singularity-CRI runtime on at least the Kubernetes worker node with the Slurm (or Torque) login capabilities and Singularity software installed on all HPC compute nodes to manage containerization on the HPC side.

The wlm-operator software can automatically discover Slurm partition resources (CPUs, memory, nodes, wall-time) and propagates them as node labels to Kubernetes by creating one virtual node (virtual-kubelet) per partition. For this the virtual-kubelet technique is used internally[10]. Similar procedure is followed for Torque queues. Each Slurm partition (or Torque queue) is represented as a dedicated virtual node in Kubernetes. Those node labels will be respected during Slurm job scheduling so that a job will appear only on a suitable partition with enough resources. The communication protocol between Kubernetes and Slurm (or Torque) is based upon a gRPC proxy, named red-box, which takes place on the worker node that operates the Slurm (or Torque) login binaries. Furthermore, on that Kubernetes worker the user to submit jobs will have to be created on the HPC site and have the rights to submit and monitor jobs.

In order to bridge the communication between Torque and Kubernetes. Torque-Operator extends the wlm-operator with Torque support [3]. Both operators share similar mechanisms, nevertheless, their implementation varies significantly as Torque and Slurm have different structures and parameters. The Torque job script is encapsulated into a Kubernetes yaml job script. The yaml script is submitted from a Kubernetes login. The Torque script part is processed by the Toque-Operator. A dummy pod is generated to transfer the Torque job specification to a scheduling queue e.g., waiting queue, test queue (scheduling queue is a terminology of job scheduler). Torque-Operator invokes the Torque binary qsub which submits Torque job to the Torque cluster. When the Torque job completes, Torque-operator creates a Kubernetes pod which redirects the results to the directory that the user specifies in the yaml file.

By default, with the current version of wlm-operator, all submitted Slurm jobs will be executed on behalf of one user. This is very limiting in our context because we need multi-user support in order to enable individual monitoring, accounting, fairshare scheduling and other features per single user or group of users. For this, we provide a dynamic adaptation of the user context by automatically reconfiguring the virtual-kubelet and agent which is used as a pass-through for the Slurm or Torque job, along with the necessary red-box socket, on the node having the Slurm/Torque login capabilities, using the right user privileges. This gives us the ability to enable each user to use Kubernetes with her account and submit Big Data Analytics on the Slurm or Torque cluster through her account as well, hence removing the initially existing isolation and security barriers of wlm-operator. The mechanisms presented in this paper will be provided as open-source once they are considered more mature.

---

[10] https://github.com/virtual-kubelet/virtual-kubelet.

4   Environment Deployment

In our hybrid Big Data-HPC context, the Environment Deployment tool is responsible for setting up the environment for the task execution and deployment. Based on our needs we sought for the following features:

1. the ability to define the environment for any application, without need for access to the underlying system, i.e. the ability to decouple development and deployment,
2. portability across different systems, including HPC and Big Data resource partitions and
3. the ability to transparently use all available system resources, i.e. accelerators, high-performance interconnects, storage.

We based our solution on Singularity containerization and pre-built images for specific AI and Big Data frameworks and HPC resources. For this we offer a repository of singularity images with Pytorch, Tensorflow, Keras, Horovod optimized for specific versions of GPUs, Infiniband and their adapted libraries CUDA, verbs, etc. Different combinations of the above results in a number of pre-defined images that can be used as the base to deploy a specific Big Data Analytics application.

4.1   Singularity Container Creation and Deployment

A Singularity container image is a single, immutable (read-only), SIF (Singularity Image Format) file. The environment is stored within the image and can include everything from the application code/executable to runtimes to system libraries. Using Singularity, a user can build an image from either a Singularity definition file or by downloading an existing image from a container library, or from Docker hub. In the latter case, the build process transforms the Docker image to a Singularity image. We highlight the following issues and our solutions, related to container creation in the context of its usage in hybrid Big Data - HPC platform:

1. A Singularity image may or may not contain the application itself. In the repository we prepare the images to be generic and we give the ability to the users to either built their application within a new image or just use the base image and deploy their application externally.
2. Although Singularity does not require elevated privileges to deploy an image, it still requires elevated privileges to build an image. Therefore, Singularity image files cannot be built directly on HPC systems, where user access rights are limited. We build all container images on external desktops/servers. The produced image can then be uploaded to the system where it will be deployed, or a shared repository from where it can be used directly by users.
3. To make transparent usage of the network and/or the GPUs, since containers do not virtualize the system, Singularity relies on the host environment as well. For example, for the case of MPI, Singularity partly uses the host

runtime to manage MPI processes. Similarly, for the case of GPUs, it uses the host device drivers and related user-space driver libraries. This can cause compatibility issues, if the runtime encapsulated within the container image is not compatible with the runtime on the host. Therefore, even though we externally build Singularity images, we do take into account the related software versions of the underlying HPC systems, to ensure compatibility.

Once a Singularity image is created, either uploaded to the target system or pulled onto the target system from the component library, it can be deployed to execute the corresponding application task. To guarantee an optimal and simplified deployment of singularity images the following parameters need to be configured correctly for the deployment process. These are the bindmounts, the environment variables and the possibility to use instances. Since these are very closely related to the specific application to be deployed we do not provide any generic solution. Nevertheless some batch scripts examples featuring the usage of singularity deployments and best practices can still be helpful. The pre-built Big Data images along with their definition files will be provided as open-source once they have been sufficiently tested.

5   Multi-GPU Scaling of Sample Precision Agriculture Application

In order to validate the orchestration and environment deployment layers of our hybrid Big Data/HPC solution we have performed some experiments using one real-life precision agriculture application. The aim of the application is to develop a framework for automatic identification and counting of wheat ears in fields by getting data from sensors on ground that will enable crop yield prediction at early stages and provide more informed decisions for sales planning. The application consists in training a deep learning algorithm written in Python and using Fastai/Pytorch framework based on a group of RGB images (initially 138 images). In particular we deployed the wheat ears counting application upon one single HPC node testing the scaling and parallelization of the code by increasing the number of GPUs.

The experiments have been performed on a dedicated testbed where the previously described architecture of Kubernetes orchestration on both Big Data and HPC partitions has been deployed, along with the integration to Slurm and Singularity for the execution on the HPC partition. The HPC testbed is part of BULL NOVA cluster and we made use of the following hardware:

- one HPC BareMetal node, featuring a Bull Sequana S800 machine, equipped with 4X2 Intel Xeon Platinum 8253 (256CPUs), 4 TB RAM and 4 GPUs NVIDIA GV100GL Tesla V100 PCIe 16 GB,
- one Big Data VirtualMachine node, with 4 CPUs and 8 GB RAM

The execution took advantage of the singularity pre-built image for fastai/pytorch and was triggered through the orchestration layer of Kubernetes abstraction using Kubectl command line utility. In the case of BareMetal node the execution is finally submitted by Slurm, whereas in the case of VM it is submitted directly by Kubernetes as batch job. The experiment was repeated 5 times for each case and the median value is shown in Table 1.

Table 1. Execution time of wheat-ears application on 1 VirtualMachine (4 CPUs) node or one BareMetal (256 CPUs) node scaling from 0 to 4 GPUs

VirtualMachine (VM) or BareMetal (BM)	VM	BM	BM	BM	BM	BM
Number of CPUs	4	256	256	256	256	256
Number of GPUs	0	0	1	2	3	4
Execution Time (sec)	37008	7020	417	312	274	247

The usage of BareMetal node may be misleading because the execution is not done literally as bare metal. Both cases use containerization with singularity for the executions with the difference that in the second case it is done on VM while in the first on bare-metal. The results in Table 1 show the performance improvement of our application when using a powerful HPC BareMetal node with GPU instead of small VM, 100* orders of magnitude. Besides that it shows how the scaling of GPUs impacts the application performance: 10* orders of magnitude when using GPUs rather than only CPU. Our goal is to enable further performance optimizations by providing a distributed version selecting between pytorch.distributed or horovod. Furthermore and most importantly, these simple executions enabled us to validate the usability of our integrations combining Kubernetes, Slurm and Singularity in a hybrid Big Data/HPC environment for execution of Deep Learning training models.

6   Conclusions

This paper presents a prototype architecture to enable the execution of Big Data Analytics upon supercomputers using different Big Data and HPC hardware partitions and a converged Big Data-HPC-Cloud software stack. We proposed mechanisms that make use of Kubernetes as high-level orchestrator and common API to allow the deployment of Data Analytics as HPC jobs, through an integration with Slurm based on an a multi-user version of wlm-operator and Singularity containerization. Furthermore we proposed an environment deployment tool bringing pre-built images of Big Data and AI frameworks (Pytorch, Tensorflow, etc.) specifically adapted to targeted HPC resources (GPUS, Infiniband, etc.) which can be used as base to further built environments to be used for different types of Data Analytics on HPC.

These mechanisms are aimed to be used as the basic building blocks to provide supercomputers abstraction targeting data-scientists with no-HPC expertise. For this we aim to deploy Cloud-level software such as the Spring Cloud

Dataflow workflow manager[11] and the LeanXscale database[12]. These tools can be used to create hybrid Big Data-HPC workflows, with the necessary data management, to be deployed transparently, for a data-scientist, through the common Kubernetes API and the aforementioned techniques to the underlying supercomputer. Further optimizations will be researched for the multi-user support of the Kubernetes integration with Slurm and for this we will explore the possibility to use the newly introduced Slurm REST-API[13] which will allow a more direct communication with Cloud services. The support of specialized Big Data frameworks such as Spark and Flink need the usage of a resource manager. This role can be played by Kubernetes [10] and this is another direction that we are exploring. In this context we are studying ways to allow the collocation of Big Data and HPC jobs by making use of Kubernetes to deploy Spark applications on Slurm clusters through a non-interfering method of low-priority jobs [9].

Acknowledgments. This project has received funding from the European Union's Horizon 2020 research and innovation program under grant agreement NO. 825355.

References

1. ETP4HPC. Strategic research agenda (SRA4) for HPC in Europe, March 2020. https://www.etp4hpc.eu/pujades/files/ETP4HPC_SRA4_2020_web(1).pdf
2. Perakis, K., Lampathaki, F., Nikas, K., Georgiou, Y., Marko, O., Maselyne, J.: CYBELE - fostering precision agriculture & livestock farming through secure access to large-scale HPC enabled virtual industrial experimentation environments fostering scalable big data analytics. Comput. Netw. **168**, 107035 (2020). ISSN 1389–1286
3. Zhou, N., Georgiou, Y., Zhong, L., Zhou, H., Pospieszny, M.: Container orchestration on HPC systems. In: IEEE CLOUD (2020, to appear)
4. Casalicchio, E.: Container orchestration: a survey. In: Puliafito, A., Trivedi, K.S. (eds.) Systems Modeling: Methodologies and Tools. EICC, pp. 221–235. Springer, Cham (2019). https://doi.org/10.1007/978-3-319-92378-9_14
5. Hightower, K., Burns, B., Beda, J.: Kubernetes: Up and Running Dive into the Future of Infrastructure, 1st edn. OReilly Media (2017)
6. Xavier, M.G., Neves, M.V., Rossi, F.D., Ferreto, T.C., Lange, T., De Rose, C.A.F.: Performance evaluation of container-based virtualization for high performance computing environments. In: 21st Euromicro International Conference on Parallel, Distributed, and Network-Based Processing, pp. 233–240 (2013)
7. Plauth, M., Feinbube, L., Polze, A.: A performance survey of lightweight virtualization techniques. In: De Paoli, F., Schulte, S., Broch Johnsen, E. (eds.) ESOCC 2017. LNCS, vol. 10465, pp. 34–48. Springer, Cham (2017). https://doi.org/10.1007/978-3-319-67262-5_3
8. Zhang, J., Lu, X., Panda, D.K.: Is singularity-based container technology ready for running MPI applications on HPC clouds? In: Proceedings of The10th International Conference on Utility and Cloud Computing, Association for Computing Machinery (2017)

---

[11] https://spring.io/projects/spring-cloud-dataflow.
[12] https://www.leanxcale.com/.
[13] https://slurm.schedmd.com/rest.html.

9. Mercier, M., Glesser, D., Georgiou, Y., Richard, O.: Big data and HPC collocation: using HPC idle resources for Big Data analytics. In: BigData, pp. 347–352 (2017)
10. Spark - Kubernetes integration. https://spark.apache.org/docs/latest/running-on-kubernetes.html
11. Boettiger, C.: An introduction to Docker for reproducible research. In: ACM SIGOPS Operating Systems Review (2015)
12. Yoo, A.B., Jette, M.A., Grondona, M.: SLURM: simple Linux utility for resource management. In: Feitelson, D., Rudolph, L., Schwiegelshohn, U. (eds.) JSSPP 2003. LNCS, vol. 2862, pp. 44–60. Springer, Heidelberg (2003). https://doi.org/10.1007/10968987_3
13. Godlove, D.: Singularity: simple, secure containers for compute-driven workloads. PEARC **24**(1–24), 4 (2019)
14. Muscianisi, G., Fiameni, G., Azab, A.: Singularity GPU containers execution on HPC cluster. In: ISC Workshops, pp. 61–68 (2019)

Author Index

Printed in the United States
By Bookmasters